From

# "KNOTTED

# STRINGS"

To

# TALKING

# BIBLES

From
# "KNOTTED
STRINGS"
To
# TALKING
BIBLES

*HARVEY T. HOEKSTRA*

*William Carey Library*
Pasadena, California
*www.WCLBooks.com*

Published by
William Carey Library
P. O. Box 40129
Pasadena, CA 91114
(626) 720-8210

ISBN 0-87808-453-3

Cover design: Crooks Design Co.

*PRINTED IN THE UNITED STATES OF AMERICA*

# CONTENTS

# DEDICATED

To my wife, Lavina, so beautifully genuine, unpretentious, never seeking acclaim — a missionary-mother with a servant heart, able to convert mud-walls or sticks and grass with dirt floors into an attractive home in which there was contentment and love and where our people in Africa knew they were always welcome and could find help in times of need.

To our six children, Denny, Jim, Dave, Carol, Mark and Paul who shared our adventures in Africa and the pain we experienced as a family during those long months of separation while away from home in a distant, mission, boarding school.

To my missionary colleagues with whom we were privileged to live and work and without whose encouragement and help our task could not have been accomplished.

To God be all the honor and praise for the incredible privilege He gave to us that we should be Christ's missionaries in Africa for nearly thirty years among people who might otherwise never have heard of Him! And we praise Him for the dozen or more years He gave us to serve Him in many other countries prior to the founding of Audio Scriptures International in California.

*****

I want to express my heartfelt thanks and appreciation to Marion Stipe who read and carefully edited the entire manuscript for publication.

And I am most grateful to those who read the manuscript and are commending the book to our readers.

1

Akobo in the Sudan where the Hoekstras lived was 750 miles south of Khartoum, 90 miles north of Pibor Post and just 3 miles from Ethiopia's furthers border in the West, as is indicated by the map. Where Harvey and Lavina later lived in the rain forest among the Majang was approximately 325 miles southwest of Addis Ababa and 50 miles east of Gambela, located on the Baro River. During those years Gambela was an Ethiopian government post in which, interestingly, the British *colonializers* continued to have a mile square enclave over which they flew the British flag..

Dr. Harvey and Lavina Hoekstra

Harvey and Lavina with their six children
when Mark and Sandy were married in 1982

3

*"Go, swift messengers,*
*To a people tall and*
  *smooth-skinned,*
*to a people feared far and*
  *wide,*
*an aggressive nation of*
  *strange speech,*
*whose land is divided by*
  *rivers."* Isaiah 18:2b

# FOREWORD

As you read this book a marvelous story will unfold, and the wonderful love of God for the nations will be seen through the eyes of one of God's faithful servants. My father, Harvey T. Hoekstra made a commitment to serve the Lord when he was just a child, and the Lord made a commitment to hold my father in His hands during the entirety of his life. God's love for the nations spills out of my father; everywhere he goes and in everything he does, he does it in such a way as to show God's love for the many different kinds of people in this world. My father wants everyone to know just how deep God's love is for each and every one of us. God loves all the people in the world so much that He gave His only Son to die an agonizing death on a cross so that all who call on him might have the free gift of eternal life.

This free gift for everyone must be heard by everyone. My father's personal experience with Jesus and God's love in his own life made him eternally grateful and willing to dedicate and spend the rest of his life making sure as many as possible could hear that good news about Jesus. My father wanted everyone to know this, from those living in the rain forest of southwest Ethiopia to the person sitting next to him on a flight to Michigan from California, he wants everyone to know. My father's life and the story you are about to read is the story of God's sustaining love for an individual man, his wife and family during a life long walk with God.

There are many wonderful testimonies of those who have been saved from a life of sin and evil to become followers and sometimes great warriors for the kingdom's sake, but for me the best testimony is that of a man like my father and others who have lived a pure life dedicated to their Lord and savior Jesus Christ. The Lord blessed my father with one of the most significant tasks in the history of the Christian movement. From a small farm in Minnesota, God called a servant named Harvey T. Hoekstra. When the call went out "Who will go to Africa?" My father responded with a resounding "Yes, here am I, send me!". I do not think that he had any idea at that time what really lay ahead.

5

During the early years on the mission field while the Christian movement was putting a great deal of money and effort into creating written languages for the various oral cultures around the world, reducing them into written form and translating the New Testament, God opened his eyes to see something not many others had seen or embraced. For many years he was like a man shouting in the wilderness. Like John the Baptist, my father envisioned something too awesome, something too crucial to the success of the great commission to not shout it from every part of his being. While most of the energy for Bible translation was being put into teaching people how to read the new translations, he was advocating a different approach. Most everyone can hear and most people without exception from oral cultures communicate orally by talking and listening. My father saw something much deeper in the plan for the nations and the way the Lord was bringing about the great commission. He saw the need for audio Bibles for non-readers.

We are living in the most exciting time in the history of the Christian movement. The good news about Jesus is traveling to new areas faster then ever before in the history of the church. More people are coming to Jesus every day than ever before. There are more people in prison for their faith today and more people are being killed and murdered for their faith these days than ever before in the history of the church.

Many of these new believers are people coming to Christ from oral cultures. There is a strong missionary movement among these illiterate people groups. They are the warriors of the future. They are the army of tomorrow in the great battle for the souls of men. Because of the great missionary movements and mobilization efforts to reach the unreached people groups in recent years, millions have come to the foot of the cross. Millions of new believers all acknowledging Jesus as the Son of God. All professing him to be their personal Lord and Savior. The good news is now reaching into the final frontiers where people living in darkness do not embrace reading as a part of the culture. A great deal of money and energy has been put into teaching people to read the new translations yet less than 1% of the people will ever learn to read the New Testaments that are being translated. They are Bible-less people, hundreds of thousands, in fact millions of people without a Bible. The new warriors are without a Bible because they do not read. Those needing to be strengthened by the Word of God will have no access to it unless it is in audio because they cannot read it for themselves and there are not enough readers to read to them.

My father saw this coming years ago and has been working diligently for over thirty-five years to make sure that all those translations that have been so painstakingly prepared do not go to waste, just sitting on a shelf somewhere because few can read them. Give an illiterate person an audio Bible and soon they will be trying to read a printed Bible. Give an illiterate person a printed Bible and soon it will collect dust in the corner. For many missionaries, local evangelists and local pastors in these non-reading parts of the world, it is very clear to them that most non-readers will remain non-readers for a lifetime. They see how important audio Bibles are for the non-reading church.

In 1948 when my mom and dad took off for Africa, going to Africa was a big deal. Africa was a long ways away and only those willing to give up everything went to Africa. Many missionaries never came back. Africa was a hostile place, with sickness and diseases that white people could not handle very well. There were animals, snakes and bugs that could and would kill. That's not to mention the savages. . . and I do mean savages! Some African tribes were eating each other and doing all kinds of bizarre things that a young American lad from a small farm in Minnesota and his lovely wife would not understand, but God's call for someone to go to Africa and make His Word known to the Anuak people was answered by my mom and dad. My father spent twelve years translating the Anuak New Testament, a work well done, but hardly anyone could read it when the printed New Testaments finally arrived.

I am not going to give you the whole story of how he discovered the power of God's Word in audio for people who do not read. Then you wouldn't need to read this book! (It happened in the rain forest of Southwest Ethiopia.) While I was running around with just shorts on trying to have as much fun as a missionary kid could have, something else was unfolding. I never saw it until I went back to Ethiopia with my brother Paul twenty years later in 1996. We discovered that 85% of the Majang (earlier known as Mesengos) had become Chris-

7

tians, followers of Jesus. As a child I remember the pitch-black nights, so dark that if I woke up in the middle of the night I would light a match just to make sure I wasn't blind. We had candles for our only light when the generator went out. When the candle was out it was pitch black; you could not see your hand in front of your face. If you could see at night it meant there was no rain and the moon had come out. On those moonlit, hot, humid African nights came the sounds of the jungle. The sound I hear most often in my memory and the sound that still brings tears to my eyes is the eerie sound of the drums and the people wailing. The natives would gather together and dance all night, beating the drums and singing in the clearing in front of the chief's hut. The music would rise up above the forest and float for miles all the way to the mission compound and the dark little room where I slept. I could tell even as a child it was evil.

My father loved the Majang. One day an anthropologist came out of the rain forest. He had walked for days from Gambela looking for "Terry". We discovered he was not looking for "Terry" but "Daddy". All through the rain forest the Majang were calling my father "Daddy" because that was what they heard us kids calling him. They did not know what "Daddy" meant, but God did, and Harvey Hoekstra was "Daddy" to the Majang. It took twelve years of living right there in the rain forest with them for God's love to pour out through my mom and dad. God brought the Majang from darkness into His wonderful light and the saving grace of Jesus His Son. The drums and the wailing have stopped and in their place are the sounds of life and the songs about Jesus.

The story goes on but you'll have to read the whole account in the book. It all began in a small room above a pharmacy in Minnesota. In that room a frightened fifteen-year-old boy was about to die. Harvey T. Hoekstra made a commitment to follow God's will and desire for his life. This book is that exciting account of Harvey's life and ministry and God's sustaining love. The story of a Bible translator in the Sudan, a dedicated evangelist missionary in Ethiopia, an innovator in recording and producing the New Testament in many languages in Africa and Asia. I believe his greatest achievement of all was creating Audio Scriptures International's worldwide distribution center, which gave birth to the Talking Bible™. The Talking Bible™

is God's gift to my father for shouting in the wilderness when the Christian movement worldwide had not yet seen the need of the Bible-less people from oral cultures. The Talking Bible™ is God's gift to non-readers of the world. It makes putting God's Word in audio for all the translations a doable task. A dream my father has had in his heart for many years now.

I trust you will enjoy this book, it is the second edition. So many people could "hardly put it down" that the first printing has sold out. The second printing has four additional chapters as the story continues to unfold.    And there two new chapter inserts plus other additional information in this revised and expanded edition. At the time of this printing both Dr. Harvey T. Hoekstra and his wife Lavina are eighty-two years old.

Mark S, Hoekstra

*"The Lord is my light and my salvation — whom shall I fear? The Lord is the stronghold of my life — of whom shall I be afraid?* Psalm 27: 1-2

# CHAPTER ONE
# HOW
# IT ALL BEGAN

That first "knotted string" had thirteen knots on it. I had never seen one before. We learned about it while living in the rain forest in SW Ethiopia. Argeem, a teen-aged girl, a new Majang believer was back from her mother's village two rivers away. She reached in her bag — pulled out her cassette player with its dead batteries. Then she reached in once more and pulled out this "knotted string." On it were thirteen knots. Thirteen women in her mother's village had said, "Argeem take some grass and make a string. Tie a knot on your string for me. I want to become a person of your Jesus."

But, I'm way ahead of myself. We must go back to the beginning — I was on my way home from the seminary where I was preparing for the ministry. We had just been listening to a "red headed, rash, religious" Presbyterian missionary from Africa, named Don McClure. He told how he had recently come from the South Sudan beyond the Nile River, where people had never heard of Jesus Christ. God had given this man a great vision and a bold, innovative plan. They called it the "Anuak Plan" — fifteen missionaries for fifteen years to evangelize an entire tribe and then move on.

He wanted to return to Africa with competent missionary recruits. He needed a doctor, a nurse, an educator, an agriculturalist, an evangelist and someone to translate the Bible into the Anuak Language. As he spoke, my heart was strangely warmed. I sensed that God wanted me to be that person. But what would Lavina say?

# CHAPTER ONE

As I raced homeward about as fast as I thought was prudent, I fantasized that Lavina would collapse, falling to the floor in shock and that I'd have to revive her. And then, again, I'd think, "No, it's not going to be that great a surprise. We've talked sometimes, albeit superficially, about being missionaries, possibly to Japan." But, Africa was something else. She would picture lions chasing her up trees and snakes slithering in the grass waiting to strike.

Bouncing along those twenty-one miles in my 1932 Ford with its worn out shock absorbers, I also pondered the commitment Lavina had given me before we were married. I sometimes had kidded her that she wanted me real bad, because she promised she'd go with me wherever the Lord called me. She had said, "Honey, I know that ministers move from place to place and have to go wherever God calls them. I can do that with you. I'll go with you wherever the Lord calls you."

But to go out to Africa? It was still considered a dark continent and a risky place with wild animals, strange people and threatening diseases? Our image of Africa had been shaped by Livingston and Stanley. Neither of us had thought that far ahead when we were madly in love making far reaching commitments to each other. One side of my brain was racing in high gear with all these and a myriad of other conflicting thoughts. The opposite side was praying earnestly that God would prepare Lavina's heart with a positive response. -- Anyway, there would be a long while before we would have to make a final decision. I still had another year at the seminary. That would make for a total of three years driving back and forth those twenty one miles to attend classes while serving as student pastor at Bignell Chapel.

I'll never forget the flow of adrenaline and the boundless enthusiasm with which I shared what I thought God had been showing me that morning about our going to Africa. She never collapsed and I didn't have to pick her up off the floor, but it was a turn of events she had never anticipated. We prayed about it often, talked about it regularly until finally one night, when sleep eluded us, we got out of our bed around two o'clock in the morning and told the Lord we were ready to go to Africa if that was what He wanted us to do. That night, on our knees, our hearts were at peace and we heard His word of promise, "I will be with you always, even to the end of the world." The old translation came to mind because to us, that was exactly where we would be going. A scant two years later, a lion was in our front yard while we slept peacefully in our mud-walled house with only a mosquito net between us and him. We were at Akobo in the Sudan.

Our story really begins much earlier than that fateful day when God used Don McClure to spark our interest in Africa.

It begins in a tiny eight room hospital upstairs over the pharmacy where I promised Jesus that if He would make me well again, I would try to be a preacher of the Gospel.

It was November, 1935. I had just celebrated my fifteenth birthday.

## GROWING UP ON THE FARM

My boyhood home was in Minnesota. I grew up in a Christian family with five brothers. We never had a sister. I'm sure my mother must have been at least a little disappointed when the doctor said, "We have another boy here." I was number four!

We all went to catechism, Sunday school and attended church as a family. When itinerant evangelists held services nearby, our family sat near the front. We lived on a dirt road five miles from Maple Lake. The closest school was two miles away and we walked both ways except when it rained or the weather was too forbidding during the winter. Sometimes we were lucky to catch a ride if my dad or a neighbor happened to be going into town.

Ours was a small farm of eighty acres. On six or seven acres of that we grew a wide assortment of vegetables which my dad and we boys peddled on retail routes to homes in the various towns and among resort people spending their summer on one of the many several nearby lakes. We also sold to stores and vegetable markets in the neighboring towns, reaching out as far as St. Cloud some 27 miles distant. All of this was excellent preparation for learning how to communicate and make a sale. My dad was good at this and he taught his boys these same skills. I can still hear him saying, "Harvey, take a head of cabbage and run up to that house. Tell the lady it's ten cents for one and if she'll take three she can have all three of them for a quarter." That boyhood experience, trying

13

to sell vegetables and meeting people in public, was excellent preparation for a future preacher.

I graduated from grade school when I was twelve years of age, went to high school a few weeks and quit. I never went back to high school until four and a half years later. It was during those years that I promised Jesus I would try to become a preacher of the Gospel.

## ILLNESS STRIKES

On October 10th, in the evening, I was out beside the barn feeding the calves their evening milk. I began to feel ill with chills. It was the evening for our young people's meeting at church, and I didn't want to miss it. I went, but was miserable with chills and fever. I could hardly wait for the meeting to end so that I could go home and crawl into bed. Three days later when the fever had left and I came downstairs, my mother remarked that she didn't like the way I was walking all bent over. Concerned about that, later in the week they took me to old Dr. Rousseau in Maple Lake. He said that I had had an attack of appendicitis but he didn't recommend surgery.

Ten days after that first attack, the fever and chills returned. Around six o'clock, my folks took me to Buffalo, sixteen miles from home where I was admitted for surgery later that evening. On the way, they stopped at Uncle Ralph's farm to pick up my Aunt Marie who was a registered nurse. The hospital was small and up a flight of stairs above the drug store. In preparation for the surgery, I was given a spinal injection. My mother cautioned me to lie real still when they pricked me. She said, "Alfred Naagkteborn, a neighbor boy who lived across the field from us, nearly died when they broke off the needle while attempting to give him a spinal before his operation." I never moved!

During the surgery I was fully conscious and able to hear part of the conversation as Dr. Catlin and his son, Dr. Bob, performed the surgery. I recall how Dr. Catlin said, "I had hoped we could have gotten that thing out of there in time."

I knew then that I had a ruptured appendix and was a very sick boy. They saved the dirty black pieces of it and I later saw them in a little bottle floating in liquid. Eventually we threw them out!

Two weeks and two days after the first surgery, these same doctors again performed a second operation to deal with an abscess that had formed behind the bladder. I was desperately ill following the surgery and it wasn't at all sure that I would make it. This was before the miracle drugs of penicillin and sulfa had been discovered. My Aunt Marie, a registered nurse, was in the same room with me taking care of me night and day.

## A LIFE CHANGING EXPERIENCE

On November 20, we celebrated my fiftcenth birthday in the hospital. Two days later, at noon the doctor came in, pulled back the covers, tapped me on the abdomen and said, "We're going to have to go in their once more." Another abscess had formed into which they would insert a tube through which it could drain.

My favorite aunt, Ella Mae, mother's younger sister, was "baby-sitting" me keeping me company that same day. She knew that I was afraid to die. When the doctors left the room, she got out of her chair, took hold of my trembling hand, knelt down beside my bed and prayed. I don't know what she said. I only know that as she prayed I had an indescribable experience of God's grace and peace. My fear was totally gone. I felt I was bathed in God's love and goodness. My heart was inexpressibly glad. It seemed that a thousand lights were brightening up the room. I am unable, adequately, to describe the wonder of that experience. I felt joy -- waves of joy and God's peace washing over me. It made no difference whether I lived or died. It would be alright. I knew that God loved me!

Two hours later my folks drove in from the country. They had been phoned and told of the impending surgery. My mother was crying. She fully expected me to die. I remember sharing my experience with her then and telling her not to be sad or afraid. Well, as you can see, the operation was a success and God mercifully healed me. I went home on December 5th. I had been in the hospital 45 days and had lost 27 pounds of weight. But, before I left for home, another wonderful thing happened.

# CHAPTER ONE

## A LIFE CHANGING PROMISE

On one of those days after the third operation, a retired farmer, Peter Schermer by name, stopped by to visit me. He had been there once or twice before. To a boy just fifteen years of age, he looked pretty ancient. Even so, I really appreciated his coming and making my time go just a little faster.

This last visit of his, however, was surely ordained of God. Sitting just beyond the foot end of my bed, this elderly man shared with me about the experience they had with their son when he was a boy like me and was ill. He said, "I had a son like you and when he was a boy, he too, was desperately ill. One day when I came into the hospital there was a black sheet over his bed and he wasn't there. When I saw that black sheet, I put my hands in the air and said, 'Oh, God, if only you'd have spared my son, I'd have given him to you.'" He continued, "As it turned out, my son was still alive. They had put him in a room across the hall expecting him to die." And then he said, "But God spared his life and when he became a young man, he went to the seminary and became a preacher of the Gospel."

When I heard those words, I said in my heart, "Dear God, if you'll spare my life and make me well again, I'll try to be a preacher of the Gospel." It was a commitment which by God's grace I kept and from which I was never seriously tempted to turn aside. I knew that God had spoken to me through that retired farmer.

On December 5, 1935 I was released from the hospital. At home I was gradually regaining strength. Two years went by and I was still not in school. I often prayed about it, wondering how it would ever be possible for me to become a preacher. I had been called and had made a promise to God, but I was no nearer getting into school two and a half years after leaving the hospital than I was when I had promised to be a preacher.

But, God has his own timing in things like that and brings it all together at His appointed time. We don't always understand these matters, but we know it to be so.

## PLANS FOR GETTING INTO SCHOOL

In the summer of 1937 our little country church was

16

having a week of special evangelist meetings. A man named Isaac Van Westenberg came from Chicago to be the week's speaker. On one of those nights, he called for testimonies. Among others, I also shared from my experiences. This man had never heard of me, but that evening when I sat down, he pointed his finger straight at me and said, "Now, there's a young man for the ministry." It was the finger of God!

After the service a few gathered around my folks and urged that a way be found for me to go to school. The next day, I was out hoeing cabbage in the field across the road just opposite our house. A car came over the hill from the direction of the church and turned into our yard. It was Rev. Van Westenberg. He had come to follow up on the events of the preceding night at the church.

I was called out of the cabbage patch and my folks, the visiting preacher and I sat around the kitchen table. It was agreed that I should get into school and prepare. We all decided that it might be good for me to enroll in Northwestern Bible School in Minneapolis at the beginning of the second semester in January. That would allow me to help with the farm work through the busy fall months too.

When January came, my folks, my brother, Gerrit, and his wife, Glorene, who were living in the little house next door, took me and my trunk to the Bible School in Minneapolis. We went two weeks early so that I could seek out a job and support my myself. I, actually, found a meal job in the restaurant next to the Orpheum Theater on Hennepin Avenue. It looked like I was all set to become a student at Northwestern Bible College.

However, on their way back, when the folks and Gerrit and Glorene returned home the day they had dropped me off in the city, Gerrit shared with my folks that I had sometimes talked with him about wanting eventually to attend our own theological seminary in Holland, Michigan. That conversation triggered in my Dad's mind that he should visit with the superintendent of schools in Annandale and explore the possibility of my starting high school. I really don't know what I was thinking of when I spoke of going to our own seminary when I didn't even have a high school education. But, my dad realized what would first have to happen. He wasn't a strong advocate of education for his boys, but he knew that I needed one if I was to become a preacher of the Gospel.

## CHAPTER ONE

Ten days after they had dropped me and my trunk off at Northwestern Bible College, at two o'clock in the afternoon I received a letter from my father. In it he told how he had been to see the superintendent of Annandale High. Mr. Tripp, the superintendent then, had said that if I began high school immediately I could probably catch up with the others and graduate in three and a half years. There was a precedent for that kind of accelerated attempt. Henry (Hank) Schut, who later married my cousin, Hazel, had gone back to school when he was older. He had graduated in three years and I had heard a lot of people talk about what he had done. By four o'clock that afternoon I was out on the road hitchhiking the fifty miles home. Once in Maple Lake, I called my dad and he collected me. It was already past eight o'clock in the evening before we arrived home. We sat together around the kitchen table discussing this new possibility. By ten o'clock that night the decision had been made. I would go back to the city the next afternoon, Sunday, collect my trunk and begin high school in Annandale. Wilbert Schut drove me to the school in Minneapolis that afternoon.

### ATTENDING HIGHSCHOOL IN ANNANDALE

The next day, Monday morning, January 24, 1938, the school bus stopped at our mailbox to pick me up. Annandale was seven miles from home. I began my high school education that day.

Two and one half years later I graduated with honor. It had been hard work, but God had marvelously helped me. I never took an examination without asking the Lord to help me. Some sacrifices were necessary to achieve. To catch up with the other students, I spent the first few Saturdays studying the entire day in the little vacant house on our farm. It was a great challenge and I loved it. I often studied late into the evenings. Sometimes I would go to bed real early, set the alarm and begin studying at 2:30 in the morning. We always had cows to milk and chores to do as well. During my second year, I even took seven weeks off from school on Thursdays to go out alone with the truck to sell vegetables on a route I had in Monticello.

During the school year I didn't participate in most of the young people's social activities and "good times". I did continue teaching Sunday School and always attended the weekly teacher's meeting. Rev. Adolphus Dykstra, our young pastor, was such an excellent teacher none of us who taught on Sunday wanted to miss out.

## ATTENDING HOPE COLLEGE IN MICHIGAN

In May 1940, I graduated from high school. That same fall my folks and I traveled from Minnesota to Michigan in their nice 1937 Chevy. My dad always kept his car in tiptop shape, so it was a first class ride all the way! I was excited. The first hurdle of finishing high school was behind me. I was eager to start at Hope College and complete my formal education. I was highly motivated because of the promise I had made when I had been so ill. It never occurred to me that I wouldn't make it.

The college had a job lined up for me taking care of a woman's furnace and yard on thirteenth street right near the school. We met this lady in the afternoon and I expected to move into my room in the morning. My dad handed me a dollar bill just before they left for Chicago where they would visit relatives on their way home. His last word, as I recall it, was, "You'd better get yourself a haircut."

I had no idea what lay ahead. In the morning, I learned that the lady had changed her mind. I don't know whether she didn't like my looks or what went wrong! I ended up staying with an older lady named Miss Doesburg, living on Tenth Street between College and Central Ave. It was close to the college, and I liked that. My duties were easy enough. Carry in the coal for the space heater and empty out the ashes, help with odd jobs around the place, and be available in case of need.

I also found a job in the Dutch Mill restaurant where I could earn my meals. That first semester, I skipped classes three days each month so that I could read light and water meters for the city. When my friend, Howard Van Egmond, quit his job as night clerk in the Hotel Netherlands, I applied and was accepted. A boyhood friend, John Schut, from Maple Lake who was also attending Hope College, was rooming with me at Miss Doesburg's home. At this juncture he took over my responsibilities in the house. Employment at the Netherlands

Hotel involved long hours, seven nights a week, but it was a good job for a college student having to work. It gave me the opportunity to study on the job. My classes were in the morning and I slept afternoons. When I received me first grades, I was surprised to find I had done better than I had hoped for. I suspect I had set my academic sights a little too low and never thought that I might be able to maintain the good record I had finished up with in high school. But, sensing that I could probably finish near the top of my class if I really tried, I began to study more seriously like I had in high school.

By taking nine hours of credit work in the summers, I could come close to graduating in three years. I did this and finished the remaining several hours required to graduate during my first year at Western Seminary. One of my summer school courses was in Japanese history. Dr. Albertus Pieters, who had spent years in Japan as an RCA missionary and later taught at Western Seminary, was the teacher. He was retired by then but former students still talked about how they would never go into his classroom unprepared. Dr. Pieters, for some strange reason, wasn't much in favor of students working and studying at the same time. I was holding down a full time job nights while going to school during the summer. I've always considered that Dr. Pieters paid me one of my highest compliments during my college years when he gave me a grade of 99 1/4 on one of his comprehensive examinations. As he returned my paper he snorted in his mustache in his inimitable manner saying, "Mr. Hoekstra, I don't know how you do it, but I can't deny the facts." I still chuckle whenever I recall how he said it. When I received my diploma it was "Cum Laude" (with honor). I knew it was because God had helped me and I gave Him thanks and praise!

## MARRIED WHILE STILL AT HOPE

I was a very busy young man during those student years. Even so, I managed to court an attractive young lady, Lavina Hoffman, and we were married while I was still at Hope. She was God's gift to me, beautiful, sensible, supportive and never ready to give up. Looking back, we concede that getting married when we did may not have been the smartest thing to do. But, God sometimes graciously overrules for good even when we may not know what is best for ourselves.

It wasn't easy! Lavina and I were normally poor and lacking some of the amenities of life. But we had each other. When our first son, Denny, made his debut, eleven months after we were married, we knew we had our work cut out for us. Sometimes, we wondered where our next meal would come from. Many a can of soup made its way to our table. Occasionally, we would look at each other and say, "The Lord must be getting us ready for Arabia or something!" At that time, we had no idea that it was Africa.

Though the going was tough, we both worked to put food on the table and pay our way. Quitting school was never an option. It never occurred to either of us that we wouldn't make it or that I should drop out. It simply wasn't an option. We would look to God to see us through and we were willing to do whatever was required.

I think our lowest point came one day when, during the college year, out of work, I had taken a day out from classes to look for a job. All prospects for job openings had come to a dead end. Nothing was available. I finally stopped at one of the factories where a man, whom I didn't know but who said his name was Ed Boevie, gave me hope. He said I should go to the Boone Aluminum company and ask to speak to the man in charge. He said "I'll call him and tell him you'll be showing up."

This was encouraging because most of those places were simply taking names down and one never got in to see anyone at all. Eventually, I was at the little opening in the outer lobby where you filled out the forms. After waiting longer than I had hoped would be the case, in as much as Mr. Boevie was supposed to have called them, the manager invited me into his office. He confirmed that he'd been contacted.

At one point I said, "I don't care what job I have to do. I'm willing to clean spittoons or do anything. I need work."

This kind man, raised his hand and stopped me saying, "Take it easy, fellow. Take it easy. We'll find something for you."

They gave me a job working nights in the tool crib where I would sharpen tools and give them out to the workers whenever they needed to turn in their dull cutting tools for replacements. I had never seen the inside of a factory before. To learn the job, I had to skip classes at Hope for one week.

21

The following week I began at mid-night, came home in the morning after eight o'clock and changed into clean clothes quickly to get to classes at Hope.    In the afternoon and early evening I tried to sleep.

It was a good job. The pay was three times what I had earned at the hotel, and I could still study on the job. Some of the factory workers knew I was studying and tried to avoid disturbing me as much as possible.   Some even sharpened their own tools. I suspect they could do it better than this college student with his limited experience at that.    The Lord was so kind and merciful to me!        Later when I started seminary, Lavina began working nights and switched back and forth between the second and third shifts.    Denny was just a little tyke then.    Jenny Schut, a dear friend from Minnesota who was living next door, took care of him.        Jenny and her daughter, Elsie, were like a grandmother and auntie to Denny.

During one period, every morning before going to class, I would transport Denny in a basket on the front of my bike to get him over to our friends, Bill and Kay Vandenberg. If it rained, we covered him with plastic. This was when Lavina was working the day shift and I was in seminary.

## OUR FIRST SUMMER ASSIGNMENT TO PREACH

Seminary students were normally sent out on summer assignments.    Some went to help in local church ministries and two or three students always went to the Indian mission fields in New Mexico or Nebraska.    We were the only married couple in seminary at that time, so Lavina and I, with our two year old son, Denny, would be going out together. We had been assigned to Winnebego, Nebraska, but before this was finalized, we were reassigned to Bignell Chapel near Grand Haven. The change was made because during that time Lavina's mother, living in Holland, Michigan was gravely ill.

Again, we saw the marvelous providence of God at work in these events.  First of all, we met Franklin and Gladys Kieft who in later years would play such an important role in our lives and ministry.  When our summer assignment ended, this little preaching post called Bignell Chapel, where I had been preaching two sermons every Sunday, invited us to continue on as their student pastor.   They wanted us to keep on living there and serve them like a pastor until I completed my seminary training.

Every day during the school year, I drove our '32 Ford V8 the 21 miles back and forth to seminary. Every Sunday two more sermons were waiting to be preached. It was my great joy, but also my ever present burden. More than one message received its final touches well past Saturday at midnight!

It was great that Lavina didn't have to work those long hours outside the home any longer. She loved watching Denny develop and teaching him all those things a good mother does. I suspect her stories included the boys and girls from Africa. Sometimes Lavina and I talked about the peoples of the world who had never heard of Jesus. We would talk about America where the churches were so plentiful and where radio programs put the Gospel within reach of almost everyone. We sometimes spoke about our becoming missionaries to Japan, but not really seriously. We never talked about becoming missionaries to Africa. That is, until that day when Don McClure visited our seminary.

## AFRICA IN OUR BLOOD

In the summer of '46, Lavina and I attended the New Wilmington Missionary Conference in Ohio. We met a number of missionaries there on furlough and some who were new recruits. We felt right at home with them and Africa was in our blood. It was a summer that confirmed our call to Africa.

Lavina and I talked incessantly about Africa. We must have talked about the rivers, rain and mud as we speculated and tried to visualize what living in Africa might be like. That we were doing a lot of this became apparent one rainy day when we drove out to the country over muddy roads to pick up a side of pork from a local farmer. Denny was in the back seat and when the car came to a halt, he excitedly started hitting his mother on the shoulder to get her attention. What do you think he wanted to know? His question, "Is this Africut? Mommy, is this Africut?" To him Africa was a place of rain and mud and he thought we were there!

# CHAPTER ONE

## APPOINTED BY THE RCA

During this time when God was calling us to serve in Africa, the Reformed Church in America (RCA) was making it decision to expand its missionary program to include Africa. The RCA and the United Presbyterians were to become partners in the work of the American Mission (the name of the Presbyterian Mission) in the Sudan. The RCA had caught this vision from this same Don McClure. Bob and Morrie Swart and Wilma Kats would be the first to go out. We'd be following them in a few short months. But, before all that happened, there were still some hurdles to overcome and training we needed to be ready for the tasks lying ahead.

During our last year at Western Seminary, we formally applied to be accepted by the RCA to serve with the Presbyterians in Africa. The forms to be filled out seemed long and complicated. There were hurdles to overcome, but eventually one night the phone range. We were just about to step out of the house to leave for our weekly young peoples' meeting in the church. Bev Vandermeiden, a young teen aged neighbor girl, was standing there waiting to ride with us when the phone rang. On the line was Miss Ruth Ransom from the RCA's Board of World Mission meeting in Kalamazoo. She was calling to tell us that Lavina and I had just been appointed by them to serve in Africa. They wanted us to come to Kalamazoo the next day to be introduced to the entire Board and to meet with her committee to make future plans. It was a night we can never forget.

That same year in May, 1947 I graduated from Western Theological Seminary in Holland. We had had three marvelous years serving as student pastor while attending seminary. Suddenly this was all past tense. The RCA mapped out the additional preparation we should have before leaving for overseas.

After a year at Scarrit and Peabody Colleges in Nashville Tennessee and a summer at the University of Oklahoma in the Summer Institute of Linguistics (SIL) of the Wycliffe Bible Translators, we were ready to push off. But, there were innumerable details needing attention. Passport forms to fill out; inoculations that gave us fevers and sore arms; furniture, food supplies and tools to accompany us. Visits to family members and visits to a number of supporting congregations eager to

24

meet their new missionaries and bid them Godspeed. Everywhere we went, people encouraged us and tried to help in any way possible. Several men helped build wooden cases that could also serve as cabinets for furniture. Going to Africa, we needed guns and ammunition for hunting. Our meat supply was out there somewhere in the tall grass, or perhaps flying overhead. We would become expert shots as we kept meat on the table. We would be in lion and leopard country so we would also need guns for our own protection.

## SAILING FOR AFRICA

It was July 2, 1948 when we sailed for Africa. Our dear friends, Arnie and Marge Van Lummel, had come from where they were serving a church in New Jersey to see us off. Rev. Bert Bosenbroek, representing the Board, gave us their official send off and he led us in prayer.

We were on a newly refurbished freighter, named "The SS Steel Apprentice". They allowed eleven passengers. To carry more meant they'd have to include a doctor.

Late in the afternoon our friends had already left and we started moving out to sea. We were all out on the deck watching the shoreline gradually recede in the distance. It was beginning to darken. As the Statue of Liberty was fading in the distance, we suddenly felt an indescribable sense of aloneness. Nobody was with us and we were desolate. I thought to myself, "What have I done? I'm taking my family to a place I've never seen and where there are dangers I can't even imagine?" Lavina wasn't feeling that chipper either. It was the moment of truth. There was no turning back. We were committed. The bands had stopped playing! All the nice words said about our courage and how great it was that we were willing to go out as missionaries were past history. We were alone and nobody spoke to us.

About that time, we took Denny, who was five and a half years, and Jimmy, who was just three months old, and went into our cabin. We opened the Bible and it fell to Psalm 105 where we read these beautiful, unforgettable words:

> *"When they went from one nation*
> *to another,*

25

*from one kingdom to another people;*
*He suffered no man*
*to do them wrong:*
*yea, he reproved kings*
*for their sakes;*
*Saying, 'Touch not mine anointed,*
*and do my prophets no harm'."*
Psalm 105: 13-15 (KJV)

We closed the book, got on our knees together and prayed. When we opened our eyes it was like we were in another world. The loneliness and desolation had been lifted. Our hearts were at peace and we experienced His presence and peace. This terrible feeling never returned, but it was a moment we will never forget. How precious, indeed, are the promises of God to strengthen the hearts of those who lean on Him.

## DOCKING AT PORT SAID, EGYPT

Sixteen days later we docked at Port Said in Egypt. We would soon set our feet on African soil.

As we sailed nearer and nearer to our destination, we realized we had no idea of what to expect. We said, " What do we do when the ship docks?   Where do we go when we get off?"

We had no idea. Somehow, in the rush of that last day, we had failed to get last minute instructions. So, when the ship docked about a half mile from land, we would be playing it by ear.

It was around two thirty in the morning. Whistles were blowing and the ship was anchoring. Small boats were circling around on the shore side.   The ship's spotlight picked up numerous small boats.   One or two might have come out to collect passengers, but the others seemed to have traders with their wares.

This was the period when Israel and Egypt were hostile toward each other.  Because President Truman had recognized Israel as a sovereign state, Americans were less than popular among budding radicals.  The very first words we heard from people in Africa, traders in one of those small boats, still surface in my ears: "We no like um American.   We no like um

American!" Not exactly a warm welcome!

Eventually, a small contingent of the Egyptian military came up the stairway which had been lowered enabling people to board from one of the boats. These harbor police marched the length of the ship symbolizing their authority over the vessel in Egyptian waters. Others also came aboard.

Lavina and I were in our room when someone asked us for our passports. Not knowing any better and remembering we had been warned not to let our passports out of our hands, we refused. It wasn't too long when the ship's officer came with this individual and explained to us that he was a representative from Cooks Travel Agency and had come to assist us through customs and take us to our hotel. What a relief! We realized then, for the first time, that our RCA Board had made arrangements with Cooks to help us with travel arrangements from the ship to our ultimate destination, the Sudan. We weren't on our own after all. It was just that this was totally new to us and we felt as "green as grass".

With the help of Cook's representative, we collected our belongings and started toward the stairway leading from the upper deck down along side the ship to the small boat waiting below. It was a scary experience for us and Lavina was worried about Jimmy in his basket. Strong Arabs had grabbed our luggage to carry it down the stairs to the boat. One of them had taken Jimmy's basket and proceeded down the steps. Jimmy was in it and we were worried that he might get dumped out into the water. We were relieved when we were all safely in the boat and were chugging through the darkness toward the dock. This platform was about a fourth of a mile from where the ship was anchored. We were only eleven passengers on board, and only one lady with her young son had disembarked with us. They carried our things to a nearby Quonset customs shed where two officials checked and cleared us. Two old taxis were standing behind the building and we and our luggage were taken out to get into one of them. It was still pitch dark and scary. We couldn't understand a word being said, but these two taxi drivers got themselves into a fist fight over who was going to transport us. The one man ended up with a terribly bloody nose. I remember his nose was large and it was bleeding profusely. We were tickled pink when the taxi, with our things and us, drove off in the dark toward what we hoped would be our hotel.

27

# CHAPTER ONE

The streets of Port Said were dark. Only later did we realize that this was because of the blackout to protect against possible Israeli air attacks. When we arrived at the hotel, an Egyptian employee met us with a flashlight and ushered the attendants with our luggage and us into the room. By now it was about 4:30 in the morning. We hadn't slept yet. It was an eerie feeling in a strange land, in a strange hotel in the dark.

We had trouble locating the toilet but eventually we settled down and tried to sleep. Very soon we heard the loudest kind of noise coming from the street. It was new to us. The noise sounded like some old pump handle being used that needed greasing. We learned later that it was the braying of a donkey. We had myriads of new sights and sounds along with new tastes to absorb. What an adventure we had begun!

When daylight finally came, we wandered out into the garden area which was part of the hotel. The palm trees were so beautiful and stately. There were numerous flowers and shrubs. We sat at a small table on metal chairs and eventually someone brought us food and tea. We had never seen food like this before and pursued it gingerly. It all tasted very good to us, but we wondered what it was. I said to Lavina, "You know what? I'll bet we're eating fried snake!" It didn't stimulate her appetite a bit, but it was a lot of fun as we were exploring the first 24 hours in our new world. Later we learned it was probably egg plant. During our years in Africa, we would be growing and eating a lot of egg plant. It was very tasty the way Lavina fixed it with a nice batter!

Later in the morning Cook's representative met us. He spoke good English and told us the plan. We would be taken to the train that evening and would travel by rail to Cairo. The trip would take about two hours. In Cairo another Cook representative would meet us at the train and take us to our hotel. We would have a full day in Cairo and could go sight seeing, visit the bazaar or if we were too tired we could spend our time sleeping. He said we might even want to go out to see the Pyramids.

My one indelible memory of the day spent in Port Said is when one of the merchants with true Arab hospitality treated us to our first cup of Turkish coffee. It was served in a little cup without ears, black, thick, syrupy and strong enough to curl one's hair. We had never tasted anything like it, but in the years that followed, we learned to love this delicacy.

## ISRAEL'S PLANES BOMB CAIRO

When we arrived in Cairo, Cook's representative was waiting for us. Again it was dark with street lights off. They, too, were afraid of possible Israeli air raids. They had already had one or two and were preparing for more.

The next morning, Cook's representative came to the hotel to check on us. He arranged for us to go out to the Pyramids and to visit the Bazaars. All day, this representative stayed with us. He even babysat Jimmy so we would have some freedom to move around the traders' stalls and see what was going on. Later, on our first furlough, when we told our families they weren't exactly enthusiastic about our wisdom in having done that. Looking back on it ourselves, in our more advanced years, we wouldn't think of doing it again. But, at the time, it didn't seem that risky.

When darkness fell, we were back in our hotel room resting when the sirens began to scream. Israeli planes were dropping bombs. We huddled together alone, a long way from home, and we were afraid. We needed to remind ourselves during those moments of those verses from the Psalm that God have given us on the ship when we left the harbor in New Jersey.

> "He suffered no man
> to do them wrong:
> yea, he reproved kings
> for their sakes;
> Saying, 'Touch not mine anointed,
> and do my prophets no harm'."

These words comforted us then and they would give us courage now! The time for our flight to the Sudan was still six hours away. We were ready to leave!

The Hoekstra's first home in Africa would be among the Anuak People on the bank of the Pibor River more than seven hundred miles south of Khartoum.

# CHAPTER TWO

# FRIGHTENED IN CAIRO
# AND
# FRIENDS IN THE SUDAN

Never were missionaries happier than we to get out of Egypt. Those Israeli airplanes dropping bombs on King Faruk's palace and the anti-aircraft guns during our brief stay in Cairo made anything in the Sudan seem attractive. My letter to the folks, written just before we left for the airport later that same night on July 17, 1948, 1:30 a.m. tells how it appeared to us then:

*"We had a terrible, shocking and trying experience this evening when Cairo was twice attacked by bombers. (Israeli planes) Oh, it was terrible. It seemed that all hell had broken loose. Shells were exploding everywhere and all was dark except for the flashes of light from tracer bullets and powerful searchlights.*

*We all stood huddled together with our arms about each other and expected any moment to be struck. The first raid lasted about 15 or 20 minutes and then the siren blew 'all clear', but just as the lights went on, another attack began and the shells began bursting again. It is the most shocking and terrifying experience we have ever had."*

Lavina added these few words to the same letter:

*"Harvey just went to drink his tea, so I will finish with a few lines. We have enjoyed ourselves so much with the*

*exception of last night. My hands are still shaking. It really was something to go through. ... We're getting ready to leave so will say, 'Goodbye' for now."*

Early in the morning, flying toward Khartoum, I described how happy we were to be able to leave Egypt so quickly and unexpectedly. We were flying at 11,000 feet over the Sahara desert. The time was 7 a.m., July 18, 1948:

*"It is beautiful up here looking down on the endless, sand desert of North Africa. We are so very glad to be out of Cairo. We will never forget our experience last night in the air raid. Lavina and Dennis were awfully nervous and frightened. I was just plain scared to death. I honestly expected to be blown up any minute. There was a terrific noise of bursting shells. Later they told us that King Farouk's palace had been hit.*

*God has marvelously provided this plane for us. The travel agent said it was most unusual. We would have had to stay for at least two weeks if this plane were not going. We thank God and praise Him for His marvelous provision for us. Our faith was really tested last night. It was very difficult as we stood with arms about each other and softly prayed that we might be spared. How wonderful as the Psalmist says, "He knows our frame. He remembers that we are dust."*

*This plane is a twin engine Viking, a British plane. It is taking some freight as well as three other passengers. Because of this, we had enough room for all our extra baggage and trunk at a special, reduced rate. It cost me $100 extra for the baggage. We would not have it for months and perhaps never, if we didn't bring it with us. And, we would have to pay customs storage and freight. It is really cheaper in the long run this way. For this, we are very thankful."*

## ARRIVING IN KHARTOUM

We had flown all night, hitching a ride on that small aircraft flying from Cairo to South Africa. When we landed in Khartoum about eleven in the morning, we felt as if we had stepped into a blast furnace. It was 110 degrees and rising! For a moment I wondered if we had missed our calling. It was hot! It was worse than Norman, Oklahoma! We had never felt anything quite that hot before. People seemed to be lying around in whatever shade from buildings could be found. We thought everyone must be suffocating from the heat. Later we learned that this was the time when Muslims fasted for thirty days. They had been up feasting all night and were now sleeping and resting during the day. Not being permitted to drink or even swallow their own saliva during the day, was reason enough for them to be less than energetic.

It was a different world from which we had come. Wearing those wide-bottomed, white shorts I had bought in Cairo, and wearing that white, pith helmet hat didn't make me feel very comfortable. I worried a little on the plane about arriving in Khartoum on Sunday wearing those shorts. I didn't feel any more secure when sedate, impeccably dressed Dr. Shields with his wife, Mildred, met us at the airport and he was wearing neatly pressed tan trousers. I felt a little better about it when Dr. Shields came to the table the next (first morning for us) wearing shorts. But, when I made an innocent comment like, "I see you wear shorts also" and Dr. Shields responded with "Yes, when it's not the Sabbath", I knew I must have looked like a greenhorn, out of place and stupid besides! We had a lot to learn!

Dr. Shields seemed rather forbidding at first, but we later came to realize that both he and Mildred were tremendous people who cared for others and were always extremely helpful. The lesson we learned was not to be so quick to pass judgment and to learn to appreciate others however different they may be from one's own way of seeing and doing things. Coming from a somewhat parochial background, I needed to learn tolerance. I was challenged to cherish my basically conservative views and theology, while learning to be flexible in my attitudes and more readily adaptable. In a cross-cultural environment, we would constantly be challenged to distinguish between form and substance.

We survived the first shock and were told that as we traveled further south to Malakal and eventually to Akobo, some 750 miles south of Khartoum, the weather would be much more pleasant because the rainy season had already begun in that region.

There was much to learn in this difficult and forbidding country. The Shields, who had met us at the airport, ran the mission guest house where we stayed until a way could be arranged to get us further south to our destination. They took care of everything and shared from their experiences. We soon learned that one of the primary virtues we needed to learn to survive and be content was "patience". Everything would take longer and we would be dependent upon others making decisions over which we would have little control. And then, there was always the uncertainty of it all. There might be a plane in two weeks, or then again, there might not be one indefinitely. We would just have to wait and see how things developed. Don't be in a hurry! Patience!

We were shown to our room in the back where guests stayed. It was Spartan and clean except for evidences of a liberal layer of dust which had been already dealt with. We were told that this was "haboob" season and these strong winds off the desert could develop unpredictably and make a real mess of things.

Each afternoon, everyone disappeared into these rooms, shut the door, turned on that huge overhead fan and rested from about two until four p.m. At four thirty, the Shields and any other missionary guests gathered on the veranda for a refreshing "tea time". We later learned that this was a British custom which missionaries had also adopted. These were delightful times of rich fellowship when in this relaxed atmosphere experiences and plans were shared.

After this "tea break", everyone went into "high gear" and rushed off to the office or the market. Dr. Shields and I returned to government offices to finish what had been started and hadn't been completed during the cooler morning hours.

We learned that the evening dinner hour was also according to British custom. The Sudan was still peacefully ruled by the British during those years, and their good influence was exhibited in innumerable ways. Influenced by their customs, missionaries also fed their children first around six or six thirty in the evening. After the children had bathed, had their evening meal and were safely tucked away for the night, the adults had a quiet evening dinner. It began around eight p.m. and lasted for nearly an hour. During the meal, conversations stopped while everyone listened to the 8 o'clock news on BBC (British Broadcasting Corporation). Rarely was an evening dinner or a morning breakfast completed without the BBC being turned on. It was every missionary's indispensable contact with the outside world. This was supplemented by a subscription to TIME or NEWSWEEK. We soon learned that most missionaries were real news hounds!

## OUR FIRST HABOOB

We were in Khartoum less than a week. During that time, however, we experienced that inevitable haboob with its powerful wind and blinding dust.

The night it happened, we were all sleeping on the veranda. Every night those single width beds were rolled out of our rooms unto the veranda to catch the cooler night air. The rooms stayed hot until nearly daybreak. If you wanted to sleep, you slept outside. It was a beautiful experience to feel the fresh air coming in and to see the thousands of stars overhead. Dogs were barking everywhere and when daylight broke, the donkeys were braying in some neighboring Arab's yard, sounding like a dry farm pump that needed a good greasing. The bustle of people on the street getting to their places of activity was part of our new experience. It was often less than quiet when we were there because of the feasting during the night and the fasting during the day. We were there during Ramadan, the month Muslims fasted and feasted. We wondered then, how this could be!

The morning after the haboob, Lavina picked up Jimmy out of his basket, and found him covered with dust. His little eyes were okay and his one thumb had been sucked clean, but he was covered with dust. Where he had lain, was clean and you could see his shape in the basket marked out with boundaries set by the dust. Dust had gotten into our suitcases and everything else as well. Nothing escaped receiving its uninvited layer of dust. We actually thought it was pretty bad. Our hosts, Dr. and Mrs. Shields, however, insisted that this one wasn't that bad and that we really ought to see a real haboob sometime. We realized then, that the old timers knew a lot and that we young, missionaries had a lot to learn yet!

Dr. Shields knew his way around government offices in Khartoum. He knew exactly what had to be done before we could move on. Permits to travel to the south, considered a closed district by the British, required special permission to enter that area. We were told later that this was, in part, a way to control the spread of Islam in the South by restricting

35

the movement of Muslim merchants who introduced Islam wherever they went.

## STOCKING UP IN KHARTOUM

Dr. Shields took us to Morhigs, a large, general store belonging to a Greek merchant. In this store, one could find almost everything needed from lumber and nails to pots and pans and foodstuffs. This store had what we needed to purchase before moving south to Akobo. Morhigs would pack whatever we bought and ship it to Akobo. We were surprised at how extremely helpful these Greek merchants in the Sudan were to the missionaries. Most of them were genuine friends.

We bought huge amounts of staples, including big, 30 gallon, baked earthen pots called, zeers and smaller two to three quart earthen jars called, gulas. At Akobo, we would be having our water carried up from the river to the house. Every day, the person who carried up the water would fill those zeers. The zeers, in turn, would drip the water drop by drop into a bucket underneath.

We learned that these were essential pieces of equipment for our safety and survival. Without a senior missionary like Dr. Shields helping us, we wouldn't have had a clue. Later at Akobo, we learned how to clean the zeers periodically by having them emptied and rubbed down with a soft brick. Then we let them dry out well before refilling. Between cleanings they would be useable for another two or three weeks, depending on how dirty the river was before cleaning was again required. The clean water in the bucket was put on a fire and boiled, cooled and poured into the smaller, clay jars called gulas, which aerated the water and cooled it. This was a daily chore that Lavina learned never to neglect. If one did, by afternoon when it was hot, that cool, refreshing drink might become an occasion for drinking luke-warm water! We learned fast!

Supplies from Khartoum would be put on a train by the Greek merchant. His agent would transfer them from the train to the Nile steamer at Kosti, about 19 hours by rail from where they had started out. Three days later, a resident missionary in Malakal would meet the steamer and off load these supplies destined for Akobo, another 300 river miles up country. Akobo was approximately 700 miles south of Khartoum. It would take from two weeks to a month before they would arrive. At Akobo, we would be off-loading them from a provincial, paddle wheel steamer. They couldn't get there too quickly!

## MALAKAL -- JULY 17, 1948

So there we were flying to Malakal with all the business of getting supplies and permits accomplished. We were so excited to be heading south this quickly. Older missionaries commented that we had broken all records. Normally, missionaries had to travel a couple of months to reach the Sudan. God was indeed blessing us and we daily thanked and praised Him.

What a thrill to land in Malakal. There was a different feel to the air. The atmosphere seemed fresh and clean. This was rainy season in the South. We sensed immediately how much more pleasant the weather was.

Mat and Ruby Gilliland, missionaries based in Malakal, along with Robb McLaughlin, a young, short-term volunteer working as a builder met us at the plane. An earliest memory is of the beautiful cooing of a morning dove perched somewhere in one of the tall trees in front of the house on the riverbank where the Gillilands were living.

Malakal was the capital of the Upper Nile Province. In 1948, when we first arrived in Malakal, the British were in control. The provincial governor, deputy governor, a chief police officer, an education officer and a public works officer were people we came to know well. They were generally very helpful to the mission. In the field of education the government and the mission cooperated closely. The British administered a vast area covering thousands of square miles and numerous tribes, each with its own customs and language. Some of these officials were deeply committed Christians and had the welfare of the people under their jurisdiction at heart. We learned to respect them and greatly benefited from their wisdom and assistance.

Before moving south from Malakal to Akobo, some 300 river miles away, a lot had to happen first. Was there a steamer going soon? If one was going up river, could we find space on it? How long would we have to wait, if we missed the first one going? If it went too soon, would we be able to get the additional supplies we needed and would there be room for them on that steamer?

## STOCKING UP IN MALAKAL

Mat Gilliland and I did a lot of walking back and forth the quarter mile from the mission into the town. We went to and fro between government offices and between the two Greek merchants. These Greek merchants had been in Malakal a long time and were the only source of groceries and supplies for missionaries and government people.

Having just come from America, the shelves in these small Greek merchant shops didn't look like much to us. There wasn't a great variety on those shelves. One item I remember as being in abundance was a mixed canned fruit from South Africa called "Compote". We later got so tired of it at Akobo that we began to refer to it as "Compost". Not too complimentary!

We had gotten the big items in Khartoum, but not knowing when they would show up at Akobo, we had to purchase basic supplies again and with less variety available in Malakal. Now we purchased a five gallon tin of cooking oil, a two hundred pound sack of sugar, salt, kerosene, beans, rice, and powdered milk -- all in quantity.

Later, at Akobo, we learned that once a year, Lavina would be returning to Malakal to order the next year's supply of most things. These would be supplemented with orders placed by a letter or telegram we would send to these same Greek merchants who would pack things up and send them to us at Akobo. We were amazed at how thoughtful and helpful these merchants were. We were utterly dependent upon them and for the frequent good offices of the resident missionary if something out of the ordinary was needed. We would learn to help each other and depend upon each other. The mission family is unique and precious. Ties between us would become strong and bind us together like one large family working together, laughing and sometimes crying together.

Our first letters from Africa to family in America tell how we saw things then and our reactions to our new surroundings. Every day we were getting farther and farther from

38

what had been home as we slowly penetrated this strange and forbidding land. We were remembering how He had said, "I will be with you always, even to the end of the ...." We felt like we were almost there! Why not look over my shoulder and read along with me?

From Malakal, Wed. a.m., July 22, '48:

"*We arrived in Malakal on Monday morning and at 3 p.m. I was out with Mat. and Rob helping build a house. It was pretty hot that afternoon too. The local people here are very likeable. The Christian men helping build are all such happy and humorous fellows. Some of them have shoulder cloths and a few wear shorts, but many of them wear only a string of beads. They are very tall and slim, although many of them are our size too. ... I am much impressed with the bird life -- unlimited birds and songs of all sizes and descriptions. The trees are beautiful and numerous -- although on the plains they are limited. We have beautiful mahogany trees here in the front yard and some others that look much like the Florida magnolia trees, only prettier. I have never seen prettier flowers -- even in Florida. These flowers are all on the properties of the government officials and, I suppose, the seeds are imported. Right now we are living in a vacant government house with Mat. and Ruby.*

*... We haven't heard a word from the outside world since we arrived in Malakal. So be sure to write things that you might take for granted. We haven't heard a thing yet. We were hoping a letter from you folks via air might be here, but I guess we came too fast. ...*

*Today it rained in the morning and the balance of the day has been grand. Page is full. Write us soon. This is our last letter for a long time again as mail is scarce at Akobo. God bless you all. Love, Harvey and all*"

We were in Malakal only a few days before we boarded a wood burning, paddle wheel steamer, called the "TAMAI". It was painted white and was really picturesque. The first class barge on which we traveled had two small bedrooms, a dining room and a lovely screened in veranda across the front with comfortable, cushioned reed chairs. The kitchen was down below immediately beneath the dining room. It was dark and dirty and smelled like smoke. This was where a person hired for that task normally cooked the food on a wood fire. When all was ready, he would send the food up on a "dumb- waiter", operated in something like a chute in which dirty clothes are-sent to the basement to be laundered. It was brought up to the kitchen and lowered again by pulling on a rope attached to the shelf on which the food was coming up and on which the dirty dishes would be lowered. We had never seen one of these and it was intriguing to this young missionary family!

We brought with us all our food needed for the remaining estimated 300 mile, seven day journey up the Sobat and Pibor rivers. We also had on board our supplies for Akobo. Paul Musser and his wife, along with Mildred Heasty, who had grown up on a mission station and whose parents were still there, were traveling with us. They chaperoned us as far as Nasir, located on the Sobat about 90 miles from Akobo. They get off there, visited missionary friends, and we proceeded on the last 90 miles alone to Akobo, just off the tip of Western Ethiopia.

Traveling by paddle-wheel steamer was a marvelous, calming experience for us. With the gentle breezes created by the slow, forward movement of the TAMAI, we relaxed and reflected on God's goodness and mercies. So much had already happened. It was good to have time to reflect. The leisurely journey on the TAMAI provided that delightful opportunity. Ours was a rare privilege.

**THIS CROCODILE WAS A MAN EATER. IT WAS FOUND TO HAVE A MAN'S PRACELET IN ITS STOMACH**

During the rainy season, roads were impassible and rivers were flooded. Huge flooded areas were teeming with fish. And one always had to be aware of crocodiles.

Someone asked, "How do you baptize in a river like that when you know a crocodile may be lurking nearby.?"

With a twinkle in his eye, Harvey's light-hearted response was, "You baptize faster than you've ever baptized before!"

41

*"You will keep in perfect peace him whose mind is steadfast because he trusts in you."*
Isaiah 26:23

# CHAPTER THREE

# THE "TAMAI"
# OUR PADDLE-WHEEL
# STEAMER

That first paddle wheeled steamer trip from Malakal to Akobo is unforgettable, sheer delight, with good company and so much to see, restful and relaxing pure luxury to this young missionary family. We felt so privileged and the Lord was preparing our hearts for the challenge just ahead. We wondered what Akobo would be like. Would it be like Malakal with cooler weather and rains or hotter as we were traveling south? What would we live in once we got there? How long would it be before the promised mission doctor could move to Akobo? Would we get malaria and how bad might it be? How long would it take for our supplies and the things from America to reach Akobo? How difficult would it be to learn the language? What were the folks doing back home today? We had plenty of questions without answers. Our adventure and challenge was to trust the Lord and take one day at a time and to learn to be "patient".

A letter to my family in Minnesota on July 26, 1948, 5:30 p.m., aboard the TAMAI, tells how things were going:

*"Dear Dad, Mother and all, -- Greetings from our boat, the TAMAI, a provincial, paddle wheel river boat. We are all in the best of health. It has been very hot the early part of the afternoon, but now it is cooling off and very comfortable again.*

## CHAPTER THREE

*"This is a wood burning steamer and has to stop every 3 to 4 hours to take on more wood. We stopped at a pile of wood at 2 a.m. but the village people would not begin loading until 6 a.m. So we lost lots of time. We average less than 3 to 5 miles per hour...*

*"We have seen boundless bird life. I have seen countless kinds of birds, large and small, and innumerable flocks of birds sitting around swamps and in the fields. The plains are green now and there have been considerable numbers of trees so far. The cattle appear to be in excellent shape now and the herds appear to be large. Villages with grass roofed tukls are seen constantly along the river and as far back as a mile or two. My field glasses are much appreciated. They are wonderful glasses and how glad I am for them. I have seen only one hippo, but numerous crocodiles on the banks and at lease one huge snake. The river winds constantly and varies from 100 feet wide to 250 feet. It is, of course, high now. We had a big rain with some wind last evening. The rains, actually, are not as heavy as they should be by now and there is some fear among the local people. However, it really does come down when it comes! We also have heavy thunder and lightning. The clouds look much like the clouds in Minnesota."*

### MEETING DR. TRUDINGER AND KEN   RASMUSSEN

One of the thrilling experiences on that trip was when a small outboard with three people in it appeared out of nowhere and joined themselves to our barge. It was Dr. Trudinger, veteran missionary from Australia, and a young, short-term, American missionary named Ken Rasumussen. They were moving among the villages, had seen our boat and came aboard to travel with us for awhile and enjoy some Christian fellowship. As young missionaries just starting out, it was so very special to us. I shall always remember their joy as they shared from their experiences out in the villages. It whetted our appetites for the time when we would be doing similarly at Akobo.

I was privileged to lead our little group on the TAMAI for our time of worship and prayer together. This is what I wrote to my folks  the next day while still moving south toward Akobo:

"How thrilled we were to have them with us and tell of their experiences. We had a church service in the screened in veranda and I was given the joyous privilege of leading it and speaking a few words. We opened with prayer -- then sang, 'Savior like a Shepherd lead us, What a friend we have in Jesus, Jesus loves me this I know' and the chorus, 'Safe am I.' This was followed by the Scripture and the message. Dr. Trudinger told of the moving of God in these villages. (He is an elderly saint of the Lord, a medical doctor, translator of the Dinka New Testament) We then had a prayer service and prayed for the success of this mission; the mission in Egypt and Palestine and a prayer of thanks for our supporting churches and their prayers and a prayer for new recruits for the field. It was a service we shall never forget. How wonderful it was to gather in a Christian fellowship and worship God after several Sundays without others with whom to fellowship. "They were with us for lunch and the usual, late afternoon tea. We dropped them off and loosened their boat to push them off about dusk to make their way to some village to resume their witnessing in the morning. The mosquitoes must be furious in that tall grass!"

While on board, Dr. Trudinger treated the eyes of some twenty people who had problems. I was very touched by his loving, concerned attitude. ·I couldn't help but feel that a medical doctor came close to approximating what Jesus did when he ministered to the sick and those who needed help. I recall how during our first weeks at Akobo, I was tempted to consider returning to school and pursue training in medicine to become that kind of missionary. It's hard to believe that I was serious enough about it to have written a letter to Hope College to inquire what would be required for me to qualify for medical school. Interestingly, the young man on the boat, Ken Rasmussen, later returned to America, completed his theological training, came with his wife and children to the Sudan as career missionaries and then later returned to America and got a degree in medicine for that same reason! For myself, once I became fully engaged in the translation effort, I knew that I was where God wanted me and had been prepared and educated for that special task. My heart was totally at peace in the certainty of His calling.

## CHAPTER THREE

### STOPPING AT NASIR MISSION STATION

We were on the TAMAI seven days and nights. Ninety miles from Akobo, on the Sobat river, was Nasir where Presbyterian missionaries had been at work for many years. The work among the Nuer had been started there by Dr. Lambie before he moved on to Ethiopia. Dr. and Mrs. Smith were still there and about to retire, but their daughter, Mary, was now back at Nasir. She had recently completed her medical training and was serving as a medical missionary doctor. We were met at the steamer by Charles (Chuck) and Mary Alice Jordan. Chuck was a trained Agriculturalist. We didn't know then that within a few years the Jordans would be moving to Akobo and become dear colleagues of ours living in the same mission station.

Several things stick in my memory from those 24 hours we stopped at Nasir. First impressions have a way of writing themselves indelibly on the mind! The flies were so numerous as we walked from the steamer to the mission house, that the next time out, I put on my army surplus, bee-bonnet. During that time, most young missionaries going to remote areas stocked up on things like that at the army surplus stores. We had done it too. We were ready for anything!

I must have looked like an idiot and I wonder what those missionaries must have thought about this naive, stupid young missionary. The Arab merchants sitting in front of their small, thatch roofed shops must have had a good laugh too. We weren't in the Sudan many days when we realized that coping with flies was normal and one didn't wear a bee-bonnet! The missionaries at Nasir must have shaken their heads and had some hilarious laughs after we returned to the TAMAI.

Another recollection is of the food these missionaries served us. At Mr. and Mrs. Smith's for breakfast, they came out with a very dark colored porridge which hardly looked like something one would eat. It looked like mud! In fact, however, it tasted great, much like our Ralston cereal. We learned that missionaries ate this porridge almost every morning. It was their home made cereal, prepared by roasting the ripened dura (kaffir-corn). This particular variety had a purple color, and consequently the dirty looking appearance when cooked. We learned later that the dura had a number of varieties and colors and we often had beautiful tasting, as well as nice colored, porridge with which to start our days.

At Akobo, our problem wasn't the color of the porridge, but quality of the milk we put on it. Before the mission had its own herd of cattle, we'd buy milk from village people. One could never be sure that the gourd in which they brought the milk hadn't been washed in cow urine and that a little may have remained in the bottom of the gourd. It didn't take more than a swallow to know things weren't right! A few such experiences, and we missionaries were strongly motivated to have a mission herd. Each cow produced only a little, but we had good quality control and that's what was important for a good dish of home grown, home roasted, dura porridge at the beginning of every day.

On that stop at Nasir, back in July of 1948, the single, lady missionaries served up a delicious noon meal. I still remember how much better it tasted than it looked. We were served a fruit we hadn't tasted in the states. They called it papaw (papaya), deep orange in color and, as we learned in the months ahead, normally eaten when the flesh is firm. Theirs must have fallen off the tree because it was soft and gushy, not nice and firm as we imagined this unknown fruit, which sort of reminded us of a cantaloupe, should be. Once we gingerly tasted it, we found it quite good, especially when we squeezed a little lime juice on it as per their instructions as to how it should be eaten. Then at the close of the meal, they came out with a very "runny" lemon (lime) pie. It was much too thin to pass the test, but it tasted so good that no one complained. We soon learned that lime pie just was that way in this hot country and that regardless of how it appeared, it was "special". We loved it, and a good lime pie like that often graced our table in the years ahead.

Once settled in, we raised papaya all the time. We grew to love them and I suspect that we ate papaya at least 300 days out of the year. Our morning breakfast rarely lacked a generous half of a papaya with a slice of lemon beside it to spruce it up just a bit! Papaya mixed with bananas, oranges and some home grown pineapple was "missionary-desert" that can't be matched anywhere in the world! We loved it then and miss it now!

Stopping and staying overnight with the missionaries at Nasir was a great experience. These were folks from whom we could learn so much. They would become our dearest friends

47

and colleagues in the Lord's work in the years ahead. We were glad to stop, but itching to move on to complete the last 90 miles up river to Akobo. We'd been on the way for 25 days. Seemed long, but everyone told us we were breaking all records. It had taken the Swarts more than two months to make it, including their delay enroute in Egypt. So far as this young missionary couple was concerned, we just wanted to get there as soon as possible. Excitement was mounting! So, when the steamer, having unloaded its cargo for Nasir and having loaded the grain and other supplies for Akobo, blew its first warning whistle indicating a sailing time was approaching, we collected our things, put Jimmy back in the basket, and with the resident missionaries leading the way, we threaded our way through the busy local market, stepping it off in the direction of the TAMAI.

## HEADING FOR AKOBO

Finally, it happened! The narrow gang planks connecting the steamer with the shore were pulled on board. The ropes tying the steamer to secure posts were loosened and dragged onto the barge. A last whistle blew and the boat began to move. This was it! We were slowly churning our way upstream, heading for Akobo. We were alone now, just the four of us, Lavina, Dennis our five year old, Jimmy, then four months, and myself. This was adventure of the highest sort. We were on our own!

As we picked up just a little speed, the gentle breeze began blowing through the screen on the sitting veranda. It was pleasant and refreshing. We drew close to one another, put our arms around each other and praised God for His watch-care, protection and leading. We knew His good hand had been on us all the way. Our hearts sang to be His missionaries in this far away land of Africa. We were glad because we knew that He was taking us to a place where without our being there a task He was entrusting to us would remain undone. My hope and dream was to be the translator for the New Testament in the Anuak language. Time would tell!

# CHAPTER FOUR

# OUR NEW HOME
# AKOBO

## WELCOMED BY THE LIGHT OF AN ALADDIN LAMP

According to folks at Akobo, we were 24 hours ahead of schedule. It was already dark, nearly 7:30 p.m. when the TAMAI finally stopped and tied up. We discovered that we were directly in front of Don and Lyda McClure's house. It was less than 75 yards up the bank and down the short path from the steamer into their house. What a night to remember!

As the steamer was docking, we could see a bright light coming down the steep bank toward us. It turned out to be Lyda McClure carrying an Aladdin lamp to light her way. She was surrounded on all sides by about fifty school boys wearing their white shoulder cloths. Their white teeth and white cloths were about all we could make out, but the chatter of excited voices filled the air. What an unforgettable night! The journey was over! Twenty seven days -- via ocean freighter, train, airplanes and the last seven days by a slow, wood burning, paddle wheel steamer.    S c h o o l boys meant willing hands. They helped with the luggage and the supplies we had brought from Malakal.

Lyda quickly apologized that Don was not there to welcome us. They had thought the steamer was coming the next day. Don and Wilma Kats, a single missionary who was still living with the McClures until the single ladies' house was built, had gone by boat up river to shoot some ducks for meat. They weren't home yet. She explained that Bob and Morrie Swart were living in a vacant government

49

house at the government post about a mile away. She said, "They'll know you're here when they hear the steamer's whistle. They'll be joining us for dinner once Don gets back."

By this time we had made our way up the bank -- pitch dark, except for the light of the Aladdin lamp. We shall never forget the awesome, memorable experience of entering by the front door into the McClure house with Lyda and that Aladdin lamp. The room we entered was a huge round tukl. (mud-walled and round with a grass roof) Overhead was a grass roof, held in space by 2" inch coils of woven grass rings that went around and around to make a conical covering. It was so beautiful and rustic. We had never seen anything like it. The roof was made of poles, those rings of grass and thick thatch which we would see better the next day. It was poetic, pictur-esque and made an indelible impression on these young mis-sionaries. We knew then that we had truly arrived. This was Africa and these missionaries, like the Anuaks, lived in houses made from mud and grass. We were home in Africa. Praise be to God.

We soon heard the drone of the outboard approaching in the darkness. Don and Wilma came in with guns and a handful of ducks. Don apologized all over the place for not be-ing there to welcome us, but explained that we'd come so fast they just weren't expecting us for another day. Don had a great sense of humor. Having been on the TAMAI seven long days and nights, it didn't seem that we could sneak up on any-one unexpectedly. But, that's the way things were in the Su-dan. We were often in the dark. No mail! No news! And sometimes no lights!

Bob and Morrie Swart and their two little girls, Valarie and Gayle, soon arrived in their jeep. We were all so excited. Questions flew thick and fast from both directions. We learned that we would be going home with them in the jeep and that we would be living with them until our house was ready.

Lyda had a fantastic meal ready in no time, including a delicious cherry pie for desert. We learned that they, too, had been to Leggett's wholesale store in New York before coming out to purchase basic supplies of tinned fruit and vegetables. Without Leggetts, missionaries would have been hurting. We hoped *our* freight would catch up with us soon with *our* order of tinned food. Lyda had a real gift at homemaking and was known for her good cooking and creative table displays. We ate by candlelight with candlewick dishes in a mud house with a grass roof. We were pleased and surprised!

## LEARNING TO LIVE IN A DIFFERENT WORLD

During the meal we learned more about what to expect. Additional missionaries were scheduled to come in the months ahead. Once the rains ended in a few more weeks, Don and Bob would be busy with a big building program to provide houses, school buildings and a clinic. As soon as Bob and Morrie's house was built, they planned to move from the government house a mile away to the mission compound. The single ladies were scheduled to have the next new house. When completed, Wilma Kats would move out of the spare bedroom in the McClure house to be joined by a United Presbyterian missionary expected at Akobo early in the new year.

Our more permanent house was a little over a mile away in the opposite direction, downstream from the mission. That would put it a little over two miles from the Swarts. This house had been started by another mission while Don was on furlough. It was abandoned when the two missions deemed it best not to work that closely together when large unreached areas remained with no missionaries at all. Good sense prevailed and any possible tension between the two missions had been averted. God overruled it all for good and it proved to be a great blessing for us personally.

The building needed a lot of additional work on it before one could move in. It had walls and a roof only. It needed a floor, doors and window openings framed with mosquito netting until screen was available to replace the cloth. Everyone agreed that netting was good for mosquitoes and flies but not too formidable against lions! To work on the house I would be walking the more than two miles back and forth each day until it was finished. The jeep couldn't make it because the river had backed up and the swamp enroute was impassable. I later learned that I'd have to wade in water nearly up to my waist to get there. Once through the swamp things dried up quite rapidly.

So Bob and Morrie took us along with them that night and we had our first night on army cots under a mosquito net. Some new missionaries experience several weeks with their

51

stomach and digestive tracts  making an adjustment to the new environment. I was one of them! I still recall how sick the smell of fresh guavas made me feel. I could never believe then, that one day I would learn to love them and eat them in all sorts of combinations.

Lavina seemed real strong and took everything in stride. This surprised us because back home, I was the strong one and she had frequently had minor health problems. In fact, I was to give her liver shots the first few months to help her build up her iron! During those first few weeks when food just didn't sit well, I often felt I was the one who needed the shot more than she!

But, we made it, and gradually the body adjusted and we began to feel strong and eager. My leg muscles strengthened and I was able to get the house finished. I still recall the shock of being on my hands and knees mixing up mud mortar while putting in the blot on our floor. Anuaks were working right beside me and sometimes I'd hear, "Kith kany" or "Kith kanyogo". They were telling me to "Put it here" or to "Put it there". I learned a lot about Anuaks those days and I learned a fair amount of Anuak language. I also learned a lot about myself. They really meant it when they said that a missionary has to have a servant heart. This was for real! The Lord was close to us and He was molding and making us into people in whom and through whom He could make Himself known.

The physical adjustment for the body was more difficult than our emotional adjustment. We were so grateful to be missionaries at Akobo. We counted it an unspeakable privilege. Any difficulties and inconveniences were part of a missionary's experience. We remembered Paul's testimony, "I have learned in whatsoever state I am, therewith to be content." Phil 4:11. The excitement, the new things we were constantly learning, and the challenge to be available to the Lord shaped our mindset. When we were tempted to be anxious, we found ourselves often remembering the exhortation of the Psalmist, "Commit thy way unto the Lord; trust also in Him and He will bring it to pass." Psalm 37:05.

## WE LIVE OFF THE MISSION COMPOUND

Akobo mission station anticipated rapid growth. The

Anuak plan called for a total of fifteen missionaries to work among the Anuak for fifteen years. Additional stations were on the drawing board. But, in the beginning, most of the new missionaries would likely get their start at Akobo. Houses were needed. To get started, the mission would put people where there was a roof that didn't leak. And if the roof did leak, they would put them there anyway!! That's why Bob and Morrie Swart were a mile up stream from the mission where the McClures lived and we were to be a good mile down stream on the other side. We were scattered out along the Akobo river. We were connected either by walking or using a canoe or outboard during the rains and by jeep during the dry season. Later I also had a Whizzer bike with a motor on it.

Lavina and I had ambivalent feelings about living in isolation down stream from the mission. At first we were tempted to feel isolated and somewhat deprived. But, once we got our roots down, we began to realize that living off the compound at this place called Pokang, located near a large Anuak village, gave us a unique advantage. We were forced to use the Anuak language to be understood. We would learn the Anuak language more quickly and more idiomatically. Once we were able to speak a little, we had a marvelous evangelistic opportunity to share the Gospel in those nearby villages. Living there, we found our fulfillment in relationships with our new friends and neighbors, the Anuaks. Were we to live on the mission station, we would likely find our social relationships with fellow missionaries tending to take center stage. These and many other thoughts made us ponder it all. There were advantages and disadvantages to living some distance from our colleagues. On balance, we concluded that we had received a blessing and opportunity in disguise and we gave God daily thanks. Our hearts were overflowing with joy. Lavina and I were both supremely happy and content.

## LETTERS HOME INDICATE THE ADJUSTMENTS

Letters to our families during those early days indicate how things were going and what we were thinking.

September 8, 1948:

"All of us are just fine. Our bodies have made the adjustment now. Our appetites have returned and we are all feeling fine. I was pretty soft when we first came, but now my body is strong, my feet are tough and I am a real farmer. There is much physical work that must be done out here to get things organized. The village workmen help a great deal, but still there is always the special work to do one's self...

Almost three weeks ago we moved from the Swarts into our new house. It is not complete yet, but a unit of it is finished so we moved into it with odds and ends of furniture provided by the other two families. Luckily, McClures still had their old refrigerator so we are using that too. Our own things have not arrived, nor do we know yet if they are on the way. I have had word that my guns have left Egypt and are on the way. I have borrowed a couple of Don's guns for now. I use a shotgun constantly for ducks for food. I shot four in one shot the other day.

Our home is located about 1 1/4 miles down stream from the mission. It faces the river along the South side and is set back about 100 to 150 yards from the water. It is a rectangular building at present with three rooms and a washroom. The three rooms are about 12' by 16' with a hallway and bathroom between two of the rooms. The walls are about a foot thick, made of mud bricks covered with solid mud. The roof comes down low and extends out over the side about 5 feet. It is a grass roof. We have no glass. The windows and doors are full size and are covered with mosquito netting. We use one room for sleeping, one for a sitting and dining room, and the other for a kitchen. Lavina cooks on three single burner kerosene stoves. Not too handy for her.

There is a small house, formerly intended for a kitchen in back of our house. So in it, I fixed up a stove -- building it out of a type of sand brick. I made the stove pipe out of five gallon kerosene tins. I made the cover over the stove out of one tin I had opened up flat. Then for an oven I took the end out of the can and fixed a wooden and tin door in it. Well -- believe it or not, we baked bread in it yesterday and it worked slick. The bread was very good! Out here a person makes a little bit go a long way. We would not think of throwing a rag, a piece of paper or a piece of string away. I made a table for Lavina to use temporarily out of a little grocery box about 20" square. For legs I used some long sticks of firewood. For nails I used the old crooked nails out of the box. Everything is useful out here. We enjoy making things a lot. Sometimes it puzzles us just how we are going to do it, but after awhile we figure something out. For funnels we are just using a tin can bent shut on one side for a spout. And so it goes with making something out of nothing almost every day.

We like our place here very much. We are away from the mission which has some disadvantages. However, we have the advantage of being near a big village and this will give us a big opportunity to learn the language and to carry on evangelistic work. Every day we have about 20 or 25 women, men and children hanging around the yard. Often they come and sit right under the eaves of our house where it is nice and cool. When we know the language we will be able to have Bible story hours for them and what an opportunity it will be to bring them the message of salvation. Then, too, in some ways, I think it is an advantage to be more or less alone. I think one would tend to tire of living too close together. As it is we can get together whenever we want to. Don has a motor boat and we can get back and forth easily. Else there is always an Anuak canoe around and we can get an Anuak to take us. It is a common sight to see us on the river in a driving rain. We are used to that here.

We have tall grass out away from the house a ways and it is a good place for the wild animals. Every night we hear the hyenas howling. Last week one morning we had a lion track across our front yard. The following night we were both awakened about mid-night by the roaring of a lion. It is a blood curdling roar they have and he was very close by. We got up and I loaded my heavy rifle. Lavina and I each sat by the mosquito netting covered window openings looking for him. My light was not strong enough so we did not get him, but now I have a search light and car battery from the mission. We are hoping he returns. Sunday morning we had a hyena track less than 6 feet from our front door. In the evening, right after we were in bed we heard him howl in the back yard. You should have seen Lavina and me out there in the terrible mosquitoes with the searchlight and gun. He got away in the tall grass, but during the dry season it will not be so easy for him.

While building our house, one morning we discovered a leopard track right under our window. So, you see we have lots of animals around here. How would you like to sleep with just a thin mosquito net between you and an angry lion? We are so used to it that we think nothing of it anymore. Can you imagine? Even Lavina isn't afraid of them! It is just part of our life here -- as trucks and cars and airplanes are back home. I think I have seen about two or three planes since we left Malakal!"

March 17, 1949:

"I must write a word, too, about our new companions. They are the mice, rats and bats. Last night I think I was awake about three fourths of the night between the rats and the bats. One of those bats just missed my head when I was dozing off and boy my old heart pounded like ever for awhile. The rats were running around right behind the end of my bed (Lavina slept outside as it was cooler) and they make plenty of noise. Several times I put the light on and one time I saw a fat one less than four feet away under my bookcase. The light frightened him and he came right for it and I almost hit him with it. I don't mind mice but rats are no joke. They make too much noise and I always wonder if they might not bite a finger if one's arm hangs off the bed. The worst part of it is we have nothing we can do about them. For now, we have no rat poison nor traps anywhere at the mission. The McClure house is just alive with rats and ours is fast becoming that way."

June 27, 1950:

"Last night we were rudely awakened at 2. a. m. by an invasion of army ants. They were all over my study and bedroom. They awakened me first and then Dennis, Lavina and Jimmy. Do they ever bite! Scorpions were fleeing for their lives before their carnivorous march. I killed 8 scorpions which had fled out of the grass roof down the walls onto the floor. I walked in the dark the first time, not realizing their presence and missed a couple of them by a matter of inches. I think the Lord was caring for his own again. We had to spend the rest of the night on the davenport, in chairs and on the floor in another part of the house."

September 18, 1950:

"Just before coming in for the night we took the children

*down to the river to wash the mud off from them. Right now I am at my desk sitting under what I call a 'mosquito house'. It is a huge net about 7 feet high and 8 feet square, tied to the roof sticks and surrounding my desk, typewriter stand and chairs for Lavina and myself. This is our first evening with it. We are borrowing it from Lee and Kitty Crandall as their house is alright. Our house is literally so full of mosquitoes that they tend to get in our eyes and ears.*

*We have a very fine mosquito repellant made in Khartoum, and with long trousers or house coats we have managed for awhile in the earlier part of the evening, but it was pretty rugged. We think this little cage will be pretty nice."* (We soon discovered that it became very hot under there because inside we also had to have an Aladdin lamp burning and it used up the limited supply of oxygen.)

*I wish you could see just how we live out here. We so often take these things for granted, but I suppose you would be quite surprised."*

March 10, 1949:

*"We are all sick here except Jimmy. We've been in bed for a week with a burning fever and a terrifying headache in the back of the head and down the back. We have to take aspirins every couple of hours to keep going. Sulpha or penicillin don't touch it. Our doctor doesn't know what it is yet. He thinks we may have typhoid fever, but wont know until he sends our blood samples tomorrow via car and flies them to Khartoum. ... We're having a pretty rugged time of it, but don't worry about us. The Lord will most surely see us through. ...*

*Dr. Harry Hangar is here for two days and leaves tomorrow. Blood samples, were refrigerated in thermoses and taken by Dr. Hangar and his traveling companion Dr. Weber, the 185 miles by road to Malakal. These were then put on a plane and flown another 500 miles to Khartoum. A telegram from Khartoum confirmed that we had Typhoid fever. Fortunately for us, our inoculations helped reduce the pain and duration of the disease.*

March 17, 1949:

"I don't remember if I wrote it or not that our new veranda roof collapsed on us last Monday night while we were out
there sick and half asleep about 10:30 in the evening. The men
had just finished the concrete floor on this end of it so that we
had the beds rearranged and Jimmy's bed was in the house
proper for the night. Had our beds been arranged as usual, Lavina's would have been crushed and Jimmy would have been
crushed beneath the heavy timbers.

A strong wind came up and suddenly we heard a terrific
crash and that was it. I reached for the light and discovered the
end of the roof had fallen on my bed and just missed my head
and feet. A few inches either way and I would have had broken
legs and a cracked head. I really feel the Lord was watching
and not a hair of our heads was hurt.

It didn't take us long to get out of there for fear of more
coming down. It was quite a shock to say the least. The next
morning I managed to take the bed apart and set it up under the
eaves again. So we are back to about where we started. It
means lots of work again. The wood bores had eaten the poles
out already. Now we will have to look for different kind of wood
poles in the forest. That is the way we live and learn! The
Anuaks had said not to use that wood, but we all thought it
would surely last for a year. We learned our lesson! ... "

Had I thought then that my mother was saving every
letter she received and that someday I might be quoting from
them in a book, I would have been more careful in my diction
and choice of words. The value of the letters, however, though
hastily written, as many of them obviously were, lies in their
authentic testimony as to what actually happened so many
years ago and what our thoughts and feelings were at that
time.

## HOW LAVINA COPED
## THOSE FIRST MONTHS AT POKANG

Those first six months at Pokang were an extended
camp-out. We survived and thrived on borrowed pots and
pans, mismatched dishes and cutlery, army cots and impro-

vised cooking utensils.

Lavina, like all the missionaries, baked her own bread and prepared everything that went into our mouths. The bread deal was quite something. She had a 200 pound bag of flour when she started out. Gradually, it went down, but as it went down the weevils and worms in it went up! She taught an Anuak to sift it, sometimes running it through an old silk stocking to separate the weevils and worms from the flour we wanted to save and use. The sifted flour was set in the sun in large, round, eight inch high, copper wash tubs called a "tish" which we had brought down from Khartoum. Chickens and goats had to be kept away and whenever a sudden shower appeared these heavy tubs had to be brought in quickly.

At first Lavina mixed her bread and let it rise at home. But, after she had carried it that 1 1/4 miles to the mission to bake it in Lyda McClure's oven, she found herself baking unleavened bread. The rise in it was gone! To solve the problem, she took to carrying the flour and yeast and mixing it at Lyda's and waiting for it to rise there before baking it. This way she came home with some mighty fine looking bread.

But baking it in the back yard worked out much better. That kerosene tin with a partial, mahogany wooden door swinging on a nail driven through the tin on each side worked just fine. The only problem was that about every three weeks, the door would dry out so badly that it started to burn and would have to be replaced.

Lavina not only baked on that outside arrangement of bricks, but also did a good bit of cooking out there when things needed to simmer longer. This economized on kerosene and, anyway, those kerosene pressure burners were often a headache. They operated under pressure and the little pump often needed a new leather which we didn't have.

We were counting the days until our freight would arrive. Week after week went by and still no certain word on where it was or whether it would arrive before the last steamer for the season would come. In the end, our things from America made it to Malakal from Port Sudan in time to be loaded on the very last steamer before the river would be too shallow to navigate. It finally arrived at Akobo on January 6th.

The arrival of our stove, kerosene refrigerator, beds, pots and pans and dishes and cases of canned fruit and vegetable from Leggetts wholesale house in New York really lifted our spirits. We were as happy as kids with new toys. And what a difference it made in the comfort with which we lived. Never did that good food taste so delicious. Now Lavina could really cook again and bake her bread right in her own oven. She had made do with very little and had made our little house into an attractive, homey place, but now she could really enjoy some of the essentials which would make everything easier for her. She is a great cook and homemaker under any conditions, but having the essentials again, would make it so very much easier.

Lavina was a truly happy, fulfilled missionary wife and mother. She was more than busy. Each of the children was taught during their first years at home. It took a lot of skill and perseverance to keep busy children at their schooling. Still, in addition to these inescapable responsibilities, Lavina found time to help me with primer construction, teaching some of the women and just making time for anyone who came. Our home was always open and many hours were spent sharing with women and girls who dropped by. Lavina set a terrific example for Anuak women as to what it means to be a wife and mother who modeled the love of Jesus Christ. I don't recall an Anuak, or for that matter, a Majang who ever criticized Lavina for some failure in character or demeanor. She set a great example for all of us in our home and in relationships with others. Hers was honoring to Christ! In all our years on the field, I never once heard her pine to return to America. To God be the glory!

Lavina was a brave woman. She showed no signs of the fear she had once expressed about living in Africa among the lions and crocodiles. She had come a long way since that day when I came home from seminary and suggested the Lord might be calling us to "the dark continent". A vision of being up a tree in Africa with a hungry lion at the base had long since evaporated. She learned to cope with ants, rats and snakes in the house, plus scorpions that hid in the grass roof and would drop down on our beds when the army ants invaded us. Once when she was resting on the bed in the afternoon and looking up into the grass roof, she saw a snake in the grass weaving its way forward just overhead. And still another time, she was cleaning out a small cabinet we'd made out of a packing box. Immediately behind this little, three foot cabinet, she discovered a poisonous puff adder sleeping. Once she had a six foot red cobra in the dining room. She, and the rest of us too, were all so very aware of our daily need for the Lord's protection and care.

## DANGERS AND INCONVENIENCES

There were plenty of dangers and inconveniences to cope with in Africa. I sometimes said, "Everything is done the hard way out here." The modern conveniences that make life easier for women in our homes in America weren't possible out there. Clothes were washed by hand. Washed clothes were hung on an outside line to dry. No problem during the dry season, but a real headache during the rains. The responsible person always had one eye on the clouds! Ironing was with a heavy cast metal charcoal burning iron. Floors were mopped daily to keep ahead of the dust and dirt. There was no wall to wall carpeting and only a few throw rugs. Inside plumbing was a facet through the wall attached to a pipe coming out of an elevated barrel positioned on a platform. Water was carried up from the river morning and night to keep the barrels full. Another barrel stood outside the bathroom and was connected to a facet and a shower. This too was filled by hiking it up from the river. Much more could be said, but the question is, "How does a woman cope and still have time for ministry?"

The answer was found in training people for those tasks. Taking people right out of the village who wore little or no clothes and had no experience in how foreigners lived and teaching them was a challenge and sometimes a frustrating experience. People trained to help in these tasks were known as "servants" or "house-boys". Sometimes new missionaries didn't like the idea of having "servants" and would try to do all these tasks themselves. It was interesting to see how many of these idealists gradually came around and decided that coping with all these mundane tasks was taking too much valuable time and robbing one of time for an effective ministry. Servants were a necessary evil. In fact, they were a mixed blessing. On balance, we couldn't have coped without them. Many of those who worked as servants stayed for years. They enjoyed the security of their position and the benefits that flowed from it. We missionaries learned to live with servants and tried to lead them to Christ and set a good example before them.

## CHAPTER FOUR

Our servants, particularly those who worked in our houses became trusted friends -- more like family members than employees. We thanked God for them. But, had their been a choice between modern washers and driers, carpets and vacuum cleaners, we would have opted for the later.

With this background, you can now appreciate the pathos and humor of several of our experiences during those early years at Akobo.

### A SCORPION IN THE CRIB

One of the house servants normally baby sat our children when we had to be out of the house. Because we lived more than a mile from the mission, and because most of the religious and social activities were there, when these things occurred after dark, we normally left our little children home.

This particular evening we were to attend our weekly prayer meeting at the mission. Lavina and I would walk down and probably return home in the canoe. Lovely experience, but not that romantic when your pretty wife is 18 feet away in the front of the canoe and you're paddling in the rear.

Carol was just a little girl then, still sleeping in her screened in crib. Lavina had checked on her and was satisfied that she had already fallen asleep. We quietly sneaked out the back door, trying not to slam it or make any noise. We had scarcely closed the door when we heard Carol let out a terrible scream. We said, "Shucks, she heard us and has awakened."

So, before leaving, we went back in to try to get her quiet before we would leave. As soon as we saw her, we realized something was dreadfully wrong. This is what happened. She, apparently, had put her little arms over her head, which put her hands to the edge of the mattress. Between that mattress and the screen, unknown to us, was a scorpion. It had stung Carol's tiny finger.

We picked her up and carried her to the mission to keep her with us during the prayer meeting rather than leaving her with the other boys and the servant. How glad we were that we had done so. She was in such excruciating pain that she began to perspire and to vomit. We felt so sorry for this little tyke. The pain lasted most of the night. Lavina and I took turns walking the floor with her. Having a kerosene burning refrigerator, we were able to ease the pain somewhat with ice to slow the chemical action of the poison.

Personally, I was never stung by a scorpion. Lavina was stung once in the knee when a scorpion fell out of the roof on her bed and once when a scorpion in the tomatoes got her. That neither were pleasant experiences is an understatement. Chuck Jordan once stuck his finger down the sink to clean it and was stung by a scorpion that had crawled up the pipe. He said he wanted to cry and nearly did! Morrie Swart had one on the knee and said it felt as if her whole knee was being gouged out. No fun! Be careful for scorpions!

## THAT FASCINATING PIT

Servants were great baby sitters, but sometimes they let us down. I recall twice when our children played with things and in places that were out of bounds.

We had an 18 foot pit for our toilet or latrine. It was dug under the backside eave of the roof and enclosed with a mud wall. Its advantage was that we had access to it without having to go outside during the rains.

For some inexplicable reason, that little room seemed to have a special attraction, on occasion, for our little children. Once when we came home from the mission, we learned that David had been playing over the hole with my set of keys to all the trunks and doors dangling from a chain in his hand. I guess it was great fun to see the pendulum of the keys in motion until they slipped out of his hand and sank to the bottom. The keys were never recovered!

On another occasion, however, the situation was quite a bit more serious. The clothes hamper also stood, out of the way, in that same little room that had the box with the hole in it. This time, the servant was preoccupied with something, and, sure enough, the children were in there again. This time they took to dropping pieces of laundry down the hole. It must have been great sport because the hamper was nearly empty when we discovered it. With the help of a flashlight I discovered what had happened. Fortunately, the things were still retrievable. With the help of a garden rake, I think I recovered every last piece. The final solution was a hook on the door out of reach! The barn was locked after the horse had escaped!

How human we missionaries proved to be.

## A HOLE IN THE BABY'S CRIB

Before leaving these experiences with servants and our children, let me tell you of an experience that could have been tragic.

On a Sunday morning during the dry season, we all went to the morning worship at the mission. Our children were with us as they normally were. One person was assigned to guard the place while we'd be away like that.

On this particular Sunday when we returned around noon, I saw that Deng, the man who carried up the water, was in the back yard plucking the feathers off from a beautiful, spur winged goose. I was surprised and asked him how he'd managed. He said he'd sneaked up on a flock of geese and was able to hit one with a stick.

I thought this was quite unusual but gave it no further thought. Later that same day, I noticed that our davenport, a home made sofa built from the 16 foot boards that had been part of the case in which our boat had been shipped from the states, had multiple, tiny holes on the front edge. The painted, 4 inch wide board across the front on which the pillows rested was peppered with these tiny holes. It looked as if someone had taken a hammer and a small nail and had driven innumerable holes into it. I was puzzled but hadn't yet made the connection with Deng and the goose.

Later, I noticed that the screen cover over the baby's crib had a hole in it about 3/4 of an inch in diameter. Again, I was puzzled. It was only when the screen cover over the crib was lowered to hang beside the crib as it would when opened that I made the connection. The hole lined up perfectly with the peppered board across the front of the davenport.

Deng had opened the gun case in our absence and had gotten my .410 shotgun out. He must have accidentally pulled the trigger and shot through the cover of the empty crib standing in front of the davenport. Hence the peppered up board.

Conversations with Deng appropriate for the seriousness of the offence followed. For our part, we made sure that the gun case was securely locked from then on out. We'd been too trusting and possibly, even, somewhat careless. That night our prayers took on special meaning as we thanked God for His mercy! I wonder how frequently we looked back on that experience and said, "Just supposing we had left the baby home with the servant and he'd have been in that crib!"

## A GREEN THUMB PUTS FOOD ON THE TABLE

Lavina can put a terrific meal on the table but if you don't have any food in the house its impossible. Perhaps that's where a little team work makes the difference. I was challenged to provide vegetables, fruit and meat so it could happen. I had grown up on a farm in Minnesota and we had also been truck gardeners along with having cows, horses, chickens and pigs, so gardening was easy and fun for me. I have to qualify that word "easy" somewhat because nothing is really easy in the Sudan. The cotton soil was so hard where we started our garden that I added sand to the soil. The sand itself had come from a pit dug by Bob and Don along the river bank in connection with the building program. That cotton soil was so tightly packed that their sand pit went right down beside the water, going 15 or more feet below the water level only a few feet from the river, without water ever leaking into the pit.

In addition to adding a little sand, we encouraged things with a liberal does of sheep manure from the village. Then to protect the young seeds and seedlings, I put a thin layer of grass on a lattice work over each of the seed beds. These were gradually thinned out as the plants grew and needed more exposure to the sun. Water was carried up from the river by one or two Anuaks. They'd carry two five gallon tins of water, on each end of a four foot pole that they put across their shoulders. Many months later the First Reformed Church in Orange City, Iowa sent us a gasoline powered engine and pump which we positioned on a small barge floating on empty barrels. Vegetables and fruit began to thrive in abundance!

It was a lot of work to survive. But growing a garden was good for me as it gave me a useful hobby which fit in with my translation work so very handily. Eventually, I had a couple of Anuaks who could do most of the work and I would just keep eye on it, so to speak. Late in the afternoons, when the sun was smaller and the work in the office had been set aside, I enjoyed "playing" in the garden. It was a real relaxation and renewing experience for me. The other missionaries liked it too as we grew more than we needed and could often share with those whose thumbs were less green or who were so busy with other things they found little time or inclination to garden.

Lavina, the little children and I frequently moved around in the garden in the late afternoon as the temperature was beginning to go down and the sun was getting ready to retire for the night. It was family time and we enjoyed our time together so very much. Sometimes, we would get in the boat and take a little ride up the river just to cool off as the breeze we created evaporated the perspiration.

## A FISH FROM HEAVEN

One late afternoon episode in the garden is unforgettable. The river, of course, flowed peacefully with only a long inclined bank separating the garden and it. On that river scores, sometimes hundreds, of pelicans were , floating, swimming and catching their fish.

This particular afternoon, one of them took off, circled in the direction of the garden and was nearly overhead. From its mouth was dangling his catch--a live fish. It looked large enough to make us a meal. Lavina, looking up longingly said, "How I'd like that fish for supper tonight." The thought had hardly formed and the words had scarcely taken shape when that pelican dropped his fish almost at our feet in the garden. It couldn't have been more freshly delivered. And it couldn't have been delivered at a more appropriate time -- just in time for supper and providing our first meat in several days! Our thanks to the Lord for our food took on special significance that evening. Our children had a first class object lesson in our Lord's ability to meet the needs of his missionaries, even in extraordinary ways! The lesson wasn't lost on their parents either! Thirty years later, the memory of that experience still triggers the joy bells ringing in our hearts. Is anything too hard for the Lord? God is so good!

## HUNTING TO PUT MEAT ON THE TABLE

At Akobo, we missionaries had different gifts, training and responsibilities. The practical jobs were divided among us taking these factors into account. Don and Bob did a great job with the cattle. The mission herd grew steadily and after a few years we had all the fresh milk and home made butter we needed. As the herd increased, the men would sometimes butcher an animal and we would have beef instead of wild animal meat in our refrigerators.

During our early years, we depended on our ability to locate and shoot one of the numerous kinds of wild animals for meat. We would usually work all day and then around four or five in the afternoon we would go out looking for animals. Bob and I frequently went out together. We had a lot of fun kidding each other on who was the best shot. Bob had a sharp eye! He used a .306 caliber bolt action, and I had a .348 lever action because I shoot closing my right eye.

Hunting was great fun at first, but gradually it lost some of its appeal. A lot of hard work was involved in going out for meat. Once the animal was shot, we either skinned it or supervised the skinning of it. Some of the meat and all the intestines were given to the local people to divide as they saw fit. We learned early on not to try to divide the meat for them ourselves. This had great potential for misunderstanding! Sometimes the Anuaks and Nuers would quarrel as to who should get what. That really took the fun out of it.

Once the animal was skinned and each missionary home had its chunk of meat, we still had to cut it into appropriate size pieces so our wives could handle it. By the time we finished all of this, it was often between nine and ten at night. Since we also arose early in the Sudan, any night activities tended to be limited. At the mission, the generator was set to go off around nine-thirty at night.

During the rainy season, which usually lasted from late April until early October, we depended more on hunting ducks, geese and Guinie fowl. We really became excellent shots with all that practice. I had a smaller caliber shot gun, a .410 pump action. Many a spur-winged goose tumbled out of the sky and into our kettle. Ducks often congregated along the river in thick concentrations. More than once I shot five to eight ducks with one shot. Without our guns our table would have looked quite different. They were our lifeline for meat just as our garden was for vegetables. There was no meat market, vegetable stand or bakery at Akobo. Our missionary wives cooked everything from scratch. And they were all experts at it.

## TRAVELING ON THE RIVERS BY OUTBOARD

Looking back on our years in the Sudan, I have often marveled that we had no serious, life threatening accidents on the river. The river was our road to get places. We visited villages up and down the river for preaching purposes. During the rains, we would go out to shoot ourselves some ducks or geese to keep meat on the table. Sometimes we would go on picnics and stop under some thorn tree on the river bank where ubiquitous Anuaks or Nuers always showed up from nowhere. We spent hours and hours in outboards on short trips and long ones.

Several times each year we would do the trip of 90 miles each way to our neighboring missionaries working in Nasir.

Once when Lavina was ill, I left her behind at Akobo and took Jimmy along with me so that she could have the needed rest. Jimmy was about five years old then. Eager to get back home to Lavina, we turned around at Nasir that afternoon intending at least to get a start. We would go a couple of hours and then sleep in the boat. By the time we started going up the Pibor river, it was already getting pretty dark. We pulled into the tall grass beside the flooded river and put up our net in the boat to sleep. Jimmy fell asleep in the bottom of our 16 foot boat, but I never did succeed in overcoming the mosquito problem. There were just too many to cope with. Finally, after a couple of hours of this, I decided we would do better just traveling slowly up the river, creating enough breeze to lick the mosquitoes. I left Jimmy sleeping on the bottom under the net which was now serving as his blanket.

We traveled all night like that making our way toward Akobo. On a narrow, crooked river with floating logs and grass, it was really a strain. At first we went quite slowly, but gradually, as I became more brave and accustomed to the darkness our speed increased to where we were traveling at full speed. I have never been on the river when it was darker or more difficult to see. Only our defeat by the mosquitoes and my eagerness to get back to Lavina made us foolish enough to keep going. Once in awhile we would hit a floating stick. It was really difficult to see where the banks of the river were.

Finally, about 4 a.m. I thought we were passing a bayou where the river would turn in the direction of Akobo. In the darkness, I turned sharply and soon found myself stopped in the tall swamp-grass beside the river. It wasn't the place I thought it was. In veering off into the grass, I had killed the engine and had broken off the sheer pin in the propeller. Fortunately, I had a flashlight with me and was able to take the motor off in the pitch darkness, lay it down beside Jimmy who slept through it all, replace it, put it back on the boat and get back into the river again.

By this time, it was beginning to get just a wee bit lighter. An hour later we were safely home tied up on the river bank in front of the house. I carried Jimmy up, unloaded our things and crawled into bed. Lavina was so pleased and surprised that we were back already and could hardly believe it.

Less than a half hour later, a colossal rain storm crashed down around us. That's why it had been so unusually dark on the river. There hadn't been a star in the sky. But the Lord mercifully held off the rain until Jimmy and I were safely home. When I awakened and went out after the storm had passed, I discovered our boat out front was nearly sinking. It had rained some 4 1/2 inches of water. We sang the doxology in our hearts, marveled at the Lord's mercy and said, "I must never be so stupid again!"

Sometimes, we'd get caught on the river in unavoidable tropical storms of wind and rain. I recall starting out for Nasir, 90 miles distant, one morning with Ojulu in the back of the boat while I was in the front driving with a rigged up steering wheel. It was nice to get a little farther away from the noise of the motor, but it never did work totally satisfactorily.

About two hours out from Akobo, we ran into a terrific rainstorm. Our sleeping gear, typewriter and food was covered with a canvas. I was shielding myself from the pounding rain with my raincoat. Ojulu had taken refuge under the canvas. The water began accumulating in the bottom of the boat. It was apparent that we'd have to stop and wait out the storm. I looked for the first hard bank where we might make a landing. Grass, swamp-land lined the river on both sides. When I spotted a solid bank, I headed for it and yelled back to Ojulu. I'd no sooner touched the bank, when all the water remaining on the canvas and what had accumulated in the bottom of the boat rushed to the rear. Within moments the weight of the water was such that the rear part of the boat began to go under. Ojulu, scrambled over the top of the load to the front and in seconds he and I jumped into the river, one on each side of the boat. Our efforts to hold up our boat with its heavy, wet load were of little avail. We saw it gradually sink down deeper and deeper in the water. We were two and a half hours from Akobo.

While one of us struggled to hold it up to keep the entire boat from disappearing, the other unloaded gear as fast as hands could move. With everything out of the boat, we were able to drag it on the bank out of the water. When I picked up my typewriter water streamed out of the case in all directions like from the head of a sprinkle can.

AS quickly as possible, we emptied the boat of any water. The storm by this time was passing beyond us. We pushed the boat back into the river and with one pull on the cord the engine started. I had feared that water might have been sucked up into the cylinders. I can scarcely imagine being more thankful that this hadn't happened.

We reloaded our things, turned the boat around and headed for home. Lavina was surprised to hear the boat coming in the distance. She thought we'd have been approaching Nasir. It was three o'clock in the afternoon.

We hung our wet bedding and clothes on the clothesline where they dried quickly in the hot, remaining, afternoon sun, which was always hot and dried things in no time flat. Bob tried to rig up a fan and a blow torch combination to dry out my soaked typewriter. It would take a day or two to get it where one could use it again.

That night at 8 o'clock I was back on the river heading for Nasir. We started out with a gasoline lantern on the front, with an improvised shield behind it so as not to blind us. Ojulu and I hadn't traveled far before we realized the gasoline light did more harm than good. We turned it out and I went back to our old method of having a flashlight in hand and switching it on only when in doubt. On a normal starlit night, it was amazing how well one's eyes adjusted. Only occasionally would we run into an unsuspected chunk of floating grass or a small log. By six o'clock in the morning, Nasir's windmill was in sight. A few hours of sleep and we'd be ready for the meeting. Within 36 hours, we'd be on our way back to Akobo. Each trip took just under fifteen gallon of gas each way. Later, when MAF began to fly, we would be in Nasir in less than 40 minutes.

### CLOSE CALLS IN THE WATER

Reading these old letters reminds me of two very close calls in the Pibor river during our early days at Akobo. In both of these encounters, drowning wouldn't have been that difficult. Dennis and I both came close to going under together in that one experience in front of the house. This is the way I described it in a letter dated, January 25, 1950:

*"We had a very trying experience again the other day. Dennis was so very close to drowning that if he had gone down, I know I would probably have drowned with him, but God was with us again.*

*Al, Lee, Dennis and I had been out hunting ducks and were just coming home in front of the house. We were nearly to shore and Dennis had his shorts off and asked if he might jump in now and swim. We waited until we thought it was safe and then told him alright, he could jump. He was about 12 feet from shore and he came up and started paddling, but it was evident that he was in very deep water and could not do more than just stay out of water with his head.*

*Suddenly, I was seized with the awareness that he couldn't cope and I said, 'That kid cant swim -- he's drowning in there.' I jumped out of the boat and ran into the water to meet him, but the river dropped so swiftly that it was well over my head and when I grabbed him, we both went under. When we came up I yelled to Lee to come and get him. He just tore out of the boat and got hold of Dennis under his chin and dragged him in. I could paddle alright alone, but with Dennis, if the other men had not been there, we would have both drowned.*

*Dennis was just as white as chalk. Lee and I both had tennis shoes on and our shorts, which did not help us swimming at all. I shall never forget that awful sight and feeling. How thankful I was that Lavina was in the house and not there or she would have run in and drowned herself too.*

*When we came into the house, Dennis and I were so weak that we just went right to bed and Dennis stayed there without supper. First, when he came in, he lay on the davenport, and when Lavina came through the first time he said, 'Am I going to die, mother -- am I going to die?' The second time she came through the room, the dear little guy was down on his knees beside the davenport and was praying. Truly, we can say again that the Lord has wanted to speak to us and teach us how each day we must cling more closely to Him."*

A letter, dated, June 27, 1950, tells about our other close call in the water:

*"You will be thinking that all we do is nearly drown here in Africa, but it is true that three weeks ago I came closer to drowning than ever before. We were pulling the mission launch with the jeep and others of us were in the river trying to push back the grass from the bank so that the launch could pass. We had gone along for more than a mile and then got stuck. The grass was so tight here that people could walk across the river on top of it.*

*We tried to make an opening and had a small channel cleared. Don and I were in the river standing with our backs up against the grass about up to our chest in the water. Bob started up the jeep and began pulling the launch forward. Don was ahead, but I got caught between the launch and this packed grass. The launch pinned me and then started to slide by and in a flash I was under water. They yelled and Bob, who was up ahead on about 100 feet of rope, saw them waving and shouting and stopped. In seconds Don was at my side and pulled my head up just enough to breathe. I had gotten a bit of water in my stomach and up my head and windpipe, but, except for a good shock, I was okay.*

*What a dreadful experience to be pinned beneath the water. The only thing Don could say was, 'Praise the Lord.' He was as white as a ghost. After that for a number of nights, before going to sleep, I found myself tense, without realizing it, and living it all over again.*

OUR NEW HOME AT AKOBO

We are glad that is behind us and perhaps we ought to
learn a lesson or two from it. Surely life is uncertain and we are
reminded again to make full use of our time for Christ while it is
day. Little do we know when we shall be called to account for
our stewardship."

## KEEPING SPIRITUALLY FIT

In a letter written a year earlier, dated April 27, 1949,
after telling of some of the rats, scorpions, mosquitoes and
flies, I shared my thoughts our challenge to keep spiritually
alive.

April 27, 1949:

"I suppose when you read things like this back home you
think this is an awful land, but once living out here these things
become part and parcel of life and one takes them as a matter of
course. There is real danger in this for us too, in that we fail to
realize sometimes how completely dependent we are upon the
Lord for our well being. How we must pray constantly, and how
we need your prayers, that we will always be aware of how dependent we are upon our Heavenly Father's care and that we
stay in the very center of His will. The old Devil is just as real
here and attempts to deceive us just as much, even as he does
in more or less Christianized America. The final test, wherever a
Christian is living, remains the inner relationship he nurtures
with the abiding presence of Christ. It is as easy for us to drift
away from Him here as it is for you at home -- and perhaps even
a little easier, because we have so little in the way of things to
aid us and inspire us. So much, so much we need the constant
prayers of the Church at home that we may be absolutely and
fully committed to the sacred trust as Ambassadors of Christ."

## BUILDING AND MAINTENANCE

Bob and Don and, later the other men as well, often
spent weeks and months overseeing the work on new buildings
and maintenance of the old ones. During the dry season a lot
of hard work was involved in the blazing hot sun getting the
roofs in shape before the rains returned.     The men saw to it

that before another rainy season rolled around, everything was in order and the roofs had been patched or re-thatched so as to withstand the downpour of rains coming. Once our house at Pakang was finished, I didn't get involved in building activities to any great extent. I was assigned to work on the language and to work on the translation of the New Testament into Anuak. I must confess that I sometimes felt guilty about being so privileged and not doing my share with the other men in those hard tasks. But, both Don and Bob helped me by strongly encouraging me to stick to the translation and leave these things to them. I can still hear Don saying, "Harvey, you stick to that translation. It's the most important thing you can do. Our time is short and we want you to complete it before we all have to leave." Translating was truly a team effort!

# CHAPTER FIVE

# LEARNING A NEW LANGUAGE

As soon as we were moved into our partially completed house, I began a disciplined language study. We had been trained at the Summer Institute of Linguistics (SIL) in Norman, Oklahoma how to analyze a language and reduce it to writing. Without that background, we wouldn't have known where to begin. There were no grammatical aids of any kind. What little writing existed had been improvised from the Shullik and we soon realized that it was inconsistent, inadequate and incomplete.

## DISCIPLINE OF DAILY LANGUAGE STUDY

I would spend 5 hours a day with one or two informants. These were Anuak teachers or students with not more than four to six years of formal education. Their use of English was limited and was often unsure that the information given to me was accurate. One could never be certain that what you asked for and what you were told were anywhere near close in meaning. Once I asked for the word "house" and later learned I had been given the word for "horse". A little further along, when I tried to get a translation for the verse, "Surely He has borne our griefs and carried our sorrows", I discovered he was using the word "to give birth to". When we really got into serious translation, a possible miss-communication became much more significant and dangerous. The challenge to figure out what was being said and how to write it down was totally consuming. I wanted to work at it night and day!

We had been taught at SIL how to identify the different kinds of sounds found in different languages. We had learned the international alphabet so that we could write down accurately what one heard and then reproduce it by looking at the paper. We knew reasonably well how to handle the phonetics involved, but when it came to phonemics, we were pioneering in unknown territory. Our challenge was to determine what phonetic sounds were psychologically significant and should be represented in the final alphabet used for spelling and printing. They had told us that phonemics was the science of cooking the phonetics until what was pure remained. As you know, all languages have many conditioned sounds which slide and glide together.

Then, too, we had to figure out what actually constituted a "word". It was difficult at first to know what was a "word" or a "phrase". We needed to determine how words were formed, that is, what were the different parts of a "word". (i. e. the morphemes) We needed not only to determine where the "word" boundaries were, but we needed also to figure out the grammar. It was like working on a gigantic jigsaw puzzle -- totally captivating and in the back of one's mind night and day. Sometimes long periods of "pumping sand" with little apparent progress in language study was suddenly illuminated with a brilliant flash of insight which made several things fall into place and now seem simple. It was a task that never really ended before we had to leave the Sudan.

The essentials we were dealing with are technically described as matters of phonetics, phonemics, morphology and syntax. That Anuak proved to be a tonal language with words that were basically a consonant, vowel and a consonant making it one of the difficult languages in the world to speak and write accurately. The words were short. Thus the vowels were extremely important. Each vowel could be high or low in tone, short or long in length, and it could be tense or lax in quality. To pronounce or write the vowel inaccurately resulted in a difference in meaning. To complicate matters further, the quality of the vowel with respect to tone, tenseness or laxness changed according to its grammatical position in the sentence. In contrast to some tonal languages where the tone remains constant, in Anuak the tones were changing depending on where the word was found in the grammatical structure of a sentence.

To be understood, we had to learn these basic tonal

patterns of the various kinds of sentences we use in speech. Many times we had the words all correct, but when using them in the villages, people couldn't understand us. We would observe Anuaks asking each other, "What is he saying?" This caused a lot of heartache and frustration. When we conversed with mission employees and folks close to the mission, they seemed to understand us because they had learned how to second guess what we were saying in context. In the villages, it was a different matter. Visiting village folks taught us how much we still had to learn! I made visiting villages and spending nights in villages sitting around the fire with Anuaks an essential part of my language study effort. I learned a lot under my mosquito net, just listening, when folks thought I was asleep. What they said about missionaries was also instructive!

My method in studying the language was to write every word or expression on a separate 3 by 5 card. I would shuffle these cards daily, gradually separating those I could safely put "on the back burner" and review less frequently. After five hours with informants, I would normally go to a nearby village or find people outside the office with whom I could practice as I tried to speak and listen. There were plateaus of learning and sometimes it seemed no progress was made. Language study called for the most serious kind of discipline. I kept telling myself to study the language just as faithfully as I had studied for an exam in college. Without that kind of discipline, the goal of speaking, being understood and understanding the Anuak would never be realized.

## DANGER OF BEING DIVERTED

Lack of discipline wasn't the only thing that could sabotage one's language study. There was always the pressure of other useful activities. In every mission station the school and the clinic require people to work in them. Someone has to do it. Some are trained specifically for that purpose. They are medical and educational missionaries. But, in a new station like Akobo, the first missionaries, untrained for these tasks had to do them. I was no exception.

I was assigned to teach 4th grade arithmetic. I had never taught arithmetic in my life. It never occurred to me during all my preparation to serve as a missionary that I would become an arithmetic teacher. I walked back and forth to the school from our home a mile and a quarter each way every day. In the afternoons, I would sometimes walk back again to give a hand with the new buildings. Not much language study was going on during that period. I determined in my own heart that God hadn't called me to Africa to teach arithmetic. It wasn't that I didn't enjoy it to a certain extent, but I knew this wasn't my calling.

I praise God that my colleagues soon recognized this too and in one of our regular station meetings, it was voted unanimously that I should be set free from that arithmetic class, devote full time to language study and prepare myself to translate the New Testament for the Anuak people. That was why we had come and now the mission, too, recognized it and confirmed that call with their blessing by assigning me to the task. The joy bells were ringing!

This is what I wrote home to my folks in a letter dated, December 19, 1948:

*"I have been asked by the station to analyze the language and to reduce it to a proper writing system. ... Also, I have the task of translating the Bible into the Anuak tongue. My soul thrills at this glorious task. I started with three informants on Monday of this past week. ... Pray for us and may the church pray for us in this tremendous task. One feels so weak and incapable. It is really baffling. Only the same Holy Spirit who inspired the original writers can qualify us for this task. In the passage where we read that John baptized with water, but you shall be baptized with the Holy Spirit, we translated it, 'John led people to the river to wash their livers with water, but you shall have your livers washed by the spirit of light.' The Anuak have a saying, that if one is angry with his friend that he should wash his liver with his friend -- this leads us to make that translation."* (This translation later proved to be inadequate as it suggested a kind of "baptismal regeneration". It was later changed)

## LANGUAGE STUDY
## PRACTICING IN THE VILLAGES

I made rapid progress in my language study. Living near the village along with careful discipline and persistence all helped.

The letter to my folks dated, October 2, 1948 tells how I was going about it then:

*"I am getting along nicely with the language. I can see progress every day and that is encouraging. These past ten days I have been doing some real missionary work and it has been a thrill and blessing to me as well as to the Anuaks. I have been writing a simple story of the Gospel in English and then I write it in Anuak with the help of an informant. With this in hand, I go out to the various villages and get the people of the village together under a tree and tell them that I want to tell them a story. We sing a couple of songs in Anuak and then I read them the story in Anuak. This does two things. It helps me learn the language and at the same time I bear testimony to the significance of Jesus Christ. It seems to me that this is almost an ideal way to start out.*

*I wish you might see me some afternoon as I start out in just my shorts -- no shoes or shirt! I go down the trail and when I get to the village there are usually a large number of men sitting around and some kids. The kids run out to meet me and then we either call the women or start to sing so that many of them come. When the service is finished I walk around through the village and stop here and there to talk with the various men or women sitting around or working with the flour which the women pound out with a long pole in a hole in a hollowed out block of wood placed in the ground. Often they will ask for soap or a piece of cloth or for money. Other times they ask me to try to help them as they are sick. How I would love to be a doctor and be able to help them both of body and soul. It seems to me that almost the ideal way to work out here would be as a doctor going in and out of the villages healing and telling the gospel message. This would be the closest approximation of Jesus' ministry of healing and teaching.*

*When the service in one village is finished, I go on to the* next, which is usually about 1/2 to 1/4 mile away. After three or four, I turn around and come back home greatly blessed for having born witness to Jesus Christ. In all the villages visited so far I have found an eagerness for the message that is most encouraging. The door for Christ stands wide open here. If the church is not asleep she will work here now before the Muslims come and they become hardened to the Gospel. Our need here is for a consecration and for men and women."

## SOME VILLAGE VISITS WERE MULTI-PURPOSE

Some of my visits to the villages were sort of multi-purpose visit. We were always needing eggs and sometimes we needed people to come in to help with the work. One never knew what to expect. In that same October 2 letter, I wrote:

*"This was a Nuer village and they happened to be having a trial under a big tree. It was very interesting to see about 30 of these big, tall, naked villagers under the tree having their own, local court. There was one man there who spoke English, which I knew before I went down there, so I could get along alright. ... I really figured on getting a canoe ride back, but I found out that no canoes were available for that afternoon or even the next morning. The only thing to do was to hike back.*

*I started back in bare feet about ten minutes to four and it was just past six thirty when I had the given miles behind me and was home. That was some walk! I had an Anuak guide to show me the way. Long stretches of the way there was mud and slush up to my knees. Other places the path was dry and hard and really hurt my still too soft feet. Last of all, just after dark, as I was about 300 yards from our house, I stepped into one of the many ant trails here and, before I knew it, I had ants biting me from head to toe. I'm telling you it didn't take me long to get those shorts off and tear down to the river and get under water. That finished off the ants. I don't know what I would have done if I had been further back from the river.*

*On the way home, I passed through about 20 Anuak and Nuer villages, each with about 12 to 15 huts and a couple of cattle barns. We inquired for eggs along the way and ended up with 9 very welcome eggs. These eggs are smaller than ours but are very good. We always test them before buying them. We use the old method of a gourd of water and if they stay down they're okay. Right now eggs are very scarce. We haven't had eggs since then. During the dry season they are more numerous."*

## LEARNING THE LANGUAGE
## A HIGHEST PRIORITY

Learning to speak the language was one of our highest priorities. Regular hours with informants, 3 by 5 cards, memorization and practice along with regular visits to the village regulated our lives during the early months and years. While my assignment was to translate the New Testament in the Anuak language, I prayed that God would always give me the heart of an evangelist.

In a letter home, dated, November 21, 1948, I wrote:

*"This afternoon I will go to the village again for a service. I have been preaching without notes or reading now in the villages. I feel very grateful to the Lord for helping me get this language sufficiently to do this after only three and one-half months out here. To be sure there is so much one cannot say yet, but at least we have a start and it is better than reading it. There is always a thrill and joy in telling the wonderful message of Christ in these services. It is the greatest thrill that one can have on this side of glory. Unceasingly, we thank Him for calling us here to witness for Him. He is good and His grace is sufficient for every trial."*

In a letter dated, October 19, 1948, I wrote the folks:

*"... I just returned from a little service in the village. Today, I sat on a small stone in the midst of the sheep and goats and kids. There was quite a nice group gathered together. Sometimes one feels the weight of their ignorance and superstition so greatly that you just know that only the supernatural power of our risen Lord can ever change them. If we ever lose sight of that, we are sunk. Humanly speaking, the task is impossible, but with God nothing is too difficult and we feel confident in our souls that if we fully consecrate ourselves to Him*

81

## CHAPTER FIVE

*that He will accomplish through us His purpose of salvation for these poor lost souls."*

### WANTING TO SPEAK LIKE AN ANUAK

Language study with informants, spending week ends in villages to practice. listen and learns became a way of life for me. I enjoyed preaching in the villages and doing the work of an evangelist. But, my real task was to translate the New Testament to give the Anuak people God's word in their own language. Progress was sometimes slow, but gradually, I was able to understand most of what was said and could express myself effectively in the Anuak language. My goal was to speak it so well that in the dark Anuaks wouldn't know that I was a foreigner speaking.

To communicate the way Anuaks did, we also had to learn their body language and sign language. We soon learned that one never beckoned to another with the finger as we do in America. Among the Anuak as in many other parts of the non-western world, you beckon for someone to come with the hand turned downward and one uses the entire hand to motion for one to come. One points with the tongue -- a bad habit when one is home on furlough and accidentally points with the tongue to indicate to the clerk the item one wants. We learned that the size of animals and fish required the hand to be either stretched out strait, palm down, or to have the palm stretched out with the hand on its side. Chickens were indicated by the crooked finger. But, perhaps the most important use of the hand which one wanted to be sure to use correctly was when speaking about the size of a child. The Anuak never wanted anyone to indicate the height of a child by putting out one's hand with the palm down as we would in America to indicate how tall the child was. To do so, for the Anuak, was to stilt the growth of the child. On furloughs I enjoyed so much telling about these various ways of using our hands when speaking Anuak. It was a joy to challenge the children in our congregations to give their hearts to Christ and to grow up swiftly loving Him and being ready to serve Him, perhaps, even, as a missionary. I would hold up my hands as in Africa and say, Today, I'm holding up my hands (palms showing with fingers up at the level of a child's head) because I want you to grow up quickly and to be strong and ready to do what Jesus asks of

82

you. He loves you and is helping you grow up quickly so that you may go somewhere for Him; his missionary to take our places as we quickly grow too old'."

To speak like an Anuak we had to have the sounds pronounced correctly, the length of the vowels and the tones the right length, quality and level, and we had to use our hands with body movements that communicated accurately and effectively. A lifetime challenge and never fully realized!

On March 27, 1949, I wrote:

"I have discovered some very interesting things about the language and am making some needed changes in spelling, recognition of words and sentences which will make reading much simpler and save months of time in learning it as well. This is all due to good old Wycliffe in Norman, Oklahoma. Some day I hope to go back there and learn some of the things I have already forgotten or have never learned ..."

## ADULTS VERSUS SCHOOL CHILDREN

In that same letter I put down some of my concerns about what I then perceived to be a disproportionate emphasis on schools and too little effort to reach adults with the message of Jesus Christ.

"I am preaching this evening on II Corinthians 5:17-21. This morning I rode my bike, as I did last week, and went out about six miles on the trail. I held four services in different villages. There was a very good response and it thrilled my heart to tell them the wonderful message about how Christ was sent by God to save them. We just sat around under the trees, sang some songs in Anuak, and then I told them about Jesus. I prayed in Anuak and then moved on to another village. I think this is the only way to win Africa to Christ. It can never be done in the school alone. It will come through village evangelism and the teaching of adults to read so that they may read the Word of God for themselves."

The longer I was in the Sudan, the more convinced I became that missions were making a mistake in their putting

83

so much emphasis on teaching the children in the schools to the neglect of evangelizing adults. I said we should go right to the top and meet with village chiefs and elders and tell them the great truths from the Bible. These were the decision makers. If they became believers, whole villages would follow them, other heads of households, their wives and their children. Concentrating on the schools sent the wrong message to village leaders. Concentrating on schools suggested that we missionaries may have lost confidence in the power of the Gospel to convert adult people and their ability to change. Perhaps, we were, unconsciously, giving up on adults because we thought only children could change enough to qualify as Christians. There was a lot to ponder as we considered where God would have us place our effort. Years later in graduate study at Fuller's School of World Mission, Dr. Tippet helped me understand a bit more clearly what I was wrestling with in my spirit during those first years in the Sudan.

The fundamental issue was a question of power. We were dealing with a "power encounter". The question for the adult villager, especially, was a question of who has the power for good or for evil over one's life in all its aspects. The Gospel made sense when, under the Holy Spirit, those who heard recognized that Jesus Christ was powerfully alive and present and had power to protect one from every threat, including sickness, demons and death. The Gospel was seen to be fantastically good news when Christ was proclaimed as Savior and powerful Lord, alive and present to save and to protect anyone who committed one's self to Him in faith. This was a message that made good sense to adults and could give whole households a new way to live in freedom and without fear. We didn't need to teach them how to play our kind of church, but, rather to introduce them to Jesus and create the opportunity for them to look into God's written word. The Holy Spirit could be their final guide. Exciting possibilities with dramatic change, contextually relevant would occur. I was feeling things deeply as I tried to think through for myself where my priorities and emphasis should be.

While searching to better understand the most effective approach by which to reach the African for Christ, I was totally immersed in my language study, translation and literacy efforts. This is evident from my letter of July 17, 1949 approximately one year after we first arrived at Akobo. I made these comments about the work:

*"...There surely is a lot to be done. I have so much trans-
lation work .... It will take me a lifetime to get done what I want
to do and then I know I will run short of time. It surely is wonderful to have my work to do. I could live, eat, sleep, and dream
translation work. We praise the Lord for giving me this wonderful calling. It is quite a thrill to read over the new translation of
Mark and also to read it to the Anuaks. When I return I shall cut
stencils for it and have it printed. I have a new mimeograph
coming and much paper so I should be all set. I hope so much
that the new typewriter will soon be on its way."*

A letter dated, September 21, 1949 tells of the progress
made during that first year at Akobo in spite of time lost
through teaching Arithmetic and getting our house so that it
was livable:

*"Sunday morning I preached in the mission service for a
change. After the service they were all standing around, talking
about the preacher -- just like at home.*

*They said, 'Mr. Hoek has learned all the Anuak. (not so)
Now we can learn the whole Bible.' They are so surprised that a
white person has learned their language. ... This is both a
source of inspiration, but also a source of temptation to become
proud. I hope I may be spared from that. I know that my work
in the literature and translation helps me to learn it and I do
have an opportunity that the others do not have. In the villages
there is always a mummer too, 'He has learned all the Anuak.'
In Anuak it is written like this, 'Eni dha Anuak bare akwanye.'
Lavina, too is learning a lot of Anuak these days and it is not too
far off when she will be able to speak it well enough to bring
messages also.*

*A week ago Sunday, I preached five times; three times
along the terribly muddy paths and twice via boat. It was a
very satisfying day, but I was plenty tired by night. Last week,
after the morning service, Lavina and the children and I went on
a picnic up river and had our lunch in the flies under a thorn
tree. On the way back, we stopped in a big village and
preached. We had a lovely time."*

# CHAPTER FIVE

## POKANG

Pokang was a little over a mile from the mission where our colleagues lived. At Pokang we lived near Anuak villages. People were coming constantly to see what we were doing. They pointed to things and asked questions. At first, we understood very little, but it was a marvelous opportunity to practice our language skills with our many curious visitors.

Living near the people gave us a good feel for the African village. I was frequently in those villages, some close by, and later when I had an outboard motor boat, I would go further from home. I came to feel strongly about the importance of the African village and how it related to the evangelization of the Anuak, and possibly of Africa. Sometimes I wrote about it in my letters home. I tried to picture for my family what I observed then and shared my reactions with them. Many of the convictions formed during those early months in Africa remain unchanged today.

## ANUAK FIELDS AND VILLAGES

The Anuak were fastidious farmers. Seeds were planted using five or six foot sticks to make the hole in the wet, sticky cotton soil into which the seed was dropped and stepped on. Men used simple, single bladed, hoes which were about three inches in width with a small channel into which a two or three foot stick, about an inch in diameter, had been tightly jammed. They prepared their plots of land meticulously and worked hard to keep the growing crop clean of weeds. They planted both dura (kaffir corn) and maize.

When the crop was ripening, crude, temporary, six foot platforms were erected on poles and situated as needed throughout their fields to protect the harvest from the sparrow sized dura birds, so numerous that an unguarded field would be completely destroyed. The children and young people made these platforms their homes and ate and slept there during harvest season, abandoning them only during the severest rain storms.. With three foot, willowy sticks to which they attached marble sized mud-balls, these "field watchers" successfully kept their losses to a minimum.

Women, with the sporadic help of men, gathered the

ripened grain in baskets woven from grass and stored their bounty in small, circular storehouses positioned so that their bottoms were about three feet off the ground. These were covered with small thatched roofs which the women would tilt up and then lower again on days that the grain or corn was needed for pounding into flour.   Such grain holders were located close beside the houses in which people lived.

Every village had a few cows, sheep, goats and chickens.  These belonged to individual families and the cattle were frequently kept in a common building which was similar to other Anuak houses in size and shape. .

Chickens were usually in limited numbers because a brood of eight or ten tiny chicks was easy prey for the hawks. The mother hens did their best to warn and protect their babies, but only a few reached maturity.  And, of course, every village had its quota of barking dogs.

When we went out to the villages, we passed through these Anuak fields, unable to see anything except the path underfoot until we emerged  on the opposite side.  During the rainy season these paths were often muddy and some had low spots with standing water and filthy areas one had to pass through.   Canvas shoes were the shoes of choice to wade through these low areas as they could dry on one's feet.  During the dry season these same paths were baked dry and in the earlier, sticky, cotton soil there would now be deep and sometimes treacherous cracks going down a depth of several feet. One could now see great distances  whereas only a few months earlier we were "walking blind"..  It was fun to travel on these dry paths riding my small whizzer trail bike propelled by  its tiny gasoline engine.

Some of  our impressions, being formed during those early months in the Sudan, are reflected in a letter home dated, May 9, 1949:

*"The key to the heart of Africa lies in her villages.  It is in the African village with its mud houses and grass roofs with lounging men, playful children and hard working women that the real victory for Christ will be won.*

*If I could take you with me to one of our villages, you would find, perhaps, ten to twenty of these small huts.  The* walls are made of mud and sticks and are about as tall as a short man. You cannot see these walls from the outside because long grass from the roof comes down to the ground protecting them from the rains. On one side we notice a small opening. We enter but see nothing until our eyes become accustomed to the darkness.

Inside the hut we see a small baby lying on an animal skin on the floor. The mother sits nearby. Flies are crawling all over the little baby. If we look more closely, we will likely find the baby's eyes are sore and infected. How could it be different with hundreds of flies crawling over its little body every day. The marvel is that any of these babies grow up considering that they have no clothing and no protection except their mother's love.

From the roof of the hut we notice a wing or two of a bird, possibly the shriveled up head of a chicken, several horns from cattle and some tobacco hanging to dry. Each of these items has some special relation to the spirits of whom the Anuak lives in constant fear.

Walking through the village, we notice that here and there are mounds of dirt with several tall sticks on the top of which are the horns of some former cow. Tied to the sticks are ears of corn. Buried beneath the mound of dirt are the fetish bones and charms and even, possibly, the body of some relative who has died and is buried there.

To this shrine the Anuak turns at specific times to offer prayer to the spirits of the dead. They have greatest fear and respect for these shrines and in no case would they walk on them or be disrespectful to them.

Often, as I preach in the villages, I see on either side of me these pagan shrines and know that only as Jesus comes into their hearts and transforms them will the fear and superstition that haunts our people's hearts be taken away. Often I will ask them if the Gospel is not a good word from God (Anuaks ask a question with a particle that anticipates a positive answer) and they will answer, 'It is a good word.'

Then I ask them, 'Will you not trust in Jesus, God's only son, to care for you and save you.'

They answer that they want to, but then I point to their shrines and tell them that if they trust in Jesus they must throw these things out in the field because Jesus wants them to trust *in Him only. They smile and know that what Odola (that is my African name) said is true, but in their hearts they are still afraid to do so.*

*We can bring them just that far and then we know that we must wait for the Holy Spirit to take all fear and superstition away and to plant within them the new life. Pray for the power of God to be released here in the heart of Africa."*

Every village has its graves. Some are buried just beside the house where they are protected by an enclosure of thorn branches. It is normally several years later before the grave site is no longer revered and respected as a place where one communes with the spirit of the departed one. During the first few weeks after the burial, the women relatives mourn loudly and hauntingly every morning long before the sun rises. In our memory bank these haunting cries of hopelessness and despair are indelibly written.

Some burials take place in the house of the person who has died. A letter home describes what happens.

May 20, 1949:

*"Last week one day while at Bob's house we heard a lady go by wailing loudly and knew that it meant a woman was mourning the loss of a relative. We decided to walk over to the village and see.*

*There inside the grass wall we found about 25 women wailing loudly and a couple of men. We asked if we might come inside the village fence and sit down to observe. This we did and then presently saw the mound of dirt outside the hut and the man who had died lying under the cloth lying nearby. Inside the house several women were digging the grave.*

*In a short while this man would be buried inside the house. A grass mat would be put up to cover the opening into the house and the house would be sealed shut until it caved in upon the grave.*

*Another soul without Christ had slipped into eternity. Bob and I asked if we might have a prayer in the village, but they refused, saying, we weren't relatives of the man. Things like this write themselves deeply on our hearts out here. You have never heard anything quite like it at home. It makes us want to work even harder in the little time that that is ours to live for and serve our Savior."*

## PREACHING IN THE VILLAGES

MAY 8, 1949:

*"On Sundays I usually take my motor bike (a whizzer bike with a motor) and go out for five or six miles along the rough trail (worse than our cow paths in the pastures at home by far) and hold five or six services in the villages.*

*In these services we either meet under a tree or in the cattle barn. Sometimes we have the cows and sheep and goats tethered right beside us giving us competition with the message. I don't stand in these village services. Instead, I sit down with them, teach them some songs and then tell them about Jesus Christ. Often, I stop and ask questions and we talk it over as we carry on the service. Often one of the Anuak men will repeat after me each word I say. Now and again a person from another village walks by and one from our service exchanges greetings with him and they have a short conversation. Or it may be some baby is crying or children are talking in a slow, low mumble.*

*You would be shocked to drop in out of the sky to see our service but it is Anuak and the way the Anuaks gather together and we must learn to accommodate ourselves to their patterns of behavior. It isn't always easy, but there is something about these village services that reaches deep down in one's soul and moves one to preach the wonderful Gospel of our Savior who is their only hope as he has never preached it before.*

*If you folks at home could see for yourselves our people and the terrible weight of their sin, superstition and fear, it would fall upon you as a dreadful weight, and there would be no one who would not believe it worthwhile to come out hear to live for Christ. Not one of you would withhold the very best you have for Christ.*

*We are moved to shame when we think of the complacency and ease of the Church and the believers back home when thousands and millions are dying every day in the terrible fear and guilt with no knowledge of Christ, the only Savior. How can it be right that one would not sacrifice a little for these folks for whom Christ died. Our people here are waiting for the mes-*

90

*sengers of God who are coming so late. Perhaps some son or daughter back home will feel the call of God to come to a pagan land to bring the glorious message of Salvation. Do not dissuade that boy or girl. Bid them God-speed. Encourage them on their way of preparation to be His ambassadors to realms beyond the sea. God gave the very best that He had, His only begotten Son to die the shameful bitter death on Calvary for our salvation. We dare not withhold all that we are and have from Him for those for whom He died."*

The letter quoted above indicates where our hearts were as we began our many years of missionary service in Africa. Looking back, some forty five years later, our core convictions remain much the same as when we started. "There is no other name given among men by which we must be saved." Acts 4:12. True then and still true now!

## LIVING CONDITIONS THOSE FIRST MONTHS

From a letter dated December 19, 1948:

*"You would be quite surprised to see how we live and get our food prepared.*

*Every two weeks we sift all the flour to get the worms and weevils out. Then, every time we use it, we put it through a nylon cloth to get the rest of them out. All eggs are tested over a separate dish. When we bake beans, every bean must be inspected for a little worm that bores into it. We opened a package of oatmeal from Khartoum and it was full of worms. We had ten packages in that order but were never hungry enough to entice us into eating from them. We bought a sack of wheat and we wash that and dry it as we use it. I then grind it and we use it for cereal or as a potato substitute. The cabinet in which we keep our sugar stands in tins of water because of the innumerable ants. Our milk is boiled and strained each evening. Our water is boiled each morning and then it cools in earthen jars by a process of evaporation. Dates we steam ourselves.*

*And, so it goes. Everything is done the hard way and everything must be watched for worms and weevils. In a hot country these things thrive. ...*

*With so much detail work, it is wonderful for Lavina to*

*have her servants. It is a terrific job to get them trained though.*
...

*I think the mosquitoes are letting up just a bit. They have been terrible in the house these first few weeks of the dry season. I think they come in to escape the heat. Consequently, they would itch one's feet night and day. Now, however, they seem to have let up and we should have several good months. The river is going down rapidly. It has gone back a full 75 yards from the house. It seems strange to be living so far from the water."*

## LOCAL FIGHTING THOSE EARLY DAYS

From a letter dated, December 19, 1948:

*"We have found much fighting here. There is always somebody getting beaten up. Our own servant was nearly killed a few weeks ago when three men attacked him with clubs. He's still not able to work for us. The sad thing is that the people look upon these things as natural and have no conscience against them."*

## NEW WAYS OF HANDLING COWS

From a letter dated December 19, 1948:

*"I have charge of the cows here now that Don is gone. We get an average of 12 quarts of milk to a milking from 12 cows. Seven of these cows just had calves so you can see we are breaking no records! But, they only get marsh grass and water so what can you expect?*

*I saw our cattle man washing his hands behind the cow having a bladder movement the other day. It is so much closer than the river. They have a custom of blowing up the cow if it refuses to release its milk. (normally the calf is put to the cow to suck for a little while, is pulled back, and our milk is milked into a pan before the calf is allowed to finish off whatever is left) If the cow refuses to let her milk down, a man simply puts his face to her where the calf had made its first appearance and blows. He almost buries his face in the process. That is one thing I shall refuse to do. ha! ha! But it works. The cow gives* her milk. These folks handle all the manure of the cows in their hands -- and then, if away from the river, wait to wash them until a cow urinates. The Nuer also use cow urine in their hair to make it a reddish, pink color."

The Anuak either eat with shells or with just their hands. They make plenty of noise, but all they have is some dura flour and water and occasionally a fish with it. Many of them eat only once a day, although some do eat morning and evening. They consume much home made beer in the villages and moral standards are not too high."

## DEADLY SNAKES - A LITTLE GIRL DIES

From a letter dated June 9, 1950:

"Last Sunday I had five nice services. In one village I found a friend whom I have been teaching to read. His little girl, about nine, was bitten by a snake the night before. He brought her to us at three Sunday afternoon. I took them to Lillian, but she said the poison was spread through the body and the only thing now was rest.

We carried her back to the boat and home, but the next morning we had word at seven o'clock that she had died. It was so pitiful to hear the awful wail going up by those who have no hope but much fear. I have spoken to him once since then and will see him again soon to talk to him earnestly of the Eternal hope there is in Christ Jesus.

I have been dealing with another young lad who had T.B. and am trying to show him the love of Christ and his hope for a better life. Pray for us in our personal work along with the translation. This morning, he stopped by on the way home from the clinic and I stepped outside the study and sat down in front of the door on the ground and told him so simply the beautiful message of Jesus. His face was interested. Pray that God may be pleased to touch his heart. He lives in a village near our friend, Dilok.

Just this very minute I saw a blind Anuak passing by. He had a Muslim, long gown on. He is one whom the Arabs have supposedly converted to Islam. I didn't know him, but called him over and we sat down and I told him of Jesus and how he had died and rose again. We prayed and he promised

93

*to return soon to hear this new word. O, that God will give us power. I wish you could feel and see with us the tremendous challenge. How pitiful for this man -- blind in soul as well as body."*

## LOW RIVERS - FISH IN ABUNDANCE

From a letter dated June 14, 1949:

*"These past months took us through our first dry season, with our swollen river shrinking to become so shallow we could actually wade across it. The entire countryside is scorched to a dirty, somber brown. The local people kindled fires which swept across the prairies, driven by withering winds, while tall flames leap high into the air to light up whole sections on distant horizons. Men and boys have left their villages to join themselves together in small cattle camps across the river where a bit of green grass remained for pasture.*

*More and more canoes filled the narrow river hidden between steep banks, so shortly hidden by water which had now evaporated or emptied itself into the Nile. These canoes mean that father and son, or brother and brother or friend were harpooning fish now crowded in a river whose width could be measured in feet, while a few short months before it had overflowed its banks flooding thousands of acres of marshlands."*

Every dry season the Pibor river became so shallow that we'd have to cut the speed of our outboards to avoid snapping off sheer pins in the propeller caused by hitting fish. The fish were so numerous that they were unable to escape quickly enough when an outboard motor was cutting through them at full speed. There were times when fish would jump out of the water into the air as they tried to get out of the way. More than once I was struck in the chest by a flying fish. Rather painful too!

One night Lee and Kitty Crandall gave Lavina and me a ride home to Pokang from the mission following the regular mid-week prayer meeting. It was a delightful ride with the four of us in the boat -- stars overhead in a brilliant sky with a gentle breeze blowing in our faces and keeping the mosquitoes away. Under a full, bright shining moon a night-time ride in a boat or native canoe on the river was intoxicating!

But, this particular evening, when Lee and Kitty returned to the mission after dropping us off, it was far from that. With only the two of them in the boat, it was skimming the water at a good clip. Lee and Kitty were just new on the field at that time and hadn't encountered fish jumping out of the water and hitting them in the boat. Kitty soon called back over the roar of the motor that she would prefer walking. They parked the boat at the first little village, walked the rest of the way and picked the boat up the next day. We all had some good natured fun and laughs over that for several weeks.

## DRY SEASON FISHING

During the dry season, we were fascinated with the way Anuaks herded fish ahead of them in a flotilla of a dozen or more canoes being paddled side by side. Each canoe usually had a father and a son in it, with the father in front with his harpoon and the young lad paddling very slowly from the rear. The men worked the harpoons and kept coming up with speared fish. There were so many fish now concentrated in the narrow, shallow river that their chances of spearing one were extremely good. They would go about a fourth of a mile and then all would turn back in unison to do the same thing coming back to where they had started out. They actually caught so many fish that the river banks smelled from decaying fish. During this time of the year, the Anuak virtually lived on fish, cooking them along the river bank rather than back in their villages. I often wondered if Jesus and His disciples prepared fish along the water's edge the way the Anuak did.

When the rains returned and the rivers began to rise, the flotillas were discontinued, but father and son kept on fishing, using a slightly different approach. Now the man in the front used his fish spear with its sharp, curved barbs and patiently waited for an unsuspecting fish to break water in front of the canoe. In an instant the man would throw his spear. Rarely was there a day when such a team returned to the village without at least one good sized fish and possibly several. A favorite time of the day for this was late in the afternoon when the sun was beginning to go down in the west.

We missionaries frequently were able to purchase a

nice, fresh fish for only a few cents. Many a supper hour in our home saw fresh, tasty, fried fish on our table. Two varieties were known to be better than others, the Olok and the Orwedho. Once we learned the hard way that a certain type of fish had pin worms in their flesh. Needless to say, we were careful not to make the same mistake twice! One learns quickly under those conditions!

## GETTING AROUND DURING THE DRY SEASON

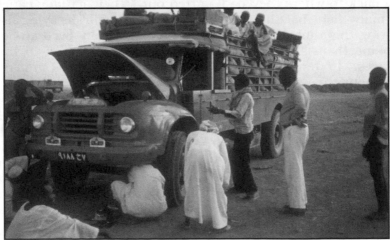

Lavina, Denny and Harvey traveling some 180 miles — Malakal to Akobo.

Before Mission Aviation began operating in the Sudan, it was really difficult to get around. We not only moved about in a dugout canoe or with an outboard motor boat on the rivers, but during the dry season, we traveled either with some kind of mission vehicle or we would hitch a ride on one of the Arab merchant's trucks. These trucks were always overloaded --stacked high we goods and people. Breakdowns were frequent between Malakal and Akobo. While the driver would try to figure out what to do, we would try to find a bit of shade to shield us from the sun, or at night we'd try to find a way to sleep in what seemed really cold weather after the hot daytime sun. We always carried extra food and water along for such emergencies. Our letters home during those early years bring back vivid memories of rugged trips.

### A MOST DIFFICULT TRIP FROM MALAKAL

From a letter dated June 9, 1950:

*"We had a rugged trip back to Akobo from Malakal. I drove the station wagon, which is a complete wreck, really, with nothing but the spring holding the back frame together. We started from Malakal in a rain storm, the fourth in four days. It took us four hours to do the first 12 miles and we were stuck several times. We had a long pry-pole in the car and when stuck, Lyda would drive and I would heave on it. We had soft roads all the way except about 20 miles.*

*First of all, we broke the bottom water hose to the radiator and I had to tape that all up. We always carry plenty of water. We had about forty gallons with us this time and 55 gallons of gasoline.*

*A little further out from Malakal we noticed a bad leak in the gas tank. By keeping it less than half full we overcame that problem. Then we hit real mud and were nearly stuck when we stopped about mid-night and threw the bedrolls on the wet ground and slept until daylight. We then cooked a breakfast and by that time the sun had dried the surface out sufficiently to move.*

*The car over-heated very badly and for a long way we were using water every two miles exactly. We were dangerously low on water -- in fact, so low that we scooped up water*

*from the old car tracks to get enough to get us to the nearest wa-
ter hole. It is quite a dangerous trip with fifty or more miles with
not a soul living there and with no water anywhere. But, we
always send a telegram when leaving Malakal just in case. If
we do not arrive in sufficient time, someone will come out to look
for us.*

*Last of all, about 9 o'clock the second night about sixty
miles from home we ran into a terrific pool of water running right
across the road and with ditches on both sides or the road. We
tried to roar through it but stalled out about four feet from the
other side. Fortunately, we were near a Nuer village. I called
for them to help, but only seven or eight Nuer women came out to
give us a hand. We put a long rope unto the front of the car.
Lyda drove and they pulled, while I heaved on the pry-pole.
Even Lavina was pulling with the Nuer women.*

*Finally, after much effort, we got out and from then on
we managed somehow to get home. The tracks had been dug so
deep by a truck that one time while traveling along about fifteen
miles per hour we suddenly came to a dead stop. We were
stuck fast on the high center. Again, the old pole and some
heaving saved the day and out we came! We arrived home that
morning at one-thirty a.m. -- ever so glad, but tired! This is just
a little idea of our trip home from Malakal."*

## DEPENDING ON MAF

Once Mission Aviation Fellowship (MAF) initiated their
program in the Sudan, these grueling trips would be past history!

MAF was vital to our mission in the Sudan. They saved
us hours and hours of time to say nothing of energy. MAF flew
in our supplies. They flew our children out to catch other
modes of transportation which would eventually get them to
school in Alexandria, Egypt. MAF enabled missionary families
to move about on business and with MAF we could leave for
annual vacations and still be rested when we arrived back
home to resume our work. If there was an emergency, we
could count on MAF to come to the rescue. Before MAF was
there it was quite a different story.

In the Sudan, road trips that took a day and sometimes
more, were flown by MAF in less than an hour. More impor-

tantly, there were many months when roads weren't useable. Because MAF had two planes, one of which was a float plane, we could get in and out during both the dry and rainy seasons.

It was interesting that when MAF first began to serve missions in the Sudan there was some question in the mission as to whether or not traveling by MAF should be considered a normal and legitimate way for us to travel, or whether we should use MAF only in an emergency. Missionaries living in remote places like Akobo opted for looking on MAF as a normal way to travel. Some missionaries living in the Malakal area at first questioned whether we shouldn't perhaps look on MAF as being available primarily for emergencies. In a few short months, the debate was academic. Everyone recognized that MAF had increased our efficiency so dramatically that it would be folly to wrestle on the roads and river with MAF there.

We used MAF all the time. And, on at least one or two occasions they came to the rescue in times of emergencies. I still recall well our concern when Vern Sikkema, Bill Roy and our son, Dennis, failed to return from a trip by Jeep to Waat, about 70 miles away. After waiting a day, when they failed to return, we called MAF on the radio and Betty Greene flew in with the float plane. She picked me up and we flew low over the road from Akobo in the direction of Waat. About 35 miles out, we spotted Vern and Denny wearily trudging toward Akobo. They looked so pitiful from the air. They had already walked some thirty miles and had a long hike ahead of them. To encourage them we dropped some cans of food and fresh water. Bill Roy had come on ahead, more quickly, to tell us what had happened, so we didn't see him on the road. But, we had the information we needed and knew that the men would be home before night. Knowing this, Betty and I continued on to Malakal for a scheduled mission committee meeting.

When I returned home, Lavina said that Dennis, then only fourteen years old, was so tired from the nearly seventy mile hike in rain and mud that he was delirious during the night as he tossed back and forth fitfully from exhaustion. It was an experience this young lad didn't soon forget. We all had a good reminder of just how much MAF meant to us.

We had one, final lesson, in the Sudan on just how much we had come to depend on MAF. This occurred only a few months before missionaries were forced to leave the Sudan by government order.

All of our missionaries from the outstations had been flown into Malakal by MAF for our annual mission meeting. We always spent a week together each year hearing reports, enjoying fellowship together and making decisions about the following year's work. These were great times in our missionary experience.    On the next to the last day of our meetings, we were in for a rude surprise. The MAF pilot came in and said he had some disturbing news to share with us. They had had a slight accident the day before in which the prop of the plane was bent. It'd take about six weeks to get a replacement propeller from England. They had no way to get us to our homes.

Dry season roads were still not useable. We'd all have to, somehow, get home by river. Pibor, the most distant station from Malakal was just over an estimated 400 river miles. Missionaries from Abwong, Nasir, Akobo and Pibor all needed to get back to their stations along the Sobat and Pibor rivers. The only way to get home would be by outboards on the river. The only person not having to get home was Bob Swart who had remained at Pibor to guard things from the flood which was threatening to inundate the mission station.

Outboards from nearer mission stations and Malakal were pressed into service. My assignment was to go on ahead by one day with the needed gasoline for the others who would be following.  I'd drop the gasoline off at agreed upon places along the river so that the boats following could carry the maximum number of people with the minimum weight of additional fuel.

I started out on the appointed morning at six a.m. in a sixteen foot aluminum boat with two outboard motors attached. I was carrying a load -- 34 five gallon tins of gasoline. When darkness fell, I had traveled nearly 200 miles and was approaching the Nasir station, now empty of missionaries who were still stuck in Malakal.

It's a trip I'll never forget. Just outside of Nasir, in the darkness I lost my way. With some shouting and sign language wherever I stopped to ask people the way, and with the help of lightning I found my way back into the main stream of the river. It was nearly 8 o'clock when I pulled up to the bank in front of the Nasir mission station. Pastor Moses Kwaich came out and welcomed me, inquired what was happening and then showed me to one of the vacant mission houses. After a time of devotions and conversation, he left and I slept.

The next day I did the 90 miles to Akobo and the following day went the remaining 125 miles to Pibor. I spent the remaining hours of the day getting rested up. Bob Swart and I started out that same night to fetch our wives from Nasir more than 200 river miles distant. Meanwhile, other missionaries and their children were making there way upstream toward Nasir in a flotilla of small boats. For the mothers with small children it wasn't an easy trip to make.

In one week, I had traveled more than 800 miles by outboard. It was as if I had traveled from Minneapolis to Chicago and back in a small boat on the river. It goes without saying, that no one among the missionaries ever has anything bad to say about MAF. Never, ever!!

## OUR FIRST PRIMER THE HARD WAY

But a lot of history would be written before that last emergency without MAF's services. Way back in 1949 we had just completed making our very first primer. Lavina and I worked together in our efforts to provide primers and books and to teach Anuaks how to read. We started from scratch, even before we had a mimeograph to run off our stencils.

During August in 1949, Lavina and I had cut stencils for our first primer. Not having a mimeograph machine, we traveled with the children via paddle wheel steamer downstream for three days, going some 200 miles to a mission station that had a mimeograph machine. Tal Wilson was living alone at Abwong where we arrived unannounced. We told him we planned to stay for at least a week and that while there we wanted to use his mimeograph. We told him we'd brought our own stencils and paper. The steamer was continuing on to Malakal and when it came back on its way to Akobo we'd be leaving again. I can hardly imagine putting forth that much effort to produce our first primer. But, it was that or nothing under conditions that then prevailed. It proved to be well worth the effort. One of those primers was used by God to teach a young man, living some 150 miles from Akobo inside Ethiopia to read. That young man later became the first Anuak evangelist out of the Pokwo station and the first ordained Anuak pastor. His name was Akway war Achudhi!

We'll tell you his remarkable story when we tell you about Pokwo.

When the steamer showed up, we boarded with our mimeograph job completed and returned back to Akobo. Lavina spent hours putting that primer together to make it useable. Beds, tables and chairs became her assembly line as pages were put in their right sequence and stapled together.

Working together in this way, we were able to begin a small literacy program at an early stage in our ministry.

In that letter of September 21, 1949, I described our humble efforts in one of the villages trying to teach people how to read:

*"I have begun daily meetings in the village near by, beginning with Bible instruction. After that I have the children dismissed and then there are 10 persons who have books now and are learning to read. I made four large 36 by 36 inch charts using unbleached white cotton cloth to help them learn. Imagine me drawing pictures of cows, dogs, people, and many common things to illustrate the words? They are just simple pictures, but it is amazing how the Lord has helped me so that I could do even that. I am amazed at it myself, because at home in the states before going to the Sudan I couldn't draw a thing. The rest of the staff here seem to think they are quite good too."* (they were, obviously, very compassionate)

## KEEPING IN CONTACT

During the dry season, when badly maintained dirt roads were passable, missionaries could get out by merchant truck or with a mission vehicle if they had one. Roads were open only a few months of the year. The rivers were too shallow for steamers during the dry season.

At the beginning of the rains between the time when the roads were closed and the steamers ran again there was a period of about two months when one couldn't get in or out and when mail accumulated in Malakal. When that first steamer came in after the rivers were up, it was quite a day of excitement with supplies and especially mail arriving. I remember a heap of our mail on the floor that was more than 18 inches high and three feet in diameter. What a boast to our spirits when the mail was opened and we heard from family and friends in our praying, supporting churches in America.

## JOY IN OUR WORK

Our contentment and joy from the very beginning of our missionary experience is indicated in my letter to the folks, dated, February 18, 1949:

*"That leads me to speak of Lavina. She has done very excellently out here. She has been a constant companion and a real missionary wife and mother. She has made a wonderful home for the children and all of us. In all the inconveniences, she did not complain or murmur. Never has she complained of loneliness or of a desire to go back home. We have all been so very happy in our work.*

*The Lord has indeed been gracious to us. He works in marvelous ways in the hearts of His children. He has given us perfect and indescribable peace in our souls. Each day is a day of rejoicing in our work. We are perfectly happy and would not exchange our work for the largest salaries and the largest pulpits in the world. I don't know how many times I remark to Lavina how happy I am in my work and what a joy we have because God called us so clearly to our work. As you look at it, everything seems hard and difficult for us, but when your soul is at peace everything seems easy and fun. I do not mean that there are not many difficult and hard trials, but when the will is in harmony with the will of our Lord, the greatest burdens are lifted off and we walk free. We praise Him again for the marvel of His grace and mercy in calling us here to suffer but a little to make Him known, loved, honored and obeyed."*

*"Be joyful always; pray continually;
give thanks in all circumstances, for this
is God's will for you in Christ Jesus."*

I Thessalonians 5:1

# CHAPTER SIX

# BAPTIZING NEW BELIEVERS

My first love and consuming passion was to master the Anuak language and to translate the New Testament. Like finding the missing piece in a gigantic jig-saw puzzle, new discoveries spurred me on to keep at it night and day. Along with this, I wanted to win Anuaks to a personal faith in my Lord and Savior. Sometimes, God gave us opportunities in the midst of the translation effort. Interruptions were never really welcomed, but they were inescapable. Sometimes, I'd say to Lavina, "I wish I had a little houseboat in the middle of the river where no one could interrupt or disturb us." How glad I was that this wasn't possible, because one memorable interruption, which I recall vividly, I would not want to have missed.

## AN INTERRUPTION IS WELCOMED

On this particular morning, we were busy at it in the little office with the narrow door. This tiny room had been added onto our bedroom veranda to make roofing problems less complicated and less likely to leak. To reach it from inside the house, I passed through the living room and the sleeping veranda.

Every day I was home, I tried to be in the office by 7 a.m. Morning prayers began at 6 a.m. with our workers and any visitors from the village. We'd have our breakfast and family prayers before my translation helpers arrived.

That morning in the office, we had barely completed the prayers with which we always asked the Holy Spirit to guide us as we handled God's Word, when there was a clap outside. Stepping outside, I was shocked. In front of me was a man so emaciated and ill that he, literally, took hold of his shriveled up, empty stomach and pulled it out, a flabby, empty piece of flesh. Still holding the extra skin and flesh in his hands, he pleaded with me to do something or he would die.

We didn't have a doctor in the station yet, so we were helping as we were able in situations like this. I often remembered Don McClure's furlough story of how he would sometimes go to the medicine chest in situations like this and say, "Ini mini maini mo" and pull out whatever bottle was so identified! I wasn't at all sure what to do, but finally settled on giving him medicine for dysentery. This would require his taking the medicine several times a day for seven days. What to do? I couldn't give him all the medicine then and there and tell him to take it to his village to use it as per instructions until the seven days were up. This would be far too risky. There was a good possibility that under those conditions, he would go home and take them all at once to be cured and made better immediately. Or again, he might just put the entire bottle up in the inside of the grass roof along with the other sacred things he had no doubt put up there at the word of the witchdoctor. I had seen those necks of chickens, backbones of fish and the sacred sticks in their houses, tucked in the grass where it came down and extended over the mud wall.

So this is what I did. I said, "Look, I'll give you medicine for now and the rest of the day. But, in the morning you have to come back and get your medicine for tomorrow. I want you to do this for seven days. ( I showed him on my fingers) This will help you and we will pray to Jesus every time you come to make you well again."

To my delight and surprise, this man, whose name was "Dilok" and who lived in a village called Wangdwar a little over a mile from our house, came back faithfully. Not only that, but he would push open the narrow office door and sit on the floor listening to our discussions about the translation we were doing. His was an interruption we welcomed!

When the seven days had passed, Dilok still kept on coming back and sitting on the floor listening to the new translation as it developed. Finally, after several weeks, we finished the last two chapters of the Gospel of Mark. We took time out to read it all aloud so that Dilok could hear it also. When we were finished reading, he quietly said," I've been listening to everything you have been saying about Jesus. It has gone into my liver. I want to become a person of Yechu Kricho (Jesus Christ) and be baptized." I can scarcely express adequately my feelings that day. Besides the joy of hearing Dilok's words, I saw this experience as God's seal of approval upon my commitment to translate the entire New Testament for the Anuaks. God's word had proved to be powerful to open Dilok's eyes and cause him to believe. One day the entire Anuak tribe could have the opportunity to similarly hear and believe if my team of Anuak helpers and I stuck with it and were faithful.

Then some strange, unexpected things happened. I had been in Dilok's village and had seen the large shrine in the center of his village. I knew that he had sacrificed many sheep and goats at that shrine and that he and his wife kept beer in that small gourd attached to the bamboo pole standing in the center of their shrine, filling it regularly to appease the spirits. How could Dilok be baptized with that shrine there? He would have to remove it before he could be baptized. Did he realize this?

I spoke to him slowly and carefully. My Anuak usage was still limited but I knew I could explain it adequately for him to fully understand. This is a summary of what I tried to say, "Dilok, our livers are filled with happiness because of what you said. But, there is one thing we need to talk with you about before you may be baptized. The shrine in your village! Are you prepared to pull up that shrine, turn away from the word of the witchdoctor and trust in the power of Jesus Christ alone to help you and protect you? If you truly trust in Jesus, you must trust him with 'one liver'. (your whole heart) No one can walk on two paths. As the paths get further and further apart, you have to choose to walk on one path or the other."

As I was speaking to him, I could see his face darken. It was as if a terrible heaviness had fallen upon his liver. He finally arose, walked slowly out the door, and without a word of explanation headed in the direction of his village.

## DILOK IS BAPTIZED

It was three weeks before Dilok returned and pushed against, our narrow office door to enter. Now his face was radiant and he was eager to speak. He said, "I want to pull up my shrine and burn it. I want to follow Jesus with just one liver. I want to walk on his path alone." How we praised God as we prayed together for this tremendous victory of faith. Dilok was committing himself to Jesus in the confidence that Jesus was more powerful than any witchdoctor or any of the spirits he had tried so long to appease.

And then, I had a real shock and surprise. Dilok said, "But, I don't want to be baptized yet. I want to wait for Odan (Don McClure) to return so that he can baptize me." Dilok wanted the top man, the chief of the mission, and no young, missionary newcomer for this momentous occasion. He was thinking like an Anuak. I learned a real lesson on how Anuaks think that morning.

When Don returned, he graciously arranged it so that I was, so to speak, his official representative and Dilok readily accepted Don's word. I had the joyous privilege of baptizing him. Dilok and I became very close friends and I learned from him, even as he learned from me and the Word.

In a letter written home following his baptism, I described it like this:

*"Last week we had a thrilling service in which I baptized my first Anuak. He was the man who I had been teaching to read and had been trying to lead to Christ during these months. What a blessed day it was!*

*We went to his village about a mile from our house for the service in this man's village. First we sang some songs and then Dilok spoke, standing beside his tall shrine . (a bamboo pole about 15 feet tall, several ears of corn tied on it, a gourd in which they would have been putting beer for the spirits, and then a mound of dirt about 14 inches high around it under which were buried the bones of the sheep which he had sacrificed)*

*He told of how he had built this shrine a couple of years ago when a witchdoctor promised him that if he did so and sacrificed sheep for the spirit there, God would cause his barren wife to conceive and he, also, would have good health. He explained how he had sacrificed ten sheep there and nothing had happened. He said he had been deceived, but that now he had learned to know of Jesus, the Son whom God had sent to save him, and he was leaving all of this and trusting only in Him.*

*He then pulled up the shrine, chopped it up and burned it. They then dug up the bones and burned them. Then he still had some charms in his house and he asked his wife to bring them out to destroy them. The were brought out along with a special stick from the roof of the house, and these were all burned.*

*Then I spoke a few words in Anuak and he knelt and I baptized him with these words in Anuak, 'Dilok, pi akithaa bat wii ni nyudhi. Yina dhanh Yechu Kricho, na ni war Jwok, ki nyeng jweiy Jwok ni en kur keere.'*

*Following a few words spoken to him and prayer, all the Christians, that is the baptized persons gathered in a circle while the non-Christian village neighbors looked on. We were having our first communion service in an African village among Anuak people. Don took this part of the service. We used pancake like food for the element and tomato juice for the wine. We used a small gourd and Don went to each one of us and each took a sip. How our hearts were knit with one another as never before and how we felt that truly Christ was among us. It is an experience, we shall never forget. Don said later, 'Harvey, it was the most beautiful and wonderful service I have ever been in.' The Lord was close to us that day as the sun began to set and we began making our way home on the trail.*

*A couple of days later I came to Dilok's village and in place of the mound of dirt and the shrine, the mud floor in the village was smooth and clean. We are expecting great things from this man. He is truly a saved man. He is learning to read and says he wants to go out to teach his people. ... Dilok is the first Anuak to be baptized who is not an employee of the mission or a wife or relative of an employee. He lives about a mile from our home and about two miles from the mission. We just praise the Lord for giving us this joy and for calling Dilok for Himself. We feel this may be an opening wedge into the hearts of the people in the villages."*

Dilok, indeed, became a faithful Christian leader. He served as an elder in the Akobo church and showed real spiritual understanding. He remained true to Christ until his death some years later when he died from what was diagnosed as cancer of the liver. He died with the testimony that he was ready to die and to go to be with Jesus in heaven. It will be our joy to meet him there one day!

## RITUAL EXPERTS, THE "WITCHDOCTORS"

Ritual experts, that is, "witchdoctors", had an enormous power over the lives of the Anuak people. They were greatly feared and were believed capable of causing death as well as giving blessings of health and prosperity. Illness, death, or unexplained threatening situations brought people to the witchdoctor to have his interpretation of what went wrong and what was needed to appease the evil spirits and bring blessing rather than their curse. Both men and women had these special powers enabling them to be witchdoctors. Some were more powerful than others, but none were to be taken lightly. If a baby was ill, the witchdoctor identified the "jwok" (spirit) and prescribed what had to be given or sacrificed to entice the spirit causing the harm to leave.

These witchdoctors had a bag full of tricks and fetishes to ply their trade. There was little doubt that these persons had connections with the evil spirit world that gave them supernatural power. Some of it was pure deception, but there was much more to it than simply being more clever than others. Often a witchdoctor was a person who had had some unusual, unexplainable experience. If one had been rendered unconscious for some reason and his "jwok" (spirit) returned, this one might well be considered to have special powers associated with witchcraft. My observation was that many of those who functioned as witchdoctors were somewhat weird and eccentric. The Anuak had ambivalent feelings about these people. On the one hand, they were looked upon as benefactors, and on the other, they were seen as sinister and self-serving.

Before telling you about how one witchdoctor, Odola Wenyari, turned to Christ and was baptized, I must say a word about amulets, charms, fetishes and shrines.

The Anuak were animists; that is, they believed that material objects had spiritual qualities. Spirits of many different kinds were identified with locations, objects, animals and things of all sorts. Certain trees were sacred locations and one never passed such places without showing reverence and usually offering a small gift of beads, a coin, or an offering of spilled beer or coffee.

Before crossing the river to set out on a journey to a distant village, older Anuaks would first make a small offering at the river's edge. If one were ill, the witchdoctor might require the villager to acquire a goat of a certain color or shape. This goat would be given special treatment in the village and given special gifts on a regular basis. These gifts might be a little beer or a little special grain -- anything to keep it happy. In that goat the spirit that had attacked the sick person would live happily and no longer cause illness so long as it was given this special attention. Sometimes, the tip of the ear of such a goat would be cut off, put on a cord and worn around the neck of the person so honoring this animal.

The witchdoctors told the people what was wrong and what they had to do to correct the situation and to keep the spirit world happy. Their prescriptions ranged all the way from cutting one's own body until blood flowed to sacrificing a cow, a sheep or a goat. Nearly every Anuak had in his hut, his village or on his person some indication that a witchdoctor had been consulted. All were very aware of the reality of a spirit world which was hostile and needed to be appeased and kept happy.

The Creator God, giver of sunshine, rain and author of life was known and frequently invoked. Special people had power to influence the God who gave rain and produced the harvest. In general, however, it was apparent that the Anuak world-view perceived God to be far distant and, while ultimately with supreme power, He was not their primary concern. Romans 1:21 accurately describes what we observed then, "For even though they knew God, they did not honor Him as God, or give thanks; but they became futile in their speculations and their foolish heart was darkened." It was the fearful, essentially evil spirit world, that needed to be dealt with. For this, the witchdoctor was the person who knew what to do. These witchdoctors had the ultimate answer to matters of life and death. It was such a person as this that Christ loved, turned around and set free from the power of Satan and his evil accomplices.

## CHAPTER SIX

## ODOLA WENYARI IS BAPTIZED

I described what happened in my letter home, dated January 25, 1950:

*"Yesterday morning I went and had a marvelous visit with a witchdoctor and feel that I was very close to leading him to Christ. My new translator said in his enthusiasm, 'If this man believes, everyone will turn.'*

*This witchdoctor said finally, 'How am I going to speak the truth. I am afraid,' he said. 'through the years everyone knows that I am Odola Wenyari, the witchdoctor. They know that I have cheated them and have taken their cows, their sheep and goats and chickens. I have deceived them all.'*

*I then pointed out to him that he must confess it all -- bring his charms to the church and burn them and all his fetish bones, and, then, I will take him to the river and baptize him in the name of Jesus. Pray for Odola. We hope that soon he may be ready.*

*Today his brother came to my translator and said, 'Why do you speak to my brother, Odola. I, myself, will never leave the pouring of the beer on the ground as a sacrifice until I die.' This man's name is Babour. I know him well. You can scarcely imagine the blinding power of sin and the devil as we experience it daily here."*

It was a great moment when Odola Wenyari, the powerful, local witchdoctor professed his faith in Christ. He said he wanted to have the service in his village and to be baptized in the river in front of his house. He wanted all his neighbors to hear his testimony and see what he would do because of Jesus Christ. His village was on the river and less than 300 yards from the edge of the mission compound.

When the appointed afternoon came, his village was crowded with more than a hundred men, women and children. A couple of local Arab merchants, who were Muslims and dressed in their long, white, traditional garments were there to see what was going on.

Odola still looked like a witchdoctor because his one eye had long ceased functioning and was focused at an awkward angle. His hair was always askew and standing up in a

112

peculiar way. His actions were always jerky and he seemed a bit eccentric. If you met him alone on a lonely path, your first reaction would be of some slight fear. That perception changed as we got to know him, but, so far as his outward appearance was concerned, it never did fade away completely

On the inside, however, everything was different. By the time the service in Odola's village ended, everyone knew it.

Odola sat on the ground in the center of his village with the crowd sitting or standing around in a large circle. Odola was sitting with his legs crossed, and in front of him was a large gourd which he was holding with the neck of the gourd close to his mouth. He spoke using his typical, short, jerky sentences.

He said, "You people all know that I am Odola Wenyari, the witchdoctor. What I am saying is being heard by God. This is no time to be lying. God will punish me if I fail to tell everything I know. ... I have deceived you by taking your cows and your sheep and your goats." .... Odola began speaking into the neck of the gourd as he had done so often in invoking the name and power of the spirits. Now, however, he was demonstrating how he had deceived the people with those strange sounds that came back from the neck of the gourd. He then, dramatically, lifted the gourd and smashed it on the ground in a hundred pieces. The people were awestruck. Unbelievers could scarcely believe their eyes. How could Odola do this and not be afraid that the spirits would strike him dead?

Odola went on to give his testimony. He wanted to be forgiven by God and to have peace with God. He said, "I want my liver to sit down." (to be at peace) "Because God has sent His son, Jesus, I have found that peace. Jesus, God's son, made the true sacrifice. We need not ever make another sacrifice of our sheep and our goats. We must all put our faith in the blood that Jesus shed. I am at peace because this Jesus was more powerful than death and those who killed him. This Jesus is alive because when his friends went to the place where they had buried him, it was empty. His friends saw him many times before he went back to God's place above. I never knew about this until these white missionaries came to tell us. At first I couldn't believe it. And, when I knew in my liver that they were telling the truth, I was afraid of what you all would do to me if I confessed how I had sinned before God and had deceived you by taking your sheep and goats. My liver was hard and I wanted to refuse to change. But, when I realized that I must fear God more than you all, I said, 'I want to leave my evil things and be baptized so I can follow Jesus with one liver.'" (with my whole heart)

With these and many other words, Odola Wenyari confessed and professed his faith. It was a day none of us who were there would ever forget. We were reminded again that the Gospel is the power of God unto salvation for all who believe.

Eventually, the broken pieces of Odola's sacred gourd and other paraphernalia of a witchdoctor were all gathered up and carried by Odola and the other Christians down the steep riverbank and thrown into the river to be carried away or to sink out of sight forever. Odola, himself, then went into the river waist deep, turned around and faced the people crowding the bank. With a radiant face and without fear he was baptized. The missionary and an ordained elder from the church gently pushed him under the water. He was baptized in the precious, saving name of Jesus Christ, God's only appointed Savior.

Odola Wenyari became a true and faithful follower of Jesus Christ. He never wavered in his faith. He became a trusted elder in the Akobo Church. He was faithful in attendance and was always at the village prayer meetings. He continued to believe that God could speak to him directly. If he experienced a dream, he unfailingly shared it in the prayer meeting and closed his account with the words, "Now God, I have told the dream. Let it be so."

## BAPTIZING IN A RIVER WITH CROCODILES

During our early years in the Sudan before the church building was done, we baptized most people in the river. Large crowds would be there on the river bank sharing in the happy event. Sometimes, people gave their testimonies of what Jesus meant to them. Not infrequently, someone had a sacred gourd or fetishes to part with and destroy. These ranged from small leather homemade sandals to pieces of wire, a shriveled up chicken head or a tooth that had been sewed in a little leather pouch and worn as an amulet. This was clear evidence that Jesus was setting people free. In the power encounter, Jesus was winning! People knew deep down that Jesus was present and more powerful than everything they had always feared. True, they still needed to learn a lot about how to live out their faith in the context of their traditions, but on baptism Sundays they had already made the fundamental commitment to trust Jesus Christ to protect them from evil and to be their one and only Savior.

The baptisms themselves took considerable time when as many as thirty or forty were baptized in one service. Things weren't always routine either. I remember well the Sunday when people being baptized seemed a bit nervous. They had good reason to as we soon discovered. Floating silently in the middle of the river was a huge crocodile. Just the knobs over his eyes were visible. We assumed he was hungry and unpredictable like all the crocodiles we had ever known. I can tell you we baptized faster that Sunday than we had ever baptized before. We thought about the Lord shutting the mouths of lions to protect Daniel in the Old Testament and asked Him to please shut the mouths of crocodiles too!

That afternoon, as I sped off to the village with the outboard, this crocodile was still in that area. Chuck Jordan was on the river bank and I slowed to yell to him, "Chuck that croc is still there. Why don't you get your gun and see if you can get him.?"

When I came back from the village about four miles out, where I had preached that afternoon, I stopped to ask Chuck how he had made out. He said, "I got him. But, by the time I shot him, he had one of our mission cow's calves in its throat."

I said, "Where is he? I've got to see that."

At that point, Chuck looked at me somewhat quizzically and said, "Don't you know that a croc doesn't come up for 24 hours after it's hit? We'll have to wait until tomorrow."

I knew that, but in my eagerness had failed to take it into account. The next noon, Chuck and I walked downstream along the river bank and, sure enough, there was our dead crocodile. It was at least 15 feet long and still stuck in its throat was the dead mission calf. God had closed the mouth of a hungry crocodile. Our silent prayers had been answered.

This experience encouraged us to baptize beside the river rather than in the river. We used locally grown gourds to pour water freely over those being baptized. Later when the church was built, we found ourselves using even less water and merely sprinkling. God seemed to honor and bless all three of these practices and, as in the book of Acts, "The Lord added to the church daily, those who believed." Well, in our case, it wasn't quite daily, but the Lord was calling His own and it was exciting to be part of it.

# CHAPTER SEVEN

# LETTERS HOME ABOUT THE CHILDREN

The Lord gave us six healthy children, five boys and a girl. The youngest and the oldest were 20 years apart. Sometimes it seems that we raised two families because of the difference in ages. Dennis was born in October, 1942 and we sailed for Africa in July of '48. Jim was born in Nashville, Tennessee in March that same year. He was just four months old and still in his carrying basket when we headed for the Sudan. The following year, Dave was born at Akobo. This gave us a pair, just fourteen months apart. They grew up having great times together. I recall how they played basketball at the Schutz, American Mission school in Alexandria, Egypt. They had quite an advantage in yelling their strategies using the Anuak language. No one ever broke their code!

Carol Joy was born in the mission hospital in Dembidollo, Ethiopia in 1953. I'll never forget how overjoyed we were to have a little girl. But, I'll save that story until later. Again, fourteen months later, running true to our pattern, Mark was born at Akobo. The story of how he arrived is worthy of being told later in greater detail.

And then, to give us an even half dozen, six and a half years later our little caboose arrived when Paul was born at home when we were living at Pibor.

Letters written to my folks during those early years bring back memories of the joys and concerns that raising a family entailed. We wrote home about the children frequently, aware that the grand parents were missing out on so much because their grandchildren were growing up nearly ten thousand miles away in the heart of Africa.

Look over my shoulder, if you will, and read with me some excerpts from those letters to Grandpa and Grandma Hoekstra in Minnesota. We'll let the last be first with a comment about Paul from Addis Ababa. By this time Dennis was already training to fly one day with MAF.

From Addis Ababa - November 16, 1963:

*"Paul just came in and says, 'Dad do you want to see my new "dinky"?' Lavina got him a little 2 inch fire truck. Do they have dinky toys in America or not? Paul loves them.*

*I said to him, 'That was nice of mother. Mother loves you.'*

*He says, 'Mother loves me?' He's a lovely child and I wish you could see more of him."*

From the same letter:

*"All the children seem happy. Jim is an adolescent now with his strong reactions -- either very happy or sad about things. He's quite a boy and has a very sensitive spirit. He loves basketball and was high scorer last game. He's working hard this year and is easily on the honor roll.*

*Dave is doing well too and is trying to up his grades. ... Both Carol and Mark did well this grade period and also seem intent to do better next time."*

The next letters take us back to the early years in the Sudan. Roads were barely passable during the dry season and were closed during the rains. The plains were flooded with standing water in the low spots and even after the rains ended, one had to wait some weeks before one could travel from Akobo to Malakal. During those weeks, until MAF had a pontoon plane, we were isolated. We were unable to get out except by canoe or outboard. To reach Malakal from Akobo would take us four days on the river. During those weeks mail piled up in Malakal until the first steamer could make its way up the rising Sobat and Pibor rivers. In front of our house at Akobo, the Pibor river had a rise and fall of at least forty feet of water between the dry and rainy season.

## BY ROAD FROM AKOBO TO MALAKAL

These letters give us an idea of what was involved to get by road between Akobo and Malakal from which all our supplies were bought or routed, when gotten from Khartoum in the North.

February 22, 1949: (written from Malakal)

*"Dennis and I are leaving this afternoon about three o'clock for Akobo on a merchant's truck. We will have to ride on the back of it on top of a load of cement. Imagine doing that over that trail for 230 miles. We will stop one half way at an Arab merchants' center. Here we will be staying over for two days. We have one blanket with us and four water canteens and some soup and some cookies, so, I think we will get along alright. I have matches in my pocket for a fire and the camp cooking set I bought in Minneapolis.*

*This will, indeed, be a rugged trip, traveling all night, but it will be a most interesting experience. It will be a little hard on Dennis, but we must get back to work and we will both be able to rest after getting home. I have my gun and field glasses with, so, it should be exciting."*

April 14, 1949:

*"We got rid of Dennis's three little Ostriches last week by taking them across the river. They got into the garden several times and cleaned out our radishes and a row of beets. They are most destructive and eat like giants."*

### DENNIS TO ATTEND SCHOOL IN ADDIS

April 27, 1949:

*"Dennis and I came in on  one of the merchant's trucks*

119

*again.* (first leg of Dennis' trip to boarding school in Addis Ababa) *We had a faster and better trip, leaving Akobo about 3 p.m. on Monday and arriving here in Malakal the next day about the same hour.*

*We had an interesting trip and rather enjoyed it, although it was very hot during the day. The temperature was around 105 again. I shot a Tiang so the fellows had meat. ..."*

April 27, 1949:

"*We decided to send Dennis to Addis this year, thinking it would be this September. However, when Don was in Addis he learned that school had already begun and that they wanted Dennis as soon as possible.*

"*It was difficult to decide what to do, but we thought it might be best for him to go. He has been quite lonely at times and we feel he needs the companionship of other boys his age with whom to play. It would be selfish for us to keep him home just because we would love to have him with us. Then too, the climate at 9,000 feet in the mountains on the edge of Addis will be much better for his health.*

*We had difficulty scaring up his warm clothes in sufficient quantity, but I think he can manage until we send some more things to him. We plan to take our vacation in Addis sometime this July so we will be able to see him then. Don says the school is a very fine, congenial place with a real, vital Christian atmosphere. We feel quite satisfied that he will get along fine and profit by his being there.*

*Lavina took it real well when we left. It is hard to be sure, but, somehow, the Lord does give us understanding minds and hearts and it doesn't seem as bad. We have the assurance that He will take care of him and that no matter where Dennis is, if the Lord is there, he is as safe as under our care. School ends next December and he will fly home in time for Christmas.*"

May 8, 1949:

120

*"Dennis is now in Addis. He left on the plane last Thursday. (Mary Euwing was on that same flight and looked after him) I was so sorry I had to return home three days before the planes left so that I could not see him off. ... We had not thought it would be so hard to have him gone, but, truly, it has been lonely with him absent. I don't know how many times each day that we don't mention him. It is so early to have him go, but we know he is in a good school and that it is really better for him. We miss him so, though. He always had so much spark and pep and was so much fun. ... I don't know, but I think the sacrifice of one's children is perhaps the most deep cutting and trying experience for us missionaries. It is especially hard for Lavina as she misses him so much, but gradually now the intensity of it is diminishing and we are reconciled to it. I know that if we truly cast ourselves upon the Lord, His grace is sufficient even for this. If only he keeps well and strong now while away. It is when they are sick that they need a mother's loving care so much."*

Commenting about Dennis at school in Addis -- July 4, 1949:

*"Dennis writes he is having a grand time in school. He is well and happy."*

## LETTERS FOR GRANDPA AND GRANDMA

JUNE 24, 1949:

*"Jimmy is still as strong and pretty as ever. ... he just loves to sing and to have us sing to him. He is really quite an affectionate and loving baby. When he finds a slip of paper on the floor, he sits down and starts rocking back and forth and sings. He sings, 'Jesus' over and over again. He's learned this because we sing 'Jesus loves me this I know' to him so often. Whenever I saw boards in the house, he either stands and*

*keeps time with the saw, or he sits down and rocks back and forth keeping time with the music of the saw.*

*This week Jimmy has had a case of sore eyes which are so common out here. They are caused by the flies which carry infections from the villages. He was awfully crabby and they are so painful. For several days they were stuck shut for more than half day at a time. It was so pitiful to see him sitting there trying to eat like a blind baby. But, they are nearly better now and he is better natured too."*

July 17, 1949: (enroute Malakal aboard the Nakheila steamer)

*"We had a couple of days delay in Nasir while they were shuttling bricks from the brick yard to the village.*

*"We are all fine. Jimmy is standing up here in his chair and jabbering his head off. Lavina is sitting on the opposite side of the room nursing David who continues to grow bigger, older and stronger each day. He still has all his black hair except a little on the top of his head and front. His eyes are real dark just like Dennis's. Jimmy has pretty, light blue eyes. He is really a doll, but he is not at all easy to handle. He is lots of work, but also lots of fun at times. Everyone remarks how pretty he is and how big and strong. He is surely husky alright. We think he bears a lot of resemblance to Ronnie. He just got hold of my sore toe and is trying to make me yell."*

September 3, 1949:

*"Jimmy and David are just fine. I should add Lavina, too, because she is so well that she weighs 144 pounds and is taking on some extra exercises to 'win the battle of the bulge.' ha!*

*She has been helping this week in checking the pages in the book which we are assembling. Several school boys came to help, but every page has to be checked, and Lavina did that. We have 150 books with 34 pages each scattered all over the living veranda. We are finishing it today.*

*Jimmy is feeling so much better natured since his dysentery cleared up. He is such a cute kid. We so often say, 'If* grandpa and grandma could only see you now, they would think you were pretty sweet.' He is, honestly, a doll.

David is getting prettier every day. He has a real sweet face with a big, deep dimple on the left cheek and a smaller one on the right. His mouth is not so tiny as was Dennis' and Jimmy's, but he has a very pretty shaped head and nose. Is he ever strong! He rolled over alone at 2 1/2 months and now at 3 months, he crawls all over that little bed or kitty coup. It is amazing how strong he is for his age."

NOVEMBER 25, 1949:

"The children are doing nicely. This guy, David, is surely advanced for his age. He crept on his hands and knees at 5 mo. 18 days, and stood up in his bed and sat alone just a couple of days later. He is just six months now and he stands up continually in his bed and walks all around the sides. He is such a good baby, too, and has a great big smile for you at any time with his big dimple. We think he's quite a darling.

Jimmy is still the capsule. ha! He is really a doll and as pretty as they come, but he is rugged to handle. He is smart and is talking all the time and still likes his thumb occasionally. He is big and strong for his age. He and David will have lots of fun. Even now they make each other laugh in their beds in the morning."

For his second year away from home, Dennis traveled with other mission children to Assuit in Egypt. They were chaperoned by one of the missionary wives or families. These trips were correlated with vacation times, which, incidentally, missionaries were required to take during those years. The weather and isolation dictated the wisdom of this mission regulation. One year, we took our holiday somewhere inside the Sudan and the next year, we had to leave the country and get away to where the climate was more favorable to good health.

On this first trip to school in Egypt, Dennis had the misfortune of breaking his arm. He was always a small little guy for his age, and we felt so badly for him when the telegram from Khartoum arrived at Akobo. We wanted to rush there to be with him to love and comfort him, but that could never happen. Like Dennis, we learned that Jesus was present to take away our fears and quiet our hearts with His peace. Our letter home, tells what happened.

### DENNIS BREAKS HIS ARM

September 18, 1950:

*"I imagine the thing you are most concerned about is Dennis. We have had another telegram from Don in response to ours. He indicates that his first telegram was apparently lost.*

*The wire read as follows: 'Sorry long letter from Kosti lost aaa Dennis fell from top bunk steamer and suffered what we thought green break left forearm aaa Exray showed arm broken above wrist and above elbow with wrist bone chipped aaa Dr. Abbot on board steamer placed splints aaa exray showed good position when cast put on aaa he suffered no pain and was in good spirits, Dr. says not serious.'*

*So that is what happened. It certainly must have been a freak accident. It is amazing that he should break it in two places. We are thankful it was his left arm. The medical book indicates that a 'green break' is similar to a young tree branch which heals very quickly and is not particularly serious. So, we feel quite assured."*

### GROWING UP IN AFRICA

In many ways, our children had a great time growing up in the Sudan. They loved to fish with the native children. They learned some of the ways the Anuak children had fun without toys. They learned to make things from sticks, grass and mud. It was great sport for them to make small mud balls, attach them to a willowy stick and sling them at birds to chase the dura birds out of the ripening dura. They would sit up on the tall stands in the middle of the ripening corn and have a great time with the Anuak boys and girls who were up there from morning until night. Sometimes, they would get a little rough, too, and have a mud-ball fight to see who could make the other person run first! We were always concerned that someone might get a mud ball in the eye.

The boys enjoyed their pellet guns and were fantastic shots. Many a rat suffered at their hands. They would spend hours hunting for morning doves and come home with up to half a dozen which Lavina prepared and put on the table for that essential ingredient in another of her delicious, home cooked meals.

The boys learned to eat like the Anuak boys too. We weren't always so excited about that because we knew how easily dysentery and diarrhea could follow.    Once, when I came in the back yard, Denny, who was then about six and a half years old, was sitting beside a little fire he had made. His legs were wide apart and he was holding a partially eaten fish. Just like the Anuaks, he was eating around the intestines and enjoying the meat. He looked up at me with a guilty grin and captivating smile that I shall never forget.   We were still pretty strict about those things those first months but seeing his endearing smile, even though tainted by disobedience, didn't make discipline any easier!

And then there was the time when I stepped out of the back door at Pibor. I was going down the back path and there, under the shade of a small bush, Dave was eating a tiny dura bird, about the size of a sparrow. He had plucked most of the feathers off and roasted it in a little fire he had going there. He looked up at me and, with the most satisfying smile,  said with his childish lisp, "Thweet, dad. Thweet." Which by way of interpretation is, "Sweet, dad. Sweet." He was translating back from Murle into English!

When David was born, the Anuaks called him "Little Akobo". When he started growing up they began calling him "David Akobo". When Carol was born, they gave her the name, "Awile", which means, "the one who changed things around". She had broken the pattern from boys to our having a girl. Her older brothers still call her "Awile" sometimes as a playful expression of love and admiration, an indication of how glad they are to have such a lovely sister.

## JIMMY AND THE ALADDIN LAMP

The children really loved the single missionary gal who lived at Pokwo with us after she came back from furlough. Having been there alone with their dad and mom for fifteen months, they were glad for a new face. Joan Yilek had a way with kids and when she would come over for a meal with us, the conversation around the table was animated and frequently hilarious.

One evening Jimmy and Dave were so excited that they monopolized the conversation and we couldn't seem to get a word in edgewise. Finally, in good fun, I said, "Alright, now it's time for the adults to have a chance to talk. I want you children to keep silent unless you have something really special to say. But, before you can talk, you have to raise your hand to get permission."

Everything seemed to have calmed down reasonably well, when Jimmy, who had had his hand up for some time and wasn't being recognized, began to sing softly, "I see something. I see something. I see something." He kept this up without our paying adequate attention. When, finally, we gave him the attention he should have had all along, under terms of the conditions playfully laid down, we saw that he was pointing to the Aladdin lamp. It was gradually going up in smoke as the wick became blacker and blacker. We had a good laugh and knew that Jimmy succeeded in having had the last word!

What fun we had as a family when the children were small and not some 2,000 plus miles away in school in Egypt. The pain of those empty beds that first night after the children left for school, has seared its way into our memories. The utter desolation and loneliness of those first nights were hard on Lavina with a mother's heart. But, we all felt it, even the little ones who weren't yet old enough to go away to school.

And then there were the letters we exchanged with our children. The school had a regulation that every child had to spend part of Sunday afternoon to produce a letter in an envelope for their parents. I suspect most kids would have written in any case. But, those letters were very precious for both parents and the children. We shared many deep and meaningful conversations in those exchanges.

Some of the letters received produced joy and laughter.

Dennis was always small for his age. He was just a little guy when he was in the third grade at Assuit in Egypt. One of his letters was unforgettable. It had only a couple of sentences but they got our attention.

He wrote, *"Please write Miss Duff a hot letter and tell her to stop opening my mail."* After a good laugh over it, we thought an appropriate letter in response would be in order!

Other letters brought concern and pain, like when one of the boys would write about some perceived injustice in the classroom because of what a teacher had said. The painful incident would be described in detail to gain our sympathy and support. But, we could sense that if we had been there, we could have helped the child appreciate some of the other factors that hadn't been taken into account. Had we been there we could have helped our child understand and the pain would have been less severe. But, by the time this kind of letter came, it was far too late to be of much help. A month would have passed. By this time they would again be having fun with friends about which they normally wrote.

June 9, 1950:

*"Lavina and the children are fine. David has had a little dysentery. ... Jimmy is so cute and good now. He is a darling and if you could hear the sentences he forms ... David says a few words and runs all over. He is all boy now! Dennis still loves to fish. He just came up with a big one, about sixteen inches long and says they want to cook it in the fire Anuak style and eat it right away. They cook the fish or broil it and then eat around the intestines native style! It doesn't look good to me, but in Anuak he says, 'It is very sweet.' Dennis hasn't grown a great deal taller, but he is huskier and well filled out now. Jimmy looks like and reminds us so much of Ronnie."* (my brother Clarence's son)

March 14, 1951: (from Malakal)

*"The weather these last two weeks has been almost un-*

127

*bearably hot. Every day it is well over 100 degrees. I had it
105 a week ago Sunday and then on Tuesday it was 107 in the
shade inside the house. The worst part of it was that the nights
were very hot too. We got up in the morning feeling like 'old cats
having over the clothesline'.*

*In the midst of it, David took seriously ill with bacillary
dysentery. It came on so suddenly about three in the afternoon.
By evening he had a terrific, burning fever. He was delirious all
evening and by four o'clock in the morning he had a convulsion.
We were so worried about him and it seemed that it might just
continue on at that increasing rate and take him. Fevers work
that way in the Sudan. One becomes ill and without stopping
the fever mounts and the patient dies.*

*We certainly praise the Lord for restoring him. Lillian
was out on trek, but Bob brought her home at four a.m.. Meanwhile, we gave him a hot mustard foot bath and put ice water
and cloths on his head. Gradually, the fever broke and by the
next night he was so very much better. With bacillary dysentery
the patient loses all the fluid in his body so quickly through the
bowels. It is amazing. Then too, he had malaria with it, but the
atabrine shot took care of that. He had malaria again last Sunday, but we gave him a course of atabrine and it's all cleared up
now.*

*"He is such a cute little kid, and now with his skin all
turned yellow his eyes sparkle even more. Jimmy and David
make a real team now. You will have lots of fun with them.
Jimmy says the other day, 'When I get to America, I'm going to
tell grandma, 'I aik you,' meaning, 'I like you'."*

## CHILDREN'S ESCAPADES AND ACCIDENTS

When Dave was about three years old, he gave us the
fright of our lives. It was late afternoon and Lavina and I were
enjoying the gradual cooling off of the day as we wandered
through the garden, commenting on how the various vegetables were faring. During this time, David had climbed up on
the steps that led up to the base where the water barrels were

positioned. These steps allowed the water carrier to make his way up there with his five gallon tins to fill the barrels morning and evening. Water from the barrels ran through a lead pipe into the house to give us inside water. We had a faucet over the sink in the kitchen, one in the bathroom and a shower. All showers were cold, and they really felt that way, too, after the heat of the day.

This particular afternoon Dave had been playing quite contentedly on the steps and having a great time. However, during one of our frequent glances in his direction, we saw him sitting on the ground and he seemed to be in distress. He had fallen off the third or fourth step, landing on his small toy crane, striking it right across his windpipe. It seemed innocent enough, but almost immediately as the swelling began, it was apparent that the air passage was rapidly closing and he was having difficulty getting enough air.

We really didn't know what to do. We carried him into the house and put him on the bed and prayed that the Lord would cause the swelling to stop. We also contemplated driving him to Pibor, some 90 miles south where Dr. Roode was stationed. Of course, that would have been to no avail if the swelling had continued. Lillian Huiskens, our Akobo nurse, was soon there and she calmly kept a careful eye on him and together we committed Dave to the Lord's merciful, saving power. We look back on that experience with great thanks to God for His intervention and how He cared for Dave and taught us afresh how totally dependent we were upon Him.

Letters home are cute telling how Dave viewed the discipline of kindergarten every day.

November 9, 1954:

*"David is in kindergarten with his mother teaching. There are rather frequent times when he shows up with 'I'm sick of school, mother. Let's not have school today.' He loves to play out with the Anuak children, roasting pigeons, fish, and corn in typical Anuak fireplaces. He speaks Anuak as if it were his native tongue!"*

Another letter dated, December 10, 1955, tells of the children's pets:

*"Last week one day Vern and I went out looking for a leopard -- saw nothing! A man had come in with a baby leopard and so we were off looking for the mother. We have this baby leopard on a bottle -- still just as tame as a kitten. Also have a little reedbuck on the bottle. You'd think we have enough kids on bottles not to fuss with animals! Actually, David does the work. It is good for the children out here. Even mother and dad enjoy it too! Jimmy will be wild about them when he comes. Dennis will enjoy the horses and soccer ball. There'll be something for each one of us.*

*Lavina cheated on Christmas a little when she got out the red jeans and a little dress for Carol. They are adorable on her. She is a cutie! Smart as they come and full of pep. Mark, too, is becoming quite handsome."*

When Dave was a little older, he and the Jordan boys, Jack and Dave, had great times together. They had an interesting debate going among them as to whose Dad's dog was the strongest. One day these boys egged the two dogs on, each side hoping to prove the other to be wrong. I suspect they bit off more than they could handle. Before this inconclusive, furious contest was over the dogs had had the last bite. Dave came home by way of the clinic with stitches and a clean, white bandage around his leg. He had gotten a little to close to the action! A prominent scar reminds him of how much fun it was before he tried to make sure his dad's dog would win!

Jim and Dave had a lot of fun together. Being just fourteen months apart they were almost like twins. One afternoon when, Jim and Dave were young lads, eleven and twelve years of age, they gave us a good scare too. Dave had a way of playing tricks on us with his delightful sense of humor, so we weren't always sure whether he was to be taken seriously or not.

I was in the office inside our house at Pibor. We lived in what was known then as "Hostetter's house". They had lived there until Paul and his family were expelled, the first missionaries on whom the ax fell, with everyone else still to follow. Missionary houses tended to be identified by the name of the first person who had occupied it.

On that afternoon of which I'm writing, Dave and Jim came into the office and asked if they could chop some wood. We always had to chop dry branches and logs for the wood burning cook store. Normally, an Anuak or a Murle was engaged to do this, but the boys thought it would be a fun experience to chop a little wood.

I looked at their shorts and bare feet and had a moment of concern as to the wisdom of their doing this without shoes, but gave it no more than a passing thought and gave them my okay to go ahead. My parting words were, "Be sure you boys are careful not to chop yourselves with those bare feet." With that they left, happy with the "permission granted" status under which they could begin.

They weren't gone more than fifteen minutes when Dave came back in alone with the words, "Dad, Jim chopped his foot!"

I thought he was kidding and responded with, "You've got to be kidding."

It was no joke! Jim had already made his way over to the mission hospital and when I arrived, Dr. Mary Smith was busy stitching up a 3" gash running right down the entire length of the foot, just off center. A quarter of an inch on the angle of the gash and he would have severed the tendon.

Again, our prayers of thanks took on special meaning. We were reminded again of how utterly dependent we were upon the Lord's loving, protecting care. It was a painful experience, but everyone learned important lessons out of it.

Dave and I were reminiscing recently about some of the boy's experiences in Africa. At one point, he said to me, "Dad, do you remember that big Nile perch we picked up that day when we were coming down from Pibor to Akobo with that old launch?" (a three day trip in an old diesel launch that had 4 bunks in it) Do you remember how we put that huge fish up on the top and how the juice from the fish oozed out and ran all over our jackets. Boy, how they smelled and we couldn't get that terrible, dead fish smell out of them? Dad, that's one of our experiences you've got to include in your book."

Our grandchildren have listened to many a story from our years in the Sudan and Ethiopia. Once, while sitting around the table with Jim's family, I got to talking about some of our fabulous experiences in Africa. At one point, Doug, then about eleven, piped up and said, "Grandpa, you ought to write a book. It'd be a best seller." Would that this young lad had prophetic blood flowing in his young veins!

Seriously, one of the reasons for writing this book is so that our children and grandchildren will be able to recall some of their incredible experiences and praise God for His marvelous, loving care as we worked together for Him in the heart of Africa. What a privilege it was for our whole family, even though some experiences were painful and threatening. Looking back, we know, beyond the shadow of a doubt, that God who called us mercifully protected us and enabled us to complete the task He had entrusted to us.

The twin-engine Rapide, MAF's first aircraft with which they flew in the Sudan.

The Pibor River was completely blocked by Sud-grass just below the mission at Akobo for several weeks that season, MAF wasn't yet on the scene. Bob Swart and Harvey spent an entire day cutting a path through the Sud to get Don McClure out to the hospital in Malakal on the small mission launch because of a serious injury Don had sustained during that time. It was very hot and uncomfortable with many leaches, flies and bugs taking advantage of their situation.

*"Blessed are all who fear the Lord,
who walk in his ways.
You will eat the fruit of your labor;
blessings and prosperity will be yours.
Your wife will be like a fruitful vine
within your house;
your sons will be like olive shoots
around your table;
Thus is the man blessed
who fears the Lord."*
Psalm 128: 1-4

# CHAPTER EIGHT

# CUSTOMS AND CONCEPTS

Almost every day was a learning experience. While trying to understand how the Anuak language was put together, I was constantly grappling with "meaning". If we were to have an accurate translation which expressed what the Bible was saying the way an Anuak would say it if he had been there and was writing it to his own people, I needed to know what Anuaks thought and believed about -- well, "almost everything." I needed to enter into their "world-view". This was an intriguing, compelling, often baffling pursuit that had to include study time with informants and village time listening and observing. On our discovering trail we were reminded of the words from the Bible itself when it says, "Even a little child shall lead them."

A letter home tells how it happened for us.

August 22, 1950:

## SPITTING TO BLESS

*"Our people are so very poor and hungry these days. They are at the door constantly begging for money to buy a little grain that the merchants had gotten a few weeks ago. The grain is more than half the normal price and our people are selling everything to get a little money together to buy it.*

*The other day Dennis gave a small tin can full of grain to an old woman who comes here quite regularly. She was so happy, Lavina said, that she took Dennis's head in her hands and spit on the top of it to show her gratitude. Needless to say, Dennis was embarrassed to tears."*

# CHAPTER EIGHT

I played a little joke on one of our guests from America over this custom of spitting on the head to extend a blessing or to show appreciation. Dr. Ed Fairman who has a good sense of humor (which always helps) was visiting us when we lived at Pokwo. Anuaks had come in from the village to see who the new visitors were and to welcome Ed and Marian and their young son, Tim. We were all having a good time and I was interpreting. I finally said to Ed, "How would you like to receive an Anuak blessing?"

Not knowing the custom, he innocently said, "Well, I guess I can always use an additional blessing." He, of course, couldn't follow the conversation the Anuaks and I were having in the Anuak language, so before he knew it, this village chief put his hands on Ed's head, pushed it slightly down and gently spit on it. This was a blessing, the memory of which stayed with Ed permanently!

On another occasion in the village, I saw a young Anuak lad, who had come in from a distance, present himself to a village elder who happened to be his uncle. The old man was so overjoyed to see the young man that he overdid it a bit. He really put a load of saliva on the young man's head. The man sitting next to him even scolded him saying that was not a proper way to bless someone! I learned that the amount of saliva was to be minimal and primarily symbolic rather than for cleansing!

## SPITTING WHEN FORGIVING

When we were searching for an Anuak word to use in the translation of "to forgive", they told me what they had used in the language of a neighboring tribe. They said those people express "to forgive" by saying "to spit on the ground". I learned that in that tribe when there was trouble, anger or misunderstanding which had been peacefully resolved and reconciliation followed, the party who had been offended would spit on the ground. The estrangement was ended and harmony had been restored. They said that when God sent His son Jesus to die on the cross, he brought the enmity between God and man to an end. Because of the price that Jesus had paid with his blood on the cross, God forgives those who come to him confessing their wrong. In that language to say, "God forgives us" they expressed it by saying "God spits on the ground." For those people, it was a beautiful, appropriate and normal way to describe what it means "to forgive".

In the Anuak language, one of the ways to express this same concept is to say, "God put His liver down." Anger, hostility, and/or estrangement cause one's liver to jump up. For the Anuak to put the liver down is to forgive. We were learning to express the great truths of the Gospel in ways appropriate to their culture and world view.

## JUST TWO COFFEE BEANS

One morning at Pokwo we were just ready to sit down to eat when we heard a clapping of hands at the back door. This is the way Anuaks let it be known that they are outside one's door. Very appropriate for the kind of grass tukls they lived in.

Two middle aged men, wearing a simple pair of shorts, as Anuaks always did, were standing outside to greet me. They said they were about to start fishing and would like to have some coffee. Since our breakfast coffee hadn't been drunk yet, I quickly assured them this would be no problem and invited them in to have a cup of coffee with us. "No, no," they protested, "We don't want coffee to drink, we want dried coffee beans that haven't been roasted yet." So, I obligingly went in and asked Lavina for a little can of coffee beans as the men had requested.

When I went out with the can of coffee beans, the one man reached forward and took just two beans out of the can. Now it was my turn to protest. I said, "Look, you can't make coffee with just two beans. Please take the whole can."

They responded somewhat condescendingly and said, "No, two beans is all we need. We're not making coffee to drink. We need only these two beans to throw into the river because when we do this the fish will really bite." I have never tried it, but my suspicion is that it wouldn't work for this missionary the way they said it worked for them.

## GREETING THE CHIEF WHO HAD DIED

One morning an Anuak man from the village and I were

137

hiking together to a distant village. We were visiting and conversing together as we walked. I was in front and he was close behind me. I had been talking, but when I got no reply, I turned around to look and establish eye contact. The man was no longer there. I turned back and soon found him about 30 feet off the path. He was on his knees talking out loud to no one visible. He was in front of a dilapidated, abandoned Anuak hut. I waited a moment before speaking, somewhat surprised to hear him talking to someone who obviously wasn't there. With no further explanation, my companion said, "I just stopped for a moment to greet our chief who once lived here before he died."

I understood better what it meant for Africans to honor the "living dead". It was important for my friend to keep on the right side of this dead person whose memory was vivid enough to cause his spirit to respond appropriately if he wasn't properly respected. Was this ancestor worship or just respect for someone they believe still to be present through his spirit? I had more food for thought as I pondered the meaning of this. We had a long trail ahead of us and plenty of time to think.

## THE MAN WHO COULD
## STAY UNDER WATER AND SURVIVE

The Anuaks have many myths and stories that they believe profoundly. One story going around during our stay at Pokwo was about a certain Anuak, still living, who had the ability to go into the river, submerge himself and come out on the river bank at another village miles further down stream. I had a lot of fun kidding and challenging them about that when we sometimes sat around under the shade of a tree and traded stories. They would always insist that it was true.

Finally, I thought, "I've got to find a way to make them show me that it actually happened or I will have to prove them to be mistaken." We couldn't both be right. Finally one day I said, "Why don't you bring the man himself to me and we'll talk with him under the tree and hear him tell us how he can do this."

To my surprise one morning right after breakfast a large number, possibly 20 or 25, grown adult Anuak men appeared outside our kitchen door. They had brought the man himself. I brought out a couple of chairs so that the important men could sit on them and I would have one for my own comfort. They insisted that this was the man. It was interesting how cagey they were. I challenged the man to go into the river in front of the house and stay under for some minutes to prove that he could really do this. "No," they said, "he can't do that for you unless there is a reason for him to do so. If there was something lost in the river, he could go under the water and stay under until he found the missing item and bring it up."

"Well," I said, "I can easily arrange that. I'll go in the house and get my gun and throw it in the river from the canoe. Then I'll come back and fetch your friend and point to the general area and ask him to go under the water and remain under until he finds it and comes to the surface with it."

With that the group turned quite serious and began to debate among themselves, discussing the matter in low, solemn voices which I couldn't fully understand. Finally, the spokesman for the group said, "No, we've told our friend not to do it because this foreigner might kill you under the water."

The meeting ended abruptly. Everyone had had a lot of fun, but nobody proved anything to anybody. Later, I gave them a can of coffee beans which they could use to either brew some coffee or throw in the river, two at a time, and induce the fish to bite. If I hadn't been there, I could never believe that we grown men spent that much time earnestly discussing such a ridiculous possibility. When the group left, they were happy and everyone felt we had had a great time! Question: How does one communicate the Gospel effectively among people with elements such as this framing their world-view of reality? It reinforced my conviction that this was a task that only the Holy Spirit could accomplish. We would keep on studying and trying to understand, but, in the end, the miracle to change the mind and to believe was His to do.

## ANUAK NAMES

We found the way Anuaks named their babies fascinating. But, before I get into that, let me say that we missionaries were all given new names soon after we arrived. I was named, *Odola, war Omot (Odola, the son of Omot)*. I was given the name of one of the ancestors who had lived on land where our house was built. Lavina was given the name, *Nyijobi,* which means "the offspring of a buffalo". I never did understand why they had called her that. She was just too pretty and to well proportioned for a name like that. But the Anuaks always insisted that it was a name of honor and great respect. I had no trouble with that and concurred that the Anuaks were very perceptive!

Bob Swart was called *Bom.* Don McClure was called *Odan.* That seemed a good adaptation because the Anuaks normally named their boys with names that started with "O". This may be apocryphal, but some of our colleagues suggested Dr. McClure was called *Odan* because the Anuaks had heard his wife, Lyda, so frequently trying to call Don in to have lunch at noon. She would have to call him more than once with a long, loud, "Oh, Donnnn! Oh, Donnnn, lunch is ready." How can we ever be sure?

Some missionary names seemed self apparent. Wilma Kats was named, *Nyikwach,* which means, "the offspring of a cat" (the leopard). Joan Yilek who was on the heavier side, and a great missionary, was called, *Nyilyech,* the offspring of an elephant. The Anuaks had done it again!

***** 

I heard that Apio had given birth to another child. Late that afternoon when my translation work for the day had been completed and the Anuak informants had left, I said, "I'll take a moment and hike down to Apio's village and see if she and the child are doing okay or not."

When I arrived, Apio was already up and about. She was pounding grain at the pounding hole. Her belly was tightly bound and kept in with a belly band of ropes tightly assembled together. She was happy to see me and glad for the excuse to sit down for a bit as her strength wouldn't be up to par for a few days yet. We had a pleasant conversation, prayed together and talked about God's gift of children. Apio was one of the stronger Christian women and known for her sincere prayer life. It was a joy and blessing to fellowship with her.

Before leaving, I said, "Well now, what name did you give to the baby?"

She responded by saying, "Odola, (my African name)

you know our custom. We haven't named him yet. We have to wait some days first to be sure he will live." I knew that, but had carelessly forgotten to take it into account when I asked her what the name was.

With light hearted bantering, I said, "Well, when was the baby born?"

She, in turn, responded by saying,"He came out yesterday afternoon."

To this I responded by saying, "Well then, I suppose you will call him, 'Afternoon'. Anuaks often named their children in association with some event the might be associated with the child's birth. For example, if a mother gave birth while traveling on the steamer, she would most likely call the child, "Steamer". If a child was weak and it appeared that he might not live at the time of birth, he would later be called, "Will not live." Normally the first two boys born to Anuak parents, were called "Omot" and "Ojulu". Girls had the same names but their names started with an "A", which meant they were called "Amot" and "Ajulu". You always knew who was the oldest and whether it was a boy or a girl. As children increased in the family, names were less predictable.

Anyway, when I met Apio on the path some ten days later, I asked her, "What did you decide to name that baby?"

With a typical Anuak response she said, "Didn't you say we should call him, "Afternoon" (Aboya)? We called him, "Afternoon." Ten years later, when we left, he was still called, "Afternoon." They considered it a good name and I had no regrets!

Our nurse, Lillian Huiskens, ran into this naming of children in an interesting way. She was constantly trying to get the women to use more sanitary methods in caring for their children. Anuak women had some sort of mid-wife system operating whenever they gave birth. This mid-wife, who was either a relative or some older person with experience in these matters, would attend the birth of the baby. They had no instruments, of course, so they just used a sharp blade of dry grass to cut the umbilical cord. Being unsterile, babies sometimes died from infected umbilical cords. The struggle was to help them understand what was happening and to call on Lillian to assist in these births that were in villages not too far away.

141

CHAPTER EIGHT

It took a long time, but eventually one lady called on Lillian when her baby was born. Lillian went out with her sharp scissors and cut that cord with her scissors instead of with a blade of grass as was customary. It was a big event. It had never happened in all of Anuak history. There had been a lot resistance to the idea. A certain amount of superstition was connected with how that umbilical cord should be cut and who was authorized to do it.

Lillian made history. We all talked about it for a long time. Its importance wasn't lost on the Anuaks either. The mother, following tradition, named the baby in association to a significant event. What could be more important than that her baby had had its umbilical cord cut with a scissors. You guessed it! The baby was named "Scissors" (*Makath*). He grew up with no bad effects from his history making entry into the world. He grew into manhood with everyone calling him "Scissors". Anyone who inquired knew he was the first Anuak baby to have had his umbilical cord cut with a clean, sterile medical scissors. After awhile, the Anuaks forgot all about how he had gotten his name, and accepted it as normal. But it would be a long time before cutting umbilical cords in Anuak country using sterile instruments was normal procedure.

I had, of course, known from the anthropologists that Africans frequently named their children with some association to events surrounding the birth. So we weren't surprised, but found it fascinating. We found people with names like "Won't live", "To be thrown out", "A bad one", "One to be chased", "He will die", " A cursed one" and "One who bites". None of these were very flattering. They didn't want to give babies names accenting the positive and the attractive, lest it draw the attention of the evil spirits who would harm their newborn babies. Being a "non-entity" was the way they perceived a newborn. And, in any case, the low profile was safer with innumerable unseen, evil spirits lurking in the shadows.

### *THERI*
### THE INFLUENCE OF A PREGNANT WOMAN

Anuaks believed that a pregnant woman cast an evil shadow on certain things and events. The influence of a pregnant women had to be counteracted. She mustn't be around the cattle or there might be miscarriages of calves. Cows would give less milk when a pregnant woman was among them.

The belief that a pregnant woman could actually cause a newborn baby's umbilical cord to pop out and not heal properly was very strong. Every Anuak believed this to be so. They called this influence *theri*. This is the way it worked.

When a baby was born, the hut in which the woman and baby were living was surrounded with a thorn fence. Three or four foot thorn branches were cut in the forest and brought home. These were stuck, upright in the ground in a circle around the hut. In a small village, sometimes the entire village was circled in this way.

Anyone passing that hut or village would know immediately that there was a newborn baby and mother there. Any pregnant woman approaching a tukl or village circled with thorns, would divert widely from the path and proceed around the village keeping a safe distance of at least forty or fifty yards from where the baby and mother were located.

Whenever the navel of a newly born baby failed to heal properly and infection set in, the immediate burning question was, "What pregnant women caused 'theri'? Who did it?" And, if the baby died, it became a matter of life and death for the suspected person. With the coming of the British colonizers, the "life for a life" with respect to *theri* was prohibited. However, in their villages, the Anuaks continued to deal with these matters as they always had. As missionaries, when we told what Jesus Christ could do for our people, we frequently told them that He was more powerful than *theri*, and that they need not fear. Jesus was more powerful than anything that tried to harm those who put their trust in Him. We longed for and waited for the day when Anuak women would no longer have their tukls circled with thorns because of their fear of *theri*. We prayed for the time when pregnant Anuak women would not need to be ostracized and live in fear that an accusing finger might be pointed at them when babies died for these reasons.

It took a along time, but eventually it began. Little by little women were being set free from fear because of Jesus. Those were great times of happiness when in the worship services or prayer meetings an Anuak mother would share and say, "I didn't put thorns around my house when my baby was

143

born. I'm no longer afraid of *theri* because Jesus is stronger. See how healthy my baby is today."

With these kinds of words they were declaring "the mighty acts of God" as they experienced His salvation. We remembered then that Jesus had said, "I am the light of the world. ... He who follows me shall not walk in darkness. ... I am come that they might have life and have it more abundantly." Our hearts were glad. To be a missionary there was totally satisfying. We praised God and worshipped Him!

In many respects, we lived as strangers in a forbidding land among a people whose ways often confounded us. Consider this experience:

I had gone downstream a couple of miles by boat with several Anuaks to see if we could get an animal for some meat. Several village people joined us as we made our way back of the village toward the swamp area on the edge of the thorn tree forest. Almost immediately we spotted a small herd of waterbuck. We could actually smell them before we saw them because of their strong body odor which tended to carry over into the flavor of the cooked meat as well. Waterbuck was our meat of last resort, but it made good gravy! Eventually, we learned to enjoy it and never really were troubled by the strong flavor.

That morning I brought a nice animal down with my .348 caliber lever action rifle. The men immediately ran to the fallen animal and were proceeding to cut its throat when it suddenly, inexplicably, jumped to its feet and began to run away. The men all followed it in hot pursuit as they disappeared among the trees. I was left standing alone, gun in hand.

After a bit I started to call out to see if someone from among them might answer so I would know where to follow them. No one responded, but shortly a man came up from the riverbank. He was passing by in his canoe and had heard me. He now joined me and called out himself. I didn't hear anything, but he said, "They're over in that direction."

I followed the man into the forest and when we came upon my hunting party, they were already skinning the animal. They had successfully caught up with it and finished what I had started.

Now, the baffling thing is this. As we stood around while some of the men were dressing out the meat, one of the village people ask me if I knew why that animal had gotten up and run away.

I responded by saying, "Well, I suppose I didn't hit him in the right place."

To this, in a condescending manner, he said to me, "No, Odola"( my African name), the problem is that one of the men in your party has a wife who is pregnant. And, whenever you hunt with a man whose wife is pregnant the animals run away like this."

Another occasion I recall is when our man who carried up the water from the river to fill our water barrels failed to do so. I went out back where his little house was and found him sitting in the low doorway. He had a bandage on his toe. He explained that he couldn't got into the water because of his bandage and therefore hadn't filled the barrels.

That was a fair explanation, but then I noticed that his house had thorns around it like Anuaks would normally put around a hut in which a mother had recently given birth to a baby.

I said to him, "Deng, I understand about the bandage, but why do you have these thorns around your house?"

He turned his head slightly and pointing with his tongue he said,"Omot's wife over there is pregnant and every time she walks past my house my toe goes like this." And then, he motioned with his hand how his toe throbbed whenever she came past his hut. It was a strange world and we had a lot to learn!

## GWITH
### A LAST WILL OR TESTAMENT

Anuaks have powerful, pivotal customs that arise out of critical junctures in their lives. One such practice is that of the "final blessing, will or testament" (gwith). When a man knows that the time of his death is near, he will call for a person he trusts to whom he can commit his final blessing.

The man sits on an animal skin beside the dying person and listens intently to each item in the blessing. He has to listen carefully because if he fails to accurately carry out the instructions of the dying person , after that person has died, the curse attached to it is most severe.

145

CHAPTER EIGHT

It works something like this: The person anticipating death speaks. He says, " I have three cows that are in the village of Ojulu. They belong to me. You must get them after I die and dispose of them in this way ......"

The man listening, repeats the words several times to fix it in his mind. He then takes a dry blade of grass about six or eight inches in length and puts it down in front of him.

Again, the person about to die might say, " I have a string of dimui beads. They were borrowed by my brother for use in his son's marriage. They must never be lost. You must recover these so that my own son can use them for his marriage."

The man listening, similarly repeats the words of the dying man to fix them firmly in his memory. A second blade of grass is laid down which is slightly different in length from the previous one.

This speaking of the testament continues until the five or six items on the dying man's mind have been addressed. Finally, when the last item has been covered and the last blade of grass has been laid down, the dying man pronounces a curse on the man to whom he has entrusted his will and testament. He concludes with the solemn warning, "If you fail to carry out my word or change it in any way, one of your eyes will fall to the ground." This has a powerful way of concentrating the mind, as you can imagine.

The person leaves with the blades of dry grass and when he reaches his own village, carefully puts them away, only to bring them out over and over again to fix permanently in his memory what the blades of dried grass represent. At the appropriate time, after the death of the person who has spoken, the testament is executed. Few, if any, would doubt the word of the man who was under a solemn oath to be truthful lest he lose his eye.

### SHI-JWOK - AN EVIL EYE

I learned a lot about the Anuak language and customs by visiting their villages and staying overnight. It was great to be under the mosquito net, continuing to listen to their conversations until I fell asleep. I was also amazed at the noise in these villages. Dogs were barking, babies crying and Anuaks

146

were stirring at different times all through the night keeping the fire going or having a smoke. There was a lot of coughing, too, as I recall.

One night in the village of Othil, about four miles from home, I slept under my net inside one of their houses. When I came out in the morning, I discovered the chief and a large group of people sitting around him having an, obviously, important meeting. They all welcomed me profusely, including the chief and the elders sitting near him. I was a bit suspicious when they all decided that the meeting was over, almost as soon as I sat down to listen in on their deliberations.

Later I learned that I had stumbled onto a meeting in which they were discussing the matter of the *evil eye*, and what to do about the baby that had been born and would most certainly grow up having the power of the *evil eye*. Such a person would be called a *shi-jwok* and would have the ability to cast evil spells on people, villages, and events. A person suspected of being a *shi-jwok* was greatly feared and people were always on the lookout for someone who might be a *shi-jwok* and have caused a misfortune.

They were discussing the fate of a little, newborn baby whose testicle had not come down. A child born with that abnormality among the Anuak was cursed and had to be killed. If allowed to grow to adulthood, this person would have the ability to curse people and cause great harm.

Normally, before the British had come to govern the Sudan, Anuaks would take such a baby, put it in a gourd and either let it float away on the river or they might put it in a swamp in the hot sun to die, in which case the vultures would have the last word.

I understood then why the meeting had ended so abruptly. They were fearful that I would report them to our local district commissioner, a British official.

Our first furlough soon followed that experience. After we returned from the states, I inquired as to the child and was told, "Oh, that baby died." My presence had delayed the inevitable, but had not prevented it. I was reminded again that without Jesus there is darkness, fear and superstition which brings death. Jesus alone can change all of that. That's the heart of the good news from God. Jesus, himself, said, "I am the light of the world." And again, He said, "I am come that

CHAPTER EIGHT

they might have life, and have it more abundantly." There is no other Savior! We are entrusted with that good news from God, and are commissioned to take this powerful, saving Gospel to the very ends of the earth and to proclaim it unashamedly to every tribe and people. And what better way, than to tell them, each in his own language.

## JWOK
### GOD, SPIRIT, LUCK, ILLNESS ...

Perhaps the most powerful concept affecting the lives of Anuaks was their understanding of *jwok*. Studying their language and customs, I found the meaning of this word most difficult to fully understand. The word, *jwok,* was constantly on the lips of Anuaks. God, the creator, was *Jwok.* A person could be a *jwok.* An individual who was ill was said to have a *jwok.* If the fish weren't biting it was because of the word of *jwok.* This seemed to imply bad luck or fate. When one was ill and dying, his *jwoks,* called *ju* in the plural were leaving his body one by one, vacating the vital organs with which they were identified. When all the spirits (*ju*) had departed, the person was dead. If one was startled, the spontaneous response was, *"Jwok"*.

In trying to understand the wide areas of meaning associated with this word, *jwok* it became apparent that this reflected a world-view with many unknowns and many things that were fearful and foreboding. The word *jwok* and its many different meanings suggested a world of unfriendly, harmful spirits. Basically, *jwok* was associated with the unknown and that which couldn't be explained but had to be treated with respect and kept friendly. Gifts and sacrifices were made to *jwok.*

It was interesting and significant that when people were learning to read, whenever they guessed how to read the sentence which said, "God (*Jwok*) is good", they would invariably say, "God (*Jwok*) is bad". They would consistently guess wrong. For them, *Jwok* was bad.

You can imagine the problems and concern this raised as to how to be sure we were using the correct word for "God". In the end, we normally added a descriptive expression so that we would be saying, "God who made the heavens and the

148

earth."

## *JWEIY*
### SPIRIT, BREATH ...

Another baffling linguistic problem arose as to the use of the word for "spirit". Like the Greek, the Anuak word we determined meant "spirit" also meant "breath". The problem was that this word *"jweiy"* which we understood to be akin to "spirit" had to be the *jweiy* of something or someone else. Whatever the word *jweiy* meant, it had no volition of its own. We always had to use a modifying expression with this word. It was the *jweiy* of God or the *jweiy* of a person or animal that had power to do something.

There was also a further complication. When this word was modified with an adjective it required a plural form. This was the word that was used in a descriptive phrase to translate the word, "Holy Spirit." The complication was that when I heard Anuaks praying for the "Holy Spirit who will live within us", I thought I heard them saying, "Give us the "Holy Spirits to live within us." I wondered how they conceptualized this expression. What was going on in their mind. Similarly, they also used a plural adjective to modify water . Surely, they conceived of water as being singular. Were they doing the same thing with the term which meant "spirit"? Was the same thing in their minds as was in mine? These were the kinds of questions we pondered night and day for months, even years as we tried to accurately translate the Biblical concepts.

## *SHIK*
### COMMAND OR "GOSPEL?"

I remember the effort to find a way to say, "Gospel." One of the early words used was *"shik"*, which, in fact, meant "message". However, the word was so strongly associated with a message from a village chief for his people to do something he commanded them to do, that it distorted what we were trying to say when teaching that God has given us His Son to be the "Giver" of our salvation. For example, the chief would send word out for the people to cut the grass off the road at the beginning of each dry season. This was a *shik* from the chief.

The "message" we had brought, however, was the "good news" about what God had done for us. We had not come with a *shik*, that was a command to obey, in order to be accepted. Using the word *shik*, in other words, made it more difficult to make clear the central affirmation we had about God's loving mercy and grace made evident in the life and ministry of Jesus Christ, which culminated in His sacrificial, vicarious death on the cross on our behalf.

The word, *shik*, approximated the expression "to command one to do something" much more closely than the expression "a message about something that had already been done". *Shik-Jwok* meant "God's commandment". To express "good news from God" (gospel of God) we came to use an entirely different expression. Literally translated, the term used for "the gospel" in our translation said, "The new, sweet word from God" (*Lum Jwok mana nyan ni met*). When Anuaks heard the message about Jesus Christ, they would frequently react to it during those early months with the expression, *Lum Jwok met* (The word of God is sweet). We had come with the "new sweet word from God." How wonderful it is, indeed!

## SHWINY
## LIVER SEAT OF THE EMOTIONS

We struggled with the concept of forgiveness for a long while too. Anuaks used *"shwiny"* (the liver) with modifying expressions to convey their attitudes and moods. We discovered that Anuaks could have many different kinds of livers (*shwiny*). One's liver could jump up, meaning: to become angry. A liver could sit down, meaning: to no longer be upset or angry. A liver could be walking around, meaning: one was restless, troubled and worrying. A liver might not yet have arrived, meaning: one was still in thought about something else. A liver could be absent, meaning: the person wasn't interest or involved. A liver could be hot, meaning: to be upset and disturbed emotionally. A liver could be cold, meaning: not to be that interested or possibly dispassionate about something. A small liver, meaning: not greedy. A large liver, meaning: to be greedy. (just the opposite of big hearted.) We had to be careful how we transferred concepts. A liver could fall down, meaning: to become saddened. A liver could be sweet, meaning: to be happy with something, to like or to love. A liver might be black, meaning: to be very unhappy and unforgiving. A liver could also be white, meaning: no ulterior motives, innocent, pure. A liver could be destroyed, meaning: one was extremely displeased and unhappy. A liver could be bad, meaning: one who was a bad person.

And this list could still go on. We learned to express the gospel and to translate the New Testament in this context. To make a translation which was the dynamic equivalent of the original language was our goal. To achieve it, the task continued night and day and never ended. No challenge could have been more captivating, compelling or satisfying.

## TO BELIEVE AND TO TRUST

How to translate "to believe', "to trust" and "to have hope" proved to be extremely difficult. At first we thought the word, "*yey*" meant "to believe". In a sense it did, but when I listened to school boys trying to share the Christian message in the village, it always came across as a response to a *shik* from God. It fit their world-view. We had to do something to keep the spirits happy so that they would *yey* us. The idea seemed to be that we had to *yey* to what God was telling us so that God would *yey* us in return. It became clear that the primary thrust of the word meant "to accept", "to agree to" or, in some contexts, "to believe that a thing is true".

To try to figure out the range of meanings words and expressions had was a never ending, all consuming quest. One was always on the alert, night and day, for new insights. Nothing, for me, could have been more challenging or satisfying.

There would be long periods when I was baffled and unable to understand what was going on. The word for "to believe" was much more difficult than one would have first suspected. I began hearing them use the word *yey* as "response". If you called to someone at a distance and this person answered back, they said he answered you. For this they used the word, *yey*. If a girl accepted the advances of a young man and agreed to sleep with him or to marry him, the word used was *yey*. It was the same word we were trying to use for "to believe". What we meant when we used it and what the Anuaks understood were two different things. What we said made good sense to them because they were hearing our words from within their world-view. But, in reality, we had a serious miscommunication of the central message of the gospel about God's grace.

Being a Nilotic language, Anuak has expressions and words which were common to other languages spoken over a very wide area. These included Shullik, Acholli, Alango, Alur and others spoken in the Sudan, Zaire, Uganda and Kenya. I tried to learn what I could from people working in those languages.

Perhaps one of the most interesting researches I made in trying to determine the right word or expression to translate the concept "to believe" was what I did in the neighboring Nuer language. The study was important to me because the three languages, Shullik, Nuer and Anuak in which our mission had translators working, all had light to share on my search for the right term to use in Anuak.

It was the Nuer language that intrigued me most. I had become aware that the Anuak word *yey* was translated *nhok* in Nuer. I was reasonably sure that in Anuak the term *yey*, in its central meaning, conveyed the idea of "to agree to, to be acceptable to, to respond to affirmatively, or to accept as being true". I learned that at that time in the Nuer translation of the first epistle of John, they had consistently used the Nuer term *nhok* to translate the word "love". I was suspicious that in using the term *nhok* to translate the concept "to love" that they might actually be expressing the concept "to accept or to agree to". The way in which the word *nhok* was used for "to love" in Nuer and the way the word *yey* was used for "to believe" in Shullik agitated my mind and spurred me on in my attempts to express these and other concepts accurately in Anuak. I was confident my colleagues working on those languages had wrestled with these same concepts and had determined their translations were correct in those languages.

For months, this probing and searching for "what are they really meaning?" occupied my conscious and subconscious mind. I wanted to be equally confident with whatever conclusions I would eventually come to in Anuak as were my colleagues translating in the other languages..

During this same period we were wrestling with how to translate "to trust". We first used the Anuak word, *ngadho*. But, we soon became aware that this word, *ngadho*, was much more akin to our idea of "to hope so". When using that word, they were meaning something more like, "I have been hoping so." To trust or to have faith was much stronger than that. We struggled to understand what was in the Anuak speaker's mind when he used words like that.

In the end, we found it necessary sometimes to use descriptive phrases or to combine terms to express the true meaning of the Biblical terms. By combining *yey* and *ngadho* in one expression, we approximated the central thrust of what it means "to believe in" or "to trust" or "to have faith in" in Anuak. An entirely different term was used to express the concept "to love".

There is much more to be said, but this will give you a feel for what was involved. Every Bible translator will know what I've been attempting to describe.

In many respects, the Anuak language was a beautiful work of art. The grammar was extremely complicated, but, for the most part, regular and predictable. Part of the process of understanding the grammar involved making long lists of words that acted in certain ways under similar conditions. We called them "form classes". Some such groupings had a common rationale, but others just seemed to belong in that category with no obvious explanation. They were neither masculine, feminine or neuter!

The Anuak language made extensive use of the subjunctive mood. They used beautiful nuances to express the mood or feeling of what was being said. They also had a propensity for using the passive voice. Instead of saying, "He did it" they often said, "It was done by him."

### THE INCLUSIVE AND THE EXCLUSIVE "WE"

The "inclusive" and the "exclusive" use of the word "we" was something, I had not previously encountered. There were two words for "we" depending upon whether the person you were addressing was meant to be included in what you were saying or not. For example, if we were together with a group and I said, "We'll be going to the village tomorrow," I would have to use either *wani* or *awni* for the word "we". If I used the word, *wani* it meant that I was speaking of a group that included me and my party, in which others were not included.

From my choice of the word, *wani* for "we" they would know that I had not included them in what was going to happen the following day. However, had I chosen the word, *awni* for "we", they would know that they were included and that they and I would all be going together to the village the next day. It took a little practice to get the hang of it, but once one did the ambiguity of what we might mean by "we" in English was totally eliminated.

Interestingly, how to translate the "we" passage in II Corinthians was one of the most baffling and intriguing challenges I encountered. If you'll examine Paul's second letter to the Corinthians you will see what I mean. Check it out for yourself. In those first five chapters, every time you encounter the word "we", ask yourself, "Does Paul mean just himself and his apostolic party or is he including the Corinthians to whom he's writing the letter?" The clue to the correct answer lies in one's study of the context and those verses in which the meaning is clear. In English the reader can be "sloppy" and not really answer the question, but in Anuak the language itself allowed for no ambiguity. One had to say either *wani* or *awni*, the exclusive or the inclusive "we". Once the decision had been made, the final translation in Anuak is, actually, more meaningful and easily understood than is the English with its imprecise "we".

Perhaps a couple of passages from II Corinthians will help us more readily understand this intriguing feature in these kinds of languages. In chapter 5:14 Paul writes, "For the love of Christ controls us." We need to determine whether Paul is speaking about himself and his Apostolic companions or is he including, intentionally, the Corinthian believers. If it is the former, and if he were speaking in Anuak, he'd use the exclusive "we", *wani*. If he were speaking a general truth in which he has both the Corinthians, himself and his companions in mind, he would use the inclusive "we", a *wni*.

Frequently when we read this passage in English, we probably, too quickly, tend to consider it as a general truth Paul is affirming to the Corinthians and which we, therefore, readily claim for ourselves. When we translated the "we" of this passage into Anuak, we concluded that Paul, in this particular passage, was speaking specifically about himself and his Apostolic companions. In Anuak we had to make a definite choice. We chose the word for the "exclusive we", *wani*, because the context indicates Paul was speaking about his apostolic ministry.

In II Corinthians 5:20 the answer as to which Anuak word to use for "we" is more transparent. Paul says, "We are ambassadors for Christ, God making his appeal through us." Here the apostle is, obviously, referring to himself and his companions. In this case with no hesitation, we translated Paul's use of "we" as requiring the "exclusive we", *wani..*

When we translated verse 21 into Anuak we used the "inclusive we", *awni.* It appeared to us that Paul was including the Corinthian believers in this general statement of truth when he said, "For our sake he made him to be sin who knew no sin, so that in him we might become the righteousness of God." Admittedly, this was a matter of interpretation. Someone might argue that this also required the "exclusive we", *wani.*

The only reason I bring these passages into the discussion is to give you a feel for what this entailed. These passages illustrate the problems involved for the translator when he has to decide whether these "we" passages are understood to be either the "inclusive we" or the "exclusive we". In Anuak there was no neutral ground. We had to determine precisely what Paul had in mind when he said "we".

I found that being forced to interpret Paul's mind precisely in order to translate these "we" passages correctly was, in some instances exceedingly difficult but ultimately wonderfully rewarding.

In addition to trying to figure out the meaning of words and expressions, we also needed to write them down accurately and consistently. Word boundaries and consistent spelling of words was a real challenge. Gradually a dictionary and lexicon were being built up, but the spelling of words changed when used in different grammatical positions. Before one understood fully what was taking place, one struggled to hear accurately and to spell these words consistently. It took years before many of the inconsistencies were recognized and standardized. We missionaries shared insights and correctives in this whole process. I was indebted to my colleagues for their valuable suggestions, yes, and sometimes correctives.

## CHAPTER EIGHT

## TO FORGIVE

Before, leaving this little excursion in which I've taken you behind the scenes, let's briefly return to the problem of how to express the concept of "to forgive". At first we thought we could use the liver concept with an appropriate modifying expression. We knew that if a person's liver had jumped up, that this individual was angry and upset. When that person had caused his liver to return downward again, the anger was gone. Sometimes, persons trying to reconcile two quarreling persons would beg the participants to "put their livers down".

Upon deeper reflection, we concluded that we couldn't use this colorful expression because of its larger implications. The two expressions when used in this context implied that those whose "livers had jumped up" were out of order and making an issue out of something over which they ought not to have been upset or angry. Were we to use this expression of "to put your liver down", we would inadvertently be implying that God, Himself, was out of order in being displeased with our sins. Using this term would make it more difficult to teach correct theology that said, "God is justly displeased with our sins." In the end, we used a term which proved to be so correct and close to the meaning in the original Greek. We simply said that God would "leave off dealing with our sins" for the sake of what Jesus did in his sacrificial death as the lamb of God. In Anuak we could simply express it in these few words, *Jwok moa bacho awie.* How beautiful it became to hear Anuaks praying to God, the Creator, to leave off dealing with their sins because Jesus had shed his blood for them on the cross. Anuak believers had no problem in understanding that Jesus was the perfect lamb of God who takes away the sins of the world. They understood that because of what Jesus had done, they need never make another sacrifice of cattle, sheep, goats or chickens to be at peace with the spirit world. Jesus had made the only sacrifice that was sufficient or needed and He had all power to drive away the spirits and to protect all who committed themselves in simple faith to Him as Savior and Lord.. That was fabulous, fantastic good news. We learned to express it in the Anuak language. What we did in Anuak can be done in any language for people of any culture. The Gospel is universal and can be beautifully and accurately expressed in any language. "O the depth of the riches and wisdom and knowledge of God!"

## THE TRANSLATION PROCEDURE ITSELF

Our translation team normally had two persons and myself. They sat across the desk from me. One of the two men knew no English, but was extremely intelligent and alert in Anuak. Having Othow War Adier, a non-English speaking person on the team, forced us to carry on most of our conversation in Anuak as we discussed the verse being translated. It contributed toward our achieving an idiomatic translation which sounded the way an Anuak spoke rather than as a translation from another language. If Othow couldn't understand and repeat the translated verse back to us without stumbling, it needed further refinement. Sometimes it was a tedious, painstaking process requiring huge amounts of time and patience.

Across the years, I had a total of three, different, full-time, English-speaking informants, Jok Deng, James Buya, and Ocala Alero. None had more than the equivalent of an eighth grade education. Their English usage, especially in the beginning, was limited. Much time and patience was required as we worked together and they tried to understand the meaning of the English text.

To make things convenient, I always had two book stands in front of me on my desk . One held my Greek New Testament and the other a New Testament in English. Stacked up on the right hand corner of the desk were copies of as many translations as were available at that time. Among them, were the translations by Goodspeed, Moffet, Weymouth, Williams, Phillips and others. These served as instant reference commentaries.

Before every translation session, we earnestly prayed that God would give us understanding and insight. We asked that our translation would have the same quality of inspiration as did the other translations. We asked that what we put on paper would, indeed, be the very word of God. We asked God for help that we not become professionals and become calloused or indifferent to the fact that we were handling the Word of God, written. We asked for the help of the Holy Spirit. Sometimes, when we didn't know how to express it in Anuak, we stopped and prayed again for the Holy Spirit to help us.

It was a demanding, exhausting, exhilarating task. It required discipline and determination to patiently see it through, verse by verse -- each on a 3 by 5 card, typed up each day into a growing manuscript to be evaluated, corrected and improved upon. It would take a dozen years to complete it. But, for me, every day was a dream coming true. I cannot adequately praise God for that unspeakable challenge and privilege.

During our later years of translating, beside my desk there was an IBM electric typewriter, a lead acid car battery and an invertor to convert 12 volts into 110 volts of power to run the typewriter. A young Anuak man by the name of Stephen Omot Didumu, whom Kitty Crandall had earlier taught to type, took the 3 by 5 cards each day and typed them into the manuscript. At night when the generator was running, the battery was charged up so that Stephen had power to run his typewriter the next day. When the translation was finally ready in its final form, this young man typed every word of it in triplicate so we could send it off to the American Bible Society for printing.

## CHECKING THE FINAL TRANSLATION

When the last verse had been translated and all the limited test-printings had been used and reviewed, one essential task remained. We brought together a committee of Anuak speakers from the three different areas where Anuaks lived -- the Baro River, Pochala, and Akobo areas. Several of these young men walked over a hundred miles to get to Pibor where the conference was held.

Every day for six weeks we went over the translation, verse by verse. All three areas with their dialectical differences had to be taken into consideration. Sometimes we discovered that words carried slightly different meanings depending on where one lived. For example, the word used in the book of Acts to translate "storm", the storm that destroyed the ship on which Paul was traveling, accented a meaning of "a strong wind" to speakers along the Baro, whereas to people living at Akobo it meant only "very cold weather". By the time the wind had reached Akobo it was minimal, but the "cold" was the main thing this word conveyed. In such cases, additional modifying expressions were added to clarify the meaning so that wherever Anuaks lived they would be able to understand the meaning readily.

And so it went for some six weeks. When the review and modifications required had been completed, the young men returned to their villages. Some of them had a walk of a hundred miles ahead of them. They left, eager for the day when the printed New Testament would be returned from America, when they would have in their hands God's precious word in their very own New Testament in their language.

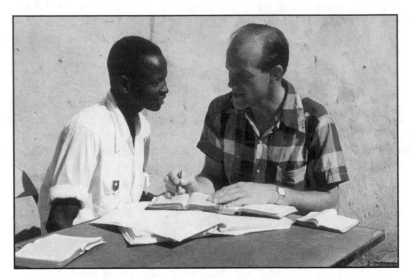

Harvey studying the language in 1949 with James Buya in preparation for the translating of the New Testament into the Anuak language.

Harvey spent many nights in villages like this listening, practicing and learning both the language and the customs of the people.

# OUR FIRST FURLOUGH

We took a shortened, nine-month furlough our first trip back to the states. Two reasons dictated we do that. The mission wanted to stagger furloughs so that everyone from Akobo wouldn't be scheduled to be away in the states at the same time. We were assigned to take an early furlough to get that schedule going and to permit me to return to the Summer Institute of Linguistics in Norman, Oklahoma. This would enable me to check out my analysis of the Anuak language and seek answers to several perplexing questions about which I was still unsure.

## CHECKING MY LANGUAGE ANALYSIS

The most basic question that I needed answered was the question of whether or not I had analyzed the language correctly in concluding that we should write it morpho-phonemically. Put in simple terms it was the question of whether or not we should write the words as they sounded when spoken or whether we should write the basic form of the word before it had been influenced by neighboring sounds. The Anuak words were very short with basically a consonant-vowel-consonant stem. To this basic stem one added suffixes, prefixes and infixes to indicate personal pronouns, tenses for verbs etc.

The problem was complicated in that in Anuak I had observed that tense indicators sometimes seemed to be attached to the particle or word preceding the verb itself. It seemed strange to me that whether something happened in the past or in, let's say, the future would be indicated by adding a vowel to the word preceding the verb rather than that it would be treated as part of the verb. This problem kept me awake many nights at Akobo and I wasn't absolutely certain that I had come to the right conclusion.

It was a tremendous relief when at SIL, they confirmed my analysis as being correct and that this phenomenon was not unknown in some other languages with which the Wycliffe Bible Translators had worked. They confirmed the correctness of writing the basic, unaffected sounds or morphemes because in doing so the graphemics or identity of the word would remain stable and the conditioned sounds would be, as it were, automatic when the words were pronounced in the sentence patterns. To have spelled the words according to the conditioned sounds would, as I had reasoned, cause readers to sound out words as they read, rather than identifying words in sequence. By writing the basic morphemes making up the individual words, the reader would be able to identify the words without having to sound them out. When reading aloud, the conditioned assimilated sounds would be reproduced naturally as in normal speech.

You will recall that I have in an earlier chapter spoken briefly about phonetics, phonemics, morphology and syntax. Phonetics deals with all the sounds. Phonemics deals with the phonetic sounds which are to be represented by letters in the alphabet. Morphemes are those phonemes, individually or when combined with other phonemes that have meaning. Syntax relates to phrases, sentences and paragraphs etc..

Admittedly this will likely be a bit confusing, but seeing the paradigm that follows should help to clear things up a bit. My example comes from the Anuak word meaning "to give". It illustrates the difference in spelling when a word is written phonemically from when it is written morpho-phonemically.

The word "To give" in Anuak is "moch". To say, "I give" one says, "mocha." The "a" means "I". So if we write, "I give, you give, he gives, we give, you (pl) give, and they give" the morphemes spelled out as additions to the stem "moch" change to indicate that difference in meaning. Those word endings illustrated by the word to give, "moch," which indicate which person is doing the acting are exhibited in the Anuak verb and related grammatical patterns throughout the language. Hopefully the paradigm in Anuak which follows will make this more transparent..

## A PARADIGM

| English | Morpho-phonemic | Phonemic | |
|---|---|---|---|
| I give | mocha | mocha | |
| you give | mochi | mochi | |
| he/she gives | moche | moche | |
| we give | mochwa | moijwa | (ch > j before w) |
| you (pl) give | mochu | mochu | |
| they give | mochge | moidge | (ch > d before g) |

This paradigm illustrates how sounds are conditioned or assimilated by their relationship to other sounds. One can see readily that when a "ch" sound was followed by a "w" sound, it was conditioned or influenced to sound like a "j". Similarly, the "ch" followed by a "g" sound was assimilated to sound like a "d". At SIL they called this "regressive assimilation according to the point of articulation!"

Writing morpho-phonemically, one writes the spelling of the original morpheme. In this case "moch" is written rather than the conditioned sound "moij" or "moid" caused by the "w" or "g".

When reading the column that is written morpho-phonemically, the pronunciation is the same as what is written in the phonemic column. When reading anything written morpho-phonemically, the reader automatically pronounces these words as in normal speech. Rather than sounding out words from the spelling, the reader recognizes the basic, correct spelling of the word ( i. e. the morphemes) and pronounces the words without having to sound them out. Spelling has everything to do with word recognition. Morpho-phonemic writing facilitates that and makes for smooth reading. It proved to be the right way to reduce the Anuak language to writing.

It has been over fifty years since we were taught these things. I hope my recall has been reasonably accurate. Let me suggest, however, that you not look on my commentary about this all as "a law of the Medes and Persians." So now, let us move on with the easy to read, uncomplicated, exciting story I want to continue sharing with you.

CHAPTER NINE

## STUDYING AND SPEAKING

After the summer, we had moved to New Jersey where we lived in the Reformed Church in America's comfortable missionary residence on the campus of New Brunswick Theological Seminary. The John Muilenbergs were in the other half of the duplex. We enjoyed a good many late night cups of coffee sharing from our overseas experiences.

Living in New Brunswick permitted me to take several courses at the Princeton Theological Seminary. One of my joys then was to study Greek under Dr. Bruce Metzger.

Lavina was pretty busy during all of those months with three lively youngsters. She had to hustle to keep her home organized and have us all on the road Sunday mornings and often on week nights for speaking engagements. There was a lot of interest in what RCA missionaries were doing in our latest and newest mission field. All of this was sheer delight.

I remember one rather frightening and unexpected speaking engagement I had while in the East. I was extremely busy with studying and frequent speaking assignments. Apparently, I didn't always read our mail too carefully.

On this occasion I had spoken in the Albany area of upper New York state on Sunday and had returned on the overnight train to New York City. I slept as best I could in my "Sunday suit". The connection was close. I carried my suitcase with me to the door of the famous 5th avenue, Marble Collegiate Church where Dr. Norman Vincent Peale ministered.

I was met at the door by Mrs. Weber, Morrie Swart's mother. She said that I had better hurry because the meeting was about to start. I had assumed I was speaking to a group of women somewhere in the basement. Instead, I was led into a packed church, filled with women from all over the state. It was a statewide RCA women's gathering.

Once on the platform, I learned that there would be two of us speaking. The other guest speaker was Andrew Branch from Broeton, Alabama. As I waited my turn to speak and try to adjust to this unexpected turn of events, I couldn't help but wonder what my dad and mother would have thought if they could have seen that little farm boy from Minnesota preaching in Norman Vincent Peale's church. I thought to myself, God certainly has a great sense of humor to have me where I am this morning. It turned out to be a fun experience, even when I sipped tea with a box lunch with ladies who were culturally much more sophisticated than I was from my humble origins and more recent experience of living with mud and grass.

## INOCULATIONS NO FUN

Our worst experience that furlough was probably the day we all had our inoculations in preparation for returning to Africa. Lavina and the three boys and I all had one of those "shots" late that afternoon. We stopped in a restaurant for a bite to eat on our way back from New York to New Brunswick. We entered the restaurant feeling just fine. While we were eating, one by one the children and then Lavina and I, also, put our food aside and were feeling too ill to eat. Once home, we all went straight to bed, but for Lavina and me there was to be no sleep. The children were all burning up with fevers and just plain miserable and sick. We learned an important lesson that night, never ever would all of us have our "shots" at the same time. Somebody has to be well enough to take care of the sick! It was all part of being a missionary! And we all survived, none the worse for it today!

## ANOTHER PERSON'S OPINION

It was quite a trick to travel from Africa to America with five children ranging in ages from still being in the basket to young teenagers. We always tried to arrange our luggage so that some of the pieces were small enough for everyone except the little guy in the basket to carry something.

We will never forget the sidewalk experience out in front of the hotel in New York City. Denny, who was already in college at this time, had flown in to meet us. So, in actual fact, we had all six children with us when we left from the hotel for Grand Central Station. We had arranged for two taxis to transport us from the hotel to the station. When the taxis pulled up, we had our twenty-two pieces of luggage, large and small, piled up outside and waiting. It took a little juggling of bags to get everything in.

A man was standing on the sidewalk about twenty feet away watching the whole operation. Finally, he wandered over to give us his sage advice, saying, "You know, if I had to travel like that, I think I'd stay home!" I'm sure he meant it!

We had a good laugh over his remark and responded saying, "Well, sir, we've come ten thousand miles so far and we have only a thousand left to go. We think we'll make it." It was true. Only a missionary would travel like that. But, traveling like that was only a small part of the story of things only a missionary would do. Ours was a daunting challenge and a rare privilege. No one ever need feel sorry for us! We might even be "fools for Christ's sake".

But now, all those furlough experiences had swiftly ended and we were heading back to the Sudan. We would soon be back in a different world. We loved them both, but our hearts were in Africa where God had called us.

## HEADING BACK TO AFRICA
## FEBRUARY 1952

We returned from furlough to Akobo in February, 1952. The trip back was rugged. Just before we left Holland, Michigan, Dennis came down with the measles. He was well enough to travel, but we knew that Jim and Dave would likely get them about the time we reached Khartoum

They surprised us and this complicated our travels considerably. The night before we were to get off the Queen Mary in Southampton, both of the boys developed a burning fever. We knew exactly what it was, but hoped we could unobtrusively board the plane in London the next day and fly on to Khartoum.

During the night, before the morning we were to dock, David's fever was so high that he had a frightening convulsion. Never having seen one, we were scared to death. Our only thought was to find the Ship's doctor as speedily as possible. Having had no experience with seeing someone have a convulsion, it appeared to us that he was dying.

The doctor examined him and reassured us that this was not uncommon with genuine German measles. He told us what to do, but when the ship docked in the morning, the first thing we saw was an old model black ambulance at the dock waiting to take our two little boys away from us and put them into quarantine. We were told they would be well cared for and that we shouldn't plan to travel further for at least two weeks. They said, "Our experiences is that it's best if you leave the children to us and not show your faces until it's time to collect them. The children make the adjustment better if the parents don't show up. Go to London and enjoy yourselves since you have to wait anyway."

## DELAYED IN ENGLAND

It seemed rough to us, but what could we do? We took their advice and Lavina, Dennis and I took a train to London where we stayed in the Victoria hotel. Sounds much more romantic than it was, in fact. No central heating. It was cold. At night they put heated stones under the blankets in the foot-end of our bed to keep us warm.

We chanced to be in London on a very historic occasion. This was the time when King George of England died and his daughter, Elizabeth, then in Kenya, came to the throne. We were on the street when all of London fell totally silent and everything stopped as a token of respect for their departed sovereign.

We visited Westminster Abbey and other historic places, but our hearts were restless for the children. And, this being one of England's coldest winters didn't brighten our spirits either. We couldn't have been happier, when they told us we could fetch the children and be on our way. Two solid weeks had elapsed.

These little tykes hadn't forgotten us either. They were so happy to see us they could hardly contain themselves. Jimmy and David both had blisters on their right thumbs from sobbing and sucking. Jimmy said, "I cried for Daddy and Dave cried for Mommy." We hoped it would never happen again!

## FURTHER DELAYS CAIRO TO KHARTOUM

That evening we flew out of London for Khartoum by way of Cairo. When we landed in Cairo, a strong wind was blowing. After refueling, we were on our way, but remembered that it was so windy they had had some difficulty closing the door on the plane. It was about 8:30 in the morning. Khartoum was at least six hours away.

# CHAPTER NINE

As we flew south toward Khartoum, we were counting the hours until we would arrive. It had been a difficult and tiring trip. But, our difficulties weren't to go away quite so easily. About one thirty, just after having our lunch on the plane, the steward came through and announced that Khartoum was in the grip of a powerful wind and haboob. If things didn't clear up in the next half hour, we would have to return to Cairo. Our hearts sank when we felt the plane bank to head back. We said, "What next?"

It was about dark time when we approached Cairo and were diverted to Cyprus. The wind of the morning had developed into a full blown sandstorm in Cairo too. We landed in the darkness in Cyprus on a dimly lighted airstrip they had used during the war.

I had bought four pounds of apples in London the treat our missionary hosts upon arrival, but these were now taken away from us and confiscated by customs. We were all herded into a gasoline lamp lighted Quonset hut to check our papers. The other 25 passengers and we were eventually loaded unto a bus and we struck out for Nicosea some two hours away. It was now eleven o'clock when we reached the hotel and it was cold. In the morning at four o'clock we were all back on the bus and heading back to the plane. The two little boys didn't think they had anything to be really happy about and they made their feelings known! Dennis took it all in stride as he was by then nearly ten years old.

## RETURNING TO A HOT COUNTRY

You can scarcely imagine our joy when we finally landed in Khartoum. From there it was on to Akobo and home in the Upper Nile.. The change in climate was staggering. We had left my folks in Minnesota with a temperature that day showing twenty degrees below zero. Now it was over 100 degrees night and day. We thought we would die and started advising other missionaries never to be so foolish as to come back from furlough during the peak of the hot, dry season.

But, in just a week or two our bodies adjusted and we were eager to begin where we had left off. Of course, it wouldn't be quite the same because while we were heading for home on furlough our brand new grass roofed house, built on the mission compound had burned to the ground. Everything we owned outside of what we had in our suitcases had gone up in smoke and disappeared in ten minutes. They told us how swiftly a grass roof burns. We were starting over again.

We were amazed at how little that supposedly major loss affected us. The initial shock was considerable when Dr. Luman Shafer had asked that first night upon arrival in the states if he and I might take a little walk together. I remember how uncomfortable I felt when he suggested this and wondered, momentarily, if I had done something wrong and was going to be instructed about that in some way. But, almost immediately as we walked the hallway in the hotel, while Lavina waited and wondered, he said, "Harvey, I have some bad news to share with you."

My first reaction was, "Somebody has died."

He said, "Your house at Akobo was destroyed by fire. It happened even before you got on the ship in Alexandria, but we didn't want to spoil your trip home with this sad information and, so, we withheld it from you until we could explain what happened to you in person."

It was a terrible shock. The floor seemed to be rocking. I thought, "What will Lavina say?"

My first question was, "What about my books?"

He said, "They are all gone. Everything was burned. Nothing was saved"

I wanted to cry, but held it in. Later we shared with Lavina, and she rightfully cried for us all.

But, now we were back at Akobo and eager to resume my work of translating the New Testament into Anuak. Bob Swart had worked desperately hard to rebuild our house and have things as nice as possible for us upon arrival. The old metal bed frames were still useable and new springs had replaced the burned out ones. The metal chests of drawers were still useable. A little brown paint and they would be as useable as before. Bethany Reformed Church in Grand Rapids, Michigan had replaced my books with a basic reference library. The New Era Reformed Church had given Lavina a new set of pots and pans. Gifts of money and materials had come from many friends throughout the church.

We soon put the losses from the fire behind us and

were none the worse for it. God's grace was more than sufficient. Lee and Kitty Crandall, whose things were also burned in that same fire, testified similarly. We said, "We must learn to travel lightly." The only things we really missed were the burned photographs, the first locks of the children's hair and my college and seminary papers. Fortunately, my language materials were all with me in America.

This is the house that replaced the one that burned to the ground while the Hoekstras were on furlough. This is the home in which they lived most of their years at Akobo.

# CHAPTER TEN

# POKWO - VILLAGE OF LIFE

## PART 1

The year was 1953. Pokwo station on the Baro river was now started. The necessary government papers had all been processed and Don McClure and Lyda were already there building the new station. Pokwo was on the Baro river about 140 miles, as the bird flies, East of Akobo. It was situated on the river about 21 miles from a place called Gambela.

This trading post was a mile square enclave given by Ethiopia to the British by treaty for trading purposes. It was as far as Nile steamers could go into Ethiopia itself. Two or three times during the height of the rains a flotilla of some five or seven barges would make its way from Kosti and Malakal into Ethiopia. They brought salt, sugar, cooking oil and other supplies in and went back down stream with coffee. To make it around the bends in the river, barges were dropped off while part of the flotilla continued on up stream. These were then tied up and the steamer would return down stream to bring up the others. Quite a process. Sometimes these barges got stuck on the sand if the river dropped too quickly. I'm sure the captain and crew had some anxious moments sometimes wondering if they might not be stuck for the season until rains returned the following year.

Pokwo station was on a beautiful, strategic location. Bob and I had made the first survey to explore its feasibility. But, now Don and Lyda were getting started and a lot of hard work was involved. Starting in tents, moving into grass and finally into a permanent building in a remote area is no small feat. Don was a pioneer at heart and seemed to love it.

But, it was furlough time for the McClures and they had to find a way to keep that fledgling work open and going. The pool in which there were possibilities for personnel was the Akobo mission station. Nobody was volunteering. We all loved our work and our location.

So, when Don approached Lavina and me and said, "I think you and Lavina should come to Pokwo and fill in for us while Lyda and I go on furlough" our instinctive response was, "Not if we can help it." We didn't say this to Don, of course, but we both knew that this is how we felt.

## LAVINA AT AKOBO -- HARVEY IN THE CONGO

About this same time, I was a member of a four person team chosen by the mission to study mission work in eight different missions in the then Belgian Congo, Rwanda and Uganda. The team was made up of Milton and Peggy Thompson, Dotty Rankin and myself. I would be gone eight weeks, sleep on 31 different cots or beds and cover 4,100 miles before the study was completed. It was a tremendous challenge to try to learn how other missions did their work successfully. Our mission was made up of mostly young, inexperienced missionaries. Those who were older wanted us to have the learning experience this would be for each of us, and also to report back to the mission on our findings with recommendations.

Christmas eve the four of us in our party were on the Nile steamer heading toward Juba. It was an eight day journey. On board was the Ford station wagon that would carry our gear and the four of us. We wouldn't be back until the last week in February.

Lavina was left alone at Akobo with Jimmy and David. Dennis was in school in Egypt. I missed them so painfully. I'm sure they had lonely days and nights as well. Many times I thought, "I wish somebody else had been chosen to make this trip. Life is too short to be separated from my family like this." That was real negative thinking! And such thinking is never productive. At times, I would remind myself that God understood. With the Psalmist I would say, "He knows our frame; He remembers that we are dust." Then again, when the sun was shining, we would be singing George Beverly Shea's song,

"Every step every mile of the way."

We learned so much from other missionaries during those weeks on the road. Some of the lessons affected my entire missionary career. In retrospect, the separation, the work involved in making the study and producing our report, was imminently worth the effort and cost.

## GOD GIVES US WILLING HEARTS

But, now to get back to the unresolved question about our being reassigned to Pokwo. Lavina and I didn't want to go, but we had agreed before I left on that tour that we would both keep on praying about it and discuss it further when I returned. We did just that.

Both Lavina and I had had a change of heart. Without being able to discuss the matter because of the great distances that separated us, we had both come to feel that God wanted us to help out at Pokwo. We were at peace with each other and with the Lord. Our hearts were united and both of us were happy.

Don was so pleased that we were ready to come. He made all the arrangement with local officials about our living there. He said, "You don't need a visa. The local governor is willing to let you come and live down here in the country without having to go through the government offices in Addis Ababa. We learned later that this would create problems for us when the government in Addis became aware that we were at Pokwo and Don and Lyda were in America.

We had another slight complication before we could get settled as a family inside Ethiopia at Pokwo. Lavina was happily expecting our fourth child. Complications with the others suggested she shouldn't live in isolation at Pokwo during those first uncertain weeks. Our mission doctor said she should spend some time in Khartoum near medical facilities and then proceed to Pokwo by way of Addis Ababa.

This was done. At the same time, I want on ahead with Dennis, Jimmy and David to overlap with Don and Lyda for a few weeks before they took off. The station was so new that I helped Don screen his house and did other jobs to help them get away on schedule for furlough. When they left, I was there alone with the children batching it. Our closest medical facility

173

was about 50 miles as the crow flies over the mountains toward Addis Ababa. In Gambela was the British government officer living in the enclave, a one mile square territory under British rule. Two or three Greek merchants and traders also lived there. We got our groceries and supplies through them and our mail came in via Gambela. To get there, we normally used an outboard, but during the short dry season the road was just barely passable for three or four months.

When Don left for furlough my parting words were, "Be sure to come back on time now." Don had a reputation for taking long furloughs. He was such a popular speaker that he just couldn't seem to get away. I wanted him back so we could return to Akobo.

The boys and I were alone for about six weeks. Lavina was cleared to travel and did so by flying to Addis Ababa. I had previously been in Addis and with a Herculean effort had secured a one time permit for Mission Aviation to cross the border from Malakal in the Sudan to land in Dembidollo to fly Lavina over the mountain to Gambela.

All the missionaries said we had made history that happy day when the old Rapide, twin engine bi-plane landed inside Ethiopia. The children and I had traveled to Dembidollo a few days earlier on one of those big, ten ton diesel trucks that hauled salt up the mountain and coffee back down. We were there to welcome Lavina off the plane. She looked so beautiful and it was like a little bit of heaven had come to earth to have her back. The children and I were all equally excited and thrilled.

We flew to Gambela where there was a grassy, government airstrip, as most of the airstrips in that part of the world were then. We traveled home the 21 miles by outboard. The MAF pilot and engineer spent the night at Pokwo and I drove them back in the outboard the next morning. The Hoekstra family was together again. We would spend some 21 months at Pokwo before Don and Lyda returned. These would be among the happiest, most productive years of our ministry among the Anuak. We had surrendered to the Lord's leading. He never failed to keep His promises. Our hearts were supremely happy.

## THE CHALLENGE AND EXCITEMENT OF POKWO

Pokwo station was an exciting challenge and responsibility. I wanted to carry Don's work forward in such a way that he would be proud of us when he returned. I respected and admired Don and had some qualms as to whether or not I could come near filling his shoes.

We had some marvelous experiences and a wide variety of them during those 21 months at Pokwo. We soon discovered that the Anuaks living along the Barro were wilder than the Anuaks with whom we had been working at Akobo. The men all had both guns and spears. The Ethiopian authorities didn't exercise the same authority over them as the British did in the Sudan. More killings and beatings occurred. Stick fights between different age sets were common. It reminded us of what it may have been like in the days of Robin hood. Rivalry and killings between the younger age sets and the older men were not uncommon. The Anuaks along the Barro were more prosperous, the soil was fertile and beer parties were held in connection with all their social events. Their drumming and singing went on into the night and we would fall asleep with these distant drums beating rhythmically in our ears. There was both danger and romance.

We lived in the new McClure house with its round tukls and large connecting, screened in verandas. Lavina's wood burning stove was out under the big tamarind tree located about 25 feet from the back door. Once when she was sterilizing milk on that outside stove, the horse came along, and without our knowing it, pushed off the lid and drained the kettle. That same day, my office door to the tukl on one end of the house accidentally stood ajar. When I returned to my desk, a freshly laid egg was there in the middle of it. A hen had wandered in and done her thing right then and there!

Snakes sometimes sneaked in also. One night I was in Gambela overnight and Lavina and the two boys were home alone. They were all in their beds on the veranda when Lavina heard the dog's tin, eating dish swishing around on the floor. She had a flashlight with nearly dead batteries beside the bed and decided, out of curiosity, to find out what was going on. To her amazement, she made out the form of a six foot, red cobra beside the dog's dish. Quickly, she ran back to bed and jumped up on it safely out of reach. She began to call and both Anuaks and the single lady missionary, Joan Yilek, approached the house to see what was going on. Lavina alerted them about the snake. Joan went back home and returned with her 16 gage shot-gun. She was hesitant as to what to do. Lavina said the Anuaks kept saying, "Shoot, shoot it so that it doesn't get away." Joan heeded their advice, took careful aim and pulled the trigger. The snake was cut in half by the blast. The McClure's refrigerator carried the pocked shell indentations from the ricocheted pellets ever afterward! Lavina and the kids slept peacefully and couldn't wait until I returned to share the excitement with me.

There were only ten or eleven believers on the station and none in the surrounding villages when we arrived. The believers were all workmen engaged to help open the station. Several of them had been brought along from Akobo. Having help that knew what was expected was extremely useful in a pioneer situation.

On that trip to the Belgian Congo I had determined that if I ever had the opportunity, I would try to put some of the things I had learned there into practice. I wanted to have a mission station that was first of all a teaching center. The workmen should be given the opportunity to learn to read and have in depth Bible teaching as part of their daily schedule. It wasn't right to have workmen spending all their time working and being viewed as a burden rather than seeing them as an opportunity for teaching.

Being at Pokwo provided that chance. We had a program with a daily schedule of time for Bible study, learning to read, working on mission jobs or working in small fields of land we designated for them to grow their own corn from which they could supplement their meager income. It was marvelous to see how God was blessing that. But, first, let me tell you about Akway War Achudhi.

## THE FIRST ANUAK EVANGELIST

Very soon after I arrived at Pokwo, I met a young Anuak on the compound sitting under a tree. He was reading from a green covered, mimeographed copy of the First Epistle of John. He looked up at me and said, "You don't remember me. But, I remember you. When you were in Gambela several years ago

176

with another man you called, Bomb, you ate supper at the home of the man I was working for. (it was a young Norwegian, living in Ethiopia at that time and serving with the Bank of Ethiopia) Before you left, you a gave a little book to this man. With that book, he taught me to read. When Odan came here, I learned more about Jesus and was baptized."

I was overjoyed to hear his story. Bob and I had been in Gambela nearly three years earlier. We had come into the area from Akobo to survey the possibility of opening a station on the Barro river. At that time, we were totally frustrated by the local Ethiopian officials. Although we had proper papers, including a paper signed by his majesty, emperor Haili Sellasie himself, the local official said, "Where is my name?"

We were refused permission. Bob and I had spent ten days, hoping and waiting, but very frustrated. We wondered how we could have missed the Lord's leading.

Finally, on that last night, this young Norwegian, a committed Christian had invited us to his bachelor home to eat with him. It was then that he had asked for a primer as he wanted to teach his servant how to read. Bob had remained behind then to proceed to Addis to see if he could get the coveted paper. I drove the jeep back to Akobo, going some 200 miles down along the one side of the river, then crossing over on the only ferry near Doleib Hill and going back an additional 175 miles on the opposite side of the river to Akobo. Little did either of us know how God was at work in and through our frustration. I have often reflected on those days and praised God for the way He turns apparent defeat into victory to those who try to do His will.

Some weeks later when we called the small little band of Christian workmen together, we challenged them as to whether or not there wasn't someone among them who could do the work of an evangelist in the many unreached Anuak villages. I explained how my task was to translate the Bible and that I needed to be near my family as well as needing to be around to care for the sick who came into the clinic we were holding under the tree each morning..

To that question about an evangelist they responded with a typical Anuak reply by asking, "Is there anyone besides Akway War Achudi?" This Anuak response meant that Akway was their choice. He could do it. He was the young man who had been the servant of that Norwegian banker. He was the

177

one who was reading under the tree.

The next question was, "But, how can he do this? He will be among people who are not his relatives. He will need a mosquito net, a blanket and a way to get his food."

## TEACHING ANUAK BELIEVERS HOW TO TITHE

It was then that I again remembered something from my experience in the Congo. There was one station in the Presbyterian mission that everyone talked about. Missionaries in different stations would say, "Wait until you get to Bulape (a Presbyterian mission station). There is a station that taught its people to tithe?" And it was so.

As I met with our few believers at Pokwo, my heart burned within me to challenge them to learn how to give the tithe. There was still no offering of any kind in the worship services. I explained how the tithe worked. I said, "Each of you earns 30 piasters a week. Three of those piasters belong to the Lord. If each of you would give three piasters every week from what you get, Akway, the Lord's servant, could go and be your evangelist in the villages."

They weren't at all sure about doing this. In fact, they would have preferred not to. I spoke to them a second time and suggested that they try it just for one month. If at the end of one month they found they were becoming poor, we could meet again and discuss it.

To this they agreed. To help them get started, I took small pieces of paper and stapled them in the shape of an envelop. When they received their pay on Saturday, 3 piasters was in each envelop and 27 piasters was outside the envelop. It was a crude way to do it, but the object lesson was clear.

On Wednesday evenings, the group met on our sitting veranda for prayer, Bible study and worship. One of the Anuaks had a record book. The names of the tithers was recorded along with the three piaster amount. Everyone was excited to be doing this. We sensed that it was pleasing to the Lord.

The Lord has a marvelous way of giving us an object lesson at just the right moment. During that following month, a group of Christian workers and I took the truck to an Anuak chief's village, Itang, about ten or twelve miles in the down stream direction from the mission. I had hoped to return early. Instead, we were forced to wait a couple of hours before the chief returned to the village. Consequently, on our return to the mission as we were passing through the large swamp where the animals frequently came down near the end of the day for water, it was the exact, right moment.. As we approached, we saw a large herd of waterbuck. I stepped out of the truck and moved cautiously forward, put the gun to my shoulder, took careful aim and pulled the trigger. When we ran over to the fallen animal, David Okwier looked at the other fellows, stretched his arms out and up and said in Anuak, "Look how God is blessing us." He related the provision of meat in abundance to their decision to tithe.

The question of whether or not they would continue tithing at the end of the month was never raised. Later as new believers were added to the flock, all became tithers from the moment they made their profession, even before they were baptized. The paper envelopes gave way to small cloth envelopes sewed by one of the women believers. Each envelope had the name of the person who was tithing written on it bold black letters. The Wednesday evening prayer times became times of great blessing and joy as the tithes increased, were recorded and they decided what to do with the extra money. God's blessing was upon us. Our hearts were glad. Incidentally, the horns of the waterbuck measured 27 inches from their tip to the base at the head.

## GOD BLESSED THE WORK AT POKWO

We had a neat program going during our months at Pokwo. I looked on the station as being an adult, non-formal education institution. The boys' school would wait until Don returned from furlough. Meanwhile, we would try out what I had learned on that tour. Young men came in from the Gila river area and other distant villages seeking employment. We took about 25 into the program at a time. Each young man was given a plot of land along the river on mission property for growing his own corn. These young men spent part of each day in their own fields, part of the day in working on the compound, and part of the day in literacy and Bible teaching classes. Each day began at six a.m. with a time of worship, singing and Bible study. God blessed with visitors from the nearby village frequently attending. When the challenge was given to turn away from the old ways and commit their lives to Jesus Christ, some would stand and profess faith right then and there. I often came home to breakfast with happy experiences to share with Lavina. By then she had the oatmeal or dura porridge cooked and the coffee pot was always enticing. Jimmy and David were waiting for Daddy so they could eat.

During that period, we taught the first 51 Anuaks how to read. From this group of young men came several of the first Anuak evangelists like Akway and David Okwier. When the men returned to their villages they spread the good news about Jesus to others.

### OLOK OMOL -- ONE TIN FOR THE LORD

Several incidents stand out in my memory. I recall a Sunday when we had been worshipping under the huge Tamarind tree on the compound. I had preached the sermon that morning flanked by a goat that had wondered in. Several dogs were lying around among us also. Babies cried until the mother gave the child another "sip" which was always available upon demand.

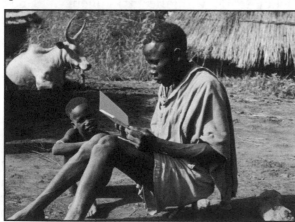

Olok Omol learning to read at Pokwo.

The service had now ended and most everyone had gone. Still standing there was a five gallon empty gasoline tin now full of beautiful shelled corn. I wandered over and asked Olok Omol, who also took care of our mission cows, what the corn was for.

He looked at me with a quizzical smile and said, "Odola, didn't you tell us that if we got ten tins of corn that one of them belonged to the Lord. I had ten tins and this one belongs to Him."

I was chagrined and ashamed. I had taught them how to tithe and when the evidence was in front of me I was spiritually too insensitive to recognize it.

I'll never forget our last Wednesday night prayer meeting at Pokwo. We were to return to Akobo as Don was expected back from America any day. Meanwhile, Joan Yilek would bridge the gap until the McClures returned.

## A SECOND ANUAK EVANGELIST

On the last such meeting in which Lavina and I participated, we challenged them to be faithful in their tithing and to pray for and encourage Akway who was evangelizing in the villages. I remember saying, "Isn't there someone from among you who could join Akway for just two months to encourage his heart?"

A tall, handsome, muscular young man stood up. He arranged his cloth carefully as they would often do when one had something important to say. It was David Okwier. This is what he said. "I have been here nearly two years. The first summer when I went home to my village, I still hadn't learned to read. People wanted to know what I had learned and I was unable to tell them accurately. This time, when I came back, I determined to learn how to read well. I've done that, but I've never really witnessed to my people. I will help Akway for two months just as you have suggested."

David Okwier was that same David who had stretched his arms out when that animal fell and said, "Look, see how God is blessing us." David never stopped helping Akway. When the two months ended, he just kept right on doing the work of an evangelist. As the Christian group grew, they began to support David Okwier financially along with Akway. Instead of one evangelist they had two.

David became known for his eloquent and forceful preaching. People talked about him with pride. But, David fell ill with tuberculosis and before long his strong body was weakened and he was a skeleton of his former self. Everyone knew that his time was short.

## DAVID OKWIER GOES TO BE WITH JESUS

To conclude our account about David, we need to move ahead five years to 1960. We were now back in the Sudan living at Pibor. One morning, we heard a clap outside our door. A young Anuak called Ochan Cham was at our door. He had walked nearly a hundred miles to tell us. David Okwier had died.

This was his story. The night before David died, he called his Anuak brothers to his bedside in that little African hut. He could hardly speak because of his weakness and terrible cough. But, this is what he told them. "When Okwier dies please don't wail and mourn like the Anuaks do in the villages. Rather, be glad. Tell them that Okwier has gone to be with Jesus. Please go through the villages and say that Okwier has gone to be with Jesus." Before morning, he did just that.

Ochan Cam had been on the way for more than a month. He was going through the villages as David had asked. The message traveled with Ochan from Pokwo to Pibor. God be praised! Ochan, himself, was suffering from tuberculosis. While we were on furlough in 1961, Ochan, too, 'went to be with Jesus' and was there with Okwier. When we heard it, we wanted to cry and sing praises to God all at the same time.

## OBEDIENCE BRINGS BLESSING AND JOY

Our years at Pokwo were among our best. And to think that we might have missed it, had we refused to obey the Lord's leading by stubbornly insisting on remaining at Akobo. We saw the Lord pour out his blessing upon us and on our ministry. It was challenging and satisfying to be laying solid foundations for the future development of the Anuak church. The real foundation was Jesus Christ, Himself. We were co-laborers with God and He alone could give the increase.

Our experience confirmed the truth of God's word. The Gospel was God's power to bring salvation to all who had a chance to hear and would believe. We knew that something was happening in the lives of Anuaks in Pokwo because we were there. It fit in with a basic point of view that has rather shaped our lives and various "missions" all through the years of our life. We have wanted to make an essential difference for Christ. We have wanted to be somewhere doing something essential for Him that wouldn't happen unless we did it. We have wanted to be available to Him for whatever He might have in mind. I hope we will, by His grace and mercy, never see things differently.

Our experience is that when we hold nothing back and are truly available to Him, everything changes. Burdens become lighter. Sacrifices fade into insignificance. We find ourselves echoing the words of the Apostle, "Indeed I count everything as loss because of the surpassing worth of knowing Christ Jesus my Lord ... That I might know Him and the power of His resurrection." And again, no matter how forbidding the moment we can say, "I can do all things in Him who strengthens me." And, yes, "I have learned in whatsoever state I am, therewith, to be content." O, to be sure, we stub our toe and fall miserably short, but in our best moments, these are the springs of our motivation and strength.

## JIMMY AND DAVID HAVE SCARLET FEVER

We lived at Pokwo from April in 1953 until May, 1955. Sometimes things were pretty rough living alone, down stream 21 miles from the nearest contact with the outside world. Without medical care, we were on our own, trusting the Lord to care for us and our little children. Jimmy and David were four and five years when we moved there.

I remember one Sunday noon when Jimmy came in from playing and flopped on his bed. He had a raging fever. Within half and hour, David did the same thing. We treated them for malaria. The rule of thumb was always treat for malaria first.

This time, the malaria medicine did nothing. The fevers kept right on burning their little bodies night and day. We were worried about polio because only a few months earlier a little missionary child, Chris Arnold, had died at Akobo from that dreadful disease. At that same time, another missionary child, Phil Roode, our doctor's son had also had it and came out of it with a limp arm and shoulder. Could this be polio striking at Pokwo?

Finally, on Wednesday, in the middle of the night at 2:30 in the morning, I went out where your young men were sleeping and called in a young, trustworthy Anuak to carry an urgent note cross country, across the mountain to Dr. John Cremer, stationed in Dembidollo. We asked the doctor to come. I would meet him on Friday at four in the afternoon on the river bank in Gambela. We knew he would be there. No question about it.

Meanwhile, we began searching the "World Book" encyclopedia that the McClures had on their shelves to try to discover what the children might have. We also started giving them penicillin injections. The fever began to break. I told Lavina, "I think these boys have scarlet fever." I had noticed that their tongues had a strawberry like appearance.

The doctor was there sitting on the riverbank waiting for me with his medical kit in hand when I pulled up on schedule with the boat. He asked how the boys were doing and then we were speeding downstream toward Pokwo. In an hour we were there. Immediately, he took each child and had them say, "aah," while he looked into their mouths. When he'd completed his investigation, he turned to us and said, "These boys have scarlet fever. They'll get along alright now. Just keep up with the penicillin a few more days."

Lavina and I looked at each other with a sigh of relief. The tension broke and I light heartedly said, "I think the "World Book" people ought to give us a free set for being able to diagnose accurately what these boys had from what was written in the "World Book".

The next morning, I took Dr. Cremer back to Gambela. It took a little longer going against the current. He got in his Jeep and returned the 46 miles on the "staircase" mountain road to his family and hospital. I picked up the mail and a few supplies and was home by noon. The crisis was over. We felt relieved and gave thanks to God.

## PART 2

### FRIGHTENING EXPERIENCES AT POKWO

We had some good scares during our time at Pokwo. The Anuaks in that area were pretty rough at times.

### LAVINA AND THE ANGRY MAN WITH THE GUN

I often hunted for our meat. I would normally go out late in the afternoon on horseback a number of miles back from the river in the flat grassland near what we described as saddle mountain. I would carry my heavy rifle with me and get down to shoot. A young Anuak would hold the bridle. Sometimes, if an animal was wounded I'd pursue it on horseback at a fast clip. Once, I jumped off the horse and pursued the wounded animal on foot. It would run, turn around and threaten to charge me. The adrenalin flowed freely. When this animal, a medium sized hartebeest turned and ran again, I pulled out my hunting knife, eventually got hold of its tail, slowed it to a walk and while still holding the tail was able to knife it and bring it down. Once, while chasing the animal with the horse, I lost my pith helmet and only stumbled unto it some weeks later on another such trip.

This particular afternoon, I had left home around three o'clock. When I returned after dark, the compound was humming with excited voices. I sensed, immediately, that something unusual had happened. Lavina had quite a story to share with me.

She said that soon after I left, Ateng, who helped us in the clinic came in and speaking in English said, "Madam, there is going to be a big trouble. A man has come from the village and is looking for his wife who he says ran away from him. He thinks she's on the compound but hasn't found her. He just left to go back to the village to get his gun and says he's coming back to find either his wife or kill the man who is hiding her."

Lavina said she and the children were in the back yard and Ateng advised them to get into the house so they wouldn't be hurt. She said that is what they did and kept an eye on the

185

path toward the village. It wasn't long and this man was on the compound with his old Italian, heavy rifle, which most adult Anuak men owned and used in marriage talks. The man slipped shells into his gun as Ateng went toward him and tried to persuade him not to come on the compound with a loaded gun. At that moment, the man raised his gun and pointed it straight at Ateng. He pulled the trigger, but fortunately it was a faulty shell and didn't go off.

As the man began dashing in and out of huts on the mission compound, Lavina discovered that her house was full of women. They had come around the down side of the house and entered by the front door. The woman the man was looking for was inside our house in the toilet room on the far end hiding. Meanwhile, on the other end, Lavina discovered that several of our young people had gone into my office where Don McClure also kept his gun case. They had gotten the door of the gun case open, guns out, and were proceeding to load them. Lavina persuaded them otherwise and managed to get the guns back where they belonged.

In the middle of all of that, she heard a vehicle in the distance. Now, trucks almost never came down that rarely used, ill kept road. God's timing was perfect. Someone ran out to the road, hailed the truck, and on it was the captain of the Ethiopian police post at Itang, some 15 miles down river from the mission. He was quickly told what was taking place. As the truck turned into the compound, the angry Anuak with the gun ran off the compound to escape, calling over his shoulder that he would be back that night to kill everyone, including these foreigners (missionaries).

The Ethiopian police captain went to the village itself, down stream from us about a fourth of a mile. They took the chief from the village hostage and announced he would be held at Itang until the village turned over the culprit.

Once the truck had gone, other men from the village came and found the woman in question. They tied her hands and led her off to the village. "Her crying and screaming were so pitiful," Lavina said, "and there was nothing I could do to help her."

That was what all the humming conversation was about when I returned from hunting. Lavina had been through a terrifying experience with the little boys and I hadn't even been aware nor was I available to assist.

We were plenty afraid that night. It was nearly ten o'clock before the Anuaks and we stopped talking about it just outside our back door. When finally, we crawled into our beds on the veranda. sleep was long in coming and when it did, we had only little "sleeps" and then we would be awake. We expected someone to come sneaking out of the nearby papaya grove or out of the bananas any moment. Never was daylight more welcome!

Before the week was out, the guilty man was located and turned over to the police. He paid a fine of a young cow, the chief was back home, and we were back to normal. Every such experience threw us upon the mercy of God and we knew that He had to keep us safe if we were to make it. Looking back, we praise Him for doing just that.

## FABRICATED FEAR

Some of our fears were of our own making. Living in isolation, it is amazing the tricks one's mind can play on a person. We had one, now seen to be humorous, such experience.

We were just sitting down to our Sunday noon meal. A clap at the door interrupted our eating. Three men were at the door. This was there story:

They had come from a village located mid-way between us and Gambela. On the preceding day there had been a gunfight in the village and a man had been shot in the thigh. He was very badly injured and they wanted me to come.

I immediately mixed up the gas and soon this party of three and I were headed up river toward the village. Upon arrival, they took me to the hut where this badly injured man was propped up in a sitting position. He had lost large amounts of blood. The wound was gaping and uncovered. It was agreed that we should transport him to the mission where we could give him the care he needed.

Once back at the mission, we put him in the grass house on the river bank where we held our classes and Bible studies. Less than an hour after we arrived, one from among them came to the door announcing that the man had died and would I take them all back to the village again.

As they carried the man to the boat, I noticed that they had put a new pair of shorts on him. This, I learned later, had some superstitious significance and was part of their ritual to put a curse on the man who had killed him.

The boat was heavily loaded and it took us longer than usual to cover the distance involved. By the time we arrived, a huge tropical storm was about to descend on us. It would bring a very strong wind and a cloudburst of water. Wanting to get away before the storm broke, I apologized for not helping them carry the body from the boat to the house where they would take him.

With that I sped away down stream. With the boat now light and empty I outran the storm and was home safely in no time flat.

There was just one problem I hadn't solved. I came home with a guilty conscience. I chided myself for fleeing the storm and not helping them carry the dead man into the village and trying to comfort them. Not only that, but perhaps they might even think I had something to do with his dying so quickly on the compound. I said to myself over and over, "Odola you are so stupid. What's the harm of a little rain. You've been wet before. You should have stayed with them and helped them." A classic example of the workings of a guilty conscience!

The following Saturday, I had to go past this village into Gambela where I was picking up supplies. It was after dark before Ojulu and I were ready to head for home. Ojulu was in the front of the boat, our load in the middle, and I was at the back steering. The motor made lots of noise so we could only shout at each other occasionally if we wanted to say something. As we approached the village and were going by, I wondered what they might be thinking. My guilty thoughts were still plaguing me. Right in the middle of that, I heard what I thought was the shot from a gun. Almost immediately, Ojulu turned around and shouted, "That was a gun." He turned around to the front and quickly turned back toward me again and shouted, "That was a gun. The bullet shot narrowly missed the boat." I had a lot to think about the rest of the way home in the dark.

Anuaks on the compound always came down to the river to meet the boat. They would help unload and carry supplies into the shop or house. That evening was no exception. The only thing different was that Ojulu had news to share that he couldn't wait to tell. We had been shot at by the people in

188

the village from which the dead person had come.

The people were shocked. They just couldn't comprehend that their missionary was shot at and in danger. Conversations centered on just one thing, "They shot at Odola."

Lavina had supper prepared and as soon as we were around the table I shared what had happened. Very soon, while we were at the table commiserating over the situation, Anuaks began coming in and sitting on the floor and on the ledge next to the screen. There was a lot of fear and apprehension.

I wanted to go that night yet and report it to the chief who lived across the river upstream about a half mile. The Anuaks cautioned against it and urged that I wait until daylight. I was all for clearing up the misunderstanding as quickly as possible. I knew I'd sleep better if I could go to the village immediately. I was outvoted, however, and Lavina voted with the majority!

After a fitful night during which Lavina and I both had visions of the worst that could happen, morning came. At the crack of dawn, one of the young men and I sped away by outboard to share with the chief what had happened. The chief refused to believe that it was so. He said, "There is some misunderstanding. Please take me to the village where the gun was fired so I can get at the bottom of it. The Anuaks would never harm you."

It was great to have the chief in the boat with us and we took off for the village in the direction of Gambela. As we approached the village, I saw a canoe with three men in it start out from there to cross the river toward the side where we were traveling. My knee began to bounce up and down uncontrollably. I was sure they had heard us and were coming across to shoot at us as we went by. I was really nervous. Almost that quickly, we were directly in front of the village on the opposite side of the river. As soon as we had touched the bank the chief jumped ashore and rushed up, over the bank and disappeared from view. I stayed in the boat fiddling with the motor. It wasn't long before the chief was back with two men from the village. This is what he said, "Here's the man who fired the gun. They were having an argument about whether or not the bullet in question was any good or not. Just as you went by they shot the gun into the air. They weren't shooting at you."

Our fears had been entirely of our own making. My guilt feelings, negative thoughts, and a gun fired at a particular time and place fueled my fears, and all added up to something that proved to be utterly false. That the bullet had narrowly missed our boat was pure imagination!

Before returning to Pokwo, we all crossed the river, and visited the village in which the dead person had been buried. They couldn't have been friendlier. They held no grudge because of my leaving to escape the storm.

Lavina and I had a good laugh over our self-made, fabricated fears. More than once we nearly laughed ourselves sick when we brought the subject up and made fun of ourselves. The concluding remark always was, "Can you imagine being that stupid?" How human missionaries are! "For He knows our frame; He remembers that we are dust." We knew that the Psalmist was right. We echoed the Psalmist's words.

## STOPPING A REVENGE KILLING AFTER DARK

Lavina, and I had just finished our Bible story time with the children and had concluded our prayers. It was about eight o'clock in the evening. Four men came out of the darkness and were at our front door. They were from the village of Pokwo, downstream about a quarter of a mile. Standing outside in the light from our Aladdin light, we could recognize them and subsequently invited them in.

There was uproar in the village. A messenger had just arrived from the down river village over which their chief also had jurisdiction. The messenger alarmed and angered the older men in our village by his report telling how the younger men, the "jo lwak," had killed someone from their older men=s age set, a person from the 'jo bworo" group. Tempers were high and they wanted to kill a young man from the "jo lwak" living among them in revenge. They wanted to do so before daylight.

The men at the door each had an old Italian army rifle in his hands. They had come because they were not in favor of doing what the hot heads were proposing. So they had come to ask if I would accompany them back to the village and try to persuade the men in the village to calm down.

There chief was away in Gambela and had stopped by

before leaving, as he often did, and had asked me to "watch his village" while he was away.

I looked at Lavina and could tell she was uneasy about my going. I wasn't that comfortable with the idea either but felt I should do so. So, I pumped up the gasoline lantern, lit it, and stepped out into the darkness with the four Anuak men. We had barely started when we spotted two young men, presumably from the *jo luuak*, barely distinguishable in the darkness. I could make out that they each had a heavy rifle in their hands. It didn't make me feel any more secure with those fellows in the dark and we in the bright light of the lantern. Such were my thoughts as I left the compound and started down the trail beside the river. My Anuak men had already put bullets into the chambers of their guns.

The river was on one side and tall, eight to ten foot grass on the other the entire distance. The lantern made it hard to see anyone in the darkness. I was truly afraid that someone might take a shot at us before we reached the village.

Once there, it was immediately apparent that the entire village was stirred up with anger. Loud voices and a steady murmuring of conversations came from all directions. I was taken to the area where some fifteen or twenty of the older age set, the "jo bworo" had collected themselves. I greeted them in Anuak, but said nothing for some little while. Finally, I found the words to speak and said, "I have heard from the men what has happened to one of your people. I understand why you are angry. But, it is not good that you do something in haste or in anger. It will be much better for you to do nothing until you have all slept and the sun begins to shine in the morning." I was hoping that by morning better judgment would prevail. I continued, "You know that your chief is gone. You also know that your chief came to see me before he left for Gambela. These were his words to me, 'Odola watch my people until I return. Don't let them fight or kill someone.' " With that, I said, "Because of the word of your chief, I forbid anyone to leave the village or to kill a young man before morning. Tomorrow, I will return and we can decide together what should be done."

With that nearly everyone agreed and said, "Odola, that is good talk. We agree that we will do nothing before the sun shines tomorrow."

Only one person disagreed and said loudly so that all

191

could hear him, "Why should we listen to the voice of this foreigner. He has now power over us."

But, God was in it and this man was rebuffed and overruled. I immediately left and headed for home, lantern in hand brightening the path. Few women were ever happier to welcome home their husbands than was Lavina that night. At our bedside, we thanked God that He had used us to save a life and that He had protected ours. We prayed for the day when the Anuak would have surrendered their lives to Jesus Christ and the drunkenness that led to fighting and the anger which followed with killings would have stopped. We thanked God for the privilege of being there to tell them that through Jesus Christ their lives could be made whole.     We  slept  peacefully.  In the morning good sense prevailed.  Tempers were calmed and, hopefully, the village would remain at peace until their chief returned.  Looking back to those days, I fear that eventually some young man, perhaps totally innocent of wrong doing, paid the supreme price.  Revenge killings are no respecter of persons!  However long it took, normally someone paid the price.

### TRANSLATOR - DOCTOR - DENTIST

We maintained a heavy work load at Pokwo.  Besides early morning prayers, Bible teaching and literacy classes, helping in the clinic and translating until one o'clock when we had our noon meal,  after a short siesta, we had another go at it in the afternoon.  Lavina had sewing classes with the Anuak girls and was teaching them to read.  I would be at the desk with two informants directly across from me six days a week. The translation work continued along with other station programs.

While we were busy translating, people were coming in from the villages to be treated in the clinic.  I had a good helper, but reserved the matter of giving needed injections and seeing the more complicated cases for myself.  Sometimes I could hear them grumbling as folks waited for this missionary to come out.  The sun was hot and they couldn't figure out why he spent so much time in the house with his wife.  Normally, I tried to stick to the desk until eleven o'clock, but if the pressure became unbearable, I would give in, dismiss the informants until later in the day, and go out to see the sick.

Once we had the captain of the Ethiopian police down at Itang come in with pneumonia. Lavina invited him and his a wife to stay in our spare bedroom until he was better. They were with us for the entire week. Every day I gave him the needed penicillin injections. It was a privilege to serve the Lord, meeting the needs of the sick, even as Jesus had done. When first in the Sudan, I had seriously considered returning to the states to qualify as a missionary doctor. That lasted only a few weeks and disappeared completely once I got into the work of translation. Even so, I always enjoyed "playing doctor" and in doing so was able to help a lot of hurting people.

My "medical practice" included being the local dentist. These poor folks had no way of dealing with painful, decaying teeth other than to knock them out or dig them out, sometimes using a fish spear. Before, I had proper dental tools, we used a pliers out the truck without anesthesia. I hate to think of it now! Two or three would hold the patient, while I extracted the tooth. Sometimes, it took a couple of weeks before the victim felt like blessing me, Anuak style -- just a gentle spitting on the head with a minimum of saliva. Just enough to make it authentic!

## LEOPARD INTERFERES
## WITH THE TRANSLATING

Once when I was translating, a couple of men came to the window and begged me to come with them to help them kill the leopard that had been in their village during the night. This leopard had taken one of their goats and they were afraid for their dogs and children. Leopards were said to be especially fond of dog meat.

I agreed to go and saddled up the horse, taking with me my heavy .348 caliber rifle, a canteen of water and a book to read. We went together to the village and tied the horse there. They took me back of the village about an eighth of a mile to a big, dry swamp where the grass was more than ten feet tall. There I found a man sitting with his heavy rifle on his lap. About fifteen feet away was a dead dog which he was using to allure the leopard. I sat down beside him. In about a half hour, he began complaining about the hot sun. He doubted the leopard would come anyway and decided he had enough of it. I was just new and told him I was going to stay.

After they all left to go back to the village, I was alone with the dead dog. I dragged the dog a little farther from where I was sitting and waited. I had my gun across my knees with the bullet in the chamber. I started reading but kept wondering whether that leopard might come from behind me out of the tall grass. It was scary and I don't remember a thing I read. You will never believe this, but within fifteen minutes of the other man leaving, a huge male leopard came out of the grass about sixty feet away from me and started coming toward where I was sitting. I don't believe he ever saw me. I remained sitting, raised my gun to my shoulder, took careful aim and pulled the trigger. The leopard fell over dead in its tracks. I had shot it through the heart.

In less time than it takes to tell you, it seemed that the whole village was out there. They looked at the leopard. They looked at me and then, again, at the leopard. Their joy was boundless. They could sleep in peace and not be afraid for their children and dogs. I felt like someone probably feels who pitches a "no hitter" in the big leagues.. It was great sport and a far cry from sitting behind the desk translating the Bible into Anuak.

They soon brought the horse and we draped this huge leopard over the horse just in front of the saddle. I went riding home like a great white hunter. Anuaks were singing and dancing for joy as we came unto the compound. Lavina and the boys came out to welcome us back. She had heard the shot from our back yard. Who knows, in protecting the Anuak village, perhaps we had also protected ourselves. The skin was so large that when we hung it on the wall, the head came close to the top of the wall and the tail was nearly touching on the floor. In the afternoon I was back at the desk.

You will recall that during our first weeks at Pokwo, Lavina was in Khartoum and the three boys and I missed her terribly. When she finally reached us, it was so wonderful to have her with us again. We had had a great summer with our three boys, Dennis, now eleven and Jimmy and David. Jimmy was five and Dave was just fourteen months younger.

When the summer was over and Dennis had to go back to school, he would be going to the Bingham Academy in Addis Ababa. He cried hard when he left and so did his mother.

From Dembidollo where they stopped for a day enroute, he wrote such a pathetic letter home. I can still see it as if it were yesterday. He wrote, "*Please watch Jimmy and Dave that they don't fall into the river. I want to come home, please, please, please ...*" Christmas couldn't come soon enough!

## EXPECTING A BABY AT POKWO
## NO SIMPLE MATTER

D-day was approaching. Lavina was great with child. Less than a month remained before the big event. We had looked at some books just in case! But, we knew we had to get to the hospital in Dembidollo if at all possible.

On the appointed day in November, we started for Gambela in the outboard. It was a rough trip because an unanticipated shower overtook us on the way and we also had trouble with spark plugs leading up. It took us most of the afternoon to reach Gambela. Once there, we were warmly cared for by a Greek, bachelor merchant.

In the morning four young Anuak fellows, Lavina, the two children and I started up the mountain. We had 46 miles to go. The road was so rough, we called it a "staircase" leading to Dembidollo. Sometimes Lavina would get out and walk up the steep hill because of the discomfort in riding. We thought this baby will come before we ever get there. As it turned out, we still had to wait another month for God's surprise, Christmas gift, our "Carol Joy".

Once in Dembidollo, the doctor did his examination and made his predictions. He said, "I can only suggest that it=s going to be another boy." I don't know if he knew anything about it or not, but he said, "The heart tones indicate that it'll be a boy." We didn't want to hear that because we already had three boys and really wanted a girl this time around. We talked about it quite a bit, rather lamenting that we would likely have another boy. Even Jimmy and Dave sensed what we were talking about. We talked about those 'heart tones' and wondered if they could really tell. Jimmy, who was only five and a half had questions we couldn't answer.

When the moment came, the tension of that special event was shattered when Dr. Cremer, excitedly and joyfully exclaimed, "We've got a girl here." I was right there and could

195

scarcely believe my ears and eyes. All the lights seemed, suddenly, to be shining more brightly. Our hope and dream had become reality. We had a little girl. Both the doctor and we talked about that unforgettable moment many times in the years the lay ahead. The boys were excited too.

Soon afterwards Mary Nell Harper, one of the nurses at Dembidollo was saying to Jimmy, "So you've got a baby sister!"

Quick as a flash, Jimmy responded by saying, "Yep, my dad changed the heartbeats." Our conversation about the heart tones had taken on added dimensions. Jimmy was as excited as his mom and dad with a baby girl in the family. Born three days before Christmas, we named her, "Carol Joy." She has never disappointed us and we know she was appropriately named. God's Christmas gift to us!

Eight days later, we put Carol Joy in a small cardboard box which served as a bassinet and put her on the front seat between us in the International pick-up truck. We started down the mountain, with Dr. Cremer and two of his sons traveling behind us in their Jeep. They didn't want us to make the journey alone.

By mid-afternoon we were at the Sako river. It was getting hotter and hotter. Under a tree there, Lavina took all of Carol Joy's clothes off, laid her on a blanket and cooled her off. By the time we reached Gambela on the river, darkness had already fallen. We learned that the river had fallen to a point where we couldn't safely reach home by outboard.

The only thing to do was to attempt it by road. The two vehicles gave us confidence we could make it. Everything went well until a little over halfway home, we came upon a swamp of water that had not receded back far enough for us to pass through between it and the river bank.

Perhaps with the four-wheeled Jeep we could make it through, but not with the International which had only a two-wheel drive. We loaded what we could on the Jeep and made it. It was eleven o'clock when we stopped by the deep ditch that surrounded the mission compound. The last 150 yards would be on foot. Anuaks living on the compound had heard us coming. They were so excited to have us back. They immediately wanted to know what God had given us. Was it a boy or a girl? When they learned that it was a girl, on the spot, they named her "Awile," the one who changed the pattern from boys to girls. With wild joy and excitement they created and sang songs fitting to the occasion. It was a night for thanksgiving to God. The house was dirty and dusty. We had been gone for more than a month. It could have been depressing, except that we came home with our bundle of love. But we were all tired and hungry and needed to eat.

Here is where Lavina shone. On the eighth day, she made that arduous trip, and at the end of the journey, prepared a meal from scratch and fed the hungry travelers. We fetched water from the river and boiled it so we would have cool drinking water the next day. Everything was difficult and tedious. How Lavina ever did it I will never know other than that God gave her special strength during those days. In our prayers we told the Lord how much we recognized this and how unspeakably grateful we were. We were glad to be His missionaries at what seemed then to be "the ends of the earth." We had experienced again that He keeps His promises. He had said it again in our hearts. "I will be with you always, even to the ends of the earth." This gave us the strength and courage we needed. It was one o'clock in the morning before we all lay down for the balance of the night.

Breakfast in the morning! Then it was to fetch the International from where we had abandoned it the night before. By late afternoon the Cremers were making their way back over the mountain. Again, we were alone. This time we had a tiny, precious, 10 day old baby to love and protect. We had prepared for it by getting film. Few babies had more pictures taken. Her grandparents were glad!

## WE RETURN TO AKOBO

Except for the six or seven months that Joan Yilek was with us following her furlough, we were alone at Pokwo. In February of '55 Don and Lyda were back in Addis and expected at Pokwo soon. Joan said she could easily cope until they arrived. We should leave as earlier scheduled.

The MAF plane flew Lavina, Jimmy, David and Carol back to Akobo. Dennis and I went cross country on horseback and with carriers. It was a journey of some 140 miles and took us 8 days. We crossed several rivers and swam the horses beside the canoe. While crossing, we knocked against the side of

197

the canoe to keep the crocodiles away. This was dry season and it was hot. Dennis and I would start out each day before the sun was shining, cook our breakfast around ten thirty and then wait until later in the afternoon before starting out again. It was just too hot to move in the middle of the day. What a marvelous experience for a thirteen year old boy and his dad. Precious times for both of us. Little did we know then that one day Dennis would be back flying over this same route as a missionary pilot with MAF. His many long treks as a boy, I am sure, gave him an early appreciation for what a plane might do to make missionaries' lives more pleasant and productive.

Before leaving that long trekking experience, I need to share a couple of interesting experiences we had along the way.

The first day out, Denny and I were feeling sorry for the horses and when we stopped to rest, decided we would remove their bridles so they could eat the grass a little more comfortably. The horses, however, took advantage of our generous hearts and soon headed down the trail in the direction of Pokwo from where we had started five hours earlier. Heading in that direction, they no longer seemed tired as before and we had a very fast run to outflank them and head them off. I can assure you they ate grass with bridles on the rest of the way unless we tethered them down securely.

On our last afternoon, the horses were showing signs of fatigue. We stopped in a village and discovered they had been making Anuak beer. The left over mash from the beer making process had been dumped on the edge of the village. We took the horses over to that mash and I wish you could have seen them. They, literally, pushed their noses deep into it and gorged themselves on it. For the rest of the journey to Akobo that afternoon, we were riding on horses that had all the energy we could control. Had their been a horse officer, I suspect the horses might have been given a ticket for drunk driving. For us, it was a relief to speed on and gain an hour on reaching Akobo before dark. We laughed about our drunken horses more than once! It was good to be back at Akobo after an absence of 21 months. I would now have more time for my beloved translation work.

# CHAPTER ELEVEN

# BACK AT AKOBO
# A NEW MAF PLANE

Lavina had flown with MAF from Gambela to Akobo with Carol, Jim, and Dave. We were expecting our fifth child and the new little Hoekstra would be arriving in a few short weeks.

## DISAPPOINTMENT UPON ARRIVAL AT AKOBO

We'd had lived at Pokwo without a doctor until the day Lavina flew back to Akobo. She was eager to get home and into her own house. But, it wasn't to be! Folks at Akobo had arranged for the plane to fly her and the children to the mission station in Nasir, 90 miles down river, where there was a doctor. Lavina and the children stayed in Nasir ten days with other missionaries until they all flew into Akobo together to attend the annual mission meeting scheduled to be held there for the first time ever.

Eight days after we had left Pokwo, Dennis and I rode up on the opposite side of the river just across from our house in Akobo. We had made the 140 mile trek, cross-country from Pokwo, on horseback.. We quickly swam the horses across the river and were home at last. I could scarcely believe my ears when I was told that Lavina and the children were in Nasir. I was so eager to see them and so very disappointed not to find them there. Fortunately, we had only the night to wait because the next morning folks began arriving for our annual mission meeting and Lavina and the doctor from Nasir would be among them.

With that initial disappointment, home sweet home, didn't seem quite that sweet. This was dry season and eve-

199

rything seemed dried up and barren looking besides. Pokwo was always lush and green, but here things looked rather dead and uninspiring. It would take a little adjusting to settle in again. Without Lavina and the children those first 24 hours, didn't raise the spirits any either.

I remember straightening things up around the yard and in the house that afternoon yet. We were really tired from the long trek but there was work to be done if we were to be ready for the influx of missionaries and their families the next day.

## MISSION MEETING HELD AT AKOBO
## 1956

We had no time to think of the "flesh pots" of Pokwo as missionaries came from the other stations. Some came by truck or Jeep and others flew in with MAF. Lavina was so thrilled to be home that morning and immediately plunged into getting the house ready for guests. The kids were all excited with their new surroundings and were soon exploring the place, inside and out. Other mission children were there for them to get acquainted with. They had so many exciting things to share and to learn from each other. They were happy with their new home.

The entire station was a bee-hive of activity getting ready for the mission meeting. Some real logistical matters had to be considered. Where would all these people sleep. How would they be fed? They had shot an animal the day before so there should be plenty of meat. But, now they were beginning to have some doubts about being able to preserve it. It couldn't all be refrigerated. Would it keep? Regrettably, the answer proved to be "no". After the mission meeting, we talked about the catastrophe of the spoiled meat and the awful smelling gravy on numerous occasions. Folks involved were given an "A" for effort but an "F" on results. It was just one of the problems that was inevitable in trying to cope with so many people with so few houses and facilities.

Our house was on the north end of the compound, separated from the other residences by the school, library and the banana grove. The old McClure house, where the Sikkemas lived, came next. Between it and the Swart house was the fruit orchard. Beyond the Swarts at the end stood the single missionaries ladies' house. These houses came to be identified with the first family who lived there and seemed to carry that name all through the years. In practice, we had other folks living in them at different times. The Crandalls, the Arnolds, the Roodes and the Sikkemas as well as the Jordans were all part of the Anuak missionary family at some time or other during our years in the Sudan. Things changed a lot from those first years when just the McClures, Swarts, Wilma Kats and we started out there. Bob and Morrie had arrived in April of '48 along with Wilma Kats. They had joined the McClures when returning from furlough. We had caught up with them three months later and always felt that we had been part of it from the beginning.

We had never had an annual mission meeting at Akobo. Normally, these were held in Doleib Hill or Malakal, a day's trip to the north of us. We were always excited about going there for the mission meeting to meet folks we hadn't seen for a year. For the ladies it was a treat just to get out of the station. They loved the opportunity to get into those two Greek shops in Malakal and replenish their dwindling supplies. They would shop for the year ahead and had to plan rather carefully.

One thing I remember about those mission meetings is that many of us would be ill with diarrhea before the week ended. Temporary pit holes, food prepared in abundance, and masses of flies made it almost inevitable. We, who had been so eager to come, now could scarcely wait to get home and become well again.

This year the Akobo folks had bravely invited their colleagues to meet in our station. We knew it was planned, but just arriving from Pokwo made the hustle and bustle of getting ready, with last minute contingencies and unforeseen problems popping up demanding a solution, seem more taxing.

They had a master plan showing where everyone would be housed. We would all eat together in the McClure house where the Crandalls were then living. Our house was to have the following people. Gordon and Jean Marshall, the MAF couple, would occupy the middle tukl on the front. Dr. Bob and Vi Gordon and their three children and Bob's father would sleep in my office and the attached storage room. Out in the back, we had a two room, thatched roof, mud floor storeroom. Lowrie and Margaret Anderson and Milton and Peggy Thompson would sleep there. In front of the tukl in which the Gordons would sleep, was a tent for our overseas' special guests and speaker for the conference, Dr. Ed Fairman his wife, Marian, and their young four year old son, Timmy. The place was full. There was no more room in the inn! We, ourselves, would sleep on the sleeping veranda on the bathroom end of the house.

## MARK STEPHEN BORN WHILE MISSION MEETS

And then, guess what? During the middle of the conference, about 3 a.m. in the morning, Lavina says, "Honey, this is the night. Maybe you better go get the doctor."

What a time to decide to have a baby! But, it was out of our control! I quickly dressed and ran down to the mission to crank up the generator. When I did so, every light on the compound came on. The generator always shut itself down with the help of an alarm clock turning a spool on the back to shut off the flow of diesel fuel.

Immediately, of course, everyone was awake and knew that "the party" was about to begin.

What a setting in which to have a baby. Lavina was terrific and took it all in good humor. We didn't have just one doctor, we had three doctors and two nurses in attendance.

Here's the picture. Guests in our back yard. Guests in our end tukl. Guests in the middle tukl. Guests in a tent in the front yard. Our four children asleep on their beds on the sleeping veranda. In the end tukl, just off the bathroom and bedroom, Lavina is having the baby.

At twenty minutes to five in the morning, the party was over. Mark Stephen had been born. The children slept through it all. How kind and merciful is the Lord!

When I went down to join the others for breakfast, they all wanted to know what the big idea was of waking everyone up in the middle of the night with those lights. They had a great time "pulling my leg". It was celebration time. God had given us a beautiful, perfect little boy. After breakfast, all the mission kids wanted to come down and see what a brand new baby looked like. They stood in awe as they looked at this red faced little guy in the basket. Gayle Swart commented, "Boy, he sure has big hands." In that basket, unknown then, God had placed another missionary. What a cause for celebration and thanks to God.

Lavina joined the crowd in no time. Even, Mark was soon on display in his little basket on the edges of the mission meeting. Later in the week, the business sessions gave way to fun and games. That night, our "party" came in for a lot of good ribbing. Mark was number five for us. The Treasurer of our RCA board at that time was Dr. Henry Bovenkerk. He was great but missionaries joked about how he "pinched pennies" for the Board. We all had the impression that he didn't like missionaries having large families because it cost the Board too much money for children's allowances. Our salaries varied those years according to the number of children one had.

That evening during the charades, a faked telegram, purportedly to us from Dr. Bovenkerk was read out -- *"Congratulations ... stop ... repeat .... stop ... signed Bovenkerk."* Missionaries have a great sense of humor and we were having fun!

## GOOD TIMES AT AKOBO

Lavina and I had a promising ministry underway at Pokwo. We loved it there and had there been a need for us to continue, we would have been happy to do so. It wasn't until we had again settled in at Akobo that we realized what blessings and joys we had missed out on at Akobo.

God gave us a wonderfully, compatible group in our station and in the Presbyterian mission. It was a joy and a privilege to be members of the team. Each of us knew why we were there and what was expected of each of us. Over the years, we had many fantastic times together. In our work, we complemented each other's contributions. In our social relationships, we played and prayed and worshipped together. A variety of activities brought us together.

The weekly teas followed by volley ball were a sheer delight. We had our mid-week evening prayer meeting, taking turns in the different homes. Sunday afternoons in the hour before dusk we had an English worship service in either the McClure's or Swart's home. English speaking teachers and school boys, our British district commissioner, Dick Lythe and his wife, Nora, with their children and missionary colleagues made up the congregations. Wilma Kats, Joan Yilek or Morrie Swart played the small portable organ. Sometimes Morrie and Bob sang us a beautiful duet or Bob played his trombone. We took turns preaching. One of the sermons by Don McClure has always stuck in my memory, it was based on Revelation where it says, "Let no man steal thy crown." We missionaries loved each, worked well together and upheld each other in our prayers. At Akobo we were greatly blessed by being joined together with colleagues we found compatible and supportive. We were a family. Our children called the adults "Uncle" and "Aunt". These ties became so strong that they vied with blood relatives in attraction. On furloughs our children sometimes had difficulty sorting out who was a "real uncle and aunt" from who was a  mission "uncle and aunt". We were truly an extended family straight out of Africa.

## FURLOUGH - A NEW PLANE FOR MAF

It would soon be time for our regular furlough. I was pressing hard with the translation effort. You might say that we were burning the candle! I was more tired than normal. My heart was beating irregularly. Doctor's weren't sure whether I had a serious heart condition or not.

Once in America, it was determined that a little more relaxation and a little more recreation and rest was all that was required. A change of pace, better food and living conditions and I was back to normal.

Two things of significance occurred during that furlough. During the first months in the states, we lived in the missionary residence in Grand Rapids. It was during that time that we began dreaming of the possibility of raising funds for a plane for MAF to use in the Sudan. They were flying an old Rapide aircraft, a somewhat ancient bi-plane with canvas covering. It wasn't ideally suited for Sudan conditions and they were praying for the Lord to provide them with something smaller, more efficient and suited for their ministry.

I had never raised large amounts of money and had no idea as to how to go about it. But, the Lord has marvelous surprises and he had one for me that was full of excitement.

## SHORT ON SLEEP AND SHORT ON CLOTHES

But, first, let me give you the setting. We arrived in Grand Rapids from overseas on a Saturday evening. Friends from Bethany Reformed Church were at the airport to greet us. We were taken over to the mission house which they had stocked with food, vegetables and milk. All we had to do was crawl into bed.

It was exciting for the whole family. The children fell asleep quite easily but in the middle of the night they and we were all awake because of the time change.

Our clothes were a mess. They were wrinkled and the children just didn't have clothes that fit them anymore. But, go to church we did, regardless. We were a little late and found ourselves in about the third row from the front. When it was time for the offering, I gave each of the boys a fifty cent piece. David, who was about six years old, looked up at me with surprise and in a whisper that almost anyone within two rows of us could hear asked, "Dad, how much bubble gum can you get for that?"

After the service, we made our way out. The kids arms were much too long for the sleeves of the clothes they were wearing and their trousers were far too short. We all looked like we just come out of Africa somewhere. In fact, we had, and anybody would know that it was so. An immaculately dressed church member who we learned was a dentist came up to us and said, "You'd better take those children down to the store tomorrow and get them some new clothes." He told us where to go and said, "Just have them send the bill to me." Bless his heart. He saw a need and met it. Later, he took care of all our dental needs that furlough and never charged us a dime! Many a time we found ourselves singing the doxology! How wonderfully the Lord cares for His servants!

## "NOW DON'T YOU GO BUYING ANY AIRPLANES!"

I had been thinking a good bit about MAF's need for a different plane. It was a need I wanted to help meet. But, the man who came up to me after the service in Bethany said, "I think my partner and I can get you that Jeep you need."

I was most surprised and responded by saying, "That Jeep may not be our highest priority. Why don't you let me think it over and get back to you."

After going over it together, the next time we met, the man handed me a check for $3,500. I had never seen a check that large in all my life. It could be used toward that new MAF plane. Lavina and I talked about it all the way to the mission house.

That same week I learned of a used Cessna 180 airplane that a local manufacturer was planning to sell. I made an appointment and we talked about how we might purchase his plane. He was Charles Werner of Werner Manufacturing. He wanted $8,500. I knew I couldn't find that kind of money, but I wanted that plane for MAF so badly that I was bold to suggest that if he could let us have it for $5,000 we would find a way to pay for it. After a moment's hesitation, he said, "Well, let me talk to the boss and we'll let you know." He was referring to his wife! In fact, both of them were great people!

The next morning, by agreement, at exactly nine o'clock the phone rang. This was to be his answer. I was walking toward the phone, when Lavina (probably meaning it besides) said, "Now, don't you go buying any airplanes!"

I picked up the phone. The voice on the other end of the line said, "If you want that plane you can have it for $5,000 dollars." With Lavina's words still fresh on my mind, I didn't know what to say. There was an awkward silence. This time, Mr. Werner said, "Well, do you want it, or don't you?"

Without a moments hesitation, I said, "We'll take it." I had bought an airplane with only $3,500 on hand. I quickly made a call to a dear friend in Grand Haven, Michigan, Mr. Franklin Kieft, and told him what I had done. He said he'd see what he could do. That afternoon he came to the house with a check for the remaining $1500. He'd gone to the bank and borrowed the money. Together, we went to examine the plane. We were both thrilled with what we saw. We had bought a beautiful, hardly used Cessna 180 for MAF.

Twenty years later, Ed Stouten, the man from Bethany, who had given the $3,500 shared with me, how his partner and he had cleaned themselves out to make that gift. He told me how grateful he was to have been challenged then. He said, "It taught me how to give and to trust the Lord. If I hadn't done it then, I'd never have had the joy of giving over $200,000 since then for the Lord's work. It was your challenging me that the Lord used to teach me how to give." He was so grateful and so was I. We praised the Lord together.

Now that I had the plane, I didn't know what to do with it. In my excitement, I decided to call Stewart King, head of MAF in London. We knew Stewart well from our times together in the Sudan and I was itching to tell him. For ordinary people like me, making an overseas call in those days was a major event!

Stewart could scarcely believe what I was telling him. This was beyond his wildest dreams. More good news, would follow, but I couldn't tell him yet. It was our hope to send this plane to the Sudan with floats as well. Then MAF operate rain or shine!

Stewart suggested I call Grady Parrot, president of MAF in Fullerton, California. The day before Christmas, Grady picked up the plane and flew it to their hanger for modifications making it suitable for use in the Sudan.

Lavina, the children and I were in Minnesota that Christmas with my folks on the farm. We were just ready to step out the door to go to our little country church for its Sunday School Christmas program when the phone rang. It was long distance. My cousin, Dick Hoekstra, was calling from Chicago. I shall never forget his words. He said, "Harvey, are you still wanting to put pontoons on that plane for the Sudan?" He always liked to kid around and before I could respond, he said, "I'll put a pontoon on one side for you. Which side do you want?" He continued, "You will probably be getting in on the right side most of the time, how about if I put one on that side for you?" Four days later, there was a check in the mailbox for $2,100.

God had better things in mind with respect to that plane than we had dared to dream. MAF actually sold that plane to a group of sheep ranchers in Australia for only a little less than the cost of a brand new one. God's people kept giving us help. When the project was completed, churches and individuals had provided funds for a brand new Cessna 180, equipped with pontoons, with a spare engine and whatever modifications were required to fit it for the Sudan. This plane made a dramatic difference in MAF's ability to serve the Lord and His missionaries with safety and efficiency that amazed us all. It changed the way we lived and worked! This was God's gracious gift and we gave Him our overflowing thanks.

## GRADUATE STUDY

That furlough we moved to Hartford, Connecticut in January for graduate study. I was enrolled in the Kennedy School of Missions for their second semester.

I concentrated in linguistic studies under Dr. William Welmers, a specialist in African languages. While there I completed the necessary class room work to qualify for their PHD field degree program. When I completed the translation of the Anuak New Testament, I hoped to pursue a field degree program doing a study of "The religious vocabulary of the Anuak language as it relates to communicating the essential Christian message among animistic peoples." But, this was not to be, because during the final year of work on the Anuak New Testament, our dear friends and colleagues, Paul and Winifred Hostetter, were to become the first missionaries to be expelled from the Sudan. They had only just gotten into their linguistic work among the Murle. Paul had worked out a writing system and a set of primers, but hadn't gotten into the translation of the New Testament.

Within days of the Hostetter's leaving the Sudan, I received a letter from Bob Swart who was then on furlough. He wanted us to move to Pibor to complete the Anuak New Testament there and to begin work on the Murle as soon as this was finished. Any thoughts of earning a field degree were put aside. Translating the New Testament into Murle was of infinitely greater importance. I did not know then that seventeen years later, the Lord would give me the opportunity to earn a doctorate in the science of missions at Fuller's prestigious School of World Missions. I am reminded of the words of Jeremiah, "'I know the plans that I have for you,' says the Lord, 'plans for welfare and not for evil, to give you a future and a hope.'"

# CHAPTER TWELVE

# POCHALA

Pochala was a government, administrative post in the direction of Ethiopia. To get there, we waited for the dry season when the dirt roads were passable. There was just one road. It was ninety miles strait south from Akobo to Pibor. Another ninety miles directly East would take us to Pochala. The country in between these places was flat savannah land with tall grass, thousands of wild animals and very few trees. Only occasionally when we came near the river, were there villages. About twenty five miles from Pibor, on the way from Akobo, was a small cluster of Arab merchants' shops. Between Pibor and Pochala there were a few more trees and we passed through a number of sizeable Anuak villages, including where the main Anuak king, Adonga, lived. Low areas made the road impassable very early when the rains began.

Pochala was ninety miles East of Pibor. To reach there we went through Murle country. The Murle were quite different from Anuak and other Nilotic people.

My assignment and deepest longing was to translate the New Testament into the Anuak language. I worked at it night and day. But, I also loved to do the work of an evangelist and to preach in the villages. I always felt that this also had a side benefit of contributing to the quality of my translation effort. Off the compound, most of my preaching was in nearby native villages. Once a year we would travel greater distances from home.

We tried to get to Pochala every dry season for a week or ten days of evangelistic meetings there and in neighboring Anuak villages. Eventually, an Anuak evangelist was stationed in that area. Years later, when the civil war heated up between the North and the South, this young evangelist was murdered because of his working for Jesus Christ and the church.

We had some very good times in Pochala. I remember arriving there, traveling on an Arab merchant's truck. It was Easter Sunday morning. The only Christians in this little, mud walled, thatched roof town, were members of the police and their families who had become Christians in another province under the influence of British missionaries. They were known for their strong, Christian commitment.

We had a communion service that Easter Sunday morning in the house of one of these families. We used plain tea and a homemade, pancake like bread for elements. In that service, Jesus was as powerfully present with us as I have ever experienced him in any of our beautiful, liturgically correct services in America. We experienced in a moving way the truth he had promised when he said, " I will be with you always even to the end of the age." And again, we experienced, as we did so many times during our years in Africa, that where two or three are gathered together, there He was in the midst of us.

Once, after Mission Aviation had begun to fly us missionaries around, we flew into Pochala with our stateside guest, Dr. Louis Benes, editor of the Church Herald. It was great fun to have him there with us. We could see things as they appeared to people from the outside. It made us realized how we had changed. Things that were novel and surprising to Dr. Benes, had already become commonplace to us. A visitor helped us realize the danger of almost making too complete an adjustment to things that were different and even inconvenient.

One night we were having our service with just the light of an old fashioned wick kerosene lantern. It hung from a post helping support the grass fence around these few huts. It's a wonder we didn't burn the place down. With that dim light, we had been singing and singing Anuak hymns from our first Anuak hymn book. Bob and Morrie Swart had put that together. Finally, when we had nearly exhausted ourselves, Dr. Benes says, "Let's sing number" (and I've forgotten the number) "and then we will have sung every hymn in the book".

## REBECCA

On one of those visits to Pochala, I had a shocking surprise. Earlier in the afternoon, I had met with the family of one of the police stationed there. They had had a new baby and were wanting me to baptize the baby before I left the next day, going back on that merchant's truck. Arrangements were made for the baby to be baptized that evening. We met that night in the moonlight aided by a dimly burning flashlight.

When it came time for the baptism, I suddenly realized I had forgotten to ask for the name. So I said, "And what did you name this child?"

The father, without a moment's hesitation said, "You name her."

No question about it. I had to do it. The name that popped into my mind was, "Rebecca." On the spot, then and there, I baptized her as "Rebecca". The name took!

The following year when I returned they couldn't wait to show me "Rebecca". They said, "Come, you must see how Rebecca has grown." God's good hand was upon her!

### BAPTIZING A KING WHO HAD FOUR WIVES

Another year, three of us missionaries went together to spend a week in Pochala. We were Bob Swart from Pibor, Tal Wilson from Obel and myself. The Anuak evangelist had come in from the village to share with us in these meetings. Every day we had several services out in the open with people sitting on the ground, some trying to find whatever shade they could. This was dry season and it was hot. When we slept at night

211

the little sand flies nearly killed us. I never understood how people could live there permanently.

On our last afternoon, one of the Anuak kings who came from the same village where the evangelist had been working all year, asked us if he might be baptized. I shall never forget his words. He said, "I've been listening to all that you missionaries have been preaching all week. These are the same words I have been hearing from the Anuak evangelist whom you sent to my village. I believe all that I have heard. I want to become a person of this Jesus. I want to be baptized, but I have four wives in my village. May I be baptized?"

Bob, Tal and I looked at each other as to who would answer. There was an uncomfortable silence. Finally, because I spoke the Anuak language (Bob knew a good bit of it from his period at Akobo, but Tal was totally dependent upon an interpreter) I told him what I thought.

I said, "What you did before you heard about Jesus Christ cannot always be undone. You have four wives and children. I believe God wants you to continue to be their husband and father. You must not send them away. Rather you must show them the love that you have learned about in God's book. I, personally, think you should be baptized. The only thing is that you must make a commitment before the Lord not to marry additional wives, now that you have become a person of Jesus Christ."

We missionaries then discussed it further. Bob and Tal agreed with what I had said. In speaking up, I felt myself vulnerable. Did Bob and Tal feel as I did about this or would I be embarrassed by their contrary opinions? I recall the relief I felt when they both concurred. That evening, along with many others, this Anuak king was baptized.

We left the next day and the king and the Anuak evangelist returned to the king's village. We reported the incident, according to the rules laid down by the church when a person caught up in a plural marriage had been baptized. The Presbytery, upon hearing what we had done, sent a senior pastor, Adwok, from the Shullik church to investigate and report back.

When he returned from there, Adwok told how he had arrived at Pochala, crossed the crocodile invested river and walked many miles on the trail through the tall grass where lions were known to be hungry. He shared his fears, but he said, "When I arrived in the king's village, one of the first huts I saw, was a hut with a large cross made from poles, extending upward out of the center." He said, "I knew then that the Gospel had been preached there." Before he left, Adwok baptized 35 people, including the four wives of the king.

This never would have happened, had we not baptized that Anuak king the last night we were in Pochala. It was a right decision and we believed that God had given us the courage to make it.

## PREACHING THE GOSPEL TO POLYGAMISTS

What to do about plural marriages had been a hot item for discussion in the various missions in Africa, including the Presbyterian Mission in which we Reformed Church missionaries were serving. Our colleagues in the Anglican church further south in the Sudan had, like most missions in Africa, taken a rigid stand against baptizing men who had more than one wife. Rules varied, which sometimes allowed women to be baptized or under which men could choose which wife to keep and which wives to send away or be cared for in some other fashion. But, generally speaking, baptizing polygamists was forbidden. Our Anglican colleagues held those views, and at one stage made it rather clear to our mission that if we began baptizing people involved in plural marriages our cooperative efforts in places like Bishop Gwynne Divinity College might be jeopardized.

So our mission moved on these matters cautiously and responsibly. That is why pastor, Adwok, made his trip and reported back. His report did a lot to persuade those who had remained unconvinced that we were moving in the right direction.

Missionaries had pretty strong views on this subject. One missionary I respected highly flatly said, "If they love the Lord, they'll give up their wives." I found it hard to believe that Jesus would want these women who were mothers with children to be cast adrift like that. These children needed the strong hand of their father, which would be destroyed if a believer's polygamous family was destroyed. Then, too, the women would likely have to turn to prostitution of some sort to cope. It just didn't seem to be the kind of thing that Jesus would have done had he been there with us in the flesh. It sounded more like something the Pharisees and religious leaders with whom Jesus so frequently argued might have felt comfortable doing.

We sometimes quoted Scripture to support our different perspectives on the subject. Paul's word to the Corinthian believers was one of my favorites. "Let each of you remain in the condition in which you were called." I Corinthians 7:20. There were some situations and relationships that couldn't be untangled without doing more harm than good. We are saved by grace not by fulfilling the requirements of a law. I felt strongly on the subject and comfortable that Jesus was pleased with it.

Personally, I always pictured myself preaching the grand and glorious good news about Jesus Christ in Anuak villages where everyone would come to listen. In front of me would be the village chief, his several wives and children, village elders, many of whom had at least two wives, and others, who more because of economics than conviction, remained monogamous -- all of these and their children.

I could visualize myself urging the people to put their trust in this Jesus who had loved the world so much that he had come from heaven to earth to live among us. He had shown us what is in the heart of God. We knew that God was not far away, but that He was near because He had visited us and, while living among us in that distant land, had healed our sick, drove out the demons and even raised the dead.

I would finish my message by telling them of the perfect sacrifice, Jesus the lamb of God. The sacrifice that made it unnecessary for them to ever have to sacrifice a sheep or a goat again. And then I told them how God had accepted that sacrifice made on our behalf and had honored Jesus for what he had done by raising Him from the dead. And there was no doubt about it because he had met his friends again and shown them his hands and his side and proved that he was that same Jesus they had been with those three years. I told them how this Jesus had gone back to heaven, but before he left he had told his followers to go into every country to the most distant places and tell this good news so that people might turn away from their wrong ways and turn back to God. I told them how Jesus has given his followers power to do this and that Jesus had said they must keep on telling this good news until one day when he would again return back to earth.

Finally, I would tell them that Jesus hasn't come back yet, and his followers are still doing what he told them to do.

I felt a little ashamed when I told them it took so long to come to where my Anuak friends lived because it was a long way and a very difficult place to reach. A poor excuse! But, aside from that the climactic moment would come when I could invite all who were listening to believe and be baptized. I just could not imagine that I had to have any reservations about that at all. The Bible says so clearly that the time was coming when "whoever calls upon the name of the Lord will be saved." That moment was now.

I couldn't imagine that if the village chief stood and said, "I believe. I want to be baptized and become a person of your Jesus" that I would have to say, "O, I'm sorry. I didn't realize ... I didn't mean this for you." I could never imagine that I would have to find some inadequate substitute way to permit him to be sort of a half-way Christian because of wives he had married before he had heard this good news from God.

These are some of the thoughts that lay behind my response to the Anuak king that day in Pochala. I am totally convinced it was what God wanted me to say.

*"He who was seated on the throne said, 'I am making everything new!' Then he said, 'Write this down, for these words are trustworthy and true'."*

Revelation 21:05

# CHAPTER THIRTEEN

# PIBOR AND THE MURLE BECKON

We returned to the Sudan during the first part of 1957. We didn't know then that before our term was finished, we, like most of the other missionaries would be expelled from the Sudan on short notice. The civil war, pitting black, Southern tribes people, now either Christian or animist, against the Arab, Muslim Northerners was gaining momentum. In their efforts to forcibly Arabicize and Islamize the south, the Arab north would bring the country to disaster. When it, happened, we recalled the prophetic words of Dr. Glenn Reed, the wise missionary statesman of the United Presbyterian Church who had predicted that the time was short and that at best we might have fifteen years to work. We would be given less than fourteen!

In 1959 the Hostetters left the Sudan, the first to be expelled. The following year, Lavina and our family moved into the vacant Hostetter house in Pibor. We completed the Anuak translation there. We had scarcely finished when we began work on the Murle. Paul had done the basic spade work in the Language. We could build on his foundation. Even while Paul was still in the Sudan, he and I had collaborated on developing a writing system using Arabic symbols. Murle would be written using the Arabic script.

Way back in 1954 while we were at Pokwo, more or less academic, discussions were underway in the mission as to whether or not we might one day want to consider writing these Nilotic languages using the Arabic script. Arguments pro and con were common among us. Some thought we should actively pursue this possibility in view of the fact that one day most of the children in the schools would likely

217

be reading and writing in Arabic. Why not build on that foundation? But, could these Nilotic languages be written accurately using Arabic letters when in Arabic the consonants were accented while in the tribal languages the accent was on the vowel.

## A FUN EXPERIENCE WITH ARABIC SCRIPT

Years earlier in my free time at Pokwo, I had done a little experimenting on the side. What I did was rather crude, but it proved a point. Anuak, which was one of the Nilotic languages, could, indeed be written using Arabic letters. In my experiment, I used the Arabic consonants, and simply used numerals from the Arabic for the various vowels. I had three young Anuak men who were my Guinea pigs. Before too long I was able to write unknown words in Anuak on the blackboard, using Arabic letters. As I wrote the words on the board, they were able to call them back to me. We were having great fun.

I decided at that time to ask the mission leaders for permission to prove my point at the mission meeting in Nasir in 1954. It was agreed and I had these three men, row down stream in a wooden canoe nearly 150 miles to the Nasir station located on the Sobat river into which the Baro flowed from Gambela.

They gave me a half hour one afternoon for my presentation. The young men sat in the front row and I was at the blackboard. I would write an Anuak word on the board using the Arabic script. My young men could read virtually anything I wrote. After a half an hour, I had proved my point beyond dispute. The Anuak language, at least, could be written in Arabic script with a degree of accuracy that made reading as easy as when using the Roman alphabet.

It was a fun afternoon. I felt that a number of my colleagues had been quite favorably impressed. When the young men left, and made there way to the river to begin the tough rowing upstream toward home in Pokwo, the business meeting resumed. As we began, one of my colleagues who didn't like the idea of using the Arabic script no matter what, acknowledged, "Harvey has certainly demonstrated that these languages can be read using Arabic letters, but I remain unconvinced. The meeting will please come to order."

It was all in a missionary's day and we had a great, good time with it. Years later at Pibor, the Murle would be written using Arabic letters.

The only school for the Murle was run by the government. Because it was taught in Arabic, the Arabic script was the script the students knew. It made good sense to build on that foundation. Anyone already able to read Arabic could go on and learn to read in the vernacular written with these same Arabic symbols and a few modifications with relative ease. The argument against using Arabic letters because of Arabic's close association with the Koran, remained. At Pibor, however, there was no choice. Murle would be written in Arabic script or it would not be written at all. The decision had been made. It was for Arabic script. We purchased an Arabic typewriter, modified two or three keys, learned to type from write to left and voweled it by hand.

I made rapid progress with the Murle translation. My informant was completely bi-lingual in Murle and Anuak. We were using the Anuak translation as our basic text. Admittedly, this first translation was more of a "living Bible" type translation. It seemed possible that the entire New Testament might be completed in less than five years. Our hopes were high.

## ASSIGNED TO BISHOP GWYNNE

The mission, however, was again short of personnel. Someone had to fill in at Bishop Gwynne Divinity College where students for the ministry were being trained. The mission had wanted to assign us there on previous occasions but we had always successfully escaped their threatened "draft". The need to complete the Anuak translation always prevailed. This time, however, the Anuak New Testament was finished and being printed by the American Bible Society. Now was the perfect opportunity for the mission to send us to Bishop Gwynne. And it happened just as we had feared.

We found ourselves on the staff at Bishop Gwynne College. The Murle translation was put in "cold storage". We were told that our assignment was temporary until the need at Mundri could be met. We were not unduly unhappy. I felt it an honor to be teaching in this theological seminary. I worked night and day as I had no old lectures on which I could rely. It was a great experience and I suspect I could have been happy with a long term assignment if the need for the Murle translation didn't exist.

## RETURN TO PIBOR - MISSIONARY EXPULSIONS

My career as a professor in a theological seminary was to be short-lived. At Mundri we always had an early morning chapel hour, after which Lavina and I had our breakfast. This particular morning in December of 1961, I had no sooner opened the back door, when Lavina shushed me with upraised hand, saying excitedly, "Quiet, quiet! The Swarts and the Sikkemas have been expelled from the Sudan."

She had her head close to the shortwave Zenith radio on which we could pick up the mission broadcasts. We couldn't talk, but we could listen in and keep in touch.

We were shocked and dismayed. The ax had fallen. We had known this could happen at any time, but when the moment came we could hardly believe it.

Within the week, the mission asked us to return to Pibor to take up where Bob and Morrie would leave off. Just before we left Mundri, our dear friend, Bishop Oliver Allison, bishop of the Sudan who was visiting Bishop Gwynne at the time, stood between Lavina and me, and putting his long arms around us, lovingly committed us to the Lord for whatever He had for us in His tomorrow. We headed for Pibor.

Bob and Morrie had already disposed of most of their things among the Arab merchants across the river. Bob and I spent as much time as possible together so that I could learn from him all I could. We wanted to have good continuity with anything he had going at Pibor. We were overwhelmed with the responsibilities that would soon fall on our shoulders. The Swarts and the Sikkemas had been given 30 days to leave. Their time was nearly up.

## SEVEN DAYS TO LEAVE THE SUDAN

Bob and Morrie still had one more day with us at Pibor when the entire picture changed. The MAF plane had flown into Pibor this particular morning. At noon I was on the radio talking to Malakal. Milton Thompson was on the radio for the mission. He inquired," Did you get my letter which I sent to you on the plane?"

I responded that I hadn't opened the mail yet and wasn't sure whether his letter had come or not.

With that, Milton said, "Well, then I better give you the bad news now. You have just seven days to pack your bags."

I could scarcely believe my ears. We, too, were being expelled from the Sudan. As soon as we had returned to Pibor, the government officials realized that we had been missed because of our being at Mundri in another province. In no time, they corrected their oversight!

The words were hardly out of Milton's mouth, when I came back with, "Milt, there's no market for used furniture here at Pibor. Bob has flooded the market."

I will never understand why I said that. I suspect it was an effort to ease the searing pain with a light hearted, attempted joke. Putting all jokes aside, we knew that our ministry in the Sudan was finished. Night had fallen! We wanted to cry, but there was no time.

Even before we ate, Lavina and I started moving boxes out of the attic. Sorting and packing had begun. We had our meal in near silence. What did the Lord have in mind? What did the future hold? It would be months before some of the answers were in. During those months, we would learn what it is to lean on the Lord in a new way and to "wait" and then "wait" again with patience!

During those few remaining, rushing days at Pibor there was one agonizing question that kept surfacing over and over in our conversations. It lay heavily upon our hearts. The Anuak New Testaments! How would we ever get them into the hands of the Anuak people? We knew that the American Bible Society had printed them and that they were supposed to have been shipped. But, we knew nothing as to their actual whereabouts. Where were they? How would they ever reach he Anuak people? With all the missionaries leaving how could it happen? This was the constant, recurring cry of our hearts to the Lord. Our hearts were burdened and heavy!

Milton Thompson and Robb McLaughlin came down to help us sort out our things, get rid of what we could and start closing down the station. We carried out with us what two small MAF planes could carry. Milton and Robb packed up what would fit in an outboard and aluminum canoe to go out by steamer. A paddle wheel steamer was coming from Malakal but it could get only as far as the village of Likwangili about 25 miles north of Pibor.

John Ducker, an MAF pilot, and Milton Thompson made the run with the two boats from Pibor to meet the steamer coming in from Malakal. The river was falling fast. This would be the last steamer before the dry season.

But, alas, on the trip down stream to where the steamer was expected, the canoe got in the wake of the outboard and capsized in about five feet of water. The men fished the things out of the river, but by the time they arrived in Likwangali, the steamer had already come and gone. The only thing they could do was park our things on the river bank near one of the Arab merchant's shops. There they cooked and steamed in the hot sun until the roads became passable and a merchant's truck collected them to deliver them to the single ladies who were still working at Akobo.

It was three months later before our water soaked goods arrived in Akobo. The dear ladies did all they could, but the damage was done. They dried out and aired out what they could and repacked the whole lot for eventual transporting to Ethiopia. In October that same year they arrived in Addis Ababa where Lavina and I were now living and studying Amharic in preparation, hopefully, for use in Ethiopia if we could get a resident visa.

Sometimes, with a bit of humor, we reminded ourselves that the Lord was teaching us to "travel light". It was only ten years earlier that we had lost everything when our house burned at Akobo. This time, we left most everything behind at Pibor. In less than fifteen years, we would again leave everything behind in Ethiopia. We were reminded that our citizenship is in heaven and that here we have no abiding city.

## A LAST MINUTE BAPTISM AT PIBOR

The last morning was hectic. Last minute packing! People from the Arab shops across the river coming out of curiosity to see what was happening. A few wanting to buy small items thought useful to them. Friends among the Murle and Anuak just wanting to be near us for a little while yet before we would be gone forever.

Lavina's letter to our home church in Silver Creek, Minnesota, dated January 5, 1962 beautifully describes the impromptu, unforgettable, baptismal service that took place during our last hours at Pibor:

*"It was with tears in our eyes and aching hearts that we left our home, our work and the people whom we had learned to love. As the little MAF plane flew us over the mission compound, it was hard to realize that we would never again return. It makes me sad to think of it. I guess I am like many other people that look so long at the door that is closed behind them, they fail to see the door the Lord is opening before them. ...*

*The morning we left Pibor, I had to get away from the business and relax a bit. So I walked out to the village to say good-bye to some of my friends. I stopped to see Bur, Ocan's wife. She had come to Pibor this spring knowing nothing of the Lord and with a mother who is very much opposed to her son-in-law's new religion. Ocan, her husband, is a very dear Christian man. He is an Anuak and a tuberculosis patient at the hospital. Under Ocan's teaching Bur came to love the Lord.*

*While we were at Mundri, she stood up in church and said she believed in Jesus and wanted to be baptized. At that time Bob Swart told her that when Harvey returned to Pibor she would be baptized.*

*"I could see she was sad about something. When I asked what was making her sad, this is what she told me: 'When you were away at Mundri, I told the people I believed in Jesus. Bomb (Bob) told me that when Odola (Harvey's African name) returned I would be baptized.' She went on, 'Now you have come back, but today you are leaving and you will never return and I am not baptized.'*

*I went home and told Harvey. When he heard this, he said, ' We'll stop everything and have a service right now.'*

*So we beat the church drum, called the people together and had a most wonderful time of fellowship with the people that last morning. It was well worth the time it took. How I wish you could have seen Bur's face when she left the church following her baptism. It was radiant -- so different from when I*

*saw her an hour earlier. It was a great joy to all of us. It is ex-
periences like this that make it well worth the investment of our
lives in a land like Africa. I praise God for the privilege that has
been ours to serve in the Sudan these fourteen years."*

In this same letter, Lavina tells of the sadness felt at
Pibor by the Murle that their New Testament hadn't been com-
pleted before we had to leave. She tells of Ocan's joy that the
Anuak New Testament was finished and then she says:

*"As he praised God for this, a cloud came over his face
and he said, ' If only the Murle had it too.' "*

Lavina's letter continued:

*"Yes, that has been our dream and prayer to give the
Murle people the New Testament also. ... Konyi, a Murle elder,
pleaded with Harvey to go somewhere, 'anywhere,' he said,
'and translate the Bible for us too.' ..."*

Lavina's letter tells us of those precious, last hallowed
moments at Pibor. The service of which she writes had barely
finished when it was time to go across the river and fly out.

## GOD'S PERFECT TIMING

It was mid-day, January 10, 1962. The two
small MAF planes had just landed at Pibor. A number of our
Anuak and Murle friends were there with us at the door of the
plane when it opened.. The pilot handed me a small package.
He said, "You'll probably want to open this before you leave."

When I opened that package, inside it were the first five
printed, beautifully bound copies of the Anuak New Testament.
We handed them out to the Anuaks who were there and could
read. We will never forget the words of one of the men as he
said, "Our hearts (livers) are heavy as you go away, but you are
leaving behind God's best gift. You have given us His Word in
our language."

There were an additional thousand copies in Khartoum,
printed and shipped out by the American Bible Society.

MAF had flown in to fetch us. We took with us what we could. We had an hour and a half from when we took off until we would make our first stop in Malakal.

Alone with our thoughts, one side of the heart was heavy, and the other was light with God's joy and peace. I thought of the verse from Isaiah, "Thou wilt keep him in perfect peace, whose mind is stayed on thee." This was God's promise and our challenge to trust Him for His tomorrow. We had long since learned that God keeps His promises.

We were over Malakal now and would soon be landing. Our hearts were still in Pibor with the Murle and the Anuak savoring those last moments at the door of the plane. Over and over their words kept coming back: " You are leaving behind God's best gift. You have given us His Word in our language." To God be all glory, honor and praise forever and ever!

**"The Lord delights in those who fear him, who put their hope in his unfailing love."**
Psalm 147:11

# CHAPTER FOURTEEN

# "WANDERING IN THE WILDERNESS"

It was January, 1963. The door for us to continue working in the Sudan had slammed shut. Harvey and Lavina were marking time in Alexandria, Egypt at Schutz, the school for missionary children. Our children, Jim, Dave, Carol and Mark were students there.

Dr. Glenn Reed, the United Presbyterians' Regional Secretary for Africa flew in from Asmara in Eritrea to meet with the Sudan expellees. Our numbers were increasing. Those with children at Schutz gravitated to Egypt. The number of missionaries still in the Sudan was dwindling rapidly. Some were given a month's notice, others were given a week to get out while several were told to pack their bags and be out in twenty four hours. We had been given a week.

It was agreed that we and several other families should apply for visas to work in the mission in Ethiopia. Harvey and Lavina should plan to locate on the Gila river where the McClures were. We should continue our Murle translation, having the people I had been working with at Pibor cross over from the Sudan into Ethiopia on foot and work with us there. Pibor was probably a little over a hundred miles away using their trails. Walking this distance was not that difficult for people who had been walking wherever they went since birth. Such were our plans!

But, it was not to be! The coveted visa permitting us to live in Ethiopia and continue the Murle translation at the Gila River was denied by the government. We, along with the Adairs, who had worked on the Shullik translation in

the Sudan were denied visas into Ethiopia. We had been clas-
sified as linguists, which at that time was anathema to the
Ethiopian government which was opposed to work being done
on vernacular languages. It would take another eighteen
months before we would be granted a resident visa. This
would be our "wilderness wandering" before entering the promised land of Ethiopia. The task the Lord would entrust to us
would be difficult and sometimes dangerous. God knew what
lessons we must first learn before we would be "fit and meet
for the Master's service". Eighteen eventful but trying months
went by, months of anxious waiting and uncertainty about the
final outcome, before the coveted visa was granted.

The months ahead were especially difficult for our children. The emotional strain of moving from pillar to post created a lot of inner turmoil for them at that impressionable age.
They were frequently separated from each other and from us
as they stayed in different places, occasionally even in different
countries, with various missionary families. Even when we
were all together, they must have sensed the strain on their
mom and dad as we displayed the concerns about our uncertain future.

Letters written during those months tell the story of
Don McClure's tireless efforts and unending optimism that in
the end he would secure our visa. No matter where we were,
every ten days or two weeks he sent us a short letter or telegram encouraging us "to hang in there" and not to give up
hope. Sometimes we were buoyed up and at other times we
were prone to doubt. But praise be to God for His mercies. It
was He who sustained us and kept us from giving in to despair. A verse from the Psalms was in our hearts and frequently on our lips:

"Commit thy way unto the Lord, trust also in Him and
He will bring it to pass." *

## WAITING IN EGYPT

Our children in school in Alexandria at Schutz were
glad to have us close by on campus in one of the dorm rooms.
When it became apparent we would be in Egypt longer than
first anticipated, we moved into a third floor, vacant flat in the
mission building in the city itself. It was a dramatic contrast to

the rural setting along the Pibor river from which we had been so hastily uprooted.

That same month Bob Swart and I flew to Addis Ababa to survey future possibilities there. Lavina and Morrie remained behind in Egypt. A letter to my folks written while in Addis, dated January, 1963 describes our gloomy disposition those early days of adjustment:

*"Both Lavina and I are in need of rest. The last month has been very exhausting -- both physically and emotionally. I imagine that is why she's had pneumonia twice and I this flu a second time. Egypt seems so cold to us. The buildings are as cold as tombs!! High ceilings and thick walls and just a small kerosene burner for evenings. What a horrible place to live! I hope we don't have to live like this too many weeks.*

*Lavina, Carol, Mark and Paul were left together in the mission apartment in Alex. It's right down town and noisy as Fifth Ave -- cars, donkeys, horses and merchants calling out their wares. What a place! We're up on the third floor of this big old building. Out of doors the weather is nice in Alex, but inside the buildings are* cold cold, cold *-- that is for a warm blooded Sudanese."*

In that same letter, I shared my feeling about recent events in the Sudan. It's obvious that our spirits were disheartened.

*"It's all very sad as we look back toward the Sudan. Seventeen from our Mission had to leave between December 5th and January 30th. There are only four families and five single ladies left.*

*Pibor station is closed -- 50,000 Murle and hardly a beginning among them. And then, there's our home and all our things gone. The only things we own again are in our suitcases.*

*Leaving as we did reminded us of how it must be to flee before an invading army. The Mission, itself, will lose all its buildings and hundreds of pounds worth of equipment. Our pump, irrigating pipes and all -- left behind. My Jeep was sold and my boat and motors.*

*The one bright spot in it all was that the very day we received our notice, the printed Anuak New Testament arrived.*

229

## CHAPTER FOURTEEN

*Later I saw boxes with over 850 copies in the Bible House in Khartoum. How we praise God for this. ... This is 1963. We look to Him for grace and strength for a new year. How uncertain it is and yet under the heavy heart is His peace which the world does not know. Love, Harvey"*

### WAITING IN KENYA AND UGANDA

The four missionary families from the Sudan with newly granted resident visas from Ethiopia all left Alexandria for Addis Ababa. Bill and Martha Adair and we were left behind in Egypt. Eventually, our visa extensions ran out and we too had to leave. The Adair's decided to return to the USA and we went on to Kenya. It was already six months since we had left the Sudan. During those months in Egypt, I worked on the Murle translation materials getting them ready for the British and Foreign Bible Society. Eventually they were completed in both the Arabic and Roman Scripts and published in one book by the Bible Society in England.

The Ethiopian Mission continued seeking visas for us. In fact, they were hopeful enough to receive them that they suggested we plan to disembark in Addis should they have good news for us by the time we were to pass through there. Sadly, when we landed the word was, "Keep on moving. Nothing yet." We continued our journey to Nairobi.

Missionaries in Kenya decided to house us at Limuru, an Ecumenical conference center next to St Paul's Theological Seminary, about twenty miles from Nairobi. It was a beautiful setting but very cold because of its altitude and cold to us because of our being acclimated to warmer temperatures.

Those were days of uncertainty and frustration. Patience and still more patience was needed. Letters to my folks in the states vividly describe the nightmare of disappointment and frustration experienced during our "wilderness wanderings". Almost every letter written makes some reference to uncertainties over the mission's efforts in Ethiopia to secure our resident visa.

From a letter dated    June 15, 1963:

*"On Monday we return to Nairobi and will search for a*

230

*more permanent house. A cable from Don McClure today said, 'Visas delayed two weeks. Suggest attend conference (in Cameroons). Sorry, McClure.'*

*So it's another disappointment. I wired him back, 'Send Jimmy whenever seems advisable.' We understand Jimmy has been at Pokwo and has gone to the Gila where we'll be living. If he's not too lonely, they will likely keep him, but they are free to send him if necessary. This year is really a set-back for us, but the Lord knows our needs and He's able to provide.*

*Once housing is arranged, I'll be attending the Bible Translator's Conference in the Cameroons from June 19th through July 12th. Everything is so uncertain that it is difficult to plan. Lavina wants me to go, but I don't really like to leave the family for so long a period unless they are well situated. ... We begin to wonder if we'll ever get visas to Ethiopia. One of the missionaries here has suggested I help them in their new seminary teaching if we are delayed or denied. Sounds very interesting too. We know the Lord has a place and will open the door at the right time."*

Two weeks later Lavina, Carol, Mark, baby Paul, and I took an overnight bus to Uganda. What a trip! It often seemed that this overloaded vehicle was careening out of control, speeding down steep hills with sharp curves making it even more frightening. It was a relief, mid-day, to arrive at the campus of the Anglican Theological Seminary located in Mukono about 25 miles from Kampala. It was a special joy to meet our dear friend and colleague from the Sudan mission, Dorothy (Dottie) Rankin. We would be staying with her for several months on this lovely campus.

How and when we might receive the coveted resident visa for Ethiopia was never out of our minds. Here is part of a letter to the folks dated, July 31, 1963:

*"At this point, we are not at all sure about the future. It wouldn't be at all surprising if the visa was finally rejected. I wrote Dr. McClure that we are prepared to wait it out until a final decision is reached there (Addis Ababa) on it. At the same time, the American Bible Society representative in Nigeria, had a conference while I was in West Africa and he told me there were five or six languages in which an analysis and translation were waiting for someone. He said that if our church continued our*

support he could guarantee us work in Nigeria.

At this same conference, this Christian Reformed Missionary from Nigeria (Margaret Dykstra) who had written us while we were still in Egypt talked to me on several occasions. They are most eager for us to come and have a house waiting in Lupwe, the town where Miss Johanah Veenstra had pioneered. But, we feel at this point the Lord would have us wait and not close the door ourselves.  We are willing for either field.  Often we are tempted to tell the folks in Addis to forget about it, but I'm sure this would not be right at this time."

In a letter home dated August 31, 1963, Lavina writes of the uncertainty surrounding the visa application efforts Don McClure was making in Addis:

"A new visa application is being made for us on the basis of our opening work in a new tribe in Southwest Ethiopia, as the Swarts are doing.  If a favorable response is given, we'll be studying Amharic for a year before getting started."

Lavina and the children stayed behind here while I soon flew to the Cameroon to attend a month long Bible Translators' Workshop sponsored by the American Bible Society.   I had ambivalent feelings about leaving the family for such an extended period, but Lavina was urging me to take advantage of this opportunity.  She was sure that living with  Dottie they would be getting along just fine without me and that I needn't worry.  Great gal!  What a missionary partner and colleague God gave me to be my sweetheart, mother of our children and best friend!

The uncertainties, the added responsibilities Lavina had for the children during the times I had to be away, proved her mettle! She had great courage and a steady faith in God.  But, the uncertainty over the visa application and our future were realities with which we both had to learn to live.  On reflection, to give up, throw in the towel, return to America and no longer be a missionary in Africa was never an option seriously entertained.  This was God's grace and power to overcome our human weakness.  Even so, the letters clearly indicate our disappointment over the long delay and the uncertainties surrounding our visa applications.

## DON MCCLURE'S TIRELESS EFFORTS

We can never adequately express our appreciation for Don McClure's optimism and tireless effort on our behalf. God only knows the hours he spent in various government offices marshalling every conceivable argument to produce a favorable response. His letters to us told of his frustrations. Application forms would be lost in government offices. At the critical moment, the official having authority to act would be called away. Another week would pass. This time, the phone would ring with still another delay. Weeks dragged on into months, but always Don"s letters inspired us to "hang in there". What a man He was!

Here are excerpts from Lavina's letter to the folks, dated July 14, 1963:

*"Harvey returns on the 18th (from the Cameroons). Away for just a month. I wonder where our next home will be. Oh, how I wish it could be the Gila river. I am so very eager to have a place that we can call 'our home'.*

*A letter from Don dated June 19 explained why we had to wait another 2 weeks. When he went to the Minister of the Imperial Court to get the letter of approval he promised, he refused to give it. He said that Ethiopia didn't need linguists and he wouldn't approve. This was the third time we were refused a visa. After much talking and Don's telling him that Harvey and Bill also did many other mission jobs, he said Don could write him another letter and give us a new classification. He would then try to help. I am afraid I was ready to give us this time and I felt we should look for another field.*

*Then, yesterday, I received another letter from Don dated July 7. He said he received a letter of approval and permission for us to enter Ethiopia from the Minister of the Pen and Imperial Court. However, the letter was sent to the minister of Foreign Affairs instead of to the Minister of Education. So, more red tape. Don has to get this letter to its proper ministry and through proper channels before he can get the visa. He had hoped to get the visa this week, but I have received no telegrams so apparently he was unsuccessful again. He said there is <u>no</u>*

*doubt* that permission has been granted. *We have been promised these visas several times and always disappointed when they are refused. I am afraid I won't believe it until I put my feet on Ethiopian soil!"*

## IN ADDIS ABABA ON A TOURIST VISA

At the end of that summer, it was decided that the Hoekstras should come to Addis Ababa on a two month tourist visa. This could be extended a number of times giving us up to eight months before having to leave the country. During that time, we could pursue our Amharic language study and I could also finish up the Murle manuscripts on which I had been working in Egypt.

Those decisions were made and we found ourselves living in Addis Ababa. We started out living in with Ted and Dolly Pollock, friends and colleagues from the Sudan. After a few weeks of house searching, we located two nice new houses nearing completion. The Mission arranged for our dear friends and colleagues from Pibor, Bob and Morrie Swart, to live in the one and we would occupy the other. It was like a dream come true. It was almost like old times at Pibor when we lived within shouting distance of each other. The uncertainty about the permanent visa remained unresolved, but our hopes were high and we felt that the end was in sight.

Our children attended the Good Shepherd school and we were again together as a family. The Swart children and ours had great times together. Morrie and Lavina enjoyed each other's fellowship. The happier mood is reflected in one of Lavina's letters (no date on it), when she writes:

*"We are happily settled in our new home. It seems quite natural to be living next door to the Swarts. We had open house for the mission folks last week. We had it on our regular prayer meeting night. First prayer meeting at our house. Harvey gave such a good meditation. Then the folks could make a tour of our house after which we went to the Swarts and they toured their house. Morrie and I served refreshments. We each made 2 dozen sandwiches and a cake and had coffee and tea. Almost everyone came as well as several folks who were in from the outstations. There were about thirty five folks present. They all*

*enjoyed it so very much and we thought we had our houses looking nice!*

*Morrie and I enjoyed it too. It reminded us of old times when we used to have parties together. But, one day our ways will separate!"* (Eventually the Swarts would go to the far south in Ethiopia and we would be going somewhere else)

This same letter gives us an idea of the work involved for Lavina to get her new house in shape. She writes:

"I had to sew all my drapes by hand--nine pairs and it was a big job. I am glad that this is finished! Morrie bought a new Singer sewing machine, but we don't want to get one until we know we are going to stay. We need a little more living room furniture too but it will wait awhile. We bought two used chairs and basic furniture (the mission) bought two for us. I would like a sofa sometime as its nice to have when you sit and read stories to the children at night. I have a small apartment size gas stove -- a new one and it is really nice...."

## AMHARIC LANGUAGE STUDY

I was five weeks late in starting Amharic language study. We missionaries rode together in the mission van to where the classes were held on the Norwegian mission's compound. The entire course was divided into six steps. Milton Fisher had worked this out and it was a great help. I enjoyed language study and managed to catch up with the rest. People were amused to see how I had rigged up my little tape recorder so that it could play a two minute, continuous loop of basic frames and phrases. I had a series of spools attached to the metal posts on which the shelves for my books were attached. The recorder was powered by a six volt car battery. I was a great believer in passive learning and repetition. The machine was playing when I did other things, including our afternoon siesta time. The basic grammatical patterns were grooved into my sub consciousness so that I am still able to recall numerous Amharic expressions correctly. My approach to learning to speak a new language was to concentrate on basic frames in which one substitutes selected parts, changing one component at a time. The essential grammatical patterns can all be memorized and mastered using this method. One's vocabulary is, of course, limited, but with time the vocabulary will increase. The important thing is that whatever one says, is said grammatically correct. Learning to speak grammatically correct is a great challenge, but, with discipline, it can be successfully mastered.

## CONSIDERING ASSIGNMENT TO NIGERIA

By this time it was already early April, 1964. Our visa extensions were fast running out. Important decisions would have to be made. At this stage it seemed possible that, in spite of all of the effort by our good friend, Don McClure, and in spite of our going ahead in good faith meeting the Amharic language study requirements, we would have to give up on serving in Ethiopia.

The Bible Society in Nigeria in cooperation with the Christian Reformed Board of World Missions had requested that we come to work on one of the languages in which they wanted me to do an analysis and begin a translation of the New Testament. Our own board, the Reformed Church's Board of World Missions, agreed to our moving to Nigeria to undertake this assignment.

Dr. John Buteyn, the RCA's Regional Secretary to whom we were accountable, was to be in the Middle East during that period of time. John suggested he arrange a stop in Cairo and that I fly via Egypt on my way to Nigeria to discuss administrative details.

## ROYAL FAMILY'S INTEREST IN THE MAJANG

On the Saturday before I was to fly to Cairo on Monday morning, I met, by chance, Don McClure on the mission compound in Addis. He had astonishing news to share with me about a meeting he had just come from with Herb Schaeffer, General Secretary of the Lutheran Mission. This is what Don shared with me. He said that Herb had just come from an appointment at the palace with her royal highness the crown princess. She had spoken with him about her desire to have the Lutheran Mission open up work among the Majang people living in the rain forest of S. W. Ethiopia. The royal family claimed a large tract of land in the area where the Majang lived. Her highness was eager for that area to be developed with a school and clinic for the people. She had asked Herb Schaeffer if their mission could undertake this new venture.

Herb said that they were not in a position to do this because that territory was an area where the Presbyterians had their work. He then explained that he had indicated to the crown princess that he knew the Presbyterians had people available, but that they were experiencing difficulty getting visas for them. At that point, the crown princess had indicated to him that if the Presbyterians were willing she would be able to do something about that problem and facilitate the granting of the visa. She requested that Herb Schaeffer convey this information to the head of the Presbyterian Mission and that she would like to make an appointment with that person to discuss these matters.

I could scarcely believe my ears. This was news too good to be true. The only problem was that it probably had come too late. My tickets had been bought. I was due to leave for Cairo on Monday and then fly on to Nigeria later in the week.

Don said, " I plan to follow this up and meet with her highness, but, unfortunately, I'm unable to do so this week. We have guests coming from overseas and I have to take them to the Gila River to see the mission work there."

I was torn inside. We had waited so long for this coveted visa. Now it seemed more possible that we would eventually get it than ever before. What to do? My tickets were in hand. Reservations had been made. I was to meet with John Buteyn in Cairo in a matter of days.

Sunday afternoon, the next day, following the afternoon worship service, Don came up to me and said, "I won't be going down to the Gila River after all. A truck carrying a consignment of benzine for the mission exploded on its way to Gore. I have to remain in Addis to take care of the insurance claims."

Quick as a flash, I responded, "Then you'll be able to get in to see the crown princess."

Don's reply was, "I intend to."

I followed up on this by saying, "Don, that's great, but I have to leave for Nigeria in the morning." I explained that I had the meeting scheduled with John Buteyn in Cairo. "But," I said, "You can always send me a telegram. I can turn around and come back." He promised he'd send me a telegram reporting on his meeting with the crown princess.

## PROMISED VISA TURNS EVERYTHING AROUND

On Monday I left for Cairo and Don had his meeting with the crown princess. She assured Don that she would see to it that we were issued a visa if we were prepared to open a station among the Majang people.

On Tuesday while in the middle of my meeting with John Buteyn, the coveted telegram from Don McClure arrived. A messenger boy wearing his red Fez hat came into the room ringing his little bell and calling for a "Mr. Hoek-e-straw". The telegram from Don had come. It read, "Visa definitely promised soon." I will never forget the exhilaration of that moment. John and I ended our meeting rather abruptly and both of us felt further conversation about Nigeria at this point was not that important!

Late in the afternoon I took the train to Alexandria to visit our children at the American School. By previous arrangement my good friend Bob Swart sent me his own telegram confirming that this time it did indeed look like a sure thing. Bob knew how frequently Don had encouraged us with his optimistic expectations. Bob had agreed to do me the favor of evaluating this last possibility and to let me know. With Bob's telegram confirming Don's earlier message, I cabled the Bible Society in Nigeria that my trip to Nigeria was delayed for at least a month and that a letter would follow.

## VISA DELAYED AND FINALLY GRANTED

Once back home in Addis, it soon became apparent that the promised visa would not be processed in time to avoid our having to leave the country. This time, we settled in Nairobi, living with borrowed pots and pans from MAF folk in what was hoped would be temporary quarters.

Letters home again indicate how our anticipation, disappointment and frustration over the delay in receiving the visa dominated our spirits.

A letter dated June 16, 1964:

*"I long for the time when we will be restored to an active ministry in our own community and home. Sometimes we feel that we just cannot wait any longer, but again the Lord seems to want us to hold on. It is a real time of testing for us. Sometimes I am tempted to return to a pastorate in America, but we have no clear indication from the Lord that this would be right.*

*STOP PRESS JUST RECEIVED IMPORTANT LETTER FROM MCCLURE: 'Patience has had its reward...your letter has been promised from Min. of Education today...Praise Him. Getting it from Education is better than from Ministry of Imperial Court for it is now through regular channels. The also should follow in a couple days and I will cable it to you. It is a long, long story and both His Highness, the Crown Prince and Her Highness the Princess have been involved. Much love to you all. Don. Carol will remain here'."*

Again, days passed with no visa news from Addis Ababa. Our children were home from school for the summer and we had some great times, but the frustration and uncertainty about this promised visa dampened our spirits. Everything we planned or did was conditioned by whether or not and when we would receive the visa. Time dragged because I hadn't brought any work along, anticipating the visas momentarily.

Finally, on July 1, 1964, the unspeakably good news arrived in a telegram from Don in Addis. We were told to go to the Ethiopian Embassy in Nairobi and pick up our resident visa. Our joy and praise and thanks to God were boundless. How we praised Him for not letting us give up. How we praised Him for His grace and strength and for the way He had used His servant, Don McClure. Winding down in Nairobi, returning the borrowed pots and pans, was carried out with alacrity. We were on our way to Addis Ababa on the first available flight! Our hearts sang as we praised God over and over again. We were eager for the next challenging adventure of opening a work among the Majang, a hidden people in the rain forest of Southwest Ethiopia.

This wonderful news was conveyed to family and

friends in America in a letter dated July 1, 1964:

*"We have GOOD NEWS! This morning we received a cable from Addis Ababa telling us our visa has been granted and we are to proceed to Addis. We have reservations on Saturday's plane.*

*You can scarcely imagine how overjoyed we all are. Eighteen months of uncertainty and waiting have passed. Often we have been tempted to give up, but somehow God has sustained and prevented us. Our deepest longing is that we may prove worthy of the tremendous effort that has been made to get us into Ethiopia.*

*We are to work with a new tribe, the Majang people. I have seen some of them before in Gambela where they go to sell their honey. These folks are very primitive people. The women still wear leaves. The area itself should be very beautiful country of hills, streams, mountains and fertile coffee land. The land itself belongs to the Crown Princess, His majesty's daughter-in-law. ... imagine working for the Princess! ... It will be a tremendous challenge to be responsible for carrying the Gospel to an entirely unreached tribe. I am sure there will be many discouragements, and I have often felt that God is toughening us up now so that when the times are difficult ahead we will be less inclined to complain or murmur."*

God's providence is indeed marvelous to contemplate. In 1960 while we were still at Akobo, we received in the mail from Don McClure, then living at the Gila River and working among the Anuak people, a letter "out of the blue". In it he was saying that if we ever had any occasion to leave the Sudan, he wished we would consider coming over into Ethiopia to work among the Majang people. He said we could live in Gambela learn the language there from the Majang who occasionally came from their rain forest dwellings into the town to trade. Once we had learned the language, he said we could move into the forest to live among them. At that time, we had no intention of ever leaving the Sudan. On reflection, it almost appears that Don had some sort of premonition that pointed to our ultimate destiny with the Majang people!

# CHAPTER FIFTEEN
# GETTING READY FOR THE RAIN FOREST

An enormous burden was lifted when our resident visa was finally in hand. Boundless energy was released. All thoughts and prayers now centered on plans and preparations to facilitate our moving into the forest to live among the Majang. It would be no easy task.

Prior to moving into the forest, we knew relatively little about the Majang people. Other members of the mission who had lived in Ethiopia for some time knew the general area where the Majang lived, but knew little about their customs and attitude toward foreigners. We later learned that the Majang had a reputation for savagery with numerous killings among themselves. During our early years among them, a retired missionary, who had lived north of where the Majang lived, wrote from the states making this comment, "You are living among the people we all feared when we were in Ethiopia."

The more we learned and heard the more we realized how essential additional information was if we were to successfully open this new work. The Majang lived in the rain forest some 350 miles southwest of Addis Ababa. Using a DC3 plane, Ethiopian airlines landed on grass strips in that part of the country. Teppi was the closest airstrip some 225 miles from Addis Ababa, and about 125 miles from Jimma. The Majang were scattered over an area of 50 to 100 miles beyond Teppi. The most important chief and ritual expert was located on the Godare River approximately 50 miles west of Teppi. The mule track widened to accommodate a jeep or Landrover went in the direction of Godare as far as Metti, ten miles from the airstrip. After that, the trail was

narrow, overhung with vines and branches and there were forbidding hills, rivers and streams. But, of this we knew almost
nothing before we did our aerial and ground surveys.

Once back in Addis Ababa following our short summer
in Nairobi, our energy focused on what had to happen before
we could set out into the forest.

The mission required that I first complete my Amharic
language study. I had gotten a 98 in grammar at the end of
step four, but it was a six-step course and I had two more to
complete. Being out of synch with the formal language learning program, I plunged into study at home with a private language informant. We worked six hours a day and then spent
time practicing on the street and in the marketplace. I, mercifully, fulfilled the requirements and they kindly bent the rule
for Lavina. The mission waived the requirement, recognizing
that she was a full time mother and had overwhelming responsibilities getting ready to survive in the forest. Imagine having
to plan for months in advance as to food, dishes, pots and
pans, bedding, clothing and medicines and whatever else we
would need to survive. How fortunate I was to have married a
partner who knows how to cope and plan efficiently.

The mission was normally very rigid in its position that
every missionary working in Ethiopia meet the Amharic language proficiency standards they had set. Fortunately for us
they had to be somewhat flexible because the Royal family on
whose land we'd be establishing our station, and who had in-
tervened to secure our visa was demanding that work begin
within six months or they would turn to another mission to
begin the project.

We'd made it our goal to move into the forest the first
week in December. So, while working on my Amharic, we also
needed to purchase essential supplies of food and gear to survive in a remote area. We also had to make an aerial survey to
learn what we could about where the Majang lived. Unable to
learn all that was needed from the air, we also had to fit in a
ground survey to learn more and to select the actual site where
our new mission work would be established. There were no
roads into that area so we had to locate where an airstrip land
could be built on which MAF could land. In a tropical rain forest, this would prove to be an enormous undertaking.

## LEARNING MORE THROUGH SURVEYS

So, how did it all come together? Let's first read from some of the letters written to our families to see how things appeared to us prior to our actually beginning at the Godare River. Reading these letters makes it apparent that what we anticipated and what we later learned and experienced were quite different.

From a letter dated   August 9, 1964:

*"On Thursday of this week I am going to go by the Ethiopian Airlines plane to one of our stations in that area. After spending the night, two other men and I will be flying with the mission plane to look over the area where we will be located. I hope to be back in Addis by about next week Monday or Tuesday. I am rather thinking now that early in October I will go down alone with one of the Ethiopians and spend a week or two in the area to see what it is like. Then later, after we have had our Association meeting (meeting of the entire mission) late in October, we will be able to have a more extended ground survey to see how the country lies, and where the people really are.*

*Friday I had a short conference with the Governor General of the Province in which we will be working. He promised to write letters of introduction to the local officials. He seems to be very cooperative and appreciative of the fact that we are going to open a new station among the Majang people. One of the problems here in Ethiopia is that often it is possible to get permission to do work from the officials here in Addis Ababa, but the local officials can do so many different things to obstruct the work. They, frequently, make things difficult and act as if there is no central government. We have been more fortunate because we have the favor of the Crown Princess and we think that she will be able to help us get things underway without too many problems. The date set for our conference with her is Tuesday at 11:00. I am looking forward very much to meeting her.*

*When I meet with her Imperial Highness, I'm going to ask her if she has a small mud building in which Lavina and I can live for a few weeks when we first begin to work. This will put us within 25 or 30 miles of where we hope to locate our station., I could then go in on foot or mule for a week or two and come*

243

*back home again after that.*

*"You were asking if we will have other families with us. The answer is 'no'. The new stations are to be one-family only. We are hoping during the first few months to have a builder help us get started but the present situation is that there is only one mission builder on the field and he is all booked up to work in two other stations for at least another 14 to 16 months. We have written to our board to ask them if they would send out a builder for about six months. We have not yet heard from them. ... If we do not get a builder, we will be living in a tent longer than we had originally anticipated. I am sure that it will take some weeks to cut down the necessary trees so that we can have a landing strip. And until there is a landing strip it will not be possible for us to live there."*

## SUPPLIES AND EQUIPMENT

Supplies unavailable in Addis Ababa, had to be ordered from the states. My family was a great help to us in packing and shipping these to us through our New York office.

From a letter dated August 8, 1964:

*"Lavina has two other requests: 1) She wants a Foley food mill 2) A small feed grinder to grind grain for our porridge. We couldn't find one in the catalogue. It should be about $10.00 and weighs about 12 to 14 pounds. The last one we had was red and the hopper held about three fourths of a quart of grain. Some folks perhaps have used these to grind grain for baby chicks. I hope you are successful in locating a grinder as it has proved very useful in the Sudan for our porridge (cereal) and also for the chicks. When you write Mr. Handerson, just tell him to forward it to us with the other goods he is sending.*

*We ordered a saw, planer, and small sander, also a pipe threader, saws etc. to come via freight. Our tent, aluminum plastic chairs and a two burner kerosene stove, and a small wood stove also coming via freight. The previous gift from First Reformed in Zeeland will cover most of the freight items. We are looking at a generator here and we have asked the Board for permission and funds to purchase. Eventually, everything has to fit into a small MAF plane so we must plan carefully.*

*On Friday I conferred with the Governor General of our province about our plans. On Tuesday we have an appointment with Her Imperial Highness. On Thursday we fly out for our aerial survey. I hope to make a land trip in early October. These are exciting times of planning ... also studying Amharic six hours daily with a teacher. We are looking to the Lord to meet our needs and to guide us in our planning."*

From Lavina's letter, August 25, 1964:

*"Harvey and I are working hard on the Amharic language. Harvey has an informant six hours a day. I can only give one hour a day with all the children home and with the interference all the time it's impossible to do more than that now. When they go to school I can give all my time to language. Harvey hopes to complete the required course about Thanksgiving Day. I must work away at it until we leave and then I have been excused from the remainder. Our goal is to leave Addis for our new field the first week in December.*

*The air survey over the Majang area was a success. Now the ground survey by mules is scheduled for October 6. Three men and Harvey will make this survey. They plan to be away two weeks, going up and down mountains all around the Majang villages to find a good sight to build the station. It is a very heavily forested area and will require much hard work to cut timber to clear a strip for MAF and a road.*

*One site Harvey saw was beautiful, way up in the mountains, a heavy concentration of Majang but we would need to depend entirely on MAF as no road could be cut through the forest because of the large number of little streams and rivers to cross.*

*Another site they saw having a large number of Majang is about eight miles from the little village of Metti where the Princess has her coffee plantation. It is possible to cut a road the eight miles from Metti to the site. It is on a river so we would have a good water supply. They think the altitude is about 4,000 feet here. It isn't such a pretty site but it seems more sensible to build at a place where we could get out by road. If the MAF plane were busy or had an accident or during heavy rains one just couldn't get out in case of an emergency. All these things must be considered as they choose the site. There are so*

245

*many little details and plans that must be worked out in connection with building a station. We pray much that the Lord may lead and guide us to choose the right place and help in all the preparations that are being made.*

*All of us are excited about this new work. Although it will not be easy at first living in a tent and so forth, we are looking forward to it. Having only Paul with us at first, it shouldn't be too difficult. ... Well, it is dinner time, so must go and join the family. Much love to all, Lavina and family."*

## THE GROUND SURVEY

From another letter by Lavina, October 6, 1964:

*"Harvey left Addis October 2 to begin his survey trip. He spent the week end at Teppi, the little village town where the Ethiopian airlines plane lands three times a week. This is the place into which all our supplies will come. We have a mission station at Ghimeera, 10 minutes away from Teppi by plane. This is where Paul and I are now. We are going to spend two weeks here while Harvey is on his survey. The other three members of the survey team are from this station. So, we four wives are together while the men are out on trek.*

*I saw Harvey for a few minutes yesterday when our plane landed at Teppi. Harvey and Ted Pollock were waiting for Ralph Borgeson and Campbell Miller to come from Ghimeera to start their trek. They sent 3 mules from Ghimeera and they arrived in Teppi alright. They had given the 2 horses sleeping sickness shots and they became so sick they couldn't stand up. So they couldn't use them, but the governor at Teppi can give them 3 mules to use and take as far as Metti (ten miles away). There is a lot of sleeping sickness in the Majang area.*

*Harvey was very eager to get started on his survey. I hope they have good weather. It's been so wet and rainy here.*

*Yesterday we had quite a trip from the airport to the station. It is only an eight mile trip, but the road is terribly muddy and rugged. Only a jeep could make a trip like that! It took us 2 1/2 hours driving time to go the eight miles. We were stuck in the mud for over an hour. Mary Nell Harper drove the jeep as all the men are gone, but she did and excellent job considering the terrible road.*

*Our plane was 2 hours late in leaving Addis. We were ready to take off when the pilot said his magneto was dead. So we unloaded, got out of the plane and had to sit in the airport for 2 hours while they loaded another plane. These are freight planes with the bucket seats along the sides of the plane. They usually carry more freight than passengers. It was a long day, but it's nice to be here. This is a beautiful station way up in the mountains. I have a lovely view of the mountains, valley and river from my bedroom window. ... Pray for Harvey and the men, for their protection and care, while they make this difficult trek. It won't be easy. Much love to all, Lavina"*

We are still examining the letters for background and perspectives that went into the planning and preparations. Later it will become apparent where perception and reality parted company. But, at that stage we had to move ahead on the light available to us. On balance, I think we did quite well in our preparations so far as having the right supplies with us when we finally struck out from Teppi for the Godare River which we had selected as the place for our home and ministry.

**LETTERS INDICATE OUR PERCEPTIONS THEN**

From my letter dated November 15th:

*"The day was beautiful again as is every day here in Addis at this time of the year. It'll be quite different in a couple of weeks when we go to our new post, to be known as the 'Godare River Post'.*

*What busy days these are. The entire house is in a mess now and we have only straight chairs left to sit on. Most everything has been sacked or boxed. I bought thirty six 10 foot by 12 inch boards for boxing things and they're nearly gone. The saws and hammers have been working overtime.*

*This past week we ordered our year's food supply, four local saddles, 2 pack saddles, 8 axes, 8 shovels, 40 grass knives, 6 pick axes, three files, an umbrella tent, two folding chairs, 20 sacks, 12 smaller sacks, 40 yards of sacking, 5 bolts of unbleached cotton cloth, a used umbrella tent... Fortunately, we can go to the office and get money and put it on our account. I guess they know that once we get started the drain on funds will be over.*

*It is interesting when you buy a saddle in the native market. You buy the basic seat and then add parts of straps to it until you finally have a complete unit. All of this takes a terrific amount of time and bargaining. ... I just remembered some other items purchased this week. On Monday I spent more than half the day in the junk yard getting an old jeep rear end axle, wheel and tire assembly. This had to be shipped to Mizan Tefari (Ghimmera) later to be put under the "tumble bug", that is, the dirt remover which will go to the Godare for work on the airstrip. I also bought a used water tank and three small barrels, plus some plastic hose and a gas pump. What a world!*

*There is so much to remember. We have check lists which are constantly being revised. Yesterday, while getting hinges and hasps, I suddenly remembered we'd forgotten springs for the screen doors. Remember the time, Pa, when we ordered that Land-O-Lakes powdered milk in Minneapolis. Well, this time we bought it all right here in Addis ... 8 cases of it. Enough for a year!*

*Other activities of the week included two conferences with the Crown Princess and the Crown Prince. The land for our site is being given to us by the Crown Prince. We get a lot of kidding from our colleagues about being so close to the Royal family. The Crown Prince is the oldest son of His majesty, Emperor Haile Selassie I, and next in line for the throne. Mr. Hanna, the mission representative, and I went together. His Highness asked many questions about the Majang and then offered to help if we had need, and finally he called in his secretary and asked him to draft a letter to the Minister of the Interior granting us permission for the land and to start work immediately. He's arranging a conference for this Wednesday with himself, the Governor General of the Province and ourselves. It is all quite thrilling for us."*

In the midst of all this planning, preparations and meetings, we kept in touch with our children who were away in boarding school. Letters to and from were so very important for them as well as for us. In some of the letters we even dealt with important theological questions. Part of this same letter written to the folks and Denny at the same time, included the following discussion. I thought you'd like to listen in! Denny was training to serve with MAF. He'd earned his various aeronautical licenses, and was now at Moody Bible School in Chicago:

*"We received your nice letter, Den. You are off to a good start in your examinations. We'll be eager for the final report. Glad to hear that you still have a high regard for Reformed theology. Our church could stand more of the zeal and warmth of the non-denominational groups, but so far as the soundness of its doctrine is concerned, I personally feel we are on solid ground.*

*One has to hang unto both the truth of Predestination and Free Will. Scripture clearly indicates that man has to make a personal decision for Christ, but once it is made he realizes fully that it is because God in His wonderful grace and mercy has called him. You cannot explain it, but it is a truth that makes one strong in the time of adversity and hardship. Romans eight is a wonderful chapter to strengthen the believer....Our salvation isn't through a particular view we may hold, but through the One who holds us. You know, one's particular view can often become a source of pride and we begin to look down on others who are not so 'enlightened'. The wonder of it all is that God has saved us, isn't it, and that we are His because of a love which is beyond our comprehension. May the Lord always give us generous spirits and appreciation for the various interpretations of others too.*

*Soon it'll be time for your application with MAF, Den. The Lord will lead and I am confident that when the time comes you'll find some of our own churches ready to share in your support. What wonderful months and years lie ahead. We're all well. Mother (Lavina) is doing a great job of organizing the food boxes and stuff. We are asking the Lord for strength for each day. We know that many are praying with us these days. Just last Wed. evening at the mission prayer meeting we prayed for the provision of a tent. Two days later a good used tent was found through an add I had put in a store. Day by day, He leads and guides. Much love, Dad, mother and family."*

*"When you pass through the waters, I will be with you; and when you pass through the rivers, they will not sweep over you."* Isaiah 43:2a

# CHAPTER SIXTEEN
# FINDING THE MAJANG

Letters home to the family told of what the ground survey hoped to find. The partial account of what happened when we actually went in on foot was well reported in the Fall - 1964 issue of the mission's publication, "Ethio-Echo." Here is how the trek was described upon our return.

"A rugged journey through heavy undergrowth, forbidding rivers and streams, slippery, moss covered rocks and sloshing mud and rain into the jungle rain forest of Southwest Ethiopia began on October 6, 1964. Four missionaries, a guide, three mules, a donkey and a dozen carriers for tents and food started into the forest. The trip ended two weeks later with a mule abandoned from exhaustion in the forest, and the missionary doctor carried shoulder high on a stretcher by some Majang men, concerned for his recovery. The team of missionaries - Dr. Campbell Millar, Ralph Borgeson, Ted Pollock and Harvey Hoekstra - had walked 150 miles in search of a suitable site for the new mission post among the Majang people.

The survey team returned on October 17th wearied by the rigors of the trip but glowing with reports of God's provision and leading. A good site on the Godare River, some fifty miles beyond the last Ethiopian Air Lines airfield was chosen. Local officials had offered every assistance and encouragement. The Majang people were responsive and friendly. In its report, the survey team made recommendations which the Mission speedily acted upon. These have now been forwarded to the supporting Church in America for their approval and implementation.

As early as 1960 the Mission had its first aerial sur-

vey of this area. Now nearly four years later the work will begin. God's leading and provision in the intervening years has
been unmistakable. Permissions have been granted. The missionaries are available. The door is open and all the signals
read, 'Go, Go, Go'. Yes, He said, 'Go into all the world and
preach the Gospel.'

Every member of the team spoke with grateful appreciation for the privilege of visiting this unique, rain forest area.
The journey was made more pleasant by the cool shade of the
dense jungle. Hundreds of monkeys greeted the men along the
way with angry cries, and often the stillness of the jungle was
broken by the sweet melody of an unseen bird deep in the forest.

The journey was not without its problems. The team
soon learned that it isn't easy to change the mind of a mule!
The story frequently came to mind of the old mountaineer who
said while beating his mule, 'You may be smarter than I am,
but you're not stronger!' In the end the team learned that the
mule had them licked on both counts! One of the mules refused to move another inch. Nothing could persuade it. With
no alternative, it was abandoned in the forest.

More seriously, on the last day of the trip, Dr. Millar
became dangerously ill with an infection that got into his blood
stream. Three days earlier he had struck his shin on a hidden
rock while crossing a swift stream. Now in a matter of hours
he was desperately sick and unable to walk. To go further
seemed impossible. And still it was imperative to press on to
reach the airstrip some 25 miles ahead. The plane was due
the next morning. As Campbell was lifted from his mule that
morning and placed on a cot in a clearing in the forest, we
gathered around and knelt in prayer, committing him to God.
Perhaps the Majang who watched us saw in this simple act a
new dimension of life.

It was midnight when the balance of the party eventually reached the airstrip, for Ted Pollock had walked on ahead
to get help and medicine. The journey had been made with
carriers and stretcher, and when Campbell grew stronger in
late afternoon he was able to again ride the mule. A local official somewhere along the way volunteered his bed for an hour's
sleep for the patient. And a medical dresser hurried to meet
the party, offering his penicillin. The word had spread quickly
and during the night, runners came from the little town near

the airstrip, wanting to help. When the team arrived that night, a doxology of praise from very tired men was spoken to God. We had learned afresh how utterly dependent upon God we all are.

The survey completed, the missionary family is now moving into the forest where the Majang live. The destination is the east bank of the Godare River, some fifty miles from the last airstrip from which supplies will have to be brought in. To be very specific, the exact location for the new mission post is 35 degrees and 3 minutes East longitude and 7 degrees and 27 minutes North latitude, and it is to be called, 'The Godare River Post'.

The Hoekstras (Harvey, Lavina and their three year old son, Paul) will travel with five mules and carriers. Paul will ride in a chair on the back of a Majang carrier. They'll make quite an impressive safari with their ten chickens for eggs, three rabbits for meat, bush knives, axes, chain saw, boxes of food shaped to be useable for temporary furnishings, and other assorted supplies.

One of the most precious items will be the little Misavia transceiver. With it the missionary family will be in daily contact with the base station from which supplies can be ordered. Until the Missionary Aviation Fellowship airstrip is ready the small plane will be dropping food from the air along with whatever supplies may be needed. It all calls for a good bit of planning and coordination. One of the first air drops will include two sacks of corn for the fifty Majang workmen who will be helping to clear the airstrip. Has anyone a bright idea on how one might drop fresh eggs from the air without damage? Someone suggested dropping the hen and letting her produce the eggs later. Both would seem to involve considerable hazards!

It is hoped that the MAF strip can be completed in six weeks and that by the first of April a strip capable of handling a Dakota plane will be ready. Cutting an airfield out of a jungle forest is no small assignment.

After the Hoekstras arrive at the site, they will be sending a radio message about the trail which is to be prepared through the forest for the Jeep. When all is ready, Ed Pollock, Jr. and Ralph Borgeson plan to come in with the vehicle and a scraper for use on the airstrip. Ed will continue with the Hoekstras for six or seven months putting up the first buildings.

Ralph will return to the base station after surveying the new mission post and marking it."

## SERVICES TO BE OFFERED

"The missionaries will spend their first months in tents and temporary stick and grass buildings. From the beginning medical care will be offered, and a trained Ethiopian dresser will be working. The missionary doctor from the base station is to make visits every second month. The following dry season the mission builder, Ted Pollock, Sr. (Ed's father) expects to come in to complete the buildings for the post. A school will be opened as soon as buildings and staff are available. It is also hoped to develop agricultural work that will be of benefit in raising the standard of living for the people.

The Majang appeared to be eager for the new mission post to be established because the local chiefs offered the help of their people in clearing a road and airstrip.

The Majang are an intelligent, semi-nomadic people dwelling in clearings they have made in the rain forest. They are widely scattered over an area of 100 miles by 50 miles. They live in simple stick and grass houses, planting and cultivating roughly prepared fields of maize and durra. The soil appears to be productive, but new methods to conserve its fertility and increase its harvests are needed. The Majang make extensive use of honey from the wild bees in the forest. It is their one 'cash crop'. A single Majang may have as many as a hundred hives placed high in the trees. The hives are carved from four to five foot lengths of log and hoisted into the trees with vine ropes. Many hives are at least 100 feet high overhead.

They appear to be a musically inclined people. Many were seen walking on the trails, keeping time with a small stringed instrument they had fashioned with wood and thin metal staves. At their dance, numerous tube-like instruments, made from branches of varying diameters and lengths, were blown upon as one would blow across the neck of a bottle. The music produced was different from anything the team members had previously heard!

The Majang were obviously fond of beads and bright colors. Many were attractively decorated. The men wore leaves

254

and a loin cloth, while the women wore grass and skins or the bark of a tree.

The survey team was impressed with the apparent friendliness of the Majang toward one another. It was not uncommon for carriers who were carrying lighter loads to volunteer to exchange loads with one who had the heavier burden. Men of all age levels shared equally in the work. The team was impressed, too, with the intelligence and resourcefulness the Majang showed in coping with the problems they face in living in a rain forest with its lush growth. They have learned how to slash their way through the jungle in an efficient manner which will always be beyond the ability of their foreign guests.

## THE NEEDS ARE MANY

The needs of the Majang were apparent. One could not help but remember over and over again the words of Jesus when He said, 'I am come that they may have life and have it more abundantly.' The Majang are still waiting to share in that abundant life. We saw many persons suffering from huge tropical ulcers. Apparently shin bone injuries are common in the forest, and with the lack of medical care the slightest injury easily becomes an incurable would. An improvement in agricultural methods will make for a better diet and better general health. Surely this is part of the abundant life of which Jesus spoke. The needs are genuine and the opportunities and challenges facing the missionary are self evident. Medical care, education, improvements in agricultural methods, the message of God's love in Christ ... all of these bring the mission to the Majang people. Fifteen thousand persons (possibly many more than that) shall have the opportunity to learn of Christ and to share in the abundant life He came to give.

The challenge facing the Hoekstras is not theirs alone. It comes inescapably to the whole family of God's people. There is a task for each of us in giving, in praying and caring. So, together we shall one day hear a mighty hymn of praise ascend from deep in the rain forests of Southwest Ethiopia. May God grant that none of us shall fail to do his part!"

## THE JOURNEY TO THE GODARE
## BEGINS IN TEPPI

Such was our understanding when Lavina, Paul and I started out from Teppi for the Godare River. On D-day, we flew into Teppi on an Ethiopian airlines Dakota aircraft. With us were twenty or twenty five cartons and boxes of supplies. Behind a nearby mud house were our six mules and two horses. They had been sent over with two mule men by our missionaries in Ghimeera. I had worked with horses as a farm boy and I had done a good bit of riding on horses we owned in the Sudan. But, to work with mules was something different. I kept remembering the sage advice of an SIM missionary who had a keen sense of humor, George Middleton. He had offered his advice before we left Jimma. He said, "Harvey, be careful for those mules. They are dangerous on both ends and very uncomfortable in the middle." I learned that he spoke as a prophet. Interestingly, we had to teach the Majang people to be careful of the rear rather than the front end of the mule. They were fearful of the mouth but had no sense of danger about the rear feet. Their understanding had been shaped by their encounters with leopards, wild boars and baboons!

With the help of the mule men, we began loading the cartons. I discovered that those men knew a lot more about mules than I did. A mule has a deceptive way of expanding its girth when the belly band is being tightened. Once finished, the mule relaxes and the band is too lose and the load wants to slip to an unbalanced position. This is never pleasant, but its worse than unpleasant when one has just balanced two baskets of a hundred eggs individually wrapped in papers for protection on the way.

Here is what happened. We had just about finished loading this one mule with the precious and fragile eggs when the animal looked around at us with a glazed eye, kicked up his heals and caused the load to suddenly tip upside down on opposite sides from what we had intended. Because it was already getting late in the afternoon we didn't examine for damage, but pressed on with the process and then started out. Along with the mules for transport and the horses for riding where we could, we had at least fifteen carriers for the first ten miles down to Metti.

It wasn't until the third morning out that we realized the extent of the damage done to our eggs. Just outside our pup tent the baskets with the eggs were covered with army ants having a feast. Lavina had a painful, painstaking job cleaning up the mess and repackaging the good ones for the rest of the journey. We were learning as we went!

It was after dark when we finally arrived ten miles down the road and found ourselves in Metti. I put up our tent in the dark. It was my first experience in doing so and I paid dearly for my carelessness. About four in the morning a colosal, tropical rain storm descended on us. I had neglected to be sure I knew how to raise and lower the back flap which was designed to cover the small opening with the mosquito covering for fresh air in good weather. The rain came in terribly and I finally had to face it - get out of the tent in my pajamas and forcibly close this opening from the outside. I was drenched and it seemed extremely cold. This was a mistake I didn't make twice!

In the morning, we realized that we would have to leave some of our supplies and gear behind in Metti where there were several merchant shops and their families. This would be the last Oromo/Amhara settlement before we went into the forest proper. We arranged to rent an empty room in a de-crepit, old, mud-walled, dirt floor building. Except for termites and rats, our things could be locked in here safely and the mule men could collect from here for their second trip to Go-dare. To be sure they brought priority items, I was careful to point out to them the carton with cooking utensils and dishes.

It was well into the morning before we finally pushed off with our motley caravan of mules, horses and carriers. We eventually rounded up twenty men and young boys to each shoulder or put on their head one of the cartons, water tank, radio, live battery and charger or whatever had to go.

## UNCUT TRAILS DELAY TREK

We soon discovered that the trail had not been cut. Majang promises to have the trail cut for us had been forgotten as soon as our survey team left town! Because the trails were unkempt with low hanging vines, we had to wait for the worst places to be cut back by our men carrying machetes. We learned that Majang kept their trails uncut because of their fear that people from neighboring tribes would raid their villages and steal their children.

Because the trails were uncut, we would be on the way ten days instead of the four or five we had planned on. There were other surprises too. In fact, we were in the dark about almost everything going on around us. And we didn't have the advantage of an interpreter guide like on the survey trip. Now we were totally on our own. The only thing the Majang knew about us was the word that our survey guide had given them. He had explained to them that a white missionary, his wife and little boy would be coming in a few weeks to live among them at the Godare. They had promised to welcome us and help us get there. That's just about it! I spoke only two words of Majang and we didn't meet anyone who spoke Anuak until several weeks after we had arrived at the Godare. The Majang words I knew weren't all that helpful either. They were "agur gur"-- do it quickly! We soon discovered that Majang weren't about to be rushed and would do things in their own way at their own pace when they wanted to! But, it was great sport and a great challenge. Our hearts were glad and we knew that the Lord was with us and that we were highly privileged to take the good news about Jesus Christ with us. We often wondered how long it would be before we could communicate this fantastic good news.

At the end of this section, I will quote from a letter I wrote soon after this trip in. When I reread it after thirty years, I was astonished to realize how difficult it had really been. I have always been proud of Lavina for making that trek in there with me. The mission tried to talk her out of it saying she should wait until I had the airstrip finished and we had a shack to live in. She wouldn't hear of it. She wanted to be part of our ministry to the Majang from the very beginning. She never once complained about inconveniences except for complaining once or twice about my huge appetite.

Here is the background. In the Sudan I was sedentary, sitting behind a desk translating, using very few calories. My appetite was small and no threat to the food supply available. In the rain forest, I was putting out enormous amounts of energy doing hard, physical work from morning until after dark. I was burning up calories and was always hungry. It was tough to keep enough food on hand and on the table. We depended on airdrops and food was scarce as well as being difficult to prepare because of a lack of cooking utensils or a proper stove on which to prepare the meals. I will not fault her for chiding me with "tongue in cheek" for eating so much. I remember hearing her say once, "Honey, you never ate this way in the Sudan. Now when we don't have any food you're hungry all the time."

We both lost a lot of weight during those first months before the airstrip was finished. We knew what real hunger pangs are.

## MAJANG CARRIERS - SHORT DISTANCES ONLY

But, I am ahead of my story. I told you that we started out from Metti with some 20 carriers. When we started out I had no idea that they would only carry for a couple of hours and then be returning to Metti. The first time this happened I was dumbfounded.

We had come out of the forest proper and were at a Majang clearing where there were scattered stick and grass shacks. Our procession stopped and everyone put their loads down. Lavina and I found some roasting ears of field corn and munched on these while we took the situation in. After what seemed to be a considerable period of time, I gathered that one of the Majang there was a local chief or headman and was taking charge. One of our carriers was carrying a heavy 10" by 10" metal box with a padlock on it with hundreds of copper five cent pieces inside. Majang wouldn't accept anything other than these five cent pieces for pay. We eventually paid each of the carriers from Metti eight or ten of these coins and they left us to return home.

Gradually, people began to pick up pieces of our gear. Men, along with the women, took the larger, heavier pieces. Smaller children would carry something light like an empty water container. Once everything had been picked up, we were on our way. This whole process could take an hour or two.

And that is just the way it went all the way to the Godare. Ten days of it! Only twice did we have some fright. The first time was when the carriers all put their loads down and we saw no other Majang or a village in sight. Our thought was

-- what will we do if they refuse to go further. I don't know what we would have done. One assurance we had was that our mule men were trustworthy having come from the Ghimeera mission station.

Well, as you can see, they eventually picked up their loads and took us to where other carriers were available to go on from there.

The trip was challenging and rewarding. Very few people have had such experiences. Looking back I wonder how we dared to do what we did, striking out into the unknown in a forbidding forest with a pretty wife and a three year old child. God surely was with us giving us courage and wisdom to cope.

We had prepared a special seat for Paul which would fit comfortably on the back of a carrier. The only problem, which he soon discovered, was that Paul would be making the trip looking backward rather than ahead. It didn't take this little three and a half year old guy long to figure out that this was less than satisfactory from his perspective. He had a way to make his feelings evident and it wasn't long before the whole idea was abandoned and Paul was taking turns with me in the saddle looking ahead rather than backwards. Eventually, I found myself walking more than riding and Paul enjoyed the saddle to himself. This was inevitable and as it should be!

## DIFFICULT RIVER CROSSINGS
## AND STEEP HILLS

Crossing the rivers and swift streams was always a challenge. Since it was the dry season most of the rivers were less than hip deep. Even so, occasionally one had to cross over crawling on hands and knees on a log which spanned the swift stream. One river was so treacherous with fast water and slippery, mossy stones that we could barely keep our footing. A Majang man carried Paul across and another took Lavina's arm as we both clung to a vine stretched across from bank to bank while we struggled to remain upright.

Sometimes we were able to ride the horses across, but then there was always the steep hill on the other side. Once Lavina questioned whether the horse might make it out of the river and up the hill with her on its back. I suggested she give him a chance, which she did. Unfortunately, the horse became unwilling partway up and gradually backed down into the water, stumbled and sat down with Lavina slipping off into the water. My popularity was at an all time low for some time after that until her wet clothes dried on her body. Wet clothes nor not, we kept on moving up one hill and down anoher toward Godare. Even the monkeys, cautiously sneaking a look as they scampered for safety, were surprised!

The trails were tough to navigate. Often, even in the clearings where growth and brush were always in abundance, hidden stumps knocked one's feet and ankles as the horses made their way through these narrow openings between two stumps. Lavina's legs were badly scarred and black and blue before the ten day journey ended.

Our last night on the trail we were at a place the Majang called Konkon. There were only a few houses there and people seemed to be scarce. Our carriers insisted that they would go no further. So, using some sort of sign language with someone who appeared to be the head man, we deposited a number of our pieces in a Majang stick hut and carried what we could with the few available carriers. We left behind our tent and some other things which we thought we might be able to get along without until, hopefully, our things could be retrieved. To the Majang credit, within a few days of our arriving at the Godare, one by one people began showing up, each carrying one of the cartons we had left behind. Not one piece was lost

### MAF'S FIRST AIR DROPS AT GODARE

That last morning on the trail, I strung up the aerial in the bushes and hooked up our Misavia transceiver to contact MAF in Jimma where they were based 140 miles away. By previous arrangement, they were scheduled to make an air drop or two at Godare that afternoon. I was doubtful that we could make it on time because we estimated it would take another seven or eight hours from Konkon to Godare. Unfortunately, MAF had a heavy schedule and said they had to come in the afternoon or it would be days before they could make it again. I had no choice but to go on ahead as quickly as possible and leave Lavina and Ed Pollock to come in more leisurely fashion behind me.

I was at the Godare by early afternoon and Lavina caught up within an hour of my arrival. We again strung up the aerial and made contact with MAF. They said they were on the way and that we should listen for the engine of the plane and let them know when we heard it. They were flying up the Godare River from the Bako River and were looking for us. Can you imagine the thrill when we told them on the radio that we heard the plane and when they responded by saying, "We have you in sight and will be making our first drop."

Majang were gathering around rapidly by now and we were concerned lest one of the sacks being dropped fall on one of them. They made two drops, picking up a second load in Teppi. One of the sacks struck the little extension attached to the back of a Majang hut where a hen was sitting on its eggs. It's almost too ludicrous to describe! The hen went flying and the eggs were scattered and broken. The woman who owned the chicken was in tears and more than a little upset. So there I was, a missionary bringing good news having to comfort a Majang woman in a language I could not speak because of un-invited damage we had inflicted on her.

MAF finished its second drop just after four in the after-noon. A huge tropical rain storm was closing in rapidly as the plane sped away. We searched for the sacks, missed one, and quickly dragged the others into the shelter of a Majang grass roofed hut. The rain came down with a vengeance as we hud-dled inside trying to keep dry and warm.

When the rain stopped, we still had another eighth of a mile to go to where we would sleep and begin the clearing for our house in the morning. By the time we covered this dis-tance, it was already becoming dark as darkness falls swiftly in the tropics. Not only was it getting dark but we were soaking wet from the bushes and brush.

We had no tent because of having to leave it in Konkon for lack of carriers. After the simplest meal you can imagine, we stretched out our sleeping bags on the wet ground, put a single mosquito net up cross ways over the upper part of our bodies and heads and tried to sleep. A man whose name was Jokjok lit a fire and we eventually fell asleep on the open hill-side with the fire burning just off to the side and behind our heads. We were glad that the rain was finished and the night was dry except for the heavy dampness of the hillside and the air itself.

## OUR FIRST HOUSE OF STICKS AND GRASS

In the morning at the crack of dawn Majang began gathering in sizeable numbers. There must have been fifty or sixty men who showed up. We indicated on our arms that we needed poles for our house so that we could sleep there. Balti, the most powerful Majang chief and ritual expert, spoke the word and it was done. Majang began carrying in bundles of poles the size of one's arm and about eight or nine feet long. They selected a three foot stump and began constructing our first house. The poles were anchored to the stump which served as a "cornerstone". The poles were laced together with vines. Not a nail was used -- there were no nails, in any case. By nightfall a crude, simple but adequate shell of sticks, vines and poles had been put together to become our first house at the Godare. The following day they brought in bundles of grass and roofed it. Unfortunately, the house, although only about 8 by 10 feet, was larger than normal Majang huts. Consequently, the roof was a bit too flat and later when the rain fell it leaked like a sieve.

Using the shortwave radio, we requested the mission to purchase a canvas tarp to cover the house. This was eventually gotten in on mules and the problem was solved. I recall, also, that within a few days our small tent arrived from Konkon and we began sleeping at night where it was dry. Our larger tent from Sears arrived much later by mule, but it was there in time for the children to use when they came home from school.

We couldn't speak the language but somehow we communicated our needs. One problem was to have a container large enough to hold water for household chores. Balti the chief sent over a huge crock container that held at least 20 or 25 gallons. Normally they used this kind to make beer. Balti not only sent this huge crock over but assigned three young girls to fill it with water every day from the nearby spring.

### EARLY DIFFICULTIES CONFIRMED BY LETTER

Before continuing our account of how things went during the early days at Godare, let me share with you a letter written in unvarnished prose less than three weeks after we arrived. It corroborates and confirms the accuracy of my recollection of what we encountered on the trek in.

From a letter written December 18, 1964:

*"Dear Dad and Mother,*

*"Forgive the scrawl. I'm writing this on a small cardboard box on my lap in Teppi. Lavina, Paul and Ed Pollock, Jr. are back there on the Godare River and I'm here waiting for the children. I arrived at 1 a.m. this morning by moonlight and rain -- all at the same time! I left home on Tuesday a.m. in the rain and spent 3 1/2 days on the way -- got lost in the forest for several hours or I'd have been here earlier. That forest is treacherous.*

*The journey out took us five days (travel time not counting the five days waiting as they cut the trail ahead of us). What a trip! About eight or nine rivers to cross -- waded them and crossed one on a log. At night the army ants attacked us. Once in a pouring rain I had to get out and lower the back flap on the tent. The trail had not been cut and it was slow going. Vines and ants everywhere. Paul got caught around the neck once and really screamed -- poor kid. He got a good neck burn out of it, but its healed again. Lavina had her legs all scratched and swollen from thorns and hidden stumps. We walked a good bit of the way because the vines were too low. With tennis shoes on we waded the rivers and walked in wet feet and legs most of the way. the worst part of that was to sleep in wet sleeping bags and then dress into wet trouser legs and socks in the morning! Brrr!*

*We expected it to be difficult, but it is even more difficult than we had figured. It has rained every night since we arrived. We put up two small shacks with sticks, but they have no roofs. Lavina was cooking in the mud inside the house when I left and bearing up real well. We've been sitting on boxes to eat and using metal camp cooking utensils. Paul manages real well. The chickens survived and the four rabbits. Rex (our dog) became mad after we arrived and I had to destroy him. Rabies are so bad here in Ethiopia. We lost a mule in the river at Godare for 24 hours -- too swift for a tired mule!*

*The day we arrived, we hooked up the radio. MAF dropped two loads of blankets, sugar, salt, flour, clothes etc. ... a*

load of corn, also fresh meat and mail. We arrived one hour before MAF came. At 4:30 p.m. we had a mammoth rain. The first
days have been difficult and somewhat discouraging, but the
worst is now past. The Lord has helped us and we continue
looking to Him.

At night the army ants often attack us. Fortunately, we
have Gamexene powder and it drives them off. Boy are they
hot! They'll eat you alive if you allow them to. In the forest itself
little hot black ants keep falling into the neck. ...

I should be home two days before Christmas. Carol will
be eleven on the 21st on the trail. The trails are now being cut
and this makes it easier.

On our trip in we used over 100 different carriers, six
mules and two horses. Paul had a long, long ride and traveled
real well after he got used to it. Food is a problem, but I ate
fresh roasting ears in the fire most of the way back. Also found
an egg in one village and made pancakes. One night I had a
cold can of green beans and six wieners from a can. Sorry page
is full. Hope to give further picture later. Don't worry about us.
The Lord is near and will keep and help. Write soon again.
Love, Harvey and family."

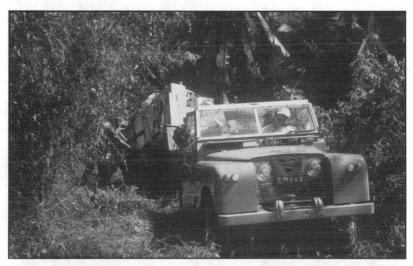

It took 25 Ethiopian men helping Bob Swart and Ralph Borgeson seventeen days to bring
in this Landrover through the forest to Godare. The distance was 52 miles..

It took 10 men three weeks to fell the tree from which this log was cut. It took another three weeks for these men with additional workmen to remove this fallen tree from the airstrip.

Majang girls wearing their typical leaves and grass .

266

The Majang men were honey collectors. This man has his gourds into which to collect his honey and he is ready to climb tall trees where their hollowed out logs were
positioned for the bees to do their thing.

Many hands make light work! Needed on logs like this to clear the airstrip at
Godare in the rain forest.

267

Harvey standing in what will become the lower end of the new airfield at Godare.

MAF'S first landing on the new airstrip early April, 1965

268

# CHAPTER SEVENTEEN

# ON THE
# GODARE - TEPPI TRAIL

We had been at the Godare less than ten days when
I had to leave to trek back to Teppi to meet Carol and Mark.
Their school vacation from Good Shepherd was beginning
and both they and we wanted to be together for Christmas.

I could safely leave Lavina and Paul because Ed Pollock, Jr. was at the Godare. He had kindly trekked in with
us and would be helping us during those first few weeks.
Ed was the son of Ted and Dolly, the mission builder family,
a sharp, capable young man educated to become an engineer.

During those first days at the Godare, we needed to
deal with the basics of how to cook, have water on hand
and a way to shower and have a toilet. We were surrounded by twisted vines, bushes and trees. It was a tangled, jumbled mass of ten to fifteen foot growth with hidden
stumps which, every day, we kept trying to cut back from
the center. Until the mules left for another load from Metti,
they were right on top of us. When we pushed out into the
entangled mess to dig our pit latrine, it seemed that we were
way out there where we wanted it. Later, however, as we
kept on clearing back we discovered that the toilet was right
in the center of things! We also put up an outside shower
by hoisting up an old tank which someone had once used
for gasoline to which we attached a sprinkle head. We put a
grass enclosure around both the toilet and shower for pri-
vacy. A white cloth hanging on the opening indicated that it
was occupied. In the shower we laced one inch sticks together for a small platform so that we wouldn't be standing
in the mud and so that the water drain hillside away.

CHAPTER SEVENTEEN

Our house had been built on a hillside. The Majangs never bothered to level the floor. It turned out to be a blessing in disguise because when the heavy rains came and the roof leaked, the water that come through the roof or that came cascading down the hillside went in one side and out the other. Even so, I saw Lavina walking around in the house with tennis shoes sticky with mud more than once those first mornings when she prepared our breakfast.

At first we had no table or chairs, but simply sat on our wooden trek boxes and ate our meals from our laps. When Carol and Mark joined us, we dragged in a 12 inch four foot log to serve as our sofa. I made a shelf in the kitchen by rail splitting a small 6 inch log. It was all pretty simple living. The floor didn't need to be swept at first because the chickens came in to find whatever might have fallen to the ground when we ate. They never found much but always felt it was worth their effort! Before making breakfast Lavina often had to go around with a small tin can to collect the huge night crawlers which came in overnight. I had never seen such beautiful bait for fishermen go to waste!

During those first days Lavina cooked on three stones the way the Majang did. There wasn't a lot to cook, but what there was had to be done that way. Later we learned to make our own charcoal and she often cooked on a small grill that fit into an empty gasoline tin from which the end had been removed and in which there was a small opening in the side for ventilation.

That was sort of what I left them with when I took off for Teppi. This was supposed to be dry the season, but it seemed to rain every night and frequently during the morning and late afternoon hours. It took me three and a half days to return to Teppi. On the way I nearly met with disaster and sudden death or, at best, paralysis.

**A NECK INJURY BETWEEN GODARE AND TEPPI**

I was making my way through the forest toward Teppi and by this time was about 30 miles from home. I was riding my horse. He was walking slowly, threading his way through a clearing where the trail was not clearly evident. I had leaned forward and was attempting to disentangle the reins   where

270

they attached to the bridle near the mouth, when suddenly I received the severest blow to the head that I can imagine one receiving and still surviving. It felt like someone had struck me a blow on the top of the head with an eight inch plank. My fingers and toes tingled and I felt faint. I slipped out of the saddle and realized that the horse on which I had been riding had walked under a large tree trunk which was still attached to its stump about six feet above the ground. Instead of going around, he'd decided to go beneath the trunk. That would have been fine if I weren't on his back, but with me up there it was a different story. Because I was leaning forward, straining to reach the bit part of the bridle where the reins were messed up, we just barely made it under the log and I took the full force of walking into it with my head.

I gradually recovered myself and remounted and proceeded ahead. The injury sustained, however, bothered me for months. Arthritis set in. I later had physical therapy on it. I was unable to bend my neck to look up properly. Finally, in July, five months later, Jim, who was home from school, and I were working on the airstrip using the chain-saw to cut large branches from felled trees. At one point, a limb sagged, caught the saw and froze the action. The sudden jerk snapped my neck in place with that same tingling of the fingers and toes I had experienced months earlier when I had first injured it with the horse. Jim, who was right beside me noticed something was wrong and said, "Dad, what's the matter. Are you hurt?"

My neck had snapped back into place. By evening I was able to look up in an almost normal manner. Three years later, ex-rays confirmed an old injury and the doctor explained how I had nearly severed my spinal column. How merciful the Lord was to me and how I still thank Him for preserving my life and my well being. Even today, I pray daily for His protection from every evil thing. And this prayer includes both the physical and spiritual dangers that threaten us.

## CAROL AND MARK HOME FOR CHRISTMAS

Carol and Mark were in school in Addis Ababa and itching to see what living in the forest was all about. Carol was eleven and Mark was ten. They flew from Addis to Teppi, about 350 miles, on the Ethiopian Airlines DC3. They were excited to get on their horses and head off toward Godare.   It was a fun trip to see their reaction to this new adventure.  They were great travelers and explorers along the way. In a few places we discovered wild gooseberries which we enjoyed eating.   The baboons and several different kinds of monkeys captivated them.

On our last night out from Godare, we stopped in the village of Konkon.  There we made a foolish mistake when we put our tent up in the green grass on the edge of which was a Majang chicken cage.   The Majang make cylindrical drums from small stripling sticks which they tie together with vines. These are about the size of a fifty gallon drum.   They hang them about five or six feet from the ground, with a pole coming from the opening on the end to the ground on which the chickens can walk to get up into this protective cage.   Once the chickens are in, the pole is removed and the trap door is fastened.   It's a safe place from the wild animals and relatively safe from army ants.

Unknown to us, the grass was infested with lice.  We scratched and scratched into the night.   And then, to make matters worse, we had a powerful electrical and rain storm. What thunder and lightning!  We thought of home at the Godare and wished we were there.   This, too, was a mistake we didn't make twice.!

The next afternoon Lavina was eagerly anticipating our arrival and had pretty well calculated that we would arrive when we did.   What excitement for all of us to be together in our new, forest surroundings.  We were overjoyed to have Carol and Mark with us.   It was a Christmas vacation that neither they nor we would soon forget.  Jim and Dave were in school at Schutz in Egypt and would be greatly missed.

Lavina and Paul had done just fine while I was away. There were many new sights and sounds to reckon with.  Once Ed, the young man helping us, came running up the hill all excited, exclaiming that he just seen a gorilla as big as a person.   Actually, it was probably one of the big baboons that lived there.   Lavina also had some interesting questions to share which Paul had asked.

One night she and Paul were in the tent each on a cot listening to the various, strange sounds of monkeys and the hooting of a nearby owl.  Paul wasn't so sure he liked it there. Finally, he said, "Mommy, do you like living in the forest?  Do you like the Majang people? Why did we come here? What are we doing here, anyway?"

She said this gave her a good opportunity to explain that we were there because Jesus loved the Majang and had sent us there to help them. She told Paul how nobody had ever come to tell them about Jesus. We were going to learn to speak their language and one day we would begin telling them that God loved them, too, just like He loves us.

She said it seemed to satisfy him and he soon drifted off into a peaceful sleep. Quite an adjustment for a little guy just three and a half years old. True to form for children, he would learn that Majang language quicker than his dad and mom!

## BACK ON THE TRAIL TO TEPPI AND SCHOOL

It was so wonderful to be home again and to have Mark and Carol with us for three weeks, but, alas, the days sped by and before we knew it, departure time had come. They had savored every moment of their short stay exploring and experimenting. With new Majang friends they had had the thrill of swinging across the sharp ravine on thirty foot rope-like vines securely entangled high in a tree. It only became risky with this cut vine began to dry out and lost its elasticity and strength.

But, for Mark and Carol, the vacation was over and it was back to school in Addis. No way to get there except to mount those horses and strike out for Teppi.

The morning we left it was raining and we had to wait until mid morning before pushing off. We had several Majang carriers with us. Around four- thirty in the afternoon, we reached a village where we could and probably should have stopped for the night. But, we wanted to make up for time lost in the morning and decided to press ahead. Before long we were again in the forest proper. Darkness, inky darkness soon enveloped us. We had to go in single file. Carol and Mark and I were up ahead of the carriers as we could make better time with the animals. In order to encourage the children in the darkness, I suggested we say the "A,B,C's". It was eerie to hear us calling out "A -- B -- C", each having a turn calling the next letter. (Carol still playfully teases about having to be the last in the procession because she was older than Mark!)

273

Everything was going along fine in the inky darkness until we came to a river we hadn't reckoned on. It was too deep to wade and the only way across was by crawling over on the log which the Majang used as their bridge to either side. I fastened the horses and crawled Carol and Mark over, one at a time. It was scary for them alone on the other side of the river. Then I tried to get the horses into the water to have them swim across. I couldn't persuade them to venture it, so I crawled back across on the log to fetch Carol to help me, leaving Mark alone in the darkness. Carol and I tried. She pulled on the bridle and I persuaded from the other end. Nothing worked. Finally, the horse jerked away, kicked Carol in the elbow and started down the trail toward Godare. Carol began sobbing hysterically, "I want my mommy. I want my mommy." I tried to comfort and reassure her. Then Mark, alone in the darkness on the other side of the river, became frightened and was calling me to come and fetch him. Eventually, I had crawled Mark back to the Godare side of the river and had both Carol and Mark with arms around them speaking words of assurance. Carol feared the horse would go all the way back home, but I was confident our carriers who were still behind us would intercept it.

In fact, within fifteen or twenty minutes they appeared with the horse in tow. With their help we all safely crossed the river and by ten o'clock we were at a village where we could spend the night.

Like a typical Majang village at this time of the night, it appeared to have no one in it. But an open sided Majang shack had warm ashes in it and when I blew on it there was even a live ember or two. We were so exhausted that I let the children lie right on the ground beside the fire where they quickly fell asleep. Around eleven the carriers arrived and I zipped the children in their sleeping bags and we all fell sound asleep. At six-thirty in the morning, we cooked a pan of oatmeal for our breakfast and were soon on our way.

We arrived in Metti around eight in the evening. Our hopes were high that we would be fetched in the morning by Bob Swart who, with Ralph Borgeson, was in Teppi preparing to start out for Godare with the new Landrover. Much to our regret, in the morning we listened to the mission transmission and were told that the Landrover wasn't reassembled yet in Teppi following its transportation by air from Jimma. We were told we would have to continue on into Teppi with our horses.

This was a real disappointment for weary travelers. We finally reached Teppi, which is about ten miles from Metti and had a reasonably good trail over which vehicles passed occasionally.

We were exhausted, dirty and tired. The children's clothes were hardly what one would like to be seen wearing upon arrival in Addis and at the school. But, there was no choice. Ralph Borgeson still talks about how bedraggled we all looked when we arrived after three and a half days on the trail. But, our hope was that by the time the children next returned from School for their Easter vacation, we would have the airstrip ready and they could fly in from Teppi in less than fifteen minutes!

## BRINGING IN THE LANDROVER

Bob Swart and Ralph Borgeson agreed to help bring the Landrover into the Godare. When we walked ia the first time, we used old Majang trails which meandered an estimated distance of some 70 miles. This time, we were going to set our compass and attempt to head straight for the Godare from somewhere near Metti.

Once the vehicle had been put back together, we started out pulling an old two wheeled trailer on which there was a barrel of fuel, flour for the workmen, a chain saw, axes, shovels, drinking water and food.

The trip to Metti was a breeze. The next morning, we assembled a crew of 25 Amhara speaking workmen who were hired to help cut our way through the forest and get us across the rivers into Godare. The entire journey would add up to fifty two miles, seventeen days with 25 men working from sunrise to sunset. It was no small task.

Bob and Ralph and I started out together from Metti. On the second or third day out, we agreed on the direction they were to go. I left them and taking eight or nine men with me started out for Godare to begin working on river crossings from that end.

The workmen and I had been going a couple of hours when I began to worry that perhaps Bob and Ralph might not be absolutely sure as to the exact direction they were to take. I decided to leave my men at a clearing in the forest and return to Bob and Ralph to make absolutely certain that we all knew what we were supposed to be doing. They were, of course, surprised to see me, and after our conversations, since it was already getting late in the afternoon, they suggested I have a bite to eat and then start out. The temptation was too great and I agreed. While eating our "picnic" supper, darkness fell and the man who had agreed to accompany me back to my men had disappeared. So, I was on my own.

Before starting out, I cut a three foot stick to have in my hand as I rode my horse. I was soon in the forest proper and it was total darkness. The horse made his way ahead, but I couldn't see a thing. To protect my head I held the stick in front of me to ward off unseen branches. This went on for nearly two hours. I began to fear that I might have bypassed my men so I started shouting like one might call out in the forest, hoping for a response from one of my men. After ten or fifteen minutes of this, I heard what I thought was a faint response. It proved to be from my men. When finally, I emerged from the forest in the clearing where the men had stopped, they were astounded that I had emerged safely out of the darkness. They literally helped me out of the saddle and kept on repeating, "Gobuz sao new" (a brave man). We were soon lying in a row like cordwood sleeping. In the morning, I awakened first and when I called them, they all sat up in unison like robots triggered by some hidden switch. It was humoros and too wierd readily to forget. Again, my heart was full of praise and thanks to God for protecting me and providing for my every need.

Earlier in the day before Bob and Ralph and I parted company, MAF had flown low over us and dropped a sack of flour. Bob had requested a special drop because it was going to take longer than anticipated. We could see that the trailer didn't have enough food along for twenty five hungry men to sustain them until they reached the Godare. We had worried that MAF might not be able to find us but everything worked out perfectly.

Back at Godare, on the seventeenth day, we had word from the Majang that the Landrover was stuck in the mud about five miles from home.

My letter home tells how difficult it was - Feb. 7, 1965:

*"The last night we were stuck in the mud, but in the morning with 35 men pushing and pulling and an apron of poles spanning 100 yards of mud we made it. We walked home the last night and Lavina had a nice supper for us. We pulled a heavily loaded tailor through the forest and up and down incredible river banks. It about gives us nightmares to think about it. Bob and Ralph stuck with the car and I came on ahead on the horse and by foot to take care of the air drops. After a night at home, I went back to meet them. We used compasses and met in the middle of the shortcut. In places the forest was so thick I had to crawl on hands and knees to follow the path of the baboons. It was a happy afternoon when I met the men. Fortunately, we had rain only two nights out. But, that forest was so thick that it took 25 men to cut through it. You simply cannot imagine it.*

*Lavina was home alone here for ten days and did well, but found it plenty difficult ... unable to talk to anyone except Paul and lots of curious people peering in. It wasn't easy, but I admire her for her courage. Few women would do that!"*

Someone questioned the wisdom of this enormous effort. She said, "They spent all that time and effort to get the Landrover to the Godare, but when they arrived they had no place to go." True enough! But, without this Landrover we could not have built the airstrip, dragged off the stumps and logs, hauled the sand up from the river, the dirt needed for the bricks, the tons and tons of stones needed for foundations of our buildings, and power the saw mill to saw the required lumber.

### REMINISCING

As work on the station progressed, I often thought of that night when we four men had arrived at the Godare on that first survey trip. We had gone as far as our government permission allowed, to the banks of the Godare river. We had seen at least two other favorable possibilities for a mission station, but here at the Godare the need seemed greatest. There was no medical care available. There was no school. And this was where the most important Majang, chief Balti, lived. Preliminary conversations that first afternoon indicated he was friendly and would not be hostile to our coming.

I thought often of that fateful night at the Godare. We four men were sitting in the darkness under the leaking roof of that open sided, dilapidated long house in which Majang men would gather. We had a flickering candle and were listing the pros and cons about opening our work at Godare. The leaking roof and falling rain along with sheer exhaustion didn't make me overly optimistic that it could be done. I argued that to be at Godare we would have to have an airstrip for MAF. I asked how an airstrip could be built in so dense a forest area. The other sites closer to Metti seemed much more desirable. But, it was Ted Pollock who said, "Harvey, you can do it. You can bring a Landrover in here to help with the buildings and the construction of the airstrip. We can cut our way through the forest and bring it in safely. It's not impossible."

Eventually, we agreed to think about it again in the daylight. We prayed together, blew out the candle and tried to sleep, but no decision had been made. We didn't know then what we would be recommending to the mission upon our return.

Daylight soon arrived. The sky was clear and the sun was shining. My mood was much more confident now it seemed. Soon twenty five or thirty Majangs came and we asked them to cut their way into the forest going down the slight incline toward the south from where we had slept. These men had short, razor sharp, two bladed knives which they carried at their waist in a protective leather shield. They could cut their way through the dense foliage and vines like cutting butter. They moved straight ahead and every fifty feet or so they would cut off to the side for twenty five or thirty feet from the center line. They did this until they had gone into the forest about 700 yards. It was apparent that if the vines, trees and stumps could be dealt with, the land was such that a plane would be able to land. The task would be stupendous, but it could be done.

With that promising information in hand, the decision was unanimous. Godare was the place God would have us open up the new work for Him among the Majang.

It was a wise decision, confirmed by the mission and never doubted during our years in Ethiopia.

# CHAPTER EIGHTEEN

# EARLY DAYS AT GODARE

Almost from the moment we arrived, we began treating sick people and bandaging their wounds. People came in with huge, painful tropical ulcers on their shins or almost anywhere on their lower legs. Some struggled to make it leaning on a walking stick, and others, unable to make it on their own, were carried. Even before one looked up, you knew that someone with a longstanding ulcer was approaching. The stench was nauseating. These poor people had had no medical care. Simple wounds frequently became tropical ulcers. They covered these with leaves tied by thin vines, but the pus just oozed out.

We soon ran out of bandages and requested women=s societies in our churches for rolled bandages. Before long, the word spread and folks came from considerable distances. You could tell who had been at our back door by the clean, white bandages they were sporting. What a relief it must have been to them to have the pain eased and the putrefying sore gradually becoming smaller and smaller. Some, however, were so large and of such long standing that they had become incurable. One young lad named Ojatiin, the first Majang to be baptized, was still wearing a bandage fifteen years after we had started with him.

At first we treated people right outside the opening to our stick house. Flies and the danger of infections for ourselves dictated that we put up a small shack to be our first clinic. We dubbed it "Godare Medical Arts Building".

People came from great distances as well as from nearby villages. Early one morning, we heard someone coming down the hill to our house wailing and crying. She was one of chief Balti's wives. He had beaten her over the head with a stick and she had a nasty wound that I attempted to stitch shut with a straight needle. This woman became quite friendly and appreciative and when we began having gatherings for worship, she came frequently. She knew hardship and sorrow. Perhaps her most devastating experience was when Balti, in a drunken rage, picked up his heavy rifle and shot and killed her son, already a young man, right in front of her eyes. The Majang could be cruel when under the influence of their fermented honey water.

## SEWING ON A FINGER

One morning only a few weeks after we had arrived, just as we were finishing our breakfast, Balti came in with a real medical emergency. He had brought a young boy in his early teens whose finger had been nearly severed. They were working on the airstrip that morning and this young lad was innocently standing with his hand on the stump on which a couple of men were digging and chopping out the roots with pick axes. Majang weren't accustomed to these long handled instruments and miscalculated. The young boy's forefinger was chopped right through the bone with only a little flesh and skin holding it on. We couldn't speak the language yet so I indicated that we would have to throw the finger away. The old chief shook his head and moved the finger to the position it had before the accident.

At that stage, I called to Lavina and said, "Honey, bring me a pan of water, a darning needle and some thread." I took the needle and fished out the crushed pieces of bone from this terrible injury and proceeded to sew the finger back on. No anesthesia was available but, stoically, he withstood the pain and never cried. Then we needed a splint of some sort to stabilize the finger. We had nothing. The only suitable board out of which to cut a splint was the plywood cover of the rabbit box in which we had brought our three rabbits. I cleaned this up, positioned it under his hand and forearm. We bandaged it carefully, leaving a small opening for air, gave the boy an injection of penicillin, prayed (in English) for him and sent them home. When they next returned, it looked just terrible. My stitches had all putrefied and the finger was deadly pale. I pinched the fingernail and found that there was still blood there indicating the finger was still alive. I re-bandaged it, continued to give penicillin and prayed for God's miracle. In about six weeks, the gaping wound had closed, the severed bones had fused and the last bandage was removed. The finger was stiff, but it was where they wanted it. I later realized that the Majang have a strong aversion to deformities of any kind. That was why the chief wanted the finger saved if at all possible.

This story has a marvelous conclusion. That young man became interested in the Gospel, became a believer and was baptized. He attended classes in school and learned to read the Bible, albeit haltingly, in Amharic. As a young man he loved to preach in the villages. I can still picture him holding his hand with that finger which never bent again in the air and calling out, "Gopan omo mo!" (There's just one way)

Years later this same young man, named Roket, by now a married man with three children, was selected by the Majang Christians to be ordained with authority to baptize. When I fell ill with severe hepatitis, Roket was chosen to minister to those who were coming to faith and needed to be baptized and nurtured in their newfound faith in Christ.

During the first months before the airstrip was completed, I had to be the doctor, nurse, dentist and midwife! Lavina was a great help as we tried to minister to human need. We were surprised at how proficient we became at recognizing the various kinds of diseases and what kind of treatment or medicine was required. We prayed much to the Lord for wisdom and that He not allow us to make serious errors in judgment. We were consciously aware of our total dependence upon God and trusting Him was our joy and comfort.

### WORKING ON THE AIRSTRIP

Ed Pollock, Jr., was a tremendous help to us during those first weeks. He was strong, energetic, and intelligent with an engineer's perspective. He was able to take charge of the work on the airstrip during the times I was trekking between Godare and Teppi.

It was a source of encouragement and assurance for Lavina to have him there when I was away.

We began the work on the airstrip with considerable

enthusiasm. Majang began clearing back the brush from their old clearing in what was to become the center of the airstrip. As the brush was cut back it became apparent that these former clearings were alive with stumps, both large and small. Every stump had to be dug out at the roots, dragged away and the hole filled in with dirt. For the first ten days, everything looked promising, but then the Majang began to show up late and, eventually, they just didn't appear. Having no idea of what an airstrip would look like and with no realization of its importance, the incentive to work wasn't there. Majang felt no need for the money we offered them as they felt no need for things money could buy.

It became apparent that we would never build an airstrip depending on Majang labor. What to do? I spoke by radio to the missionaries in our mother station, Ghimeera. They felt strongly that the airstrip should be built with local help and that it would be a mistake to bring in outside laborers from another language group. I was concerned and somewhat disappointed at what seemed to me their lack of appreciation for our vulnerable situation without an airstrip. For me, getting an airstrip had highest priority. It was obvious that it would never happen with Majang. A way had to be found or our mission would fail. We didn't discuss the matter by radio more than once or twice, but it was clear to me that they didn't want me to bring in outside labor.

In the end the matter resolved itself in a most natural manner and no one seemed to object. When we brought the Landrover in there were 25 good workmen from the Oromo speaking people accompanying it. They were now at Godare. Here was an ideal work force to employ and put to work on the airstrip. These men knew what work was and had a certain amount of accountability. Discussing the matter with Bob Swart and Ralph Borgeson, we agreed that these men were the answer to our need for workmen to build the airstrip. When offered the opportunity, most of the men stayed with only a couple returning to their homes around Metti and Teppi. Occasionally, new people from Metti showed up wanting to work on the airstrip.

With this work crew things began to look much more promising. What a joy to see the daily progress. Compared to work put out by Majang, these men were light years ahead. Oh, there were the unproductive among them, but basically, they knew what had to be done and worked hard at it.

The largest tree on what would become the airstrip itself stood near the center of the upper third of the strip. It took ten men three weeks to dig shoulder deep to get at the roots and cause it to fall. Then it took these same ten men with helpers another three weeks to chop off the limbs and cut the trunk into lengths that would allow us to roll it off the field. This tree was at least 160 feet tall and had a girth of six or seven feet. The trunk was so large that two men could stand on it facing each other with axes as they chopped their way through it. To maintain enough room to swing their axes they had to cut out sections that were two feet wide where chopping began. This cut wedge would taper down to nothing by the time they had chopped their way through the log, cutting it into manageable sections. Huge mounds of chips scattered around each of these wedges. Once cut through, the trunk was so massive that it took the Landrover and a dozen or more men with pry poles to get it to roll bit by bit. I learned that by driving a metal wedge into the trunk on the back side and then latching a log chain unto it, we could roll the log a yard or two at a time until we needed to reposition the wedge. We'd do this until, finally, the log was off to the side of the strip.

But, even more difficult than that was to get the stump itself out of the hole and removed from the field. To do this I used a ton and one-half puller on the one side and the Landrover on the other. Gradually, tipping this massive stump with its huge awkward cut roots from side to side, we could build- up underneath it with short logs or stones until, finally, the bottom of the stump was up there at ground level, allowing us to roll it over unto solid ground. It was only the afternoon before the first MAF landing that we succeeded in removing that largest stump from the airfield, making room for the plane to come in.

It was an enormous task. Other huge trees were also being worked on. Stumps of every size were dug out. We would pay children a few copper five cent pieces for small stumps the size a child might tackle. I sometimes felt that the children had it over the Majang men on jobs like that. They let us down occasionally too. I remember one little guy asked for an axe so that he could cut out a stump which we had identified along the airstrip the day before. He disappeared with his axe and in about an hour came back to collect his three coins.

CHAPTER EIGHTEEN

That afternoon, riding along that side of the strip with the Landrover, I discovered, the stump was still there. He made amends by cutting out an additional stump in due course! He and I both learned something useful that day!

The young men loved to ride in the Landrover and they were a great help volunteering to help drag logs and stumps off the airstrip for the thrill of the ride. They were a great help too in digging out and removing the stones from the central area of the strip where the incline also had an undulation. We dug out hundreds of tons of rock. Interestingly, they were hexagonal in shape and lay on the slant in clusters of eight or ten as if they had been placed there. They made excellent stones later for the foundations of our permanent buildings. When professional builders eventually arrived at Godare they said they had never worked with nicer stone.

I should mention, too, that we learned which trees were worth saving for their lumber. The "Dampay" tree was the one of choice. It was soft dark colored wood with a beautiful grain to it. We cut hundreds of logs from trees we felled, planning eventually to have a saw mill and make them into lumber.

My chain-saw was the largest that Sears sold at that time. It was roaring every day. I always had a Majang with me to watch and warn me which way a tree or trees might fall. He stood right beside me and would tap me on the shoulder if he thought there was something I should be aware of. Sometimes trees were entangled in vines and before a tree could be persuaded to fall all four or five had to be cut. It was only when the last, key tree was sawed off that they all fell together. The tangled mass of trees and vines on the ground became impenetrable. Sometimes we'd have to tackle these from the lower end of the airstrip to get at them. I marvel and often praised God then and even now that we never had a serious close call. I wore out three chains to a point where they couldn't be resharpened. The metal part one would normally re-sharpen was gone! This represents an enormous amount of work and exposure to possible accidents. But, the Lord who mercifully heard our prayers was watching over us daily and blessing as he prospered our efforts.

God so wonderfully provided the help we needed when it was critical to have it. This is illustrated by a threatening situation that developed in the early stages of work on the airstrip. This was before we had the Oromo workmen and were working with Majang.

We were cutting our way with machetes along what would become the upper right hand side of the airstrip. The area was solid brush and tangled vines with trees. As the day wore on, it was apparent that the Majang were unhappy and apprehensive. I couldn't understand their language yet, so was unable to understand what was going on.

That night after dark a young man who spoke both Majang and Anuak came to our tent. He was in the area for only a few days, but the timing was critical and God knew it. Through this young man we discovered that the Majang were angry because we were cutting in the direction where one of chief Balti's wives had been buried some years earlier. If we continued in that direction, we would go over her grave and desecrate it. If we did so, they were prepared to kill us in revenge. Needless to say, morning couldn't come quickly enough.

Early the next morning, this man who spoke both Anuak (my language from the Sudan) and Majang accompanied me to chief Balti's village about a fourth of a mile from the edge of the airstrip. We assured the chief that we had no intention of desecrating that grave and that if he would provide us with two men who could cut a path along that edge beyond which we were not supposed to go, we'd be most grateful. As it turned out, there was no need to fear. There was ample room. All ended well and everyone was happy. God's timing was perfect to provide an interpreter at the critical moment.

But, there was more to do than build the airstrip and run a small clinic. The Majang were hungry. It was a bad year for them. The rains had come early and rotted out the roots they'd normally dig out in the forest for food. They depended on these as the amount of corn and dura (sorghum) they grew was minimal. The year we arrived, we found many of them hungry and some of them would likely have starved had we not been there. I recall Raanki coming to me one morning with his four little children, lining them up in front of me and saying that they would all starve if I didn't help him. Their stomachs were distended and bloated from eating grass. He was obviously telling the truth.

We began having shelled corn dropped to us by MAF. Like everything else dropped, the contents were double sacked in burlap bags. If the outer sack broke, it was hoped that the

285

inner sack would do what was intended. We flew in many sacks of shelled corn to feed the hungry as well as food for ourselves. Normally, we tried to get the Majang to provide some work or service for the small tins of corn we gave out to alleviate their hunger. To them it must have signified something of the love of Jesus Christ that we were concerned for them in this way.

## THE MULE MEN RETURN WITH SUPPLIES

You will remember that we had to leave some of our supplies behind in Metti and that I had pointed out to the mule men which cartons were most important for them to bring on their next trip in. Once the mules were a bit rested, they had returned to Metti for a second load. The two horses stayed behind with us at Godare. With six mules they should be able to bring in most of the essentials.

After a week had passed, we began hoping every day that the mules would arrive with our things. You can imagine our disappointment when finally they showed up with only two mules rather than six. The other four had been left behind in Metti and were either sick or dying. And, instead of bringing the carton with the urgently needed cooking utensils and dishes, they came with two folding chairs, which we discovered we really didn't need, a couple of copper tishes (water tubs for washing clothes by hand) and some other things which I have long since forgotten. We were dismayed! Lavina would have to get along with just that boy-scout camp cooking set another two weeks at least.

Eventually, when the third trip was completed, we had the things we needed including the cooking utensils, dishes, a portable oven and some flour. You would have laughed to see how happy we were. That very day, Lavina mixed up some bread and the next morning, I assembled the oven, lit a fire, arranged for the oven to hang from some sticks so that it was positioned correctly over the fire and watched the bread bake through the glass window in the door. We didn't have bread tins, so Lavina put the dough in the tin cups of the boy-scout set. There we were, grown missionaries, on our hands and knees watching the bread bake in our new, little portable oven. When finally it had baked and was cooled sufficiently for us to eat it, we had the most tasty cup of morning coffee with snacks that anyone can possible imagine! Never had bread tasted so good. Far better than the choicest ice-cream cone, or so it seemed to us that memorable day!

Our letter home, dated February 19, 1965 provides the back-drop on why we were so excited at that time:

*"Things are improving steadily. When we look back on the nightmare of those first weeks, we shudder. I don't think folks will ever really understand how difficult it has been. Lavina was telling me last night that during the period I was gone she went to bed hungry many nights. There just was no food here. Then too, without meat, we felt that empty spot even after we had eaten rice or beans. Now with the garden giving us beans, lettuce, radishes and spinach things are much better. We really lost weight these past weeks. Lavina grabs at least 5 inches of extra dress in the middle and I have 5 inches of extra belt. I guess that means we were both too heavy before too! ...*

*Our view here is really tremendous. We overlook the rain forest in the valley and then up a mountain range about six or eight miles off. The scene changes constantly with smoke and haze. During the night the valley fills with fog and in the morning the fog slowly lifts with a beauty all its own. One day this will be a beautiful place.*

*The Majang people are friendly, but more like Nuer in the Sudan than Anuak. They are fiercely independent and happy to live without help from the foreigner. They do not like to work yet either. We are reminded that only the miracle of the Holy Spirit will ever cause them to believe. The power of heathenism reigns here, but Christ, I am sure, will conquer one day.*

*The main chief of the tribe is a mile from our home. He also functions as the main witchdoctor. I saw him sacrifice a chicken and sprinkle a whole family with its blood a week ago. The message of Christ's atonement should be easily understood here."*

Lavina had many unique and interesting experiences trying to provide under less than ideal conditions. On another occasion when I was away, she had boiled a pan of coffee on

287

her three stones and was just waiting for it to settle so she could enjoy it. About that same time, Odi, a Majang neighbor lady that we later got to know quite well and who lived just above us on the hill, came sauntering down, smelled the coffee and said, "Uum, smells good," and proceeded to take a good drink from the pan that Lavina had been patiently waiting too cool! We often laughed about that one.

Of course, every day the work on the airstrip had highest priority, but I also had another major project underway. The original shacks needed to come down and be replaced with a better, larger stick and grass house. By this time, we could communicate a little and MAF had dropped nails and tools I'd need for that task.

Among the tools dropped, I recall, was a hand grinder needed to sharpen the tools the men were using on the airstrip. Until then they were using files to keep their axes and machetes on edge. When the grinder came, we found a way to attach it to a solid stump. It almost kept one workman busy sharpening tools.

We were able to get the Majang to bring in round poles of the right diameter which were fashioned into handles for the pick axes and regular axes. Keeping tools in working condition was a major task.

A letter written home, dated March 14, 1965 tell us about my experience trying to build our interim house:

*"These last weeks we have been busy rebuilding our house. The old shacks have been torn down, and in their place we have two nice stick and grass roof houses. They seem palatial to us, but, actually, they are just straight 3 to 4 inch sticks with a 6 foot 3 inch wall and a grass roof. We plan to put grass around the outside too to make it more fly and mosquito proof. The floor is still loose dirt, but we will soak it down and then try to pack it. The one building is 22 by 13 feet and the other is 13 feet square. We have the living room and the dining room planned for the long one and the other one will be the kitchen. I made a nice board table in the kitchen with three legs down into the dirt about 18 inches. Around our dining room table we have some new furniture. I cut four 18 inch logs yesterday, sawed them into 17 inch lengths and they are gracing our table now*

*serving as dinner stools. We have the two aluminum chairs in the living room, and I cut 20 inch logs into 26 inch lengths for tables in front of each window opening. For our book case, I have two boards on four logs in which we cut grooves to make them fit like a single log. Things are looking up now. And with the strip ready soon we'll be getting our refrigerator in and will be able to have meat regularly. ...*

*Well, we just finished a nice supper with hot dogs from a tin and buns and beans with nice chocolate cake for desert. Not bad!"*

## MAF MAKES FIRST LANDING AT GODARE

It was the 16th of March, 1965, when MAF made its first landing. We were so eager for them to come, but I felt uneasy and nervous about the responsibility to say that we felt the strip was ready for inspection and landing. What if we were still some days away from being ready when MAF's pilot would arrive on foot to check it out prior to okaying it? If the strip should prove to be needing a lot more work on it, we wouldn't want him to waste his time while we did work that should have been done before he arrived. We discussed these matters on the mission radio. Tom Frank, a MAF pilot, and Hugh Beck, a MAF engineer/mechanic trekked in from Teppi and gave their approval. I was greatly relieved. The next day, Bob Hutchins flew in from Jimma to make the first landing.

What a day of celebration and apprehension it was. We were excited that the moment had arrived, but we were worried about the safety of our strip for that very first landing. Tall trees still surrounded the strip. The approach on the lower end had tall, forbidding trees that would make a landing tricky and perhaps make it impossible to take off. These were some of the thoughts when the fateful moment arrived. Majang had heard the plane and several hundred were racing to get to the airstrip to see it happen. We were worried that someone might run across the strip not knowing the danger involved.

Bob circled the field several times testing it from either end. Once he touched down softly in the direction he would be going when he would have to take off. He was in the air again and for a moment we wondered, would he return and make the landing or fly back to Jimma because more work was required.

What joy to see him make the big circle and head back for the field. He made a perfect landing, but when he opened the door of the small plane, I could tell that he too was nervous and glad he had made it safely. Our prayers thanking God for safety in all things had special significance for all of us that milestone day!

After Bob landed we all walked the strip from one end to the other. Bob felt he needed more clearing on the lower end before he could safely take off. Almost immediately Balti ordered every available man to go down to the lower end and cut as many trees in the clearing as the pilot asked for. That day the Majang worked as they may never have worked before. Trees were falling left and right. By late afternoon Bob said he could now fly out safely and that the men could quit. We all tried to make it abundantly clear how happy and thankful we were for the crucial help the Majang gave us that day.

In the morning, Bob made several trips to Teppi to fly in supplies. Highest priority was a wood burning cook stove! And he flew in food supplies to cook on it. We were beginning to live. He even flew in our kerosene burning refrigerator. Bending the side panels we could just fit it into the plane. A new day had dawned. We knew also that we could now get out in case of illness or danger. The essential requirement for the success of our mission had been accomplished. We were in touch with the outside world. MAF could fly us to Teppi in less than fifteen minutes and all the way to Jimma in a little over an hour. How we thanked God for MAF. Without their services, the work among the Majang could not have been done from Godare. They were God's provision to make our ministry feasible.

Our letter home dated May 2, 1965 tells of the difference MAF was making:

*"Our airstrip is completed and is a first class strip, 45 yards by 600 yards of smooth surface. The plane has been in here more than a dozen times since it opened on the 16th of March.*

*We hauled four loads from Teppi this week, including barrels of stuff, kerosene, cement etc. It is hard to realize that it took us ten days of fighting thorns, ants and rivers coming in,*

290

*when we can now make four trips in less than three hours, in-*
*cluding loading and unloading. We never cease being thankful*
*for MAF."*

## FRANK AND GLADYS KIEFT ARRIVE
## AT THE GODARE

Within a few days, MAF flew in Franklin and Gladys
Kieft, our dear friends from Grand Haven, Michigan. They had
been helping at Ghimeera for several months while waiting for
our airstrip to be completed. We met them at the plane and
willing Majang helped transport their luggage and other supplies to the back opening of our house. I shall never forget our
joy when Lavina and I joined hand with theirs under the tree
and lifted our hearts in praise and thanks to God.

Almost immediately we cleared a spot just below our
grass house and put up their tent. They lived in that little tent
until they left early in June. They not only brought willing
hands to work, but Frank brought with him a tremendous testimony of God's leading. Wherever he traveled, Frank shared
his story. I have heard it in many countries and in many different settings. It is a marvelous testimony.

Frank was born in 1906 on a farm in Michigan. He was
the oldest of ten children. They went to Sunday school and
church occasionally, but it wasn't a regular thing. They went
to school in the country. Frank says that when he had finished the sixth grade, his teacher said, "You don't need to come
back next year. We cant 'learn you anything, anymore'."
That's all the formal education Frank ever had. Spelling and
writing were always difficult for him, but he was extremely intelligent and had the mind of an engineer. I discovered there
was almost nothing that he couldn't do, improvise or figure out
when a need arose. He was a tremendous person to have as a
volunteer.

His testimony was so genuine and honoring to God.
Basically, this was how he expressed it:

## FRANK KIEFT'S TESTIMONY

*"I was the oldest of ten children. When I was twenty*
*years old I planned to build my own house and get married. I*

291

was strong and ambitious and didn't feel any need for God's help. I didn't want any preachers shouting at me. I could make it on my own.

About that time, my mother was desperately ill and taken to the Muskegon hospital for surgery. She had a bowel obstruction and was full of poison.. After the surgery, my dad called home and said that if we wanted to see mother alive once more, I should bring all the children with me and come to the hospital. The doctor had said she wouldn't make it through the night.

With the help of a neighbor woman, the kids were dressed up and I took them all in our 1926 touring Ford to the hospital. I remember walking past my mother's bed and feeling as if a powerful hand was on my neck saying, 'Take a look and go home.'

The neighbor lady again helped get the children to bed. The youngest one was only two years of age. I found myself unable to climb the stairs to go to bed. Instead, I found myself circling the old pot-bellied stove. I went around it three times and went out into the kitchen, fell on my knees at this wooden chair and cried like a baby. At that chair I promised God that if he'd bring my mother home from the hospital so that she could raise her children, I'd do anything He asked me to do the rest of my life.

In the morning, the phone rang. My dad called from the hospital and said, 'Ma made it through the night'.

She lived another 35 years and raised her children.

I had promised God I'd do anything he asked me to for the rest of my life if He'd bring my mother home alive. At that time, I had thought that meant I'd have to stay out of trouble and attend church on Sundays. I had no idea of how God would challenge me to trust Him and the blessings He had in store for me. ... I often felt overwhelmed when asked to do something in the church, but each time I had to go back to my promise and say, 'God I promised I'd do anything you asked me. I cant do this by myself and you'll have to give me the grace and power to do it. ...' That promise I made at that kitchen chair has been on me all my life. I have to be available to God. .... I stand amazed at what God has done. ... I'm only a 'farm boy', but God has poured blessings into my life beyond anything I could have imagined. He's given me responsible positions in the church *world and in the business world. He's taken me around the world several times where I've been privileged to share my testimony. He's given me financial success so that I've been able to help the mission programs of the church. ... I can only say with the writer to the Ephesians as we find it in chapter three, verse twenty, 'He is able to do exceeding abundantly above all we ask or think.' "*

What a testimony to God's grace, goodness and power! How frequently God has blessed Lavina and me, personally, through this humble servant. For Frank it all began with a promise made as a young man at a kitchen chair. For me it began with a promise I had made as a young boy in a hospital bed. Whenever Frank talked about that kitchen chair, I thought about that hospital bed. Frank made his promise on his knees at a wooden chair, I made my promise in that hospital bed. Frank had said to God, "...I'll do anything you ask me to do for the rest of my life." I had said, "...I'll try to be a preacher of the Gospel."

Frank and Gladys and Lavina and I, with our children, were in Ethiopia because of those commitments made so many years earlier. Each of us had surrendered our lives to God trusting Him for whatever He had for us to do in His tomorrow. How marvelous to be available to Him! How wonderful are His ways! Ephesians 3:20.

We frequently spoke together of the marvelous ways of God in our lives. When the heat of the day had subsided and the cool, damp evening air moved in around us, there was time to share. On more than one occasion I would read one of our favorite chapters from the Bible. Psalm 103 was high on the list.

In the nearby forest, the monkeys would call back and forth. A forest owl would plaintively hoot and call. Occasionally, a rat ran slowly across the rafters. Eventually the little midges and mosquitoes became intolerable and we each went for the protection of our mosquito nets. We knew that God had blessed us through another day. We would be safe in the night because we knew that He "neither slumbers nor sleeps." God be praised for His manifold mercies!

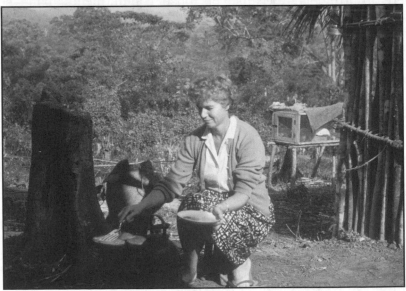

The Majang built our first house during our first few days at
Godare. The first few weeks Lavina cooked outside on stones.

# CHAPTER NINETEEN

# "KNOTTED STRINGS"

It happened by the light of a flickering candle. Lavina and I were sitting there in our stick shack trying to read a little by the inadequate light of the candle. We couldn't sit there very long because the mosquitoes were working on us. We had no doors or windows, just openings. During the day Majangs crowded the doorway and leaned in at the window openings, curious to know what was going on. Only gradually, we taught them with sign language that whenever we ate, we wanted them to back off. They got the message and would move back twenty or thirty feet, still straining to see what they could as they shared their observations with animated speech and gestures explaining to each other what they thought was going on. But, as soon as we were off our trek boxes indicating the meal was over, they came storming back. Once even one of the mules came in to investigate. And, inescapably, the chickens checked the place out on a daily basis. No brooms needed!

## BY THE LIGHT OF A FLICKERING CANDLE

But, now it was evening time and quiet. I was reading from a small book written by Joy Ridderhof, founder of Gospel Recordings, telling how God had led her through illness to establish that ministry. As I read her story of how God was blessing the use of disk records to reach people in remote areas, I turned to Lavina and said, "Honey, if we're going to reach this tribe, we're going to have to use those records." It was a simple statement, but was to have profound significance in shaping our ministry and the rest of our lives.

We had used Gospel Recording records in the Su-

295

dan. Working with the Anuak and the Murle we had considerable experience on which to draw. Frankly, the response among the Anuak had been less than spectacular, whereas the response of the Murle was terrific. We suspected that the difference was probably the quality of the message itself. The messages in Murle were better than those in Anuak. I could picture Nyaati, the illiterate Murle evangelist, going out with his heavy army surplus record player and gathering crowds in Murle villages who loved to hear the messages over and over. In fact, Nyaati had been judged to be so successful in that ministry that the local government officials, who were Muslim, often followed him up to arrest him and throw him in prison.

I continued talking as the vision grew brighter than the flickering candle would suggest. I said, "Honey, this time when Gospel Recordings people come out, we're going to work with them carefully and get the best possible messages on those tapes from which they'll make the records." It seemed clear to me that using those records we could multiply the occasions where the message of Jesus Christ would be heard in the language of the Majang.

## RECORDING OUR FIRST MESSAGES

When Kathy Hofmeyer, the Gospel Recordings recordist, arrived by MAF plane to spend a week with us at Godare, we had with us on the station a Majang who was completely bilingual in his own language and Anuak. In fact, we were never really sure whether he should be called an Anuak or a Majang. He was an ideal informant for me because I spoke Anuak and understood it well from my Sudan experience.

One of the interesting aspects of this effort was that Orac, the informant, was not a believer. The question was, "Could we use a non-believer to communicate the message of God's salvation effectively using the voice of one who did not know Jesus Christ personally?" My reasoning was that we would use his tongue like we use a typewriter key. We would look to God to be in control. We believed it would be honoring to Him. In any event, we had no alternative. I couldn't speak the language, that's for sure. There were no Majang believers at that stage. Theoretically and perhaps theologically it shouldn't be possible. But, in practice it worked and for that we praise God and feel certain Orac was His provision when we needed such a person most.

We prepared and recorded a dozen 3 1/2 minute messages to fit the length the records could accommodate. We began working from prepared GR scripts, but I felt a need to try to communicate more effectively from within the world view of the Majang. I wanted, from his perspective, to be able to express in different ways why Jesus Christ was good news for him. It was a great challenge -- our one opportunity during those seven days to do it right. We laid aside GR's prepared script and wrote our own messages in the light of what we knew about Majang beliefs. We prayed earnestly for the Holy Spirit to direct our thoughts as we worked out the new messages. It was a great week. When Kathy left she said, " I cant remember a time when I've ever experienced such leading of the Holy Spirit in the attitude and availability of an informant like I have this week in the way Orac helped us express these messages."

Orac soon disappeared into the forest to return to his distant village along the Anuak border. I don't believe I ever saw him again. I have often wondered if he ever came to faith in the Christ about whom he spoke so clearly and eloquently on those records.

Kathy returned to the states and the tapes were mastered and became phonographic disks in Glendale, California where GR is based. More than a year passed before the first records and our heavy army surplus record players arrived at Godare. We began using them, but by then it was already 1967 and furlough time. Larry and Betty Zudweg and their two girls would build our permanent house while we were away and hold down the station in our absence. Part of the time the Kiefts would be back helping them. Lavina and I would be visiting churches in many parts of America telling the story of how God had led us to the Majang and how we needed their prayers and support for the challenge that lay ahead.

## A NEW POSSIBILITY WITH
## CARTRIDGE PLAYERS

During that furlough, we were living with our family in Holland, Michigan in an RCA Mission house. It was a busy life and we had only a nodding acquaintance with our neighbors. One of these neighbors would have a tremendous impact on our future ministry.

Early during our furlough I was preaching on a Sunday morning in the Fourth Reformed Church just down the street from where we lived. In my message I told how we were going to be using records because it was a way we could multiply ourselves and the occasions when the message of Christ could be proclaimed. I explained how our stations among the unreached tribes in Ethiopia were one-family stations. The Majang were a widely scattered tribe, living in isolated clearings separated by an hour or two's walk. The were spread out over and area of nearly five thousand square miles of hills, valleys and rivers. It would be a difficult tribe for one family to reach for Christ. Gospel records could be carried by Majang believers to places beyond the missionary's reach.

The only problem was that the needles quickly dug down into the record grooves and the voice became distorted sounding like Donald-the-duck! But, I went on to explain, "It's the only means we have to extend our reach and proclaim the good news of Jesus Christ in the language of the people."

Unknown to me, God was at work in that congregation that morning. After the service while finishing our noon meal, the phone rang. It was my neighbor, Dr. Ron Beery, who taught physics at Hope College and directed the choir at Fourth Church. He said, "Say, I caught a vision while you were speaking there this morning. I wonder if I could come over and talk to you sometime."

Later that afternoon he shared how when I was speaking about those records and their limitations, he was recalling his meeting earlier in the week with Dr. Ted Ward, a communications specialist at the university in Lansing. Dr. Ward had been sharing with Ron about a new child's toy just appearing on the market. It was a two-track cartridge player powered by flash-light batteries. They had been talking about its possible potential for educational programs.

Ron said that as I shared in the church, he began to think of the possibility of these children's cartridge players being adapted to do what the records were intended to do. The existence of such a cartridge player was news to me. I was intrigued and could see the great value of the message being put on a cartridge like that where it would retain its fidelity. And, it appeared that the beauty of these players was that they were light weight, inexpensive and could be powered with flash-light batteries. Ron's question was "Do you think this kind of device would be of use in your kind of ministry?"

As Is recall it, my response was, "Ron, you may have the answer we are looking for." I encouraged him to pursue his vision and urged that he share with me all he learned. Praise be to God! I recall saying to Ron at one stage, "Ron, you may soon find yourself so busy you'll not have time to teach full time at Hope College." That moment came earlier than either of us could have anticipated at that time.

Before we returned to Ethiopia, Ron had formed Portable Recording Ministries. As I recall, he had three gifts of $500.00 each to put toward the purchase of the first thirty cartridge players. We contributed an additional $500.00 from a special gift for which we received the donor's permission to designate it for this purpose. We returned to Ethiopia six months later with the first 15 cartridge players. The other 15 went to our friends, the Swarts, working among the Galub people at the Omo. We were making history! We had the first "on line" cartridge ministry anywhere in the world to proclaim the Gospel.

Ron had transferred the messages from the GR records to the cartridges. We began with these twelve messages. Ron soon followed up with a player that he adapted so that we could do original recordings on the field. After some months, he even produced a cartridge duplicator for us that could do three cartridges at a time. We were on the way!

### CASSETTES REPLACE CARTRIDGES

Within less than eighteen months, Phillips corporation in the Netherlands perfected the cassette and were producing a small battery operated unit powered by four c-cells. For our purposes it was a gigantic improvement over the cartridge players. Very soon, these earlier units became obsolete and we were in a growing cassette ministry which later became known as "Teppi Tapes" and was based in the town by that name to which we had moved in efforts to reach additional language groups in that area.

299

The earliest cassette recorders had no pause buttons. We solved the problem on our 1970 furlough. Bill Klungle from Portable Recording Ministries improvised a means to stop the tape instantly while recording by installing a typewriter key-arm with a pad on it, which he had pivoted on one of the pins holding the unit together. It was so very simple, but did the job of giving us an instant start and stop while recording without producing any sound whatsoever on the tape. Later, when various manufacturers began introducing "pause" buttons on their machines, they all produced an electronic impulse so that the recorded tapes were always marred by these offensive clicks. Eventually, they solved the problem and the better machines allowed one to start and stop without that offensive electronic impulse being heard on the tape.

High speed duplicators soon followed and we were able to record our messages at will and duplicate the tapes efficiently and with good quality.

## ADDITIONAL RESPONSIBILITIES

I spent many hours with other outside chores supervising workmen on the airstrip, keeping the brush from overtaking the station, working on the road to the river, putting in the water and electrical systems and countless other time consuming tasks. By this time I was constantly preparing ten to twelve minute oral, tract-like messages and putting them on cassettes. I was also engaged in serious language study and we were more than busy with a continuing building program which required rocks, sand, water, timber, sawing of lumber and many other activities. Volunteers from America helped immeasurably, but also increased Lavina's work load exponentially. For both of us every day seemed too short. We were being challenged and were totally fulfilled in the Lord's work.

## THE MAJANG RESPOND
## TO "THE BOX THAT TALKS"

But, now, back to our story. During those early years the Majang came from all directions to see what was happening in their forest. They had never seen so large an open field as was the airstrip. They had never seen a saw which was able to take logs and turn them into planks. They had never seen bricks or concrete. They had never seen white people close up, and most of them had never heard of people who looked strange like we did. They came to see for themselves. Some, of course, came because they were ill and knew they would find help.

For whatever reasons, we felt God was bringing curious Majangs to us so that we could minister to their needs and share the good news of Jesus Christ with them.

On many occasions, once their curiosity had been satisfied, we'd sit with a group of Majang on the hillside in our yard or almost anywhere at all, put down a cassette player and let them hear this fantastic good news about Jesus Christ in their own language by one who spoke as they did. I wish you could have been there to see their reaction. Frequently someone would hold his or her face tightly, turning the head from one side to the other to hear more clearly. Some spoke back to the voice coming from the "box that talks". They were exclaiming, "Tia" ( I hear you) "Moko nyun" (It's no lie) or "Yang jet" (It's sweet). It was marvelous to behold. They were hearing the saving message of God's salvation. Mind you, there were no believers yet, but one day there would be because we knew from the Bible that "Faith comes by hearing" and "hearing by the preaching of Christ." It was happening before our very eyes and God keeps His promises that His Word will not return to him empty.

Sometimes in that kind of setting someone would ask to take the player home. They'd point across the river toward the mountains and say, "We live back there behind that mountain. We want them to hear this good news that we have heard. We'll return this 'box that talks' to you after they've heard."

What more could one ask? We'd show them how to put in a cassette and how to turn it over when it stopped talking. We told them that when the voice no longer spoke (the batteries would be dead) they should bring the "radioni" back.* In that distant village where this missionary's feet could not reach, the Gospel would be clearly heard. It could happen because of technology God had led people to develop in our time which we were harnessing in this unfinished task. What an exciting day to be alive and involved in Christ's mission to the ends of the earth. Our hearts were glad and we praised God often.

301

CHAPTER NINETEEN

At that time there were still no believers. Players were being carried hither and yon by non-believers who were intrigued by a "box that talks" and by what it was saying. Eventually, there were a few who had accepted the message and believed the good news. One of these was a young girl named Argeem, about sixteen years of age. She and our daughter Carol and the Zudweg girls, Terry and Sherry, had often played and visited together. Argeem had picked up a lot of English. When the girls were away at school, Argeem and Lavina became close friends and they often helped each other. Lavina taught Argeem numerous skills in sewing and baking. As they shared together, Argeem's love for Jesus grew and she was eager to share the Gospel by means of cassettes.

## "TIE A KNOT ON YOUR STRING FOR ME"

We discovered that the Majang had a neat way of keeping track of the days. Unable to read or write they had their way of checking off the days in relation to a specific event to indicate how many days had elapsed or how many days were left.

If a man was going on a buffalo hunt, he'd tell his family how many days he expected to be away. His wife would take a certain kind of grass, make it into a string, and tie one knot on it each day. On the day she tied her eighteenth knot her husband was expected back home from the hunt. Hopefully, he and his companions would be weighted down with a heavy load of meat for the anticipated feast.

The man away from home, in the same way, would be tying knots on his grass string. He knew he was expected back when he had tied eighteen knots. We thought they were exceedingly ingenious. I shall always remember the day Argeem returned carrying an Ethiopian Air Line's flight bag we had given her. Inside was a cassette player, several cassettes, and dead flash-light batteries. Argeem had unzipped the bag and brought each of these items out. Then she reached in one more time and pulled out a grass string on which were tied thirteen knots. I had never seen this before. She quickly explained.

"I've been in my mother's village. Every time I put down the player, my mother and other women would gather around

302

to listen. Sometimes, when the machine would stop, they asked if it would say it again. Sometimes, when the machine stopped speaking I would tell them, >I cant talk like this *radioni*, but I know that what it is saying is true because I am a person of this Jesus.' She went on, 'Before I left my mother's village, there were thirteen women who came to me and each one said, *>Argeem, I want to become a person of your Jesus. Take some grass and make a string and then tie a knot on your string for me=."* Unable to read or write, this was their way of signing on to register their commitment to Jesus Christ.

This was a day of boundless joy. I could see the tremendous potential of the cassette for evangelism. It was the key to our reaching the Majang people in the remotest places with the Gospel. It could happen because ordinary Majango like Argeem could communicate effectively using cassettes. All that was needed was a ministry like ours to help produce the messages on cassette and provide these cassettes, players and batteries in the languages required.

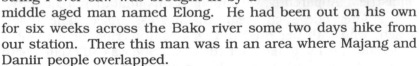

Later we saw numerous knotted strings like Argeem's. The longest string I ever saw was brought in by a middle aged man named Elong. He had been out on his own for six weeks across the Bako river some two days hike from our station. There this man was in an area where Majang and Daniir people overlapped.

Elong fingered the knots on his string coming to a larger knot near the middle. He explained, "These knots on this side are all Majangs, but on the other side of the knot -- these are all Daniir people."

Here was an illiterate barefoot Majang, a relatively new believer in Christ, who was able, with the help of a cassette player and messages in his own language, to cross the linguistic barrier and communicate the Gospel in such a way that some fifty Daniir people, said to him, "Tie a knot on your string for me. I want to become a person of your Jesus."

The wonderful thing about the cassette is that it not only enables ordinary, even new believers, to be effective witnesses for Christ, but it also is a marvelous teaching tool. While sharing the Gospel in this way, the person carrying the player is growing in his or her understanding of the essential truths of the Gospel. Initially, the cassette emboldens and enables an untrained Christian to share the Gospel among those who would otherwise not hear. In the doing of that, the believer is learning the essential truths over and over again so that at an early date this believer is able to share freely and accurately even when the player is not in hand. It is truly a tool God has given us to harness for this purpose.

## SEARCHING FOR ALTERNATIVES
## TO BATTERIES

Batteries, of course, put limitations on how often the message can be heard. But, God also led us into a solution for that problem. Hand-crank cassette players and small solar panels to power players directly from the sun were part of His tomorrow for His mission.

We missionaries shared with each other how we were using cassettes. Conversations at the dining room table in the mission guest house in Addis Ababa often included our concern about the cost of batteries. And, we wondered what might happen if missionaries had to leave and were no longer there to provide these essential components for successful cassette ministries. Apparently, we lamented this limitation frequently.

After one such meal, the hostess, Alice Jane Riderspach, who with her husband was volunteering eight months to Ethiopia, came to me after the meal. She was all excited with a solution that had come to her mind as she was listening in on our conversation. This is what she said to me: "You have got to meet my nephew. He's an inventor. He's a genius. I'm sure he could come up with a solution to your problem."

At that point, I was all ears. I excitedly said, "Who is this nephew of yours? What is his name? Where does he live?" I was eager to meet this creative genius.

Her nephew, Roger King, lived in Minneapolis, Minnesota, less than fifty miles from my boyhood home. When I met him during our next furlough, he immediately became interested in our ministry and in a few months had come up with a beautiful hand crank generator which could provide power by cranking. He had it encased in a clear, plastic case. It looked great to me, but Roger wasn't satisfied with his creation. He set it on the shelf in his office saying to me, "I think we ought to go solar."

Four months later he had designed and produced the first solar battery charger. When he sent it to me in California, he said, "Take it with you to Africa and try it."

From Africa, I wrote him, "It works beautifully. If you can produce a hundred of these for us, capable of providing 3 hours of playing time for 8 hours of sunshine, and can do it for not more than $50.00 each, we'll order 100 of them.

It wasn't long before Roger began increasing the output of the panels by adding small, shiny reflectors on each side of these units. And then, very soon, I discovered in Africa that we could play our cassette players directly from the sun with no batteries at all if we'd use these reflectors on all four sides of the panel. Then, as the output of solar cells increased, there was no longer a need for these cumbersome, unwieldy reflectors. During furloughs, as I shared in the churches, I'd share these intriguing and exciting developments.

## THE "CHARGERS"

It happened in the Menlo Park Presbyterian Church in California. I had never spoken in this church before. I had been sharing my excitement about how we played cassette players directly from the sun with no batteries required. I had in my hands one of the units we'd been using with its four reflectors. Fastened to the panel, these five by eight inch panels, bent back at an angle to focus the sun's rays, looked like a funnel, cut off somewhere in the middle before a spout had been attached. By tilting these units toward the sun and adjusting the angle every hour or so, we could play cassettes all day long wherever the sun was shining. What a fantastic opportunity God was giving us.

On that particular night, after the meeting an older man by the name of Lloyd Swenson came up to me with an astonishing remark. Out of the blue he said, "Do you know that our church could save you a lot of money!." I'd never met this man before but he had my attention. He went on, "It must require a good bit of labor time to produce one of these. This is silicon valley and we have the talent in our church which could probably put these together for you. ... Why don't you leave me one of these, and let me see what I can come up with."

I'd met others who spoke similarly, but this man was compelling. I left my unit with him. Less than a year later, he sent me his first prototype. Lloyd's vision and "drive" was contagious. From this one man, others in his church, The Menlo Park Presbyterian Church, in Menlo Park, California came forward to help. They organized themselves into a small cottage industry and, appropriately, called themselves "Chargers". Today, professional quality, attractive solar panels, powering players directly from the sun or recharging batteries for nighttime listening are being used all over the world. By 2002 more than 15,500 units have been sent out. And the count goes on!

Producing these marvelous little solar panels became a cooperative effort. Volunteers in the Community Reformed Church, in Escondido, California were soldering on the jacks and plugs. These jacks and plugs at the end of the six foot wire attached to the panel allow one to plug into the player and play directly from the sun or to charge small rechargeable batteries for night time listening or whenever clouds obscured the sun. One man in the Escondido church told me that he had personally soldered jacks and plugs on over 2,000 panels. How truly fantastic it is. These panels, the work of volunteers in two churches, are providing the energy required to tell the fantastic good news about Jesus Christ, God's only son, by the power of the "sun" He created in the beginning! They do this wherever batteries are unavailable or are too costly to use.

Pioneering in using cassettes among the Majang living in the rain forest in Ethiopia, I couldn't have dreamed of such incredible developments. And, to think that it began at a dining room table in a mission guest house of the Presbyterian mission in Addis Ababa because an alert hostess, following one of those meals, came to me and said, "You've got to meet my nephew. He's a genius. He's an inventor. He can help you." How marvelous, past finding out, are the ways of God! He often "swings His doors on small hinges"! To Him be all honor and praise!

# CHAPTER TWENTY

# "THIS IS BIG TALK"

In the wilds of Ethiopia, a Majang chief puts down his gun and listens to the story of God's love.

"Peeni cin Obiing". "This is big talk", mused the stock and obviously intelligent Majang chief. His name is Gabrekidan, the chief from Batagur, a village some three hours' walking distance on the other side of the Godare River. He and I had been sitting for more than an hour in the early evening darkness. We were sitting on the step of the "Godare Hilton" the name given to the stick-and-grass guest house where our guests slept when we had an overflow of visitors.

"This is big talk," he repeated almost under his breath as he listened intently to a taped message in the Majang language on one of our small play-back machines. "This is bigger talk than the other 'radioni' spoke when I heard it across the river," he continued. He was learning more about the wonderful things about Jesus.

Our first contact with Gabrekidan had come on one of those unforgettable days. We met under the most inauspicious circumstances more than two years ago. On that particular morning we looked up from the breakfast table and saw many Majang crossing our back yard. Most of them were carrying two spears rather than the usual one. Two spears spell fighting and bloodshed.

About mid-morning, I went to Chief Balti's village, which is less than a fourth of a mile from the mission compound. I found a large gathering of sullen tribesmen planning their revenge for a fight that had started the previous day over a wife dispute. The fight had been broken up by Bakle, the chief's oldest son, who was something of a hothead himself. He had waded into the group beating anyone unfortunate enough to be caught by the lash of a hippo tail he was flailing about. During those wild moments someone had also struck Balti, the chief -- which is quite unthinkable. The tension was compounded the following morning when Balti awakened suffering from a severe attack of malaria. His body shook convulsively as he tried to tell me the source of the trouble.

As I spoke to them, I reminded myself that I came with no authority but that as a man of God, I wanted to tell them what God's Word said about fighting and killing. And I told them of God's great love and Jesus Christ, and how we are to love one another.

Before I left that morning, they all assured me that they would not leave the village to go out to kill. If they were not attacked, they would remain in their homes. But sometime that afternoon a messenger came to the door. He had come from Balti who feared the people were getting out of hand. The new factor was the arrival of the chief from Batagur with twenty of his men. Seeing Balti's weakened condition because of his malaria, they jumped to the conclusion that it was because he had been jostled the day before and they were sure he would die. They must take their revenge without waiting to see what the outcome might be.

While we were discussing the matter with the messengers, drums began to beat and the trumped screamed its call for others to gather in the chief's village. We were frightened, to say the least. Since it was late in the afternoon, many would have been drinking and I didn't consider it safe to go and try once again to bring peace.

About this time, our little boy, Paul, came running into the house. The mother of one of his playmates had come quickly, snatched up her child, and had run off into the forest to hide. On such occasions it's a life for a life, and no one is safe, however young or innocent. Women and children were gripped with fear.

We stood in the doorway watching the messenger disappear down the trail. The shouting and confusion from the village could be heard plainly. It seemed that anything could happen. Straining to interpret the shouting, we saw a large group of Majang coming down the path toward the house. Paul dashed into the bedroom and crawled under the bed to hide. Lavina followed him into the bedroom and sat on the bed, quietly trying to reassure him. By then the men were at our back door, headed by the chief from Batagur. This was my first meeting with Gabrekidan.

They appeared to be friendly enough and we invited them into our living veranda. They all had guns and spears. For nearly an hour we reasoned with them and tried to persuade them not to kill. We urged them at least to wait until the next day. We were confident that by then conditions, now inflamed, would have had time to cool. It was not at all certain that Balti would die, we argued. Why should they take revenge without waiting? With God's help, sense prevailed. Somewhat reluctantly, they agreed to wait. And when their spirits had quieted, I had a wonderful opportunity to tell them about Jesus Christ. Gabrekidan was hearing the Gospel for the first time. God, through strange experiences such as this, often opened a door of opportunity for us to bear witness to Him.

Two days later was Sunday. Peace had returned to our community, and everyone was grateful and relieved. We met for worship on top of the hill near the center of this beautiful clearing in the forest. The sheer beauty of the day made it difficult to realize that two days earlier we were all gripped with fear and faced violence and death.

There were seventy-four present. Sitting in the center of the group was my new friend, Gabrekidan, the chief from Batagur about ten miles from here and across the river. With his heavy old Italian rifle stretched across his crossed legs, he listened intently as I preached from the First Epistle of John, chapter four. They heard of God's great love and learned that we cannot love God and hate our brother at the same time. God seemed especially near that Sunday, and the message appeared to fall on listening ears. Some days later I crossed the river and walked through the deep forest to Gabrekidan's village. We sat together in his barn and talked about Jesus. He asked penetrating questions about why they had never heard of Jesus before. I was ashamed and could not bring myself to tell him we had been too busy with other things. As we visited together, I discovered that here was one of the most intelligent and ambitious Majang that I had met. Even his newly planted fields of corn seemed to reflect his desire for things that were worthwhile.

When I left his village, he spoke earnestly, saying,

"Odola, you are going to your country soon. Don't stay away for a long, long time. If you do, we will forget these good words you have told us. Come back when the corn is ripe." And just as I was about to disappear in the forest to head for home, he called, "If you'll come back, I'll have my men cut the trail so that you can come riding on your horse."

Now as we sat together on the steps of the "Godare Hilton", evening had become night and it was already too dark to see each other's faces. But the language from the heart some-times expresses itself best without the aid of a lamp. And Gabrekidan was baring his heart to me. The sweet word of the Gospel made sense to him, and it was apparent that he deeply desired to know it better. It would only be a matter of God's own choosing when he would know Jesus.

"This is big talk," he said, unconsciously, thinking aloud. "Before you came, we had never heard this. We Majang were told that the Melineer* had come from a rock and were the offspring of God. We thought that the Melineer were our gods. We never knew from where the world came and how people began. The way of God has been lost to us."

That night before we parted with prayer, he said, "Odola, I want all my people to hear this talk. If you will come and spend a week with us, I will call all my people and they will come to listen to this word about Jesus." He went on, "Tomorrow I go to Teppi (seventy miles on the trail). I would like to carry with me a 'radioni', so that I can remember how to tell this talk to my friends with whom we'll be sleeping along the way."

Early the next day, he picked up a play-back. Three weeks later it was returned. Scores had again heard the "big talk" from the "radioni" that speaks Majang and tells about Je-sus. Gabrekidan seemed not far from the kingdom. But we remember the word of Jesus who said, "Except a man be born again, he cannot see the kingdom of God."

In Gabrekidan's village, as in others, stands a crude shrine. It seems simple enough -- an emoy plant, a few stones piled up, the horns of a buffalo or two, and a few beads and bracelets scattered about. The stones are stained from the of-ferings of beer that have been poured out and from the blood of the sacrificed chickens which has been sprinkled about. It all seems crude and unkempt. But it is the tribe's link with the spirits of the ancestors. This is the seat of power and blessing and lies at the center of the life of the community. The ritual expert who receives the offerings and can announce blessing or curse is the Melineer chief. Ignorance and superstition link hands together at the shrine. Only Jesus Christ can set them free! He is the light of the world!

\*\*\*\*\*

Typical, extraordinarily beautiful, early morning fog during the rainy season viewed from our grass house on this hillside.

A Majang chief, Gabrekidan, who said, "This is big talk!" when he listened to the cassette player telling of Jesus in his own language.

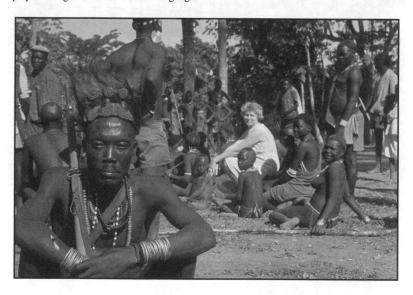

Worship services in Majang village clearings looked just like this.

# CHAPTER TWENTY-ONE
# A "ONE-FAMILY" STATION?

The Godare River Post was a "one family" station. But, that doesn't mean we didn't have many additional people involved in opening up the work and during our years in Ethiopia. Godare was one of the mission stations identified in the Illubabur-Kaffa (I-K) project. Others being opening during those years included the work at Chebera by Bill and Betsy Muldrow, the station on the Omo river being opened by Bob and Morrie Swart, and the work among the Surma people being opened by Don and Ginny McClure. There were to be a total of seven stations among seven different tribes, or language groups. Each was to have one family and be part of a network of stations in which Ethiopian staff would work with the missionary in the school and clinics. Missionary staff from larger stations in the Presbyterian mission would fly into these one family stations periodically to supervise the Ethiopian staff. The idea was to set the resident missionary family as free as possible for evangelism and ministry in general. All of this was made possible because of the services of Mission Aviation Fellowship based in Jimma.

Our stations were linked together by a morning and evening schedule on the two way radio system. These radios linked us to each other and to MAF. With these transceivers we ordered our supplies from Jimma, which in turn were flown in by MAF. In cases of emergencies or illness, a doctor from one of the other stations would come on the radio, diagnose the illness and prescribe the medicine to be taken. More than once we were on the air asking advice not only for ourselves but about some patients who needed medical skills beyond our own. Sometimes we'd have MAF fly in to transport seriously ill patients or those who required surgery to the mission hospital in Mettu or Dembidollo. These hospitals were north of us about 30 minutes by air from where we lived.

Educational missionaries and medical missionaries appointed to supervise the medical and educational work at Godare normally flew in on a bi-monthly schedule. They would spend one or two days with us and we found this to be an excellent plan. Missionaries with the special skills required gave direction to this aspect of our ministry and set us free for other areas of ministry, especially in the area of evangelism and working with the growing Christian community.

From a letter to the states, dated October 23, 1966 we were given a progress report on how the work at Godare was progressing:

*"The heavy rains are over and the sun is shining here at Godare this beautiful Sunday in the rain forest. Lavina, Paul and I have just walked home from our regular Sunday worship service. Birds were singing melodiously and from deep in the jungle came the regular call of the chime bird. Today at the service were 53 Majang people, dressed in leaves with a small patch of cloth or grass for covering. Slowly, almost imperceptibly, changes are taking place in the life of this people, and deep in their hearts God is at work. The seed is being sown and there is promise of an abundant harvest. On this day we again praise God for calling us to be His messengers to the Majang people. ...*

*This has been a year of exhausting physical work, coupled with language study, witnessing and preaching. Of necessity a great deal of time and energy has gone into establishing our base. The long airstrip to accommodate a DC3 aircraft is completed. Hundreds upon hundreds of trees entangled by twisted vines and covered with hordes of biting ants have been felled, stumps dug out, holes filled in and dragged smooth. Paths through the jungle have been cut allowing the Landrover to be used to haul water, sand, rocks and timber for buildings. Thousands of bricks have been pressed. The houses for the clinic dresser and teacher have been completed. The school and clinic buildings are nearly finished and our own permanent house has the foundation in. ...*

## A "ONE-FAMILY" STATION

*How sharply this year contrasts with our previous work and way of living in the Sudan! There, for 15 years the bulk of my time and energy was spent in sitting translating or in visiting in the villages absorbing language and culture and witnessing and preaching. Here there has been little time to sit, but each day has been too short as we have been involved in exhausting physical work, taxing one's energies to the extreme, and living under conditions that leave much to be desired. We, ourselves, are amazed that God, who gave us such joy in our work in the past, continues to fill our lives with joy and satisfaction in this entirely different kind of ministry. Truly it is of God's goodness.*

*It is a great joy to us to observe the changes taking place among the Majang. New people are moving into the area. Villagers are taking banana shoots and papaya seeds from us and growing them for themselves. Many have begun growing larger chickens from eggs we have given them. They are tasting just a bit of the material blessings that come through Christ. Increasing numbers are coming to the daily clinic for medical care. This is only a beginning. We thrill at the wonderful things the future holds for this people to whom the Gospel is now coming. In Christ all things can become new!*

*During recent weeks we've been doing considerably more visiting in the villages, making friends, witnessing and preaching. It is our goal to reach all within walking distance before we leave for furlough next July.*

*The Majang live in family units with several simple houses situated within a distance of a hundred yards, joined by ill kept paths with brush, stumps and logs obstructing the way. But the quietness of these homes, hidden in the forest, offers a marvelous opportunity for personal witnessing to the things of God. This is quite in contrast to the Anuak village of the Sudan with its many people congregated in one place and the inevitable distractions which follow.*

*The Majang seem to be genuinely interested in the new message. With humble boldness we make bold to proclaim that God has sent us as His messengers. The God whom they know only dimly has now come near to them ... and then we tell them all what God intends for them and what Christ has done for them and what he will do for them if they will turn from their former way to Him. I don't think anything can be more satisfying than to try to make the Gospel known to a people such as this who have never before had the opportunity. And this we*

315

can do in the confidence that God has sent us here and has purposed to reveal Himself through our witness. Can any greater privilege come to one than to be His witnesses!

The Majang will not be easy to reach with the Gospel. The physical barriers are many. The paths are incredibly difficult. The rivers are many, the mountain ranges are formidable and the people are scattered in isolated villages for distances up to 100 miles. And then the old customs do not change easily. The witchdoctor has a tremendous hold upon this people. The power of superstition, ignorance and custom hold the people in a vise-like grip. But Christ is greater than all these things. And it is He that we proclaim. With keenest anticipation we look forward, anticipating the wonderful changes that will come in the lives of this tribe because of Him. What a rare privilege is ours!"

## THE KIEFTS ARE BACK

We were greatly helped by the large number of volunteers and short term assignment personnel that came and worked with us for periods ranging from a few weeks to as long as two years. They came to work with us and often to do the tasks that enabled us to devote our energies to the real reasons for our being there. I could not have visited the villages, spent time with people, written those messages for the tapes or produced the cassettes which later played such a vital role in our effective witness to Christ if these people had not come to relieve us of the tremendous work load involved in opening work in the rain forest.

I think of Ed Pollock, Jr. He was that young college graduate who gave several valuable weeks of his time in the very beginning. He walked in with us and helped to get the work going on the airstrip and clearing out the initial camp site. He was able to rough it, sleeping in a hammock in the trees. He was nearby so that Lavina and Paul weren't left alone during those first weeks when I was frequently on the trail between Godare and Teppi.

Frank and Gladys Kieft made their first trip to the Godare within a few months of our arrival. They had arrived in Ethiopia even before our MAF strip was ready. When the Ethiopian airlines stopped in Teppi that first time, Frank wanted to trek into the Godare on foot to help us. The mission, however, knew this was not practical or safe for folks who were new to the country and already approaching sixty years of age. They had to fly on to Ghimeera and were a great help to Bob and Morrie Swart. There they worked with Ted Pollock prefabricating building materials that would fit into the MAF plane so that the Swart's house could be built at the Omo River. They also went in on one of the first overland trips from Ghimeera to the Omo River. Frank was a great help as they cut their trail through thorn trees to reach the Galub people and open that station on the Omo River. But, his ultimate goal was always to help us at the Godare.

Within a few days of our first MAF landing, Frank and Gladys flew in and stayed with us for several months. They came with their boots and work clothes, some pots and pans and lived in a small tent on the hillside just below our grass house. During their entire stay we never heard one murmur or complaint from them .

Frank was incredibly strong and had a head full of knowledge. He knew how to build, lay out plans, work with bricks and stone and fix and repair anything that broke. When MAF brought in the parts for a saw mill no longer being used by the Maji station, Frank figured out from scratch, without a manual, how to assemble it. Can you imagine the challenge of constructing a long wooden framework on which to assemble the 30 inch blade, pulley, chain and hand crank to move the log into the blade. Everything had to be aligned precisely or the sawed boards would be tapered and unusable. This would require extraordinary skills under normal circumstances, but with no boards available and the saw mill which could give us the required boards so that there could be a saw mill not yet assembled -- I'd say Frank had a problem!

It was solved when Ted Pollock came in with his chain saw and an attachment which enabled them to saw boards off from stationary logs by moving the chain-saw over the log itself and slicing as one went. I got involved in this myself for the couple of days required to have enough lumber to build the long table for the saw mill assembly. I still recall being nearly stone deaf those evenings from the terrible noise from the saw we were struggling to push along the log.

Frank was able to make brick, lay cement, build fireplaces in the clinic outpatient houses and in the school dormitory. Together, Frank and I built a peer out into the river from

317

small logs, and we spent days and weeks working together digging sand out and hauling it up the hill some seven or eight hundred yards to whichever new building was being constructed. It was no small task. And before that phase of the work could begin, we also had to cut a road for the Landrover through the ant infested vines and brush between the River and the compound.

Frank helped me lay out the station. What became the cleared station area with a clinic, school buildings, out patient houses, a clinic dressers house, a house intended for short-term staff, and the workshop, was originally so dense that one couldn't walk through it. The vines were so tangled that trees refused to fall even though they had been cut off. These vines were so strong that once or twice they lifted the back end of the Landrover off the ground rather than giving way. Then, too, this previously uncut forest, was alive with little, black, stinging army ants. The Majang refused to cut around several trees severely infested, but Frank dove in and stuck with it until the trees fell. He paid for it though because the ants were in his shaggy beard. He tore off for the house faster than ever before and finally solved his problem by shaving off his entire beard.

Frank and Gladys were great fun to have with us, a great help and always an inspiration and example to us. The only complaint is that he worked us hard from sunrise until after sunset! They came out on four different occasions for periods of five to six months each. Once when they left, as the little plane was disappearing from view, I turned to Lavina and said, "Honey, let's take a day off!" More seriously, we can never adequately express our gratitude to God for the Kieft's contribution to our lives and work. They came to work. When they saw a need they tried to meet it. Once, Frank even flew out a heavy cement mixer and paid the transportation charges from America. He said, "What good is it to you if that thing comes by sea and arrives six months after you need it. I'll see to it that you get it before it's too late." That cement mixer was like pure gold to us. What a relief after mixing cement in a half barrel with a hoe and a shovel! God be praised for lay people like the Kiefts.

## YOUTHFUL VOLUNTEERS LIGHTEN OUR LOAD

There were others, similarly eager to help, who came out to make an essential difference.    The first of these were Don Sill and Jim Cetan.    Don was a graduate from Hope college and Jim was a pre-med student.    Jim helped in that first clinic shack on which one of the volunteers put a sign reading, "Godare Medical Arts Building."  Jim, also, supervised the digging of ditches on each side of the road that ran through the compound connecting our airstrip with the living area where our house was to be built.  We dubbed this little stretch of road "Cetan Ave".  We so appreciated Don and Jim who put up with less than adequate food and lived under very primitive conditions.

Our first MAF plane had landed on March 16th.    During those ensuing weeks, the plane was in and out, often several times a day and sometimes several times a week.    What a joy to receive supplies that hadn't been damaged by being dropped from the air.   The only thing we missed was the excitement of seeing those double sacked supplies hitting the ground and then flying and bounding along the ground of what was becoming the airstrip. Some of those bags scooted along some fifty to sixty feet.  I will always remember soap bars flying in all directions when a carton of 200 bars without protective sacking was dropped.

Lavina remembers vividly her experience with air drops too.   I had trekked into Teppi to help with the loading and to help in making the drops.    In lieu of roses, I had wrapped a glass jar of pickles in several rolls of toilet tissue and dropped it with a nice little "love note".   It is good that I did, too, because on that same drop one of the sacks with a carton of beans landed in a stump hole and had no way to scoot along the ground to lessen the shock. Lavina reported that 23 of the 24 tins of baked beans had ruptured.  She had no can opener but used a pliers and screw driver to pry the tins open.  She said she ate beans ( not her favorite food) three times a day for three days before they soured and had to be thrown away.

But now with the strip open, that was all past history.   However,  a great deal of work on the strip still remained.  We had determined that it would pay in the long run for us to extend the strip so that a Dakota aircraft could land.  This would make the building program so much easier and we wanted the larger strip because of some pressure for this from the Royal family.

## TIES WITH THE ROYAL FAMILY

Her Highness, the Crown Princess with her two daughters, personal secretary and body guard came into the Godare on a special chartered flight one day to visit us. Lavina scrambled to figure out what to serve for lunch at noon. This was fasting time for the Orthodox Christians and Her Highness wouldn't be eating meat, eggs or any animal products. I thought Lavina was extremely creative with her menu. Almost everything came out our garden which had an abundance of vegetables and fruit. Our missionaries at Pokwo on the Baro river helped immensely by sending up tasty, frozen filets of Nile perch. We were greatly honored to have members of the Royal family as our guests. Dr. Don McClure had set that up and accompanied them on their visit to the Godare. We lived in the afterglow of this special day for quite some time!

We also had the privilege of being entertained by the Royal family at the palace in Addis Ababa. Once we were invited out to their summer palace at Lake Bishoftu for a royal dinner with the Crown Prince and his entire family along with special guests from among their ambassadorial representatives. After our humble circumstances at the Godare, it was rather daunting to sip and dine with the finest cutlery and glassware!

We always had a lot of good humor with our fellow missionaries on days such as that. I suspect they were just a little envious of us so we would tease them saying that to shake our hand after returning would call for an extra dollar. After all this was a hand that had only recently shaken the hand of the Crown prince or of her Highness the Crown princes, no less! I have often marveled at the tremendous variety of experiences one has as a missionary. They range from the humblest to the most sublime!

## A THOUSAND METER AIRSTRIP NO EASY TASK

Building a thousand meter airstrip was a gigantic task. Sometimes I wondered if it was worth the enormous effort. I recall standing on the upper end of the strip which sloped gently down hill away from us, identifying some of the huge trees out there beyond the end of the strip that still had to come down for the approach. They were way out there beyond where we had reached in our clearing. I identified one of those trees and went with workmen and my chain saw to tackle it. It was several hours before the tree we were working on finally fell. At noon when we returned up the strip toward the compound, we turned around, surveyed the situation and discovered that the tree we thought we were cutting down was still there. All morning we'd been working on a totally different tree. It really didn't make that much difference to us, in any event, because before the task was completed, they all had to be felled. But it does indicate the enormity of the task.

The largest tree we ever took down measured two hundred feet. It stood near the lower end of the strip and was about ninety feet from the edge of the runway. Ethiopian Air Lines had flown over the strip a couple of times to check it out and told us that unless that tree was felled they'd not be able to land. This tree was so huge that we hardly knew how to deal with it. Frank Kieft and I once measured it. The huge webs from the trunk going down as massive roots into the soil measured sixteen feet from one side of the base to the other. The trunk itself was eight feet in diameter and went up eighty or ninety feet before its first huge branch. It was a tree I was loathe to destroy, but we had no choice.

We determined we'd have to burn it down. A Majang man worked at this for many days and finally decided he needed a companion to help. Eventually, the men came to me saying they thought that if I came with my chain saw, we could get it to fall. I went and discovered that their fire had burned away much of the lower trunk except for an eighteen inch core at the center as well as several of the webbed roots. There was enough burned away so that I could crawl under the tree and work on it with my chain saw while lying on my stomach. It was scary, but I knew which direction the tree would eventually fall because of its leaning slightly toward the airstrip.

I began chain sawing and after some time saw that the groove made by the cutting was beginning to open ever so slightly. I continued sawing a bit longer and when it was apparent that the groove was continuing to open very, very slowly, I crawled under away from beneath the tree and we all stood back about fifteen or twenty feet to watch. After a minute or two this gigantic tree fell with a tremendous crash, burying pieces of mammoth, broken branches two feet in diameter in the soil on the side of the airstrip. This again created a Herculean task to remove this debris from the strip itself.

But, our experience with this tree doesn't end there. Late in the afternoon just before dusk, the two men who had worked at burning it down came to collect their pay. I gave them the agreed amount and went into our grass house. In no time flat, I heard the most terrible commotion outside just up the hill. The two men were fighting over the division of their pay and were actually threatening to kill each other. I rushed out, calmed them enough to get the money back from them. We then, in the darkness, all walked over to Chief Balti's village and I explained to Balti what had happened and asked him to settle it between them. I gave the money to Balti and, without my assistance, he brought order out of chaos. It was a night to remember!

The work was made more pleasant by four young fellows from the states who came out in 1966 and spent the summer with us. They were Harry Miersma, Duane Laman, Ted Wyngarden and Bill Van Eenenaam. They were all college age, full of fun and eager to work. They came with boundless energy, curiosity and a readiness to work and live under less than ideal conditions. It was a tremendous help and inspiration to have them with us. We had great times at work and great times sharing, especially after the work and heat of the day was over and on Sundays, pondering together the meaning of life and what God had in mind for each of them. It continues to bring joy to our hearts when we realize that Harry married and became a full time missionary and that Duane felt God calling him to be a pastor and went ahead with his theological training. Both men, with their families, are in the Lord's service today. We like to believe that their summer experiences living among the Majang and seeing their need for Christ and how missionaries were attempting to make a difference, perhaps in some small way, influenced them in making those large decisions that shaped their lives to be available to Him.

The memory of the companionship and vitality of those young men are precious to us even now, some thirty years after the event. With the joy comes a tinge of sadness when we think how Bill, a few years later, was tragically killed in a plane crash, leaving behind his wife and two children and family. He was always special to us.

## THE VOLUNTEERS FROM KALAMAZOO

Larry and Betty Zudweg with their two daughters served at the Godare for two years. Mary Swart, our daughter, Carol, and Lavina are all there under the big tree to welcome the Zudwegs who arrived via MAF.

Larry and Betty Zudweg and their girls were with us for two years. Larry was skilled in building and had finished part of what was to become our permanent house when Haven Reformed Church in Parchment Michigan sent us five men to help finish it and to work on many other projects then underway. These men all left their families behind to give us five wonderful weeks of their best efforts. We had great times of fun and fellowship along with hard work. They slept in our "Godare Hilton", a mud floor, stick and grass-walled building situated about twenty feet from where the new house was going up. Lavina and Betty scrambled to keep food on the table. Cooking with damp wood in the iron range didn't make it all that simple! I can still see them blowing on the stubborn flame to encourage it along.

We shall always be grateful to the families of these five men -- my cousin, Dr. George Hoekstra, Frank Spitters, Brad

Stonerock, Bill Smith and Ron Houtman, for their willing spirits in encouraging their husbands and the fathers of their children to come.

These men were all skilled in their various professions back home. At the Godare they proved to be equally skilled as builders and mechanics. I can still see them laying out on the ground lumber we had sawed on our own mill, as they constructed those large wooden trusses for the roof of the house. Without lifting equipment, they figured out how to move them and position them in a standing position on the walls.

It was these men that speeded the time when we moved up the hill from our grass house. This old house had served us well for three years but it was past time to move out. The roof leaked and the rat population hadn't diminished. In the new house it seemed pure luxury for us to have a clean, cement floor underfoot and to sleep with regular beds and mattresses again with no need for mosquito nets.

Even so, it was with some nostalgia that we tore the old grass house down. Our children lightheartedly complained, "Dad, you're spoiling the place, making it too modern." Perhaps they were thinking of the fun times we had had as a family when the children took turns with the pellet gun shooting rats off the rafters.

## A MISSIONARY'S CHILDRENS STORY

This brings back a fond memory. We always had marvelous evening times sharing in a Bible reading and prayer before calling it a day. It was during those quiet moments when I was reading the Bible that a rat or two would frequently appear on the sill or on the rafters. Sometimes one of the children couldn't resist the temptation and interjected into the reading, "Dad, there's a rat." I would keep on reading, but sometimes the pressure increased. "Dad, there's a rat!" At that point, I would give in and say, "Okay, get the pellet gun and be sure you don't miss."

That was fine except it could sometimes lead to a bit of confrontation between contenders for the gun. A minor war zone would erupt with one missionary child contending with the other as to whose turn it was. "Dad, it's my turn, he shot last night" Great fun! Missionaries and their children -- no different from normal people! There was no telephone to disrupt, but some demonic angel seemed to instigate those rats to appear just when they could inflict the maximum disruption in our quiet time together. That may not be good theology, but there were times when I almost thought it might be so!

## FOND MEMORIES FROM THE OLD HOUSE

That old house has many memories. But here is one experience from the very first shack in which we lived. We never bothered putting grass around the outside so the sticks laced together gave plenty of room for insects and bugs to enter. And with no doors or windows at all, just openings, almost anything could get inside at will.

Not having a way to bake bread, Lavina frequently made pancakes and we ate these with honey we could get from the Majang. Bees loved that honey and we would often have eight or ten bees sipping at the edges of our tin plates while we were carefully trying to eat without irritating them unnecessarily. With bees like that partaking from the same plate, one learns to handle the fork quite expertly!

The second generation grass house was much more spacious and after Frank Kieft came it had screen doors and screens over the window openings. This helped a great deal but mosquitoes and tiny midges often drove us to our cots early. These midges would itch between the fingers so intensely that one had to give up the battle and retire early.

Frequently, Lavina would put out on the kitchen work table a plastic pitcher of milk to sour overnight for pancakes she would prepare in the morning. The pitcher was always carefully covered with a cloth to keep out any droppings from wall lizards or the rats. There was one morning, however, when we would have no pancakes. During the night rats had pulled the protective cloth off and had gotten into the pitcher -- all three of them. Two had drowned and the third one was still frantically treading milk with his nose just above "water" trying to survive. I don't remember what we had for breakfast, but I know it wasn't pancakes.

CHAPTER TWENTY-ONE

## UNPLEASANT IRRITATIONS

Army ants also had a way of invading our houses. Even the new house wasn't a match for army ants. They would come in, marching two abreast, and fan out everywhere. Their sting was so hot that one couldn't really tolerate it. The only answer was to try to contain them in one section of the house by sprinkling either ashes or Gamexine powder as a barrier to a room that might not have reached yet.

Another contender to make life difficult for us, was the little jiggers we called "bojulies". During the dry season, they multiplied in any dry, powdery soil. Walking with bare feet was an invitation to them to latch on, burrow in and hatch. When this happened, the "nest" would grow from a tiny pimple to something as large as a small pea. They itched furiously and frequently became infected. Having several in one's foot at the same time wasn't at all uncommon. They had to be tackled with a pin or needle to dig them out. Afterward we would soak the infected foot in a pan of warm, antiseptic water, put a bandage over the place, and try to remember not to walk with bare feet again!

Among the most unpleasant irritations we had to learn to live with was what the mango flies did to us. The Majangs taught us which trees attracted these flies and warned us not to linger under them. Before we knew this, we were hanging our laundry directly under one of those trees with disastrous consequences.

These flies would lay eggs, especially on anything damp like laundry when hanging out to dry. Before we discovered that every piece of laundry had to be ironed, for which we used our charcoal burning irons, we found ourselves getting maggots under our skin. We made our discovery when I had what appeared to be three large boils on the shin of my leg. They were extremely painful and we got on the radio with the mission doctor who suggested I keep the leg elevated and apply hot packs to it. I followed the doctor's orders and later applied a bandage with drawing salve. Imagine my astonishment and horror the next morning when I removed the bandage and tried to get the core of the boil to pop out. What actually popped out was a large, full grown living maggot. Two others followed in rapid succession.

We learned that if we carefully ironed every piece of laundry, no exceptions -- even wash cloths, towels and socks, we reduced the chances of this happening. Even so, we contended with them frequently, especially during the first few years. Once Carol, who was about twelve then, came running up the hill to me saying, "Daddy, look what's coming out of my eye." Coming right out of the eye lash area a maggot had emerged. We had thought she had a sty in her eye and never dreamed it might be one of those miserable maggots.

Once when the boys were home from school in Egypt, Jim discovered that his blankets had gotten wet when the rain sent water cascading down the hill and into their tent. Without thinking, he hung his bedding on the line to dry and put it back on his cot late in the afternoon. Three days later his entire back was saturated with tiny pimples which gradually developed into maggots. He squeezed out some seventy of them.

During the early years, especially, whenever a pimple appeared anywhere on our bodies, we were on the alert for these maggots to develop. A sure indication that the pimple was, in fact, the beginning of a maggot was when, periodically, one experienced a burning sensation lasting ten or fifteen seconds. We knew then that it was a tiny maggot just getting started and that it wasn't an ordinary pimple which hot climates tend to facilitate. Normally, we would allow this pimple with its resident, developing maggot mature for three days. We discovered that we could deal with them with maximum success on about the third or fourth day.

We learned that we could use a lighted candle and let a drop or two of the melted, hot wax drop on the pimple where the maggot was maturing. The trick was to get the hot wax close enough, but not too close or it would be very uncomfortable. Another trick was to hit the right spot. Once these two hurdles were surmounted, it got to be rather interesting to see this hidden enemy try to get through the wax for air at which point we would squeeze it like one would a pimple and it would come popping out. That whole procedure was quite distasteful and uncomfortable.

New people and volunteers always seemed more vulnerable to them. I thought that perhaps our systems were building up an immunity or antibody because as the years went by they became less and less troublesome.

It was never a pleasant experience for our young men

volunteers to have to submit to my squeezing these things out. However, because of the expertise one develops in knowing just how to do that, the requests kept coming to me on a regular basis!

## LIVING IN THE FOREST A NEW EXPERIENCE

These were all interesting challenges and provocations. Sometimes, we had additional excitement, and it was a lot more fun, when wild pigs invaded our compound. We tried shooting them by the light of a flashlight when they got into the sweet potatoes. Once, I even shot through the screen when these wild pigs awakened us by their chomping on fallen, ripe, guava fruit right near our bedroom window.

Living in the forest was a totally new kind of experience. What we gradually took for granted would be terribly frightening and threatening to newcomers. We accepted being awakened by the coughing of a leopard. Once when we awakened in the morning, we discovered that a leopard had eaten the large chunks of meat from the hind quarter of one of our cows that had died late on the preceding afternoon. This cow had died mysteriously less than fifty feet from our bedroom. Being late in the afternoon, I'd done an autopsy but hadn't had time to remove the carcass. This nearby, previously unseen leopard, enjoyed his feast while we slept right through it.

The forest was alive with strange, frequently haunting sounds during the Night. The Calobus monkeys chattered like machine gun staccato as they called back and forth to each other from trees on opposite sides of our clearing. Baboons could scream bloody murder when they engaged in their savage brawls. And there was a forest bird we never saw that would, only rarely, pierce the normal forest environment with a blood curdling, piercing cry like someone terrified and calling for help. But, early each morning long before daylight the innumerable variety of jungle birds would begin to sing. The choir of the most beautiful songs one can imagine was our daily delight. Several times I arose early to go down the hill into the wooded area between us and the river. The variety of songs the birds were singing was out of this world. How privileged we were to be there in that unique place.

## SNAKES A DEADLY THREAT

We were always on our guard for snakes. The small, deadly poisonous green mambas were in the trees and bushes. On the ground were the cobras and the pythons. The largest python we ever killed measured sixteen feet four inches and was about four to five inches in diameter.

The red cobras were dangerous, even deadly. One day just before lunch, Majangs came in with a little boy about ten years of age. He'd been bitten by a red cobra. It was really too late to give him anti-snake medicine, but we did it anyway. A large crowd was present, anxious for the boy's life.

We put him in front of one of the inpatient houses near the clinic, prayed with them and advised them not to allow the boy to sit up or move about.

When I returned after lunch, I found them leading the boy, walking him around slowly. His cheek bones were all cut with small grooves. They had seen the quivering of his cheeks because of the reaction to the poison. They cut the cheeks with many small slashes to allow the spirits to escape. On the mat where the child had lain there were several coins and several short strings of colored beads. These were gifts to appease the spirits and induce them to leave the boy alone.

Balti, the chief and ritual expert, was there with the relatives and other onlookers. I spoke sharply to him and told him they had to make a choice now between entrusting the boy to us and the God who had sent us to Godare to help, or in their old methods. I carefully and understandingly tried to show them that they couldn't have it both ways. They had come for our help and we were happy to do what we could. We had prayed to God and now we must trust Him for His miracle. God, the creator, who had sent His son to show us what was in His heart, was powerful and able to save this boy's life if He so choose. It was a moment of great decision for them, but, thanks be to God, they made the right decision. Balti ordered the people to entrust the boy to our care and not to disturb him further. Balti's word was law and having him on our side was always our goal.

The story has a happy ending. The young boy was mercifully spared and recovered fully. I always looked upon it as one of God's signs to convince the Majang to turn from their pagan ways and believe this good news we had come to bring. The clinic was a place of great opportunity to make that clear. We never hesitated to affirm that the good things happening for the Majang through the clinic were happening because of Jesus Christ in whose name and under whose instruction we had come to bring the news of God's salvation.

## SMALLPOX AT GODARE

One summer our daughter-in-law, Sheryll, came out. It was such fun to have her. All the strange sounds at night were very threatening to her good sleep. It was interesting that when she first arrived and found we had evening devotions and Bible reading each night as a family, she thought we had "church" every night. At first, teasing playfully, she would inquire, "Are we having catechism again tonight." Before the summer ended, if there was the slightest hint that we might be cutting that devotional time because of some intruding factor, it was Sheryll who spoke up saying, "Dad, aren't we have devotions together tonight?"

Sheryll loved helping in the clinic and gave many small pox vaccinations that summer. We were experiencing the last outbreak of smallpox in Ethiopia before it was totally eradicated. I had never seen patients with smallpox before and it wasn't a pretty sight. Oozing pus filled sores covered large sections of the body and there were high fevers. It was a dreaded disease among the Majang.

When the disease first struck our area, Chief Balti, who was also the chief ritual expert (witchdoctor), discouraged people from coming to the clinic to be vaccinated. Instead, he put up a small stick trestle about three feet wide and seven feet tall over the trail between his village and the clinic. He lived about a fourth of a mile from our mission compound. Balti assured his people that if they walked under the chicken he had sacrificed and spread with wings outstretched at the top of the trestle, they would not become ill.

Well, it didn't work and Majangs gradually came to realize that the only people safe and secure from the disease were those that Sheryll and our clinic dresser had pricked with the needle. Eventually, Balti himself, was pricked in the arm and began to tell others to follow his example. During our years at

Godare, Balti was a frequent visitor to our clinic and encouraged others to come. Balti had a severe, incurable case of shin ulcers, made worse by his elephantiasis. We put hundreds of bandages on his legs and each time he heard the message of Jesus love.

## JOHN BOEREMA HELPS INSTALL THE TURBINE

We owe a lot to John and Harriet Boerema too. They came out in 1968 and spent some nine months with us. John and I had talked by phone from the airport in New York just before we left for Ethiopia. We had spoken together briefly when we had visited Iowa. During our conversation John had said he would be open to helping us. I thought a call before we left might be just the encouragement he needed. It proved to be so and in a few months they had made arrangements for their feed business and the farm, and were winging their way toward Ethiopia.

We enjoyed them both tremendously. Harriet and Lavina did many things together and had great fellowship. For Christmas they baked mounds of cookies and threw a lawn party on the hillside in front of the house for the Majangs. We had great fun over that after the party was over. Didn't take long! There must have been twenty or thirty who came. They had no idea about taking one or two cookies and a drink of juice. Each one loaded his or her paper plate with all it would hold before moving away from the table. In no time flat the table was empty! We laughed and laughed over our first Christmas party with Majang guests. I don't believe it was every attempted along those lines again!

John and Harriet were there doing those months I was installing the electric turbine and hydraulic ram. When those four young, college age volunteers had been out, Harry Miersma and Duane Laman had written a letter to their folks in California suggesting a turbine would be useful and had presented an idea on how the loop in the river could be cut with a channel to give a head of water sufficient to power it. I still remember how excited those fellows were when they shared a letter with us from their folks saying their church, First Reformed in Artesia, was excited about their proposal and wanted to make it a project for which they would provide the funds.

We had since checked the various kinds of turbines that would operate efficiently on a low head of around five to six feet of water. The unit we purchased would use up to 680 liters of water per second. The amount of water needed determined the width of the channel we would have to dig. The order had been placed in Germany and the unit was now in the station waiting to be installed when John arrived. He was exactly the man we needed. John was patient, careful, creative, and methodical. When the job was completed, the turbine operated flawlessly without vibration.

Once the turbine and the water system were completed, our Ethiopian staff and we shared equally in its benefits. The water system provided the entire compound with a constant supply of water as near as the faucet itself. An overflow pipe enabled nearby Majangs easily to fill there pots from the overflow instead of having to walk the seven or eight hundred yards to the river and carry the heavy pots filled with water back up the hill.

Having electric power twenty four hours a day made it possible to have lights in each of the staff houses, clinic and school. Eventually, we brought in an electric freezer where we could store meat for staff and ourselves to share alike. A tiny Reformed Church in Colton, South Dakota gave this useful gift to the Godare station.

In order to have fresh meat available, we purchased young bulls and steers in Teppi on market day. Once or twice a year Majangs would walk in ten or twelve animals. These grazed on the airstrip where grass was in abundance. They helped keep the grass down and provided meat for the freezer as they were butchered one by one.

Animals were a problem in the forest. The entire area was infested with tsetse flies and animal sleeping sickness was endemic. Every animal brought into the Godare had to be injected periodically to protect against sleeping sickness. Cattle responded well, but horses, mules, donkeys and dogs were never completely immune. Across the years we eventually lost every horse and dog we ever brought to the Godare. This always saddened us because we needed these horses to get around, but knew that their fate was sealed. During the final stages of the illness, the animals began to stagger about aimlessly, eventually went blind and either died or had to be destroyed. One morning right after breakfast while we were still standing in the back yard, one of our big, seemingly strong horses, without warning, took off galloping wildly. He made a big circle, turned back toward the shop area and crashed headlong into a tree. His neck was broken and he died almost immediately. We assumed he had gone blind and lost his mind, resulting in this pitifully tragic accident.

In trying to figure out what had happened, I recalled how on the previous evening this horse appeared to be acting strange. Lavina and I were sitting in front of the house in the darkness except for the light from the stars. This horse was just outside the compound fence when it took off and thundered off at breakneck speed in the darkness down the trail toward the river. After some time, when it returned up the hill I went over to have a look. He was perspiring profusely and I remember saying to Lavina, "That horse acts like he's had a nervous breakdown."

### TEACHING MAJANGS HOW TO GROW COFFEE

The Majang were learning many new things. We introduced them to bananas, pineapple, mangos, peanuts and sweet potatoes, teaching them how to grow these things. We undertook an ambitious program of helping Majangs learn to grow coffee as a cash crop. I had learned what I could from coffee plantation people near Teppi about planning the spacing of seedlings, how to prune the growing trees and how to go about harvesting the ripened coffee beans. They told me how much of the forest should remain uncut to provide shade for the coffee trees. I passed this information along to the Majangs as we worked with them. The MAF plane brought in thousands of seedlings which Majangs planted in their villages. On the compound itself we had a demonstration plot with about 100 coffee trees for teaching purposes. As I write this, I'm reminded of a 200 pound bag of coffee beans we left behind in the storehouse in 1976 when we had to leave Ethiopia because of the take over by the communists. Coffee improves with age, so this should be really prime quality coffee for roasting and grinding by now! (first edition 1995)

## AL SCHREUDER, THE MIERSMAS AND LAMANS

Al Schreuder came out to help us one summer and later came back with his lovely wife Susan to spend an internship in Ethiopia as part of his theological program from Western Theological Seminary in Holland, Michigan. Al was strong and pleasant and was willing to live the most simple lifestyle. He had the markings of an excellent career missionary in the making. We could see that Al and Sue would be "top of the line" missionaries that God would mightily use.

That same fall Henry and Susan Miersma and their pastor, Dave Laman and his wife Lois came out to help for about three weeks.

We had just returned from furlough ourselves and Larry and Betty Zudweg, with their girls, had been holding the fort in our absence. Larry was a good builder and had finished our permanent house while we were gone. We were amazed to see the beautiful, quartz stone fireplace he had put in the living room. Larry had run across a stretch of rock in a clearing just off the compound. I suspect ours may have been one of the few quarts fireplaces in the world! Larry's specialty in the states was fireplaces and he couldn't resist the temptation. We were the benefactors of this labor of love and appreciated it immensely. Whenever we had guests our unique fireplace was a sure conversation piece!

## LACK OF FOOD POSES A PROBLEM

We had arrived home from furlough just a few days before the guests from America were to arrive.. Food supplies were low. The Zudwegs were using up the supplies and hadn't replenished the larder anticipating that we would bring in what was needed when we returned from furlough. Somehow we hadn't realized how low their stock was. The problem was further complicated when we removed the lid from the barrel in the outside storeroom in which we had left a good fourth of a barrel of sugar. Imagine our horror and revulsion when we discovered that the cover had somehow slipped off at some time or other and a rat had fallen in. We discovered his shriveled up carcass of bones and hair. Our imagination told us of what had occurred between the time we found him in this condition and when he had fallen in. It couldn't have been pleasant! You may be sure that we used sugar on cereal very sparingly those days until fresh sugar could be flown in!

The Miersmas and the Lamans were to bring in numerous supplies including our new dog, Zadick, They would be coming on a DC-3 with a full load of whatever was needed including food and staples. Unfortunately, the pilot became lost and about the time they should have arrived, he was asking our traveling guests if they had any idea where the Godare was. Eventually, the pilot gave up, turned back to Jimma and landed with minimal reserves. This could have ended in tragedy!

So instead of coming with numerous supplies, our guests came in the next day with MAF and minimal supplies. Having four additional people to prepare food for when there is none poses a real problem when the closest food store is a hundred and twenty five miles away. We shared our plight by radio with the other missionaries. It was Maji station that came to the rescue and sent what they could with the MAF pilot who diverted from his course to drop them off on his way back to Jimma. They must have heard Larry on the radio one morning saying, half in jest, "Either fly in food or prepare to fly out the bodies!" It was serious enough that our guests huddled one morning and seriously discussed leaving on the first MAF plane available because of fearing they were a burden to us because of the food crisis. Lavina and I talked them out of it and food supplies did reach us and everyone lived happily ever after!

We had a great time with the Miersmas and Lamans. The women enjoyed each other and pitched in planning and cooking for all us hungry men. We still talk about the morning when, as we men came through the door into the kitchen, we found Susan scooping up a freshly baked mulberry pie off the floor. It had slipped out of her hands as she pulled it from the oven. She had a mind to throw it away, but we restrained her and said, "Not on your life, lady. The floor was just mopped this morning. We don't get mulberry pie every day in this house. You don't go throwing that away." I cant remember a homemade pie tasting better!

Henry and Dave erected the fence around the fruit orchard and house area. We had brought in metal posts and adequate barbed wire. They did a first class job like people used to do on the farm.

The other important task accomplished was putting in the headgate in the channel to the turbine at the river. We had been using the turbine, but the headgate itself still had to be put in. Like good soldiers, Henry and Dave stuck with Al Schreuder and me at the river until ten o'clock one night. We had to complete that task in one pouring of cement. They were dog tired guests accompanying a very weary missionary as we trudged up the hill the seven hundred yards with a two hundred and fifty foot climb to the house. I can still see young Al Schreuder jumping into the rain barrel half full of rain water standing under the eave at the corner of the shop. He had a good bath, but, as I recall, the rest of us did it with a little less noise and less water.

## PAUL HAS RHEUMATIC FEVER

Sleeping was somewhat difficult for lack of covering and space. The forest was always damp and sleeping on the floor could be quite chilly for a little guy like Paul. Weeks later, I recall my returning from Ghimeera following a couple of days of meetings. Lavina had been alone with Paul and was very concerned. She described how Paul had a fever and that his joints seemed to be hurting him. She said that he couldn't stand the weight of a bedsheet on his toes. Without knowing more, I suspected rheumatic fever. When we finally got him to the doctor, it proved to be just that. Lavina had a very sick little boy in bed for three months. Part of that time was spent in Addis Ababa where medical care was available. The Lord mercifully spared him from perceptible heart damage. Much concern and many prayers were said for his full recovery.

## THE KIEFTS, BROUWERS, STAUBLE AND OTHERS

The Kiefts were back at the Godare for a five month stint when Carlton and Warren Brouwer from North Holland and Harold Stauble from Kalamazoo came to help. Carly and Warren were both professional builders. Carly, Warren, Frank and Harold put up a beautiful little mud and cement brick house for short term staff we anticipated in the years ahead.

During this same period, Harold took our old Landrover and completely overhauled its engine. Hours and more hours on the saw mill and the rugged use to which it had been put on the airstrip and hauling sand, rocks and dirt for the bricks had taken their toll. It had only a few miles on the speedometer, but long hours on the engine. When Harold finished his work, the vehicle looked as old as ever, but it ran like new!

Roger Koppenol from Michigan and Tony Heinen from Wisconsin came out to help us build the itinerant airfield at Keto. Right after my first landing there, the men from Keto invited me to one of their homes. It was a simple mud-walled, grass roofed house but it had a spectacular view out across the valley. We were about ten or twelve of us and I was sharing the Gospel as one would share good news he had recently heard. I was telling them that because of what Jesus had done in giving His life on the cross, God would freely forgive the sins of anyone who was sorry, turned away from them and asked God's forgiveness.

While I was sitting among them sharing, one of the men suddenly spoke up. He said, "I'm so glad that we didn't quit working on our airstrip. We almost gave up because the work was so difficult. If Mr. Roger and Mr. Tony hadn't come to help us, we'd never have completed it."

And then another spoke as he asked a question. He wanted to know if God would forgive him. He said, "I've quarreled badly with my neighbor. Every year we'd quarrel over the boundary separating our land. One year the rocks would be moved over by my neighbor and the following year it'd be my turn to resent the stones making the division between our fields. We cheated each other and we hated each other. If we confess our wrong to each other and to God, will God forgive us?"

Yes, I'm glad, also, that they never gave up. Without that airstrip they would never have heard this good news of God's readiness to forgive all who repent and believe the good news centering in Jesus Christ.

## DAVE BAST AND DAVE PETERSEN

A couple of choice young fellows who came out for a summer, were Dave Bast and Dave Peterson. They were there when the astronauts made their first landing on the moon. Dave Bast later said that at that time when he was deep in the jungle rain forest in Southwest Ethiopia, the men on the moon could reach home before he could. ... We had a great and wonderful summer with these two Daves. They were of sterling character and fun to be around. I knew Dave Bast's father, Henry, well and often said to Lavina, "He's sure a chip off the old block. His mannerisms are just like his dads." I consider that observation to be a first class compliment to both Dave and his father. His dad had been one of our dearest friends. It often seemed that just when we needed a special word of encouragement, a letter from Dr. Bast would show up. The Lord knew!

David Petersen was a young man whose behavior and disposition reminded me always of the passage from the Gospels where Jesus said of Nathaniel, "Behold, an Israelite indeed, in whom is no guile." He was sincere, considerate and tender of heart ... always thoughtful of Lavina and her work load in trying to keep hungry mouths filled under less than ideal circumstances. Twenty years later the two Daves still speak fondly of the wiener roasts on the hillside, late Sunday afternoons when we opened tins of anemic wieners to put on home made buns that Lavina had baked in her wood oven!

Dave Bast returned to the states to prepare for the ministry, After serving several churches, he was chosen to succeed Dr. William Brownson as Words of Hope's radio minister. Dave Petersen went on to become an outstanding surgeon who specializes on the hand.

## AL AND BETH SMITH FROM MINNESOTA

Another great couple who came out to help us for two full years was Al and Beth Smith. They came out as Christian Service Corps missionaries. Their coming overlapped one of our furloughs and they held down the fort at the Godare while we were gone. They deserve special praise for sticking it out alone at the Godare when the radio went bad and they had no contact with the outside world. Only a few could have tolerated the isolation and potential danger facing them under those conditions. They were good soldiers and met a real need to man the station, working with Ethiopian staff and nurturing the growing Majang church. Al had grown up on a farm less than a mile from where I had lived as a boy in Minnesota. Beth also had close ties as her mother and I went to the same little church and Sunday school when we were children.. Al and Beth did a great job and are included among our dearest friends.

## HARRY AND PAT MIERSMA

Finally, last, but by no means least, are Harry and Pat Miersma. Harry had once come as a volunteer, but was now back with his lovely wife, Pat, who was also a trained nurse. They took over from us at the Godare when we moved to Teppi to establish a new base from which to reach several other un-reached tribes using the MAF plane and cassettes. Harry and Pat came out as RCA missionaries and were God's provision to carry the work among the Majang forward so that we might be released for the new Teppi Tapes cassette ministry which was based in Teppi.

Other volunteers also helped us get that station opened but we will wait to speak of their contribution until we come to that part of our story. Then and now, we praised God for His faithfulness and help in providing us with the means for the task and for the people who came out to help us. We praised God then and still do for the churches that assisted volunteers and short term missionaries by providing finances that enabled them to come. Godare a "one-family station"? I would say, with overflowing thanks, that it was much more akin to the celebrated "extended family" so common to Africa.

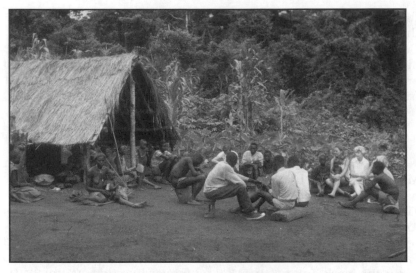

Worshiping on a Sunday morning with the Majang

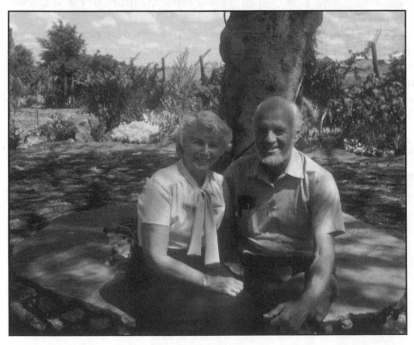

Harvey and Lavina during a vacation time somewhere in Kenya, East Africa.

# CHAPTER TWENTY-TWO
# HOPES AND FEARS

Bakle, chief Balti's oldest son and heir apparent, wasn't living in the Godare area when we first moved in to open our station. This had important implications affecting our relationships with him once he returned to the Godare some eighteen months after we first arrived. When he appeared on the scene, he came with a hostile attitude. We had the feeling he wished we weren't there!

Our dealings were with Balti. It was he who had assured us of his cooperation and that he welcomed our coming to the Godare. From the beginning, it was apparent to us that Balti had enormous power and influence over his people. At times it appeared that he had the power of life and death in his hands.

When we first arrived, nothing happened without Balti's involvement and approval. If he told people to help us, they helped. When we paid helpers their wages, they counted them out to Balti and he took a few for himself. During the early months, no one worked more than a day at a time. Usually, it was far less than a day and no one ever worked by the week. At the end of each day's work, however long or short the day, we had to pay each one his or her wages. Payment was always in 5 cent coins.

As we came to know Balti and the Majang people better, we began to understand their world-view. The Majang believed that the Creator God was far away. They recognized His existence and acknowledged him as the giver of sunshine and rain. However, they didn't worship Him and on a daily basis their concerns were about keeping unfriendly spirits satisfied and at bay.

The Majang had many superstitions. Some where quite humorous. Our son, Mark, as a young boy loved to hike, fish, hunt and explore with Majang boys his age. After returning from one of those hikes visiting villages across the river, Mark shared with us a strange experience. He said that when they came to a certain place where the path suddenly veered off in another direction, his Majang friends all stopped. They picked up small switches and began to switch their buttocks, threw these switches on a pile in a certain fashion, and then moved on. He said they had told him that a leopard had crossed the path there and they did this to protect themselves from him.

In the early days when we were exploring the river for possible sites where we could put our hydraulic ram to push water up the hill into the station, I had asked Balti to provide a man who could help me research this. Balti kept dragging his feet, so one day, growing impatient, I was able to get one of the men to take me to a nearby falls so I could check it out. That evening when we returned, Balti was so furious with this man that he threatened to kill him. I learned that Balti claimed a mysterious power over these falls and that he had some superstitious views about spirits who resided in that place who also gave him special powers.

## THE COFFEE TREE INCIDENT

Another strange thing occurred when workmen from Teppi located a coffee tree just off the compound. I had told the workmen that I was very interested in learning where wild coffee might be growing. I hoped that eventually we might assist the Majang in helping them grow coffee as a cash crop.

On this occasion, Lavina and I had just returned from our first trip out to Addis Ababa with the MAF plane. Upon our return, the workmen from Teppi were excited to show us a coffee tree they had located nearby. In fact, they had already planted several volunteer seedlings they had found growing near this tree. When they showed me the tree, I was surprised at how scrawny it looked and decided I should prune it so that it would become more productive.

I thought nothing more about this as the tree was actually growing in the midst of vines and brush just off the compound. It wasn't long, however, when we discovered that Balti wasn't at all happy with what we had done. I had no idea that this tree was anything other than a wild tree growing in the forest. I learned differently when Balti and his man, Alemayu, and I pushed our way through the undergrowth to visit this scrub tree which was only about ten feet tall. I was astonished to see these two men kneel down and begin talking to unseen spirits. I learned that it was a sacred tree which had connections with someone who had died long ago. I never fully understood, but it was apparent that it was more than just a wild tree growing by itself. They thought I had been disrespectful when I cut its branches. I don't know whether I was fully successful or not in trying to indicate that I had pruned it so that it would produce coffee beans. They had no interest in harvesting coffee from it and I'm not sure they believed what I tried to explain to them. My usage of Majang language at that stage didn't make for the most efficient or certain communication. I did know one thing, however, and that was that the Majang saw things far differently than I did and that I'd better learn all I could about them if we were to communicate the Gospel to them effectively.

## BALTI,
## CHIEF AND RITUAL EXPERT

The Melineer clan of which Balti and less important chiefs or ritual experts were considered to be gods and to have power over the spirits. On our survey trek when I made my first contact with the Majang, I asked an Anuak speaking Majang in the Korme area what the Majang believed about God. We were walking along the trail fifteen or twenty feet behind the leader, the Majang chief in that area. Pointing to the chief, he said, "*Pa Jwoka eni?*" ( Is he not the god?)

In Balti's village there was a typical shrine with the emoy plant. It had some stones, a broken pot and another that seemed to still be intact. There were a few scattered beads and that was about all there was to it. When they made beer, a little of the new beer was always first spilled on these rocks. I was told that this was to honor and keep the ancestors happy.

Balti performed numerous sacrifices of chickens. People would come in carrying a chicken. At the appropriate moment, Balti, who had bad looking legs with shin ulcers that never completely healed, would come out of his hut or arise from his stool. He would point to his spear leaning up against the grass fence. Someone would fetch it. All was very informal. Someone held a gourd with a little water in it. Another held the chicken and stretched out its neck. Balti would slowly run his spear across the chicken's neck, severing it so that the blood flowed down into the gourd. The chicken never seemed to make a fuss like when I was on the farm and we would chop a chicken's head off for Sunday's dinner.

The people who had brought the chicken were squatting on their knees waiting for Balti to sprinkle them lightly with the blood and water. If someone showed up late, he would rush in and join the others already gathered there. Before the blood was sprinkled, the spear was put back to lean along the grass fence and the chicken was put on the ground. The chicken was eventually plucked of feathers and cooked but it had no relationship to the ceremony so far as I could determine. It was just another chicken for the pot.

Sometimes if a person in the village was too ill to come to Balti to have him sacrifice the chicken, he'd put some of the blood in a hollow tubular stalk. They would seal up the end with mud and sprinkle the blood on the sick person in the village.

Almost no Majangs kept sheep or goats. When you saw such an animal in a Majang village you knew it was there for some superstitious reason. I recall one Sunday seeing someone come up the hill leading a goat on the way to Balti's village. They were bringing it from home to have Balti cut off the tip of its ear to make an amulet. This tip of the ear was taken back home along with the goat. The amulet with the tip of the goat's ear was put a a string made from the fiber of the bush with the nettles and worn around the neck by the woman in the village who had been experiencing poor health. The goat itself was staked in a shady place next to some emoy plants. Every day they gave the goat preferential treatment. They spoke kindly too it and gave it beer or fermented honey water. The idea was to keep the goat happy so that the bad spirit causing the illness would leave the woman and be attracted to live in this goat.

People were constantly coming to Balti to be blessed by him. They would hand him something like a cooked Godare root or possibly a short string of beads. Usually, they knelt in front of Balti when they did this. Balti would put the object to be blessed, under one of his armpits, spit on it, remove it to his other hand and repeat the procedure under the other armpit. It often appeared that he was talking causally about something unrelated to what he was doing -- just having a normal, friendly conversation about almost anything. Before it was over, Balti would hand the item back to the person who had brought it and this individual would wrap it in a leaf of some sort and carry it back home to the village. It appears that the idea was to convey Balti's blessing and power to a particular felt need in that person's home or village.

Frequently, we would see young people come up to Balti and he would spit ever so lightly on their chest or stomachs to bless them. When I got to know him better, I would occasionally, in good humor, lift up my T-shirt and kid Balti that I could use a blessing too, always being careful to call it all off by backing away before he might think I was serious about it. Balti had a great sense of humor and loved to tease, especially the children. People loved him but also feared him greatly. He was a complex person. He was shrewd, calculating and shared in one way or another in the lives of the Majang people. His power and reputation extended to the far reaches of the tribe.

When we would be working down at the river, we'd frequently see six or eight Majang men and women passing by on the trail leading up the hill in the direction of Balti's place.. They would be carrying heavy pots of honey they had collected from their beehives which were positioned high in the trees throughout the forest. When I would ask them where they were going, they would call back, without stopping, "Weenga. weenga" (life or spirit) They were bringing these as gifts to Balti. He received many such pots of honey. Some of the honey was turned into fermented honey water into which they had shaved the bark of a certain tree to give it a drug like effect. Other pots were carried by Balti's people into Metti and turned into cash. With the cash they were able to purchase heavy, old Italian army rifles. With these they could marry, kill each other and celebrate with on occasions like marriages and especially deaths.

## A MAJANG BURIAL

We always knew when someone had died and the burial

was taking place because of the heavy rifles being fired in that place. It appeared that the more important the individual the more shots were fired. When a new mourner arrived, he would eventually aim his gun in the direction of "nowhere" and fire.

One morning we became aware of a death just over the hill beyond the upper end of the airstrip. Throughout the morning individuals or groups of two or three came up the hill from across the river. They passed through the compound and continued on the vine covered trail leading to that village. We had heard a few shots during the morning and finally decided we would go and have a look.

This is what we saw. This older man who had died had already been buried. The grave site was almost in the center of this small clearing. Women had put a small, temporary grass enclosure around the mound of the grave. There were only a few shacks in this small clearing and the forest pressed in closely. As was their custom, an area of at least thirty by forty yards had been cleared of any vines or small sharp stumps. Several women were still working at that. Most people were just scattered around, sitting there, saying very little to one another. It was all extremely unorganized and informal.

Lavina and I quietly sat down among them on a small log. It wasn't long before one of the women ran in from behind us, put her grass skirt between her knees and took a nose dive into the air, falling flat out on the ground with a crashing thud. She was stretched out full length with her hands extended beyond her head. This was the way Majang women expressed their grief. Almost immediately, a couple of women rushed forward, grabbed hold of her and restrained her forcibly, as she struggled against them, bringing her back to where she had been sitting. At this same time, other women were throwing themselves on the ground in this same way. It all seemed confusing and terribly tragic. The hopelessness and despair was overwhelming.

After this had continued for some little while, on our left and across from us, we saw a man come running across the cleared area with his spear in hand high over his head in a position from which he could throw it. He ran past the grave site to the opposite side of the clearing near the edge of the forest. Suddenly, he stopped abruptly and made menacing movements with his spear arm in several directions as if he were

346

going to throw it each time. He then turned the spear around with the shaft pointing away from him, with the two edged blade facing his own body. He took this spear and began violently and vigorously, with strong force, repeatedly coming down on the top of his head with the sharp blade, cutting his scalp deeply each time. The entire gathering seemed to be getting emotionally worked up with a gun or two also being fired. At that point, we decided it would be in our best interests to quietly slip away and return home.

In the Sudan we had witnessed this same utter despair and hopelessness when people died and were buried. The early morning wailing of the women was haunting and so extremely pathetic. Now among the Majang we were seeing this same hopelessness in the face of death. We had long before this noted the numerous cuts and deep scars on the foreheads or on the top of the heads of Majang men. It was their way to express sorrow and it was a proper way to ritually participate in such events. Both men and women also shaved their heads bare when a member of the family died.

It was significant to us that when we asked Majang believers how they would characterize or identify distinctive marks of a Christian, setting a person of Jesus Christ apart from people who had not yet accepted him, they always remarked that believers no longer cut their heads with spears. They had heard and embraced the fantastic good news that Jesus had conquered the power of death, set His people free from fear and had given them the assurance of life beyond the grave, a life which would never end or diminish. Interestingly, another distinguishing mark they always mentioned was that a person of Jesus Christ gave thanks to God for his food before he ate. And they always added that Christians no longer sacrificed the chicken. For Majangs, both of these characteristics were obviously visible and important!

In trying to communicate the Gospel, we had to know these customs and learn to express the good news of what God intended for the Majang through Jesus Christ within the context of their world-view. I was constantly asking myself wherein is the historical account of Jesus Christ and what the Bible says about the significance of His suffering, death and resurrection good news and relevant to the life of the Majang.

## ORAL, TRACT-LIKE MESSAGES
## ON CASSETTES

When we began producing the oral, tract like cassettes, nearly every message, in one way or another, began with the words, "This is good news for us to listen to. It is good news because it is in our language and we can understand it. It is good news for old men and women. It is good news for young men and for the young women carrying the babies on their backs. It is good news for our children. It is good news because it is from God, the one who created the world, the God we thought had gone away and left us.

The good news is that this Creator God never left us. And, if we will stop and think we will realize that this is true. It was the Creator God who been giving us sunshine and rain. It was He would gave us the children in our homes and supplies us with the food that we eat. But, we never worshipped Him or gave Him thanks. For this he should be angry with us and we deserve to be punished.

But, the good news is that this God loved us so much that he said, I will send my own dear son from heaven to earth to show them what is in my heart. The name of God's only son is Jesus Christ. We never knew what God had done, but He has sent people to live with us to tell us this good news. ...@

These messages, from different perspectives, told this good news from God. Each message led up to the central affirmation that Jesus Christ had given His life as the perfect sacrifice and therefore no more chickens need ever be sacrificed again. "Jesus came out of the grave having defeated the power of the evil one who destroys and kills. Jesus has great power and we need not ever be afraid again. He is powerfully present through His spirit which he sent to live with us and in our hearts. If we will put our trust in Him, He will protect us from every evil thing. And when we die, He will take our spirits to be with Him in heaven forever. This is the good news from God.

And this Jesus told His followers to go everywhere in the world with this good news. Today, this good news from God has come here too. We have heard it in our own language. We must turn away from the things we know God will not like, and give our lives to this Jesus who loved us that much. ... "

348

When the Majang heard this good news, some would respond with comments like, *"Yaang jet."* (This is very sweet) or with *"Moko nyun."* (It is not a lie).

But, it took time before some among them took the plunge of faith and committed their lives to Jesus Christ. For some, it was when they realized Jesus power to heal and experience His loving care through the clinic. For others it may have been when they saw Jesus behind the help they received when hungry and about to starve. For all, it was the divine power of the Holy Spirit who, in His time, opened blind eyes and gave the gift of faith, doing it in His own mysterious way as when the wind blows and we cannot explain where it comes from or where it is going.

### DIFFERING RESPONSES TO THE MESSAGE

For some, it was a leap of faith they found impossible to make. I recall the Sunday when many were being baptized. Among the people waiting for baptism was Gadi, a smaller witchdoctor. She had had double cataract surgery in the mission hospital at Mettu where Arlene Schuiteman was a nurse. Gadi had been greatly blessed by this. She wanted to commit her life to Jesus and had come to that service to be baptized along with the others. We had sung many of the new Majang songs of praise. The sermon had already been preached and everyone to be baptized had come forward. Gadi, remained sitting on the ground with her paraphernalia. Slowly, she arose, turned away and made her way down the hill to her stick shack below the compound. In her hands were the paraphernalia she relied on to keep peace with and have power over the evil spirit world. It was her living and her livelihood. Village women visiting the service had whispered words of fear in her ears. She was persuaded that to be baptized was to risk her life. Sadly, she turned away and to our knowledge never committed her life to Jesus.

On the other hand, there were instances of great courage when new believers were unashamed of their allegiance to Jesus. Argeem is a case in point.

Tom Nichol, from Mettu hospital, one of the medical doctors who visited Godare clinic periodically, did a double cataract surgery. He did it in our clinic on a bare wooden ta-

349

ble. I was his assistant and amazed at what I saw! After the surgery, this lady had both eyes bandaged and we carried her over to one of the vacant staff houses. Argeem offered to stay by her night and day to tend to her needs. Later she told us how non-believing Majang women would pass by, coming in from the villages, and taunt her. They would tell her she was foolish to be sitting with a woman who wasn't even a relative of hers. They said many other unkind, sarcastic things, but Argeen said, "I'm doing this because I belong to Jesus who wants me to help others." Argeem was meeting a real need and modeling the life of Jesus so very beautifully.

This woman's case was most interesting to us. After the bandages had been removed and she could move about, she still insisted that the small girl who had helped her before the surgery continue leading her with this stick which she clung to as she was being led from place to place. This continued longer than it should and we were concerned as to the success of the operations. Then, one day in our back yard, Lavina came out to greet her and chat. This woman began to recognize that Lavina was wearing a bright red skirt. Then she looked higher and saw what long hair Lavina had. At that point, she suddenly took her walking stick and with exuberant joy threw it ten or fifteen feet into the air and began shouting that she could see. It was a joyous moment of truth I shall never forget. She realized she could see again! For it we praised God with happy hearts.

## CHASED BY A DRUNKEN MAJANG WITH A SPEAR

During our years among the Majang, especially those first few years, there were times when we really were alarmed and afraid. I can scarcely adequately describe our fear and the danger facing us on that day when angry, drunken Majangs came on the compound late in the afternoon. We had had a serious misunderstanding with Balti over an incident in which a young man had attempted to drive the Landrover. (How he managed to move it, I will never understand) Later that afternoon, when Majangs were on a high from their fermented honey water drink, laced with the bark of the tree that gave a drugged like effect, they came on the compound with evil intent.

Larry Zudweg and I were sitting, casually, in front of the office across from the clinic when I saw a group of men coming across the compound in front of the school. They seemed excited and suddenly, Bakle stopped, crouched down behind a tree about fifty yards from where we were sitting. He raised his rifled, pointing it in our direction as he took aim. I jumped to my feet and said to Larry, "The man is going to shoot. Run."

Larry responded by saying, "You've got to be kidding."

Quick as a flash, I said, "I am not, man! Run!" We both took off running down the mission road toward our houses. As we began to run, a big, strong Majang, under the influence, picked up his spear and began chasing us. He ran after me twirling the spear over his head ready to be thrown. I could see that we weren't going to get away. I turned around, stopped momentarily, raised my hand and in English said, "No, man, no," wheeled around and ran.

Two women jumped out of the bushes and tripped this drunken Majang whom I later came to know was named Ocoor. He stumbled and fell and we were able to get away. Larry peeled off into the forest below on the side. By this time, our wives had heard the commotion and were making their way up the hill to find out what was going on. I nearly collapsed into their arms with the words, "They're going to kill us all." It was the most indescribable moment of terror I had ever experienced. The women steadied me on my feet and we made our way as quickly as we could to the nearest building, the outside storeroom, rushed in and closed the door. We were worried as to what had become of Larry. All I could think of was Auca Indians. What a relief when Larry, after ten or fifteen minutes, showed up unscathed.

We were now all in the storeroom along with our little boy, Paul. We learned later that several of the Majang with their heavy rifles were lying in the coffee grove waiting for us to come out. Obala, our clinic dresser, came over and advised us to say out of sight until their anger was cooled and they were less drunk. He helped with comforting words and by bringing over something to eat as we were going to stay hidden until morning.

Larry, Betty, Lavina, our little boy, Paul, and I were in

the first room of the shop where the tools were. We immediately decided we should crawl over the six foot six inch metal roofing sheets which served as a wall separating this room for the next which was the middle room having its own outside door. We are still amazed that these women managed to crawl over it and get between the low roof and that wall. Once we were all over the wall, we were locked in there for the duration.

There were barrels of supplies in there and we moved them around a little to give us added insulation should the Majang decide to shoot through the wall. We were huddled pretty closely together and sleep didn't come quickly or sustain itself. In the early part of the night we heard the Majang shouting and milling about under the influence of that fermented honey water. But it gradually diminished and before mid-night all was quiet.

We had to deal with the lack of toilet facilities in those cramped quarter so that our dignity was retained. We all managed somehow, but were exceedingly happy when morning came and Paul Obala told us he had been talking with Balti and Bakle and the other people in the village and he was sure it was safe for us to emerge. Conversations early that morning with Balti helped resolve the misunderstanding and they apologized for what they had done when drunk. They assured us that we should sleep in our regular house again and that they didn't want us to be afraid of them.

We were still skittish and uneasy about how the morning might develop when it was time to tend to our morning radio broadcast at which time all the stations checked in with Jimma. I tried to alert them to our situation without unduly alarming them. At the same time, we all felt they should know the possibilities for evil in those events. We signed off with a request that if we didn't come back on the air by noon, they should assume the worst and arrange to investigate things at the Godare. I am sure every radio was tuned in much of the morning and that when we came on the air saying there seemed no further need for worry, many prayers of thanks to God went heavenward. At Godare, we too, gave unceasing thanks to God. He had mercifully rescued and saved us from a dangerous set of circumstances which, in part, were of my own making. We had learned important lessons. I, personally became a wiser, more careful and sensitive person because of what we had gone through. In practical terms, I learned that late afternoon among Majangs was a wrong time to try to deal with complicated, sensitive issues requiring compromise and understanding.

## THE MAN WITH THE SPEAR IS BAPTIZED

But, the story doesn't end there. The marvelous, unspeakably good news is that within a year, Ocoor, the man who chased me with the spear gave his heart to Christ. It was my great joy to baptize him in the precious and powerful saving name of Jesus Christ. Ocoor became a dear friend. I once tried to purchase the infamous spear he carried that day, but he was unwilling to part with it.

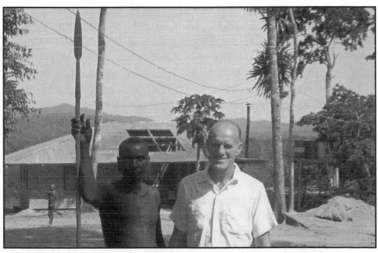

Harvey and Ocoor, the man with the spear.

Within a few months of his becoming a believer he moved with his family to an area closer to Metti about 30 miles away. He took with him a cassette player, cassettes and batteries. Later he began purchasing his own batteries in the town of Metti so that he could keep his player operating. Ocoor won a number of people to faith in Christ. Perhaps the most important among them was Elong, the son of their local chief. Elong is the man who went across the Bako river and returned after two months with that knotted string having on it over one hundred knots.

## THE INCIDENT INVOLVING BAKLE'S WIFE

The harrowing experience we had had, served us well in reminding us how to respond to various tense situations that arose from time to time during our remaining years working with the Majang. One incident I remember well, was the morning I came from our morning chapel with the staff and workmen. As we were having breakfast, Lavina said that while I was in chapel she had heard a lot of loud noise in the village just beside our compound. This was where Bakle lived.

After breakfast, I thought it might be well for me to wander over there and see what the problem might be. In doing so, I stumbled unto a situation that shocked and frightened me.

This is what I found. As I came around the corner and out of the brush into the village, I found Bakle sitting on a log with a hippo tail in his hand. Several women were huddled together near him, one of whom had her arms tied with grass rope so that her elbows nearly touched behind her back. She was one of Bakle's five wives. It appeared that she was about six or seven months pregnant. Across her bare abdomen was a nasty wound from the beating Bakle had given her and which was the noise Lavina had earlier heard before our breakfast. Two women were sitting near her with a gourd of water and they were occasionally using a smaller gourd to pour small amounts of water over her head which ran down over her bare breasts and her injured belly. It was a pitiful sight.

I sat down beside Bakle on the log. I wished I hadn't come. I was too frightened to speak and didn't really know what to say anyway. Bakle was nervous too. He was wearing knee high rubber boots, had his legs crossed and was swinging his foot back and forth nervously. His wife turned her head toward me without speaking. Her expression was so pathetic and I could see she was wanting me to do something to rescue her.

I had learned, previously, that Bakle was accusing his wife of being pregnant by another man. He had been away for months and when he returned, he found his wife to be expecting a child. He was now in the process of beating her until she would reveal the guilty person.

I finally spoke, softly and carefully. I recall telling him that I sympathized with his problem. I said that even the Bible teaches that adultery is wrong. But, I went on, the Bible also tells us that we are not to kill. I knew that he was trying to kill the baby she was carrying so that she would abort.

After, I had spoken, Bakle responded icily as he pointed to the sky, "When the sun is over there," he said, "she will talk."

I left for home and the work of the day. Around ten in the morning, I saw his wife walk ever so slowly and painfully past our back door toward the overflow pipe from the water tank. She washed her wounds and slowly returned to her village.

A few days after this incident, Bakle and a group of at least twenty grown men were at our back door. It was early in the morning. Bakle was wearing his revolver and also carrying a heavy rifle. To my knowledge he was the only Majang with a handgun. Bakle had stopped by to tell me that he and his men were heading across the river to deal with the man who had impregnated his wife. When I urged them not to kill, he assured me that "no guns will cry". He had stopped to report to me because of a somewhat strange relationship in which he respected my moral authority but feared I might report him to the government for his behavior.

By mid afternoon, we began to learn what had happened. When Bakle emerged out of the forest into the clearing in which the guilty party lived, someone fired a shot and killed one of Bakle's men. Bakle, enraged, sought out the man he wanted and shot him, cold blooded through the head. Chaos followed. People, men women and children, were fleeing for their lives. We began seeing people coming up the hill from the river and passing through the compound. These were pitiful, bedraggled women and children trying to hide somewhere to be safe.

The following morning, Bakle and his men came up the hill and walked passed the compound without saying a word to us. It was apparent that they had large guilt feelings and were fearful that I would report them to the government. Eventually, without my involvement, the government in Metti learned about this incident. Bakle was then picked up and spent about a month in jail. He was then released, after which he returned to the Godare and again lived beside us. It was some weeks before he acted normally toward us because he mistakenly assumed that I had reported him to the local governor in Metti.

## BAKLE BECOMES A FRIEND

Eventually, tensions eased and we were again on quite a friendly basis. When we began teaching Majangs how to grow coffee and brought in coffee seedlings for them to plant, Bakle took the lead in encouraging his people to take advantage of this opportunity. Bakle himself had the finest little coffee plantation and we became quite good friends. The day even came when he and his wives were baptized. On the day we left, I saw him cry because he was so sad to see us leave. God's ways are indeed mysterious and His mercy is beyond measuring.

Harvey and Lavina's home during their first three years at the Godare. Paul was three and a half years old at that time. This tent was home for Frank and Wilma Kieft during their months in Ethiopia.

# CHAPTER TWENTY-THREE

# OUR VISION GROWS

During these first few years in the forest we had learned a lot about Majang customs and habits. They were what anthropologists describe as a "slash and burn" people. With their small axes and knives they hacked down huge trees to clear small areas where they could build the simplest kinds of stick houses. Many of their houses were little more than stick shelters with open sides except for the house in which people slept. These could also be securely closed. Their houses were scattered around the clearings with no apparent rhyme or reason.

Sometimes an individual man cleared back a forest area by himself where he would build a shack or two and locate his family. Others would work communally helping each other clear back the forest for new plantings. Women had huge baked earthen crocks in which they fermented the corn mash. This was the magnet that attracted Majang neighbors to come and help someone clear his area. This beer was not that potent and, in many respects, was the stimulant to their diet needed that day for abnormally heavy work. These "working bees" were usually happy social gatherings with only an occasional time when some beer may have gotten a little too potent and an individual or two went too far.

The Majang had a most interesting way to show the depth of relationships on occasions like that by their peculiar manner of drinking from a gourd. Two persons, normally men with men, but occasionally a man and woman, would drink simultaneously from the same gourd. Two persons would be sitting side by side with a gourd of beer or honey water in front of them. While they were quietly visiting together, one of them would pick up this gourd and lift it to their lips. Their heads were side by side, facing the same direction, and their mouths close to each other, as they took a small drink from the gourd. They did this in a leisurely fashion until the gourd was eventually empty. To me it always appeared that it would be very difficult to drink with another person at the same time from the same container, but the Majang handled it with no problem. And they did this without spilling a drop!

Felling the trees for a new clearing was a big, social event, made more pleasant by the abundance of food and the drinking involved.

Once the trees were felled, some weeks would pass before the brush had dried sufficiently to be burned. Even when fired up, the logs and larger branches and stumps all remained as before. The Majang never cultivated their soil in any fashion whatsoever. Dura (sorghum) seed was simply scattered among these stumps and branches. Maize was planted using a long stick to make the hole in the soil into which the kernels were dropped and stepped on. The only hoeing a Majang did was to cut back, and that very haphazardly, those new growths that seemed to be getting out of hand. The men did the chopping and burning, but the women and girls did most of the planting.

Boys and girls guarded the fields from monkeys and baboons when the corn was beginning to ripen. Sometimes a musically inclined person would select certain kinds of sticks, split them and tie them together with vines in racks of five or six, separated by eight or ten inches. These were strung up to hang freely suspended between poles looking like our wooden fence posts on each side. Beating these crude musical instruments, they created quite beautiful combinations of melodious sounds. Apparently, it was music the baboons and monkeys preferred not to come near.

Majang, however, didn't rely only on their small, unproductive plantings for food. Men also hunted for wild pigs and they set fish traps in the rivers. The women worked extremely hard in searching for and digging out edible roots over a wide area in the surrounding forest.

The Majang were noted for their honey collecting skills. One man might have as many as forty to sixty, hollowed out log beehives in forest trees scattered over a wide area. By lacing smaller 3 inch poles up a tree trunk, Majangs had learned how to reach the first limbs of the taller trees having trunks too large to climb. Agile men climb up on these three inch poles securely laced to the larger trunk. having reached the lower limbs, they would hoist up their beehives on vines tied together like a long rope. The honey collected was their cash crop, but it was also their daily diet during long periods during the dry season. When mixed with water and allowed to ferment only a little it was a pleasant, nourishing drink for them and popular as a soft drink throughout southwest Ethiopia. But, Majangs scraped into the honey water the bark of a certain tree it had a drug like effect on those who drank it. Sometimes if there was too much bark or if the drink was allowed to ferment too long, it caused those who imbibed too much to become irritable and argumentative. It seemed that Majangs didn't stagger from this as one would expect to see when one is drunken. Instead, they seemed to become unpredictably, hostile and contentious.

Majangs stayed in their clearings for three or four years, at the most, and then moved on, clearing another small plot as before. Useable sticks and grass from their abandoned houses were tied up with vines and used again for the new structures on the new location. The old village site was left to grow over with vines and brush. Large sections of the forest had been cut back like this, making room for the Majang. It was a never ending cycle of slash and burn, staying in one place a few years, abandoning it to grow over again, and moving into a newly cleared site.

When traveling through the forest and visiting Majang villages, we'd normally spend and hour or more in thick, uncut, original growth before emerging into a Majang clearing of scattered shacks and unkempt fields. To move ahead, one followed a crooked path through this clearing to the opposite side, reenter the forest and continue on to the next clearing. During our early days, these trails were uncut with many areas having low, uncut vines making walking difficult. Majangs feared raids from hostile neighboring tribes.

Lavina and I were itching to trek out over these trails to Majangs scattered about in these forest clearings. We had good news to share with them and were eager for the opportunity to preach it to them in their language.

While John and Harriet Boerema were with us, Lavina and I could get away to do this. Once we were out for eighteen days. We had with us ten young Majang Christians who helped carry supplies and whom we wanted to train in evangelism. They could witness first hand how we went about it and our hope was that it would stimulate them and encourage their hearts.

## AN EIGHTEEN DAY TREK

Lavina and I each had a horse that we could ride or when we were tired of the saddle we would lead our animal behind us. The horses were sometimes a big help in carrying us up the steep hills. The area between us and Teppi, the direction in which we were moving, was characterized by rivers and streams flowing toward the Bako river. Every stream and river meant a steep hill, mountainous like, that one was either climbing or descending. Long stretches of level terrain were outnumbered by the hills and peaks. This made for tough going.

We had been on the way less than four hours when Lavina's horse balked. She was coming up out of a steep gully, when the animal stopped and backed down into it, with Lavina falling off. In those tight quarters with brush on both sides, her horse kicked her in the hip. It was really painful and I thought we should consider calling the trek off and returning home. Lavina wouldn't hear of it and after awhile said, "I'll be alright. Let's get moving." I admired her for her spunk, and made a secret resolution that this would be the last time this horse would kick my wife. When we reached Teppi, I would take him to the Saturday market, sell him and come back with a different animal. And, that is exactly what happened!

## KONKON

Our first big stop was the village of Konkon. We stayed there two and a half days. I preached and we mingled with the Majang people throughout the day. Lavina prepared food at appropriate times from the supplies we were carrying in our trek boxes. At night we slept in jungle hammocks we'd strung up in the forest just on the edge of the clearing. During the night we heard many frightening and ominous sounds. Dogs barked incessantly, monkeys chattered and called back and

forth to each other. We even heard a leopard coughing somewhere in the distance, and we thought we heard leaves rustling
indicating a snake or python might be moving about nearby.

But, the most exciting moment was on the morning of
the third day when we were preparing to leave. An older man,
a woman with a baby in its carrying pouch on her back and a
little child beside her came to us and said that they wanted to
become people of the Jesus we'd been telling them about. Our
joy was tempered by the fact that we were leaving and there
were no other believers in that entire area and we had no one
to leave behind to teach them. What could we say? I remember well the words that the Lord gave me. This is how I concluded our conversation. I said, "It is true that we are leaving,
but remember that Jesus is not leaving. You have seen how
we talked to him when we prayed. You, too, must talk to him
every day just as you heard us doing. He is strong and powerful and able to protect you from every evil thing. Trust him
completely. Some day somebody else will be coming to this
village with these same words about Jesus. Listen to him. He
will teach you more. Until then, we too will pray for you many
times."

We put our arms around each other and commended
them to our Lord Jesus, and then we left. Because of illness, I
never, personally visited Konkon again. But, the story doesn't
end there and we will return to it at the appropriate place.

## TEPPI

When Lavina and I finally reached Teppi, we camped on
a hillside beside one of the major trails leading out of town. It
was right near where the road turned. This was a Saturday
and the town was overflowing with people, including Majangs
from that region, who had come into the market. Such market
days brought hundreds of people from several different language groups. They came with donkeys, horses, and on foot.
They brought sheep and goats, other livestock, grains and
items of every description to bargain, sell or purchase. It was
the important day of the week when everyone dressed up and
came to town. Relatives and friends met in the market and
shared news. More than should have made their way to the
*"Tej Bets"* (shops where people sat and drank beer and moon-

shine.) More than a few found it more difficult to return home than to come.

Lavina and I had already begun a ministry in Teppi. We had opened a small book room where Bibles, tapes and a small amount of Christian literature were sold. We had also rented a room where we could keep our cots, simple cooking utensils, and a few supplies. We had come in with MAF and spent a week visiting the various *"Bunna Bets"*. (coffee houses) We had played our tapes in whatever language was needed. Most of these houses were congregated by people who spoke the same language.. Each group had its own houses that they frequented the most. On market day, we would play our tapes in the market for people who would otherwise never hear. It was a great opportunity and our hearts longed to find a way to take full advantage of it by having a permanent base in that town.

But, now, on that Saturday afternoon we were camped on the edge of town on the far side. Our ministry at this stage was focused almost exclusively among the Majangs. As we pitched our tent and spread ourselves out, we brought out the cassette player and began a tape with Majang music. We knew that Majangs loved to hear their small Majang piano boxes being played on tape. It would soon attract a crowd here too.

## CURIOUS MAJANGS IN TEPPI

Majangs leaving town turned in to see what was going on. They were attracted by the music and curious about these strange white people. Before long, we had quite a crowd, so we invited them to sit with us and listen to the "box that talks". I wish you could have seen the expressions on their faces and heard their barely audible comments. I shall never forget one old woman sitting their, legs extended and feet crossed, listening intently. I saw her turn to a woman behind her and say, "Why haven't we heard this before? I wish (and she mentioned someone's name) were with me to hear what we are."

I never ceased to marvel at the Majang's positive response to the good news about Jesus when they heard it in their language on cassettes. I was then and remain convinced now that the cassette was no accident of history, but that the cassette is part of God's provision to be utilized to proclaim in every language the good news of His beloved Son.

Eighteen days from the time we started out, Lavina and I arrived home at the Godare. We were tired, hungry and exhausted, but our hearts were glad. The young men who had helped us were excited to share from their experiences. It was good for the people we had visited and it was a catalyst to the little church developing at the Godare. That night we praised God together with John and Harriet. He had spared them during their time of danger and he had brought us back safely. And when we prayed for the new believers we had left behind in Konkon, we knew there was rejoicing among the angels in heaven. I had every intention to return to Konkon at an early date.

Our vision was growing. From the time we had first assembled our gear in Teppi for the trek into the Godare, we felt a special burden for this town. It was only a matter of time before the urge to base ourselves in Teppi became irresistible. But, before that would happen a number of important pieces had to fall into place. Could a replacement be found to take over from us at Godare? On what basis could we receive government permission to open a mission work based in Teppi? These and other important details were pondered, prayed over and awaited implementing in God's tomorrow.

## CHECKING ON NEW AIRSTRIP POSSIBILITIES

We had often flown with MAF between their base in Jimma and Godare. Sometimes it was a straight line and other times we would fly by way of Teppi. Flights I seem to remember best were those I made with our son, Denny, as pilot or with Vern Sikkema. The reason I recall my flights with Vern is that I often heard him make comments as he looked down below. He would say something to the effect that I think we could get an airstrip in there. And when we flew over the old Italian strip at Gecha about fifteen minutes northeast of Godare, he would say, "We should try to drive in there with a Landrover someday and see how much work would be involved in reactivating it."

You guessed it! The time came when Vern and I flew the old, big wheeled, Porter aircraft to Gore and borrowed Kert

Hultgren's Landrover to try to reach Gecha overland. One of the tires on the Landrover had a patch on it the size of a maple leaf. It looked unreliable, but with speeds never exceeding a few miles per hour, it wasn't a real problem. We had only one flat that last evening going up a long, stony hill approaching Gore from where we had started out..

Vehicles hadn't been over that road or trail from Gore to Teppi in years. The Italians had built the rood during their occupation of Ethiopia, but once they left, like the airstrip, it had been abandoned.

It took us more than a day to do the fifty or so odd miles from Gore to Gecha. The local governor was excited when he heard us driving in. He put on a big feast, killing a sheep and serving us their very best injira with wat that evening long after dark. In the morning, the governor, a few officials, forty or fifty local man, Vern and I walked out to the former airstrip site. There were no trees or stumps on it but it was a mess with grass humps everywhere. Cattle grazed on it and it really was a huge cow pasture without fences except for the one that crossed the strip near the lower end. I remember that one because when we eventually landed and had our first take off that fence seemed dangerously close to our wheels as we cleared it and were in the air.

The governor promised to have his men hoe off the humps and smooth the strip so that we could make a landing if we would fly in as soon as we returned to Gore.

On our way out, we gave a ride to a young man dressed in a business suit. This was unusual dress for those parts. He turned out to be a young member of the parliament in Addis Ababa. When he learned that we were planning to open the airstrip in Gecha and begin an itinerant ministry with a medical team, he said, "You have to do this in my country too." He explained that he was from the area beyond the mountainous ridge to the west. His father was one of the most important landlords in that whole region. He said, "If you'll do this for my people there, my father will build you an airstrip so that you can fly in."

The landing at Gecha was successful. About three months later, Arlene Schuiteman, an RCA nurse working at Mettu hospital, came on the radio with startling news. She normally didn't call Godare but that morning she called in, "Three five, three five, this is three nine. Do you read me?"

We said, "We read you loud and clear; go ahead."

This was her message. Peace corps people had been in that area some fifteen or twenty minutes north of Godare. They were there in connection with the drive to stamp out small pox. They were now back in Mettu and told her that two airstrips were being built in the area north of us. They were, in fact, airstrips being built under the direction of the big landlord, the father of our passenger returning to Gore, that member of parliament. Again, we marveled at how the Lord puts things together. A, seemingly, chance hitchhiker catching a ride and catching a vision resulting in the opening of an entirely new area to the Gospel. ... We thanked Arlene, signed off and pondered where it would all lead to.

## DARABATA

Less than two weeks later, Harold Kurtz, the mission's general Secretary and also a skilled pilot who flew his personal 185 Cessna called on the radio. He said he was going to check out these airstrips and see if he could locate them. He wanted to know if I would be interested in riding along. He would come into the Godare first and pick me up. I jumped at the chance and by mid-day we were flying back and forth over that ridge which sloped off toward the east into a huge valley. We eventually found what appeared to be the strip that was closest to being completed.

We began circling the field, flying closer and closer to the ground. A tall tree just off the upper end was a menace and later had to be removed. People could be seen running from their villages in our direction. There was tremendous excitement among them to be sure. Their hard work had paid off. The plane was actually there and they were wanting to see it on the ground.

Finally, after we touched the wheels once or twice flying in the direction he eventually would have to take off in, Harold pulled up and said, "Fasten your seat belt and shoulder straps securely. I think we can make it."

He flew out over the valley and turned back for his approach. We came in over where the field dropped off sharply some eight hundred to a thousand feet to the valley below. Our wheels hit the ground and the plane shuddered from the vibration. It was a rough field. The speed, to me a lay person, seemed incredibly fast. My adrenaline was flowing freely. But, it soon became apparent that Harold had it mastered and we were rolling to a stop. When we opened the doors and stepped unto the soil, the people were ecstatic. They were pushing in from all sides with people shouting and talking together with uncontainable excitement and exuberance. In that setting, my first words to Harold were, "Harold, let's give thanks to God."

Harold climbed up on the wing of the plane, sat there with his legs dangling down, and prayed in Amharic. Some understood, but most only realized he was praying to God. The language in that area was Oromo. Almost before Harold finished his prayer the people began to clap spontaneously. I have often thought, They had every reason to clap for joy. There lives would never be the same. The good news from God had also come to them. With that good news they would also receive medical care and learn how to live a better life. Our hearts were glad.

This airstrip was known as Darabata. The other strip the Peace Corps people had reported to Arlene still needed a lot of work on it. Eventually both strips were opened and we began a regular itinerant ministry from Godare. Key elements in the ministry were the visits by our medical dresser with modern medicines and the use of players and cassettes with tapes in the language spoken by those people.

The Darabata strip, like nearly every strip we opened, had undulations and a low spots that had to be corrected. Usually, after the first landing, we'd fly in our little garden tractor with its plow attachment and go to work.

## GOD'S PROVIDENTIAL LEADING

It is difficult to realize that it all started with bits and pieces coming together in Ethiopia. How marvelous are the ways of God. An MAF pilot years earlier observed, "We should be able to open a strip over there." A hitchhiker is given a lift. He talks to his father who builds an airstrip on which MAF could land. A young lad helps make the strip useable, goes off to school, gets converted in a revival among students, becomes the mission's purchasing agent's helper which introduces him to MAF. He dreams of the possibility of his becoming a pilot for

MAF. In God's timing it all comes together. So many played a part. But, it was God who made it happen. Today this young lad, now married with a lovely wife and family, is flying for the Lord in Uganda. How thrilling to be part of God's great master plan to take the Gospel to the ends of the earth. We see it happening just as Jesus predicted. "This Gospel of the kingdom will be proclaimed throughout the whole world as a testimony to the nations , and then the end shall come." Matt 24:10

Rev. Harold Kurtz, the Mission's General Secretary, pouring over visionary plans with his fellow missionaries. Harold's vision was to establish one-family stations in ten additional peoples groups. In the foreground are the late Rev. J. Robert Swart on the left and Dr. Donald W. McClure on the right.

*"In the last days, God says, I will pour out my Spirit on all people. Your sons and daughters will prophesy, your young men will see visions, your old men will dream dreams."* Acts 2:17

# CHAPTER TWENTY-FOUR
# CONTENDING WITH ILLNESS

The Godare River area was not a healthy place to live. The Majang, themselves, suffered many illness. All of the tropical diseases were evident -- dysentery, malaria, smallpox before it was eradicated during our years there, tuberculosis, sleeping sickness, colds, flu and others plus their being afflicted with infections and tropical ulcers. We saw middle aged people become permanently old following a struggle to survive a severe illness. And then there was endemic elephantiasis plainly seen in the water logged, swollen feet and lower limbs of men like Balti, Gimti and many others we knew. Certain areas were identified as having an unusually high number of women with huge goiters, larger in size than I could ever have imagined. These women could barely talk because of their huge, four to five inch growth of swelling around their necks and under their chins.

Right from the beginning we tried helping with treatments and modern medicines. Within a year we had a good clinic building and a trained Ethiopian dresser * on staff. Paul Obala, an Anuak medical dresser, came up from the Gila river station and served with us most of our years at Godare. The good news about the clinic spread and people came from ever more distant villages. Severe injuries or extremely ill patients were carried in on crude, home made stretchers.

## MAJANG STRETCHERS

These stretchers were interesting and represented a

369

lot of creativity. Usually they were five or six foot light poles tied together with vines to give a two foot base on which the patient could lie. To prevent the patient from rolling off, they fashioned a protective canopy of light sticks like a half-circle over the patient, spacing them so that three or four of these prevented the patient from falling off when they went down steep banks, crossed rivers or encountered rocks or logs on their journey.

When these pitiful stretcher cases came in, their were always fifteen or twenty people who took turns carrying. It was truly a major, desperate, last ditch effort they made to find help. All these kinds of cases sickened our hearts because of the human tragedy and pain they were suffering. Sometimes it was too late to help, but other times we saw dramatic recoveries. There were times when we would send these stretcher cases and other kinds of patients out with the MAF plane to one of the mission hospitals. Each time these crudely fashioned stretcher cases came in, we had the opportunity to share the love of Jesus with people who knew little if anything about who He was. Tape players were listened too in the outpatient houses and there were always numerous people beside the patient who were hearing this good news from God.

## CONTENDING WITH PERSONAL ILLNESS

No, the rain forest where we lived wasn't a healthy place to live. Lavina did much better than I did. This was strange, too, because when we started out for the mission field, way back in 1948, Lavina was considered to be the frail one. People in Bignell Chapel, where we had served as their student pastor for three years, were concerned that Lavina might not be healthy enough for the rigors of the tropics. They had seen her getting pneumonia and struggling with a virus for many months. During our first months in the Sudan, I gave her regular injections to build up her red blood count. But, she fooled everyone and proved to be much less prone to sickness than was I.

## MALARIA

Getting dysentery was taken for granted. Malaria was something we protected ourselves against by taking a couple of little pills once or twice a week. In the Sudan, these pills had been quite effective, The malarial strain in the rain forest was much more resistant. I remember once when Paul had it. He was less than five years old then. At breakfast time, I had made a comment about what a beautiful day it was. Around ten that morning, Paul went into his tent and his fever began to increase rapidly. At one point, not feeling at all well, he called out with a tearful voice, "I thought you said it was a beautiful day." Paul was feeling miserable. His malaria was the kind that flared up every forty eight hours. During the off day he felt quite normal, but on the following day it was a different story. With medication, it normally took a week or ten days to knock out the fever. Tiredness and listlessness lingered much longer.

I had severe malaria on several occasions. It left one really feeling unwell, discouraged and lacking in ambition. After one of those sieges, Lavina and I joined the rest of our mission in Addis Ababa for our annual mission meeting. This was six weeks after I had finished my treatment. When Dr. Mary Smith met Lavina, before Dr. Mary and I had run across each other, she said to Lavina, "Where's Harvey? I hear he looks just awful." Malaria was no fun!

## FILARIASIS

I also became infected with that nasty elephantiasis, or filariasis. Before I realized what it was, I was itching a small three or four inch patch on my shin for weeks. During our furlough a skin specialist said he thought it was some kind of a fungus. Later, back in Ethiopia, while I was in Addis, we decided to check it out with a tropical disease doctor in one of the hospitals there. He took a little snitch of skin from that area and put it under the microscope. What he saw excited him. Under the microscope was a wiggling parasite he identified as the one causing elephantiasis. He called in his students and each had a turn at observing this thing doing its antics. Although this disease is common in Ethiopia at lower altitudes, I got the impression that they didn't see these kinds of parasites under the microscope very frequently in hospitals in Addis where the elevation was well over 8,000 feet.

Treating this disease is a long term proposition. The

disease is caused by the numerous, little, black, elephant-back flies down along the rivers. When they deposit their eggs on a person's skin, one or more become host "worms" in the human body. These, in turn, spew out countless microfilaria into the blood stream and these, again, damage the lymph glads causing fluid to collect in the lower extremities of the body.

I was diagnosed as having them and treatment began promptly. The medicine used at that time was extremely toxic and required one to spent at least twenty four hours in the hospital in the event the reaction was too severe and required an antidote. The first treatment began with one fourth of a small pill. This dosage was gradually increased until at the end of three weeks I was taking a total of nine of these little pills a day. Antihistamine helped control the reaction, but even so the itching was pretty awful the first couple of days each time one took the course. I was still taking treatments for this regularly when we left Ethiopia in 1976 and continue to experience the after effects of the damage done. It is a nasty disease.

## HEPATITIS

The most serious illness we encountered was a case of severe hepatitis which put me in bed for nearly three months. At the onset, I had been feeling unusually tired for more than a week. In fact, I was so exhausted that I would have to return to the house to lie down several times during the day. I had an important meeting with the governor in Teppi that I had to keep. Vern Sikkema, one of the MAF pilots, had night stopped at Godare and said I he could drop me off in Teppi in the morning on his return to Jimma. This was Sunday morning and he planned to leave early so as to be home in time to attend church with his family.

I took an aspirin before leaving with him for Teppi. I felt extremely unwell but never suspected hepatitis. In Teppi I put up my tent, crawled in and lay there feeling terribly ill. Later in the morning, when I went out, I saw that my urine was the color of mahogany, I knew that something serious was afoot. I ate absolutely nothing that entire day and lay in the tent waiting for my appointment on Monday morning. One of the merchants, came by around nine in the evening and offered to help. He urged a sip of tea on me which he had kindly brought over.

I kept my appointment with the governor in the morning. At mid-day, MAF, by previous arrangement, landed in Teppi and flew me back to the Godare. The next morning, I spoke with Dr. Dan Reynalds who was in the Pokwo station by radio describing my situation. He said, "You have hepatitis, man. Go straight to bed and stay there. Try to drink lots of fluids and fruit juices. There's no medication for hepatitis. You need rest and more rest. It'll take weeks before you're recovered." That was bad news, indeed.

As soon as we finished talking, before going to bed, I hiked down to the river one last time to check on the turbine. John Ojulu, who took care of the turbine, went with me. I wanted to be sure it was operating well and properly lubricated. I went over everything with John, and slowly trudged back up the long hill. I fell into bed completely exhausted and stayed there until the plane came in to fly me to the hospital in Addis.

Lavina gave me the most tender, loving care anyone could ever wish for. I know it was a great strain on her to have this responsibility. She found her strength and courage in the Lord and never faltered! Those were difficult days for both of us, but the Lord was present and very precious to us while we were learning new lessons in patience and in what it means to trust Him completely.

Dr. Dan Reynalds, one of the mission doctors, was on the radio with Lavina every day inquiring as to my progress and making suggestions. The MAF plane flew out blood samples on a weekly basis. The reports were never encouraging. My liver was badly swollen. One of the doctors put it this way when he said to me, "Your liver was badly stepped on." For weeks my skin was as yellow as an old, plucked chicken hanging in a butcher shop. I lost twenty-nine pounds during those three months. I was a very sick man.

Even so, there were also times of levity and we could chuckle and laugh together. I remember once receiving a note from Mary Alice Jordan, who with Chuck was in the Adura River station near the Sudan border. She sent up a humorous little note with MAF, saying, "I hope you're not lying there thinking the Lord is pacing back and forth in His office every day wondering  how He can get along without you!"  We enjoyed it thoroughly.  In it was an important reminder that the Lord was at work in ways beyond us.

One of the great truths I learned during those days was that the Lord's work didn't stop among the Majang because I wasn't personally involved.  He was continuing to bless the witness of Majang Christians and we kept on hearing of new people coming to faith in Christ.  I had nothing to do with it. God was marvelously at work showing mercy and kindness to these people who had been in great darkness.  There was no direct correlation between my involvement and the final result. The Lord was getting along without me just fine!  It was God's mission, not mine!  An important lesson that continues to encourage our hearts even now.

## OCOOR, THE MAN WITH THE SPEAR, COMES TO PRAY FOR ME

Dr. Reynalds had told Lavina that outside visitors should be kept to a minimum.  He said, "Harvey needs all the rest he can get."  But, there were exceptions to the rule.  Let me share a marvelous experience.  One afternoon there was a clap outside our kitchen door in the back.  Lavina went out and discovered that Ocoor and several of his friends were standing there.  They indicated that they wanted to see me. Lavina told them that the Dr. had advised against my having anyone come in.  Ocoor protested that they had come because they had heard that Odola was ill and they wanted to pray for him."  With that, Lavina couldn't resist and invited Ocoor and three of his friends to come in.

They came into the bedroom.  They sat on chairs and someone sat on the floor.  Then Ocoor said, "Now we are going to pray for you."  He identified the men who were to pray.  One of the two men selected got stuck in the middle of his prayer. At that point, Ocoor put words in his mouth and the man prayed line by line the words Ocoor was giving him..  It was a moving, beautiful, unforgettable experience and we praised God.  You will recall that Ocoor was the Majang who had tried to spear me on that dreadful afternoon several years before. How wonderful is the grace and power of our Lord Jesus Christ.

After a month in bed at home, Lavina was concerned that I get to a hospital for whatever help they could give. Denny was flying in an area just north of us that particular day. He and his mother were on the radio as he flew. Den suggested that he fly in Dr. John Cremer from Dembidollo to have a look at me and decide what should be done. He flew in that same afternoon and decided this missionary needed to get into a hospital in Addis without delay. The next day, MAF flew in and I was carried on a cot by four Majang men to the plane and we were on our way to Addis Ababa.

An excellent tropical disease doctor from England began caring for me in the Haile Sellasi hospital. Lavina stayed in the mission guest house and made it out to the hospital twice every day. Our dear friends, Bill and Marilyn Vineyard who were with the American Embassy in Addis, were able to get all the canned fruit juices I needed from the government canteen. They probably don't realize how important their special contribution was to my recovery.

The Lord mercifully restored me to the point where, thirty days later, I could get out of bed and go the mission guest house in Addis. At first, even with Lavina to lean on and using a sturdy cane, I could barcly walk.. Recovery was slow and I spent most of the next thirty days in bed.

But, God has marvelous blessings for us through adversity. How marvelous and, yes, strange are His ways sometimes.

## THE VISIT BY DR. CLARK AND MR. OGILVIE

By this time we were back from Bishoftu, a beautiful, relaxing vacation and conference center operated by the Sudan Interior Mission (SIM) located on a beautiful crater lake about forty miles outside of Addis Ababa. Now I was spending the best part of every day in bed in the mission guest house, trying to gradually recover my strength. Dr. Roy Clark was in from his hospital at Mettu during this same period. He was concerned with my slow progress.

One morning he came to the room where I was lying in bed and Lavina was sitting on a chair beside me. With him, Dr. Clark had brought a man I had never met before, but of whom I had heard. His companion was an older, former SIM missionary by the name of Ogilvie. This man was known for his eccentric ways and was also recognized by some to have an unusual spiritual gift of healing. There were many stories circulating about this man and how he wandered about from place to place casting out evil spirits and healing the sick. He was an unusual person, to say the least.

These two men said they would like to anoint me with oil and to pray for me. I had no objection and was greatly pleased. They took the little vial of oil and anointed me. Placing their hands over my liver area they began to pray for me. I recall how warm their hands were -- much warmer than an ordinary hand normally would feel. They prayed for me in English and they prayed for me in tongues. Then Mr. Ogilvie began to prophecy, speaking in beautiful poetic English. He was saying that the Lord is healing you of this disease. He is leading you into a larger ministry etc. etc. Then he turned to Lavina and speaking in poetic form again said to her that the Lord was healing me, leading us into a larger ministry and that she shouldn't be concerned about anything because God was leading and would supply our every need.

When the men left the room, Lavina and I looked at each other and both of us knew that God was in it. God had sent them to minister to us. What these men didn't know is that during my illness, I had frequently shared with Lavina my burning desire to open a new work at Teppi from which we could reach out to four or five unreached peoples groups using cassettes. Each time I talked to her, Lavina had seemed less than enthusiastic about it. She kept urging me to not worry about those possibilities yet. First I had to get well and then we could talk about possibly opening a new station.

These were the kinds of differing viewpoints we frequently shared with each other. But when these two men left our room that morning, both Lavina and I were at peace over this matter. We both recognized that God was calling us to open that new station and that in His perfect timing it would happen. What a marvelous experience for us. The Lord had ministered to us in this unusual, somewhat unconventional way. I wasn't healed instantaneously, but felt then and now that a healing process began that day which was directly related to the men who anointed me with oil and prayed over me in English and in tongues. Six months later, when I again met Dr. Clark he shared this with me. He said, "When we came in to anoint you with oil and pray for you that morning, I felt sure that you had cancer of the liver."

Only God knows! But this we do know, that whereas once I was weak and ill, I am today strong and well. It was Jesus Christ, the great physician, who mercifully restored me to health. My deepest longing was and continues to be that I be available to Him for whatever tasks He has for Lavina and me to do for Him!

The bout with hepatitis had an enormous impact on our lives and ministry. It was apparent that my complete recovery of strength and vigor was going to take years rather than months. We were going to need to rethink how we were to minister to those who became believers in villages where this missionary would not yet be strong enough to reach Hiking over rough terrain, climbing steep hills and crossing river and streams was beyond me. But by this time we knew that some of God's most fragrant flowers are often found among the thorns of life.

## PERGATIIN GOES TO KONKON

Let me share one of the important events of that period. You will recall how in the village of Konkon, Lavina and I had preached and shared the Gospel on our eighteen-day trek. You will remember how we had committed those two new believers to the Lord and promised them that one day somebody would come to their village and teach them more.

It was a young man by the name of Pergatiin from the village of Dampay, about four miles out, that God raised up to visit that village. One day Pergatiin came to me and said he would like to go with a cassette player and teach the people of Konkon. Pergatiin, himself, was totally uneducated. He was a young man of about twenty years of age, but he had never been gone to school and had never learned to read. We sent him off with a cassette player, a double set of batteries so that he would have a second set when the first ones went dead, and we gave him a number of different cassettes with the essential Christian message. Occasionally, Pergatiin came in to pick up fresh batteries.

Then came that wonderful day when Pergatiin came in with a knotted grass string having 37 knots on it. He reported

377

that there were 37 people who had believed in Jesus and they were wanting to be baptized. This was exciting good news but it posed a problem. How were they to be baptized when this missionary was too weak to make it those eight hours to that village? It didn't seem right that they should be denied baptism because this missionary couldn't reach them.

It seemed that we had two options. We could tell those people they had to wait a year or two until this missionary was sufficiently recovered so she could come and baptize them, or we could consider ordaining a Majang whom the growing church at Godare could identify and commission for that responsibility.

## ROKET IS ORDAINED

I discussed these matters with Harold Kurtz, our General Secretary. He had taken some courses at Fuller's School of World Mission and was eager to have our mission take bold initiatives to help the developing churches become truly indigenous in their application of the Gospel.. He was most open to the possibility of doing something very unorthodox. Harold and I were both firm believers in indigenous leadership guided by a contextualized theology.

With Harold's blessing and encouragement, I began meeting with Majang Christians worshipping at Godare to share with them the need I saw for someone to be chosen whom we could train and entrust with administering the sacraments. I explained to them why I felt it was important for the Konkon believers to be baptized and share in celebrating the Lord's Supper. They understood that I was unable to walk that far and that without selecting and commissioning someone for that task, these believers would have to wait far too long.

It was beautiful to hear them discuss these matters and finally select the person they felt we should train and entrust with this responsibility. Do you remember my telling you about Roket? He was the young lad whose finger I sewed back on during our early days at Godare. He was the young man who preached in the villages with his stiff finger, holding it high overhead and saying, *"Gopan omo mo!"* (There just one way)

Their unanimous choice was this young man, Roket.

By now he was a married man with small children. He had learned to read Amharic in the school and was beginning to understand more and more when he read from his Amharic Bible.

On an appointed Sunday, Harold Kurtz was with us for the special ordination service. What joy to share with Harold in laying hands on this choice young Majang. In that same service, Roket baptized his first new believers. He did some things a little differently than I would have, but I was determined to allow him to make his little mistakes and to find his way in his new responsibilities. He also led his first communion service in which we used tomato juice and native, pancake like bread.

When Roket returned from Konkon, he had written the names of all the new believers in his little record book. I never baptized another person from among the Majang. They were now able to perform the essential tasks to enable a church to grow and mature. In retrospect, the decision we had made was probably one of the wisest decisions we could have made. I have no doubt that the Lord had led us in making this unorthodox decision to ordain a man who had never been to a theological seminary or a formal Bible school. When all missionaries left Godare and Teppi, the young church was able to function in every respect. We had set in motion a totally indigenous pattern with indigenous leadership which the Holy Spirit could prosper and use. God blessed the Majang in unusual ways after we all left and today it is reported that more than 90 percent of this tribe have come to believe and are within the Christian fellowship. To God be all the honor, glory and praise!

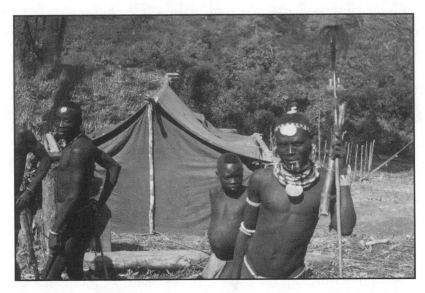

Harvey and Lavina slept in this tent on their trek to the Godare. It was their bedroom those first few month living in the rain forest among the Majang.

Majang women collected certain roots for food which they carried in these large baskets.

380

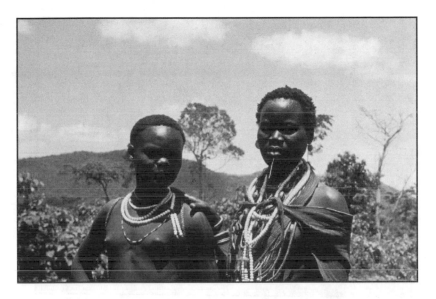

One of chief Balti's wives and daughter. They were there that Sunday morning when Balti shot and killed his son.

MAF made frequent airdrops with essential supplies before the airstrip was

The Majang had no medical care. The Hoekstras, of necessity, became like doctors and nurses ministering to these needs. After some months, they established a clinic and brought in a trained Ethiopian medical person to manage it.

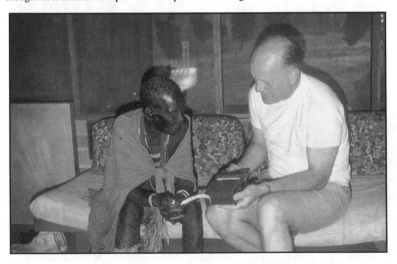

With her dirty bandaged leg-wound, Gadi loved to come and listen to the cassette messages in her own Majang language. This is the person who was frightened by others and never returned to be baptized.

# EXPANDING THE MINISTRY FROM TEPPI

Teppi was always on our hearts and minds. From the very first time we stopped in Teppi, it seemed the Lord had created within us a sensitivity to the challenge, needs and opportunities there. By this time in our ministry from Godare, we realized that Teppi would be an ideal location to base a cassette ministry. In Teppi we would have access to five or six additional language groups. For one thing, this would facilitate our production of master cassettes in these needed languages. Teppi would also be an excellent place from which to fly out with MAF to airstrips we could open in strategic places among these language groups. Teppi already had an excellent airfield on which the Ethiopian Airlines came in at least twice a week. During the coffee harvest they flew in five or six times a day hauling out those precious beans.

## A REPLACEMENT FOR GODARE

But, before we could get serious about relocating in Teppi, we must have a replacement to continue the work among the Majang. God wonderfully raised up Harry and Pat Miersma to fill this need. Harry had been there before when he came out for that summer with those other three young college students. Pat would be a tremendous asset with her nursing skills. Harry's church, The First Reformed Church in Artesia, California was behind them. This church had already made a tremendous contribution to the work at the Godare. They had provided the hydroelectric plant and Harry's folks had been out there along with their pastor, Dave and Lois Laman. The Reformed Church General Program Council approved and with supporting churches, Harry and Pat soon were ready to come and set us free to open the new work in Teppi. We could see God's leading and were constantly praising Him.

## GOVERNMENT APPROVAL FOR TEPPI

The other hurdle that needed to be dealt with was the basis on which we might receive government approval for a station in Teppi. Normally the government required a commitment from the mission to operate a school and a clinic before receiving approval to open work. In Teppi, however, there already was a fully staffed, upgraded health center as well as a large school with grades from one through eight. The challenge was to offer something to the government they would recognize as important to warrant their giving permission for us to open a work in Teppi. We were constantly talking about and praying over it.

The thought finally came to me that we could offer the government a unique language learning program using cassettes. Most of the other language groups outside of Teppi knew little or no Amharic, the official language of Ethiopia. We would offer a program in which we prepared oral, language learning tapes enabling people to learn Amharic, moving from the vernacular to the national language. We could offer this valuable service so that people coming into the market would understand Amharic and when government officials spoke and gave out orders the people could understand what was said in Amharic.

The moment came when I was in the proper official's office in Addis Ababa. I was sitting across the desk from an important official in the ministry of education. I carefully shared what I have just described. This man was greatly interested and even became excited as we discussed these possibilities. I told him that the ideal place from which to launch this kind of program was Teppi because of the government airstrip there and the ready access to the vernacular languages needed as part of the language lessons from the vernacular to Amharic.

As our conversation concluded, this official stood up

behind his desk. He extended his outstretch arms toward me and with considerable emotion said, "Mr. Hoekstra, this a program that all of Ethiopia needs. ... can you suggest a ten year plan for the whole country. ... We will give you blanket permission for your district." He promised and did write the necessary letters of introduction to the local governors in whose districts we would be carrying on this ministry.

This official, like most government personnel, was an Orthodox Christian. Before parting, with some hesitation, I shared with him my observation that while many of the people in those rural areas where we would be working were nominal Christians, many had little or no real understanding about the Christian faith. I asked if their would be any objection to our putting the essential Christian truths on cassette in the vernaculars as part of this program. I said, "We don't want to wait until they learn the Amharic language to tell them this good news from God which both you and I believe." He raised no objection and I took that to mean we could go ahead but not to raise the matter officially.

I left his office on cloud nine. I was ecstatic with praise and thanks to God. The door to beginning our cassette ministry from Teppi was open. God had not only provided the personnel needed to ensure that the ministry at Godare was in good hands, but He had opened the door for us to move to Teppi.

## MIERSMAS, HETRICKS AND TERPSTRAS BUILD THE NEW STATION IN TEPPI

The next question was where to locate our base in Teppi itself. I knew that we wanted to be as close to the airport as possible. Our larger plan was to continue opening new airstrips into which we could fly with MAF from Teppi just as we had begun at Godare. If at all possible, we should be right beside the Teppi airstrip itself.

Again, the Lord was going before us. We were able to purchase a small plot, sufficient in size to accommodate two houses, an office and recording room and a storage, workshop building. To avoid a great deal of time consuming effort, we and the Mission agreed that we should erect prefabricated buildings available from a German firm in Addis Ababa. But, before making the move to Teppi we must first take our furlough in 1971. After that, Lavina and I would return and make the move to Teppi. When the moment finally arrived, Harry and Pat Miersma were already on the field. They would help us open the new station. Harry was an excellent builder as well as a great young missionary. From the states, two volunteer couples came from the First Reformed Church in DeMotte, Indiana, Steve and Laverne Terpstra and Larry and Linda Hetrick. They came out and with the help of Harry and Pat, during their month in Teppi, literally built the new base, including erecting a protective fence around it..

## LAVINA WAITS AT THE GODARE

Lavina remained at Godare during those first weeks to relieve the housing problem. She would have given anything to be with the gang in Teppi but common sense dictated otherwise. She says it helped her a lot on those days when Denny, our son, was flying in the area. He would come on the radio and say, "Mom, I'm flying overhead this morning. How about my dropping down a few minutes and see how you're doing. And, I'll be ready for a cup of coffee with you by that time." Lavina would scurry around the kitchen and by "coffee time" she had turned out a delicious, home made cake or a batch of cookies. Denny knew he could count on that.

Later when we were all settled in our new place in Teppi, Jim and Betty, Denny and Carol and the little ones all flew in once for a week end. It was really something special to have two of our sons and their families working beside us in Ethiopia as missionaries. When they came with the MAF plane to Teppi, we would open the wide double gate and Denny would taxi in. He would tie down right in front of the house with the plane secure behind the closed gate.

But I am ahead of myself. We are still back there getting started living in tents with volunteers doing the work. A lot would happen before Lavina and I were home together in our new station and work.

Before the big trucks arrived from Addis with the prefabricated buildings, the men had laid the cement floors of the two houses. There were two because the program also called for a medical person to be based with us in Teppi. Each airstrip opened would have regular visits by trained Ethiopian medical dressers equipped with modern medicine. A nurse would occupy the second house to supervise that aspect of the ministry. The competent nurse who came to do that was Leatta Weidenbach. She came to us from the Dembidollo station but had previously served for a number of years in the Presbyterian mission in Yaoundi in the French Cameroon. Important health lessons were also put on cassette and were an integral part of the medical program.

## A SERIOUS LEG INJURY

On the Saturday afternoon of the day the trucks arrived from Addis bringing in the pre-cut houses, I suffered a serious accident with my trail bike in Teppi town. I had gone from the site into town to purchase some small item needed. The town itself had one main street running through it on each side of which were mud-walled, metal roof shops where cloth, soap, salt, sugar, tea, coffee, cooking oil and other basic supplies were sold. Interspersed among them were *"Tej Bets"* and *"Bunna Bets"* where people gathered to drink and visit.

The market area itself was nearly deserted by this time in the afternoon and the trails leading out of Teppi were crowded with men, women, children and animals making their way home. Some of them would be traveling for several hours and would arrive home well after dark.

But, many were still crowding that street in Teppi as well. Some had stayed a bit longer than they should have in the drinking houses. As I threaded my way, ever so slowly, through this crowd on my trail bike, one man suddenly grabbed my handlebars rather than making room for me to continue moving along. I put my foot out to keep my balance and stop. Somehow, in doing this I twisted my leg in such a way that the femur crashed into the head of the tibia and I fell. The pain was excruciating and unbearable. I was going less than five miles an hour and it hardly seemed possible one could receive a serious injury under those conditions. I lay there moaning and groaning. People tried to assist me but I begged them just to leave me and I would be alright. After lying like that for a minute or two, I thought I had better try to get back on the bike and head back to our site across the airfield.

Standing on one leg I managed to get my injured leg over the seat and start the bike with its electric starter. I hadn't gone more than a couple of feet when I again fell. Apparently the pain was too severe and I simply couldn't manage by myself. Again, I lay there with unbelievable pain.

About this time, Harry and Pat drove up with the Landrover. Someone had run from the town to the base and reported what had happened. In due course, I was placed on a cot just under the eaves of the workshop which had been the first building completed.

You will recall now that the trucks from Addis had just arrived before I left for the store. A storm was building up rapidly and the men and their workmen were working furiously to get the supplies under cover before it struck. Within moments a colossal, late afternoon, tropical rain storm descended on us. The wind was blowing so furiously that the tents were threatening to blow down. Everyone, both the men and the women, were struggling frantically against the elements. The rain was now coming down in sheets. I was under the protection of the overhanging metal roof, but the water was running off on me and I was helpless to move. It was too ridiculous to describe. When the folks discovered my plight they came to the rescue, but later we had many good laughs over that chaotic scene.

At that time, I didn't know how serious my injury had been. We only knew that the pain was almost unbearable and we had only aspirin to relieve it. I shall always remember, with unspeakable gratitude, the way Harry and Pat, nurse that she was, kept coming to me during the night to inquire how I was doing and to give me more aspirin. Whenever they came, I was awake! It was a very long, dark night!

In the morning MAF came in on an emergency flight and flew me to the hospital in Mettu. Poor ex-ray film failed to indicate the extent of my injury. The doctor put a cast on it and the next day I was flown home to be with Lavina at the Godare. The swelling and pain became unbearable and we had to cut off the cast to bear it. Finally, a week later, we decided I should get into Addis Ababa and have it looked at in the hospital there. I was sent to the Leprosarium where a skilled Indian born, British, orthopedic surgeon again ex-rayed the knee and said I had smashed the head of the tibia. Surgery would be required.

After the surgery Dr. Fritchie said the injury gave the

appearance of a parachute accident. He was extremely pessimistic. He said he couldn't bring the tibia back to where he wanted it because it was already nine days since the accident had occurred. He told how cartilage and large amounts of blood poured out of this hugely swollen knee when he operated. He said, finally, "I've tried to give you a leg on which you can get upstairs, but your mule riding days are all over." He was so dismal in his prognosis, that his Indian wife, who was also a doctor, rebuked him and said that with God all things are possible.

## ART AND FRIEDA VANDERPLOEG

Teppi station would be opened without my help. My leg was in a cast for seven weeks and when it came out it was as stiff as a plank of wood. Physical therapy followed and bit by bit improvements followed. This was the period when Art and Frieda Vanderploeg were volunteer host and hostess operating the mission guest house. Art was God's gift to me during those weeks we had to be in Addis. Lavina and I stayed in the guest house during which time I waited for the cast to be removed and continued with physical therapy.

I recall how I would lie on my stomach on the floor in the mission house with perspiration rolling off my forehead as Art put his knee on the back of my leg where it was supposed to bend. He would pull up on the foot, release it and pull again until it moved a little. I could barely stand the pain. Eventually, it bent far enough so that I could sit on a chair and pull the foot back by myself. Every day, for one solid month Art drove me to the physical therapist, a competent Swedish lady to whom I owe so much. When I finally began trying to walk with the help of the bars, it was obvious that there was too much wobble at the tibia for me to get along without a helping brace. For six months, I walked with a cane and every day dressed myself with a heavy metal brace which was anchored in the heal of my shoe, hinged at the knee and strapped around my leg with a six inch belt just above the knee. It seemed likely that I would need this sort of brace the rest of my life.

## CHAPTER TWENTY-FIVE

## LEARNING TO WALK AGAIN

Eventually, we were back at Teppi. Our volunteers had done their job well and had long since left for America. Harry and Pat went back at Godare among the Majang. Lavina and I were back at Teppi settling into our new home and ministry. I was walking with a brace and the help of a cane. Every day I tried to force the knee to go a little farther until finally I had almost achieved the full range of what it originally could do.

One day, I decided not to put on the brace, hung it up in the outside shop and never donned it again. I still walked with a cane, but my pain was minimal and I knew that God was gradually giving me back my leg.

I may never fully know why this kind of accident happened when it did. I believe, however, that even in the tragedies of life, God overrules them for good. In ways we cannot chart or predict God receives honor and glory through it. Sometimes we cannot understand but accept by faith what God says in His word, "All things work together for good to them that love God and who are called according to His purpose." For myself, I can only praise God for lessons sickness and injury have brought into my life. Some of His best secrets and insights were shared during my most difficult experiences. And, we are absolutely certain that nothing in life or in death can ever separate us from the love of God which is ours in Christ Jesus our Lord."

## "YOU'RE THE MAN WITH THE MIRACLE LEG"

This accident happened in February of 1972. Seven years later Lavina and I were in South India visiting in the home of Sunjeeve Savarirayan and his wife Esther. Sitting beside him was another guest who was a personal friend of the surgeon from India who was in Addis during the time of my accident and had operated on my knee. As we were sharing together, this other guest suddenly leaned forward and said excitedly, "Then, you're the man with the miracle leg!" Dr. Fritchie had told him how when we had been in India the preceding year we had visited his leprosarium and he had been amazed to find that I was walking without pain and without a limp. He recognized it as a miracle of God. I totally agree!

When I think of my marvelous recovery, however, I sometimes think of the story I heard about the man who was being complimented on his lovely garden saying something about it that only God alone could make such a beautiful garden. The man, whose garden it was, responded by saying, "When God was doing the garden by Himself, it didn't look nearly as nice as now when God and I work at it together!" I did what I could to help, but seriously, I know that without God's, powerful, healing hand, I would still be a cripple today. To Him belong all the honor, glory and praise!

The work in and from Teppi prospered. New airstrips were opened in the surrounding area. Eventually we had seven airstrips into which MAF flew our medical dresser, and an evangelist with cassettes and players. The vernacular messages about Jesus Christ were always more popular than the language learning lesson tapes. But, both were an integral part of our ministry and without either it could not have been happening.

We had some great experiences at those airstrips. Normally, just our Ethiopian staff did these itineration flights. They would go out on a Monday and return on a Friday. They had a regular circuit to complete before returning and starting all over again. Occasionally I was privileged to accompany them. It was always an inspiration to see how God was blessing their outreach and how people were being helped in the name of Jesus.

## TED POLLOCK'S PREFABRICATED STRUCTURES

I recall the week we were improving the Gecha airstrip. We had already put a small prefabricated building on the edge of that strip. Ted Pollock, the mission builder at Ghimeera, had designed these so they would fit into an MAF plane and could be transported to the site. Ted had helped us put this one together. Two or three of us, with a couple of local people helping, would have one of these prefabs ready to sleep in by nightfall.

Ted was a creative genius as a builder. He figured out building structures that would fit into the MAF plane so they could be transported from his workshop in Ghimeera to whatever new post needed them. All our first buildings at Godare had come in that way. Once Ted and three of his children had come in to spend a week with us putting up the staff houses, clinic building and the school buildings. We supplied the home made bricks, sand and cement needed, and Ted was there with the roof structure, roofing, doors and windows. Every mission station benefited from Ted and his wife Dolly's skill and dedication. And when their children came out, it was an entire family making an inestimable contribution to the Lord's work.

I really appreciated those prefabricated, one room structures beside the airstrips. Before we had them, I would sleep wherever the local people found an empty room. Often, it'd be in some abandoned trader's storeroom or in some un-used shack no longer needed by the local folks. Their hospitality was enviable, but the only problem was the rats. I learned that if I would bring with me a rat trap and start trapping just about dusk time, I could catch as many as three to five in an evening in my room where I would soon be sleeping. This seemed to discourage the rest of them and I could get quite a good nights sleep. ... Army ants were another problem. More than once I had to abandon where I was sleeping and wait else-where for morning to dawn. With the small prefabricated buildings, we had a wooden type floor and it could be locked securely during the day when I was out. Another big advan-tage was that our medical person and the evangelist and I could all be rooming and eating together and enjoy each other's company.

### GECHA AIRSTRIP

But, now we were there at Gecha with Harry and Pat, my teen aged son, Mark, and myself. Pat helped the medical dresser and served as our cook and dietician. We men kept the little tractor and plow running from morning until night. We plowed that entire airstrip, six inches at a time. Much of that week we experienced periods of showers and rain. At sixty five hundred feet it was chilly cold when the rain was falling. Heavy fog settled in periodically. Frankly, we were all eager for Saturday when the MAF plane was scheduled to collect us and fly us home. But, alas, Saturday it rained most of the day and their flight was canceled. By the end of the week our mood was somewhat gloomy. The bounce was gone! We had worked hard. Our food supply was greatly diminished and we were ready to take off. But, God had other plans. We would know better in the morning when the sun was shining.

Sunday morning came and early in the morning while we were still sitting around eating, we saw a single individual coming across the airstrip carrying a ram's horn. He walked out in front of our temporary clinic to the edge of the airstrip, put this thing to his mouth and we heard a piercing call that echoed and re-echoed in the surrounding hills and mountains. He did this several times. It wasn't long before people began coming in to where we were camped. Some were ill and wanted medical care. We had been there all week. This was Sunday, a day of rest. But we knew we couldn't say, "There are six days in which to be healed!" Human need had to be met, Sabbath or no Sabbath. The medical dresser began seeing sick people.

When nearly a hundred people had gathered, I began to preach, speaking in Amharic with the help of an interpreter. My Amharic wasn't that extensive, but out in the country I dared to manage. Eventually, I asked Yisahak, the clinic dresser to prepare his heart to preach. When he joined us, he preached awhile and when he grew tired, I would try it again. Near the end, I remember saying to them that this scene in front of me reminded me of the days of John the Baptist. I told how the crowds had come to hear him and how John had said it was time for the people to repent because this was God's time and this was the time God was coming to visit and heal His people. As I spoke of the need to repent from our sins to receive God's salvation, one of the men stood up and began to confess his sins. This led to several others sharing similarly until finally someone said, "This will take too long. We all have sinned against God. We should all confess our sins to God together."

I was amazed to hear many of them pouring out their hearts to God. Eventually, we all bowed our heads, closed our eyes and I led them in prayer. When I opened my eyes, I discovered that a huge tropical rainstorm would soon be upon us. The people scattered quickly and headed for their villages. It was a morning I shall never forget. Our disappointment in not getting away the day before was turned into joy. How wonderful, mysterious and decisive are the ways of our God. Indeed, His ways are past finding out. On Monday morning, we were all back home.  Our hearts were full of joy!  How good God is!

## SALLI AIRSTRIP

Once on another airstrip, at Salli, the evangelist, medical dresser and I had come in on Monday.  I had spent many hours improving the strip with our small garden tractor and plow.  But now it was time to leave.  The plane had come in, the door had been taken off and the seats of the plane were on the ground.  The men were busy loading the tractor and gear.  At that moment a man came up saying he had a toothache and wanted to know if I could help him.  I decided I could extract it and relieve him of his pain.  In the early days I extracted teeth without Novocain just using a regular pliers.  But my cousin, Dick Hoekstra, in Chicago had a neighbor who was a dentist.  While visiting Dick and Clara, he brought his neighbor over and this kind man provided me with four dental forceps and showed me where to inject Novocain to deaden the pain.

So when my patient sat on that MAF plane seat beside the plane, I injected him with Novocain, waited the right amount of time, and then rather skillfully extracted his tooth.  People standing nearby saw that it didn't appear to be that big an ordeal and before we left, I had extracted a total of five teeth in half an hour.  I used to say facetiously that I charged each one fifty cents and that all bills were still outstanding!  Seriously though, having a toothache for those people was no laughing matter.  Their methods of dealing with it were quite primitive.  I was only a "quack" but to them I was a real professional!  Which reminds me that the definition of a expert is "an ordinary person giving advice or services away from home"!

Lavina and I went together to some of these airstrips.  Sometimes we lived in our little yellow tent and at other times we set up shop in a local school building   during vacation times.   During some seasons of the year, fog would come rolling in and we would literally be "living in a cloud".  I remember one morning after we had finished our breakfast, Lavina and I were having our devotions together.  When it was time to pray, we both bowed our heads, closed our eyes and talked to God.  On this particular occasion,  when we'd finished praying, we couldn't tell where we were.  The fog had moved in during those few minutes when our were eyes closed and completely enveloped us. The fog was so dense that we couldn't see but a few feet from where we sat. We were amazed and completely surprised! We knew that very soon the sun would be fierce and chase the fog away as if it had never been there at all. So it was on our itineration airstrips!

## DR. CREMER AND THE WOMAN
## WITH THE TUMOR

The strangest experience I ever had on one of those itineration airstrips occurred when Dr. John Cremer from the Dembidollo hospital and I went out together with Yisahak and Getachew, the evangelist. We were living in a tent on the Gecha airstrip. One afternoon around four o'clock a group of people showed up with a woman who had an enormous, abdominal tumor. It was huge and she was extremely uncomfortable. Dr. Cremer examined her and decided he could drain off a good bit of that fluid making her feel a lot better. He explained that this wouldn't solve the problem because it would come back again, but, at least for now, it would help her immensely.

So we invited her into our tent and put her on the airmattress on the floor. Dr. Cremer tapped her abdomen and began draining fluid off into our twelve quart bucket. He explained that he had to drain this fluid off over a period of two or three hours lest the patient go into shock. You will never believe this but I carried out at least two buckets of fluid and dumped it out in the bush.

By this time, it had already become dark. There was no way we could send her away as she would have to walk back to wherever she had come from. It was much too cold for her to be put outside. There was only one thing left to do. She would spend the night in the tent with us and her entourage could make there way to the village and collect her in the morning.

John and I laughed over our ridiculous situation the rest of the week. Here were two missionaries spending the night with a strange woman breathing garlic in their faces while we protected her from the cold and permitted her to gain strength so she could leave in the morning. When morning finally came, her relatives were back. She got up off the air mattress, went outside and they all slowly began to head out toward their village. We never saw her again and I have often wondered if she saw the humor in the situation like John and I did. We had truly become all things to all people in the hope that we might at least win some, even as was said by the Apostle Paul when he wrote to those Corinthian Christians so long ago.

## THE MINISTRY IN TEPPI ITSELF

We had a small, compact, neatly laid out compound in Teppi. Located directly beside the airfield and up about a fourth of the way from the lower end was an excellent spot. Ethiopian Airline planes touched down almost directly in front of the house and were barely one hundred feet off the ground at that point on take off. The MAF plane could taxi and stop right in front of our large gate. When they night stopped, we opened the gate and they taxied in, parking safely in our front yard. We loved it.

In the center of the compound between the two identical residences was my office, recording studio and supply room for the medicines. The medical trek boxes were inventoried and restocked in that room.

My office was a place where we kept our records and accounts. Here I could read, study and prepare lessons, conduct Bible studies or meet with callers. I had an excellent library with a complete set of Calvin's Institutes, Lenski, the International Commentary, Hastings' Dictionary of the Complete Bible, the Gospels and the Church. My Greek lexicon, word studies and the International Bible Encyclopedia were my frequent companions. In this same room, we did our high speed duplicating of cassettes.

Between these two rooms was our recording room. It was never insulated as well as I would have liked, but it served our purposes adequately and many beautiful cassettes in Kaffa, Mocha, Oromo, Shako and Amharic were produced in it.

Amara, a keen young Amhara speaking man with great sensitivity about the nuances in Amharic and the languages in which we were working was my recordist. I had trained him from scratch and he did well with the state of the art available to us during that time. One of the larger projects we undertook was to do an oral translation of several books of the New Testament from Amharic to Shako. Kani Naro, one of the evangelists who was almost completely bilingual, narrated the text on tape in his language. It was recorded verse by verse by Amara -- slow, methodical and tedious but they got the job done. This oral translation proved to be a great blessing to the Shako people, most of whom were illiterate.

The recording room wasn't as acoustically acceptable as we wanted, but the major problem came from a friendly rooster outside. Invariably it seemed that when this rooster knew we were in there, he would march right past the back window, stop and crow lustily several times. He eventually paid for his folly by appearing on our Sunday dinner table!

There was an Orthodox church on the north side of town. We didn't have a church building of our own in Teppi, so we rented an abandoned trader's shop down the dirt road leading out of Teppi to the south. Before that, we had met on Sunday mornings on the veranda of our house with Getachew doing the preaching. Getachew told me that he first met us in the little book store we had opened years earlier in Teppi. He said he had come in and wanted a Bible in Amharic very badly but had no money to buy one. He still remembered with great thanks to God that before he left, we had given him a free copy. Getachew at that time was just a young man trying to earn a living by teaching the children of Amhara officials during vacation time so that they would have an advantage over the rest of the students when school resumed in the fall.

Getachew had gone to school in the SIM in Addis Ababa. He knew and loved the Lord. He was excited that we had moved to Teppi and was eager to help us in any way he could. He also had artistic ability and our volunteers from America were able to put him to work painting the inside of the new houses.

## TEPPI WORSHIP SERVICES

Getachew loved to lead those worship services on our veranda and to preach. He used an empty oil drum for his pulpit. Right from the beginning, by his own initiative, he organized prayer times and developed a choir. During one of the summers Solomon Gizaw, the lad who became an MAF pilot, was in that choir singing and playing his guitar. How marvelous and wonderful are the ways of the Lord!

When we began in that rented building, we put in crude, log benches held off the ground by five inch forked legs. They were later replaced with solid benches made by skilled carpenters. That little church was often packed with as many as twenty or thirty walking sticks leaning against the wall just outside the door on muddy days. Sometimes a dog or two showed up with the worshippers and it wasn't unknown to have a goat or sheep tied unto the building.

We saw wonderful things that God was doing in those services. We witnessed first hand the effect of demons on people there when sometimes one or even two or three would begin laughing like hyenas and were making disturbances. On such occasions the service continued normally, but other members would quietly usher these persons outside and lead them to the little grass prayer room situated about twenty feet away in the back. While Getachew was continuing his message, we could hear folks praying in that little room that Jesus would drive out the demon and heal these disturbed persons. I personally witnessed persons who had been making those disturbances become calm and quiet in that prayer room. But, before this happened, the individual under the power of prayer would suddenly fall over from a sitting position and lie there as if death had come. After perhaps a minute or so, the person would open his or her eyes, sit up and be perfectly normal.

In the main service, we also saw people moved by the Holy Spirit to confess their involvement in devil worship. Some took off bracelets that had been put on their arms by a witch-doctor. Others had heavy brass bracelets opened and removed after the service. God was marvelously at work in this church. It was not at all uncommon for Getachew and a small group of deeply committed young people to spend entire nights in prayer. Healings of sick in answer to prayer were frequent testimonials.

## PRAYING FOR THE SICK

I still remember the morning when a man came across the airfield, through the gate and to the office where Getachew, several others and I were having our morning Bible study and prayer time. This man wanted Getachew to come and pray over his brother. The sick man had been in bed for some days and was unable to walk.

Getachew and his companions invited me to accompany them. We soon found ourselves in the back of one of those small merchant shops. The sick man was lying on a cowhide strung bed on which there was a thin cotton mattress and a sheet. Chairs had been arranged for us to sit. After exchanging pleasantries briefly with the brother who had fetched us and had gone on ahead, Getachew opened his Bible and read the passage from Luke where it tells us that the power of the Lord was on Jesus to heal.* He spoke briefly of Jesus great power to save, his power over demons and sickness and exhorted us to have faith and to pray.

At that point, Getachew and his three companions got up and quietly surrounded the sick man's bed. They laid their hands on this person's body and began to pray. They all prayed at the same time. Sometimes they were praying in their own languages and sometimes they were praying in tongues. These men were literally agonizing in prayer to the point where they were perspiring profusely. After fifteen or twenty minutes, they stopped praying, urged the man to believe in Jesus' power to make him well and then we all left.

Two days later, the man who had originally come requesting Getachew to pray for his brother, came excitedly across the airstrip, through the gate and into the office where we were again having our Bible study. He was exuberant. His brother was walking. Our response was a time of praise and thanks to God! Good news like this travels and no doubt contributed to the growth of the church and the acceptance of the Gospel in that area.

With the participation of these keen young men, we also started other preaching centers. One of these small worshipping groups was loaned a cassette player. Every Sunday, a different woman would take the player home for that week. Each morning when the women met, as was their custom, to drink coffee together in one of their homes. The woman would bring her cassette player and they had a time of listening. This was a marvelous way for them to grow in their understanding of the Christian faith and the one who had the player during her week considered it a great honor to have been entrusted with it.

## CHAPTER TWENTY-FIVE

### DISTURBANCES WHILE PREACHING

During the dry seasons, these young people and we would go out with the Landrover to a place on the northeast corner of Teppi. People from this small center of shops and homes would gather around as Getachew or I would preach. It was amazing to see the tricks that Satan used to bring confusion into those times of preaching. Dogs would get into a vicious fight, or an animal might threaten to wander off. One Sunday there was a young woman who was acting very strangely. They said she was crazy and that normally she was chained inside the building. On this occasion she was sitting on the dirt and pulling her dress up in unseemly ways. She also made strange noises we didn't understand. The woman seemed to be attractive, but was mentally unstable or possibly demon possessed. I shall never forget how Lavina quietly sat down beside her, took hold of her hand and placed her arm around her. Eventually, they were both standing and Lavina was lovingly embracing her until the service ended. Lavina's loving touch was used by God to quiet this poor troubled soul's heart, quieting it with His peace. It was remarkable to observe. We left that village heavy hearted because we feared that after we left they would treat her as before, chaining her and keeping her like a dog of whom everyone was afraid.

### KANI NARO DOING THE WORK
### OF AN EVANGELIST

Kani was a Shako speaking young man with about three years of formal education. He loved the Lord, knew Amharic and read his Bible avidly. In the late afternoons Kani would frequently visit different areas of the town and surrounding villages with his cassette player. On one such occasion he found himself in the village of a local witchdoctor. This ritual expert was willing to listen, but the young woman who prepared his food and participated in some of his ceremonies was very resistant and tried to make disturbances. This woman's name was "Workit". We had first been introduced to her years earlier by her father. On one of those treks that Lavina and I made into Teppi, spending several days in our rented quarters, Workit was brought to us by her father. She was a young girl then and severely crippled by polio. The father offered me a bull if I could send her to a hospital and have her legs straightened. This poor girl's one leg was frozen in the position it would have if one was sitting on one's buttocks with knees bent. The other leg was twisted out of shape in another contortion. She could only move about by putting one hand on the ground and waddle along with her skirt dragging in the dirt or mud.

## WORKIT RESPONDS TO THE GOSPEL

This same Workit was the young woman that Kani Naro, ten years later, was contending with each time in the witchdoctor's village. Local people said she was demon possessed. Workit was the assistant to the witchdoctor. She lived in her own house nearby. It was Workit who brewed the coffee, participated in the rituals and frequently poured the beer on the special stones honoring the ancestors.

One day when Kani was in her village he said, "Workit, come here once and sit beside me. I have something important I want to tell you." Although she had never showed interest, on that occasion she responded and sat quietly as Kani carefully told her the message of salvation in Jesus. Before Kani left that afternoon, he asked Workit if she would like to keep his cassette player overnight. She accepted his offer and he gave her his player with the Gospel of John on cassettes in her Shako language.

She listened intently to the cassettes, listening over and over again until the batteries were dead. Her heart was drawn to the message from this beautiful Gospel. In the morning when Kani returned, she begged him to leave his player with her so that she could learn more. Kani, however, said, "No, but if you will go to the missionary, she will give you a player that you can keep in your house and listen further."

The very next morning Workit and a small girl who always walked on the trail with her, came to Lavina. Kani explained to Lavina what had happened and how eager Workit was to learn more about Jesus. Lavina gave Workit a cassette player with several cassettes in her language, and demonstrated to her how to operate the machine. Workit took the machine home and began listening carefully. Eventually, she surrendered her heart to Christ and was baptized

Lavina shows Workit how to operate the player.

This terribly crippled young woman came to be a very gifted, influential, charismatic leader. She eventually had in her house a box with a cassette player and every cassette we produced in the Shako language. Her friends and neighbors were frequent guests in her home or yard listening to these cassettes. On Sunday mornings, before the church service began Workit had a listening time with her growing circle of new believers. Every Sunday you would see Workit leading this Bible listening group from her home down the dirt road to the church, a fourth of a mile away. This severely handicapped woman went out as far as four or five miles to reach people with the message of Christ on cassette. Always she had some young girl beside her carrying the player and the tapes for the day. Workit was truly a triumph of God's mercy, grace and saving power in Jesus Christ.

Kani Naro, the Shako evangelist, also made extensive use of cassettes as he reached out in the direction of the coffee plantations southeast of Teppi. He would begin in an area by visiting homes and playing his cassettes in the Shako language. Eventually, he would identify some person who appeared more interested than others and who might be a natural leader. Even before this man became a committed believer, Kani would entrust him with a player and cassettes. This individual loved his recognized status and enjoyed inviting others to listen with him.

This freed Kani to move on to another area and repeat the process. Occasionally he would return to the village in which he entrusted this village leader with that player. Using the cassette players and the personal confirmation of the messages like this was greatly blessed by the Lord. I know of at least three areas where Kani had gotten groups of people to accept the message and commit their lives to Christ. It was a pattern I believed evangelists could use to plant churches successfully almost anywhere in the world. Years later I discovered in Bangladesh that they were using this same approach very successfully with five evangelist using fifteen players.

## MANY OPPORTUNITIES IN TEPPI

In Teppi we had many opportunities to share the Gospel using cassettes.

### WITH STUDENTS

On the opposite side of the airfield across from where we lived was a large government school with hundreds of students. We let it be known that students could come in the afternoon and pick up a player to use in their homes in the evening. They would pick up cassette players after school was dismissed and drop them off in the morning before their classes began. We had several players going out like this on a regular basis. In this way the Gospel was getting a wide hearing. We knew that the cassette was making an essential difference and that the Gospel was being heard where without the players it wouldn't be happening. The cassettes in the hearer's own language was the tool of choice to plant the seed when an overt Christian witness might not be welcomed.

### WITH PEOPLE REQUESTING PLAYERS

Sometimes individuals we had never seen appeared at our door and asked if we would loan them a player and cassettes in their language. Some professed to have come from a distant village and wanted their people back home to hear this good news. We frequently gave players out to folks who came like that, but I must confess that I was often a bit nervous and wondered if we might ever see that player again. At the Godare, we never doubted that our players would be returned, but Teppi, being a town with people of different cultures and backgrounds, raised some questions about the wisdom of our doing this.

## IN THE MARKETPLACE

On Saturday the town was filled with visitors from villages in all directions -- people who were in town because it was market day. These market days were extremely popular, almost like holidays when people got together for business and for social contacts. Our evangelists went into the market area every week with cassettes in whatever languages were represented there. They were careful not to play their cassettes up close to where the sales and trading was taking place lest they antagonize those who wouldn't appreciate any additional distractions. Normally, they found shady places under trees where people gathered who were waiting or just socializing. Countless numbers heard the Gospel who would otherwise never have heard. A seed was being planted. I could picture an evangelist or another Christian eventually visiting those distant villages from which some of them had come. When this visitor would begin speaking about Jesus, the seed would have been sown and the comment might well be, "That's the same message we heard in the market when we heard it from the machine."

This kind of thing actually happened once when Mel Vandevort was out preaching in a distant village. As he shared the Gospel, one of the men came forward and said that he had heard this same message when he had stayed in the clinic in Ghimeera many years earlier. At that time he had been seriously ill and heard the good news about Jesus over an extended period of time. During that time he had never embraced it personally, but on that day when Mel preached in this man's village his heart was ready and he believed. I was confident this same kind of response would happen over and over again because of people having heard the Gospel clearly from cassettes on market day in Teppi. Ours was an unspeakable privilege to be there and sharing the good news about God's powerful, appointed Savior, Jesus Christ.

Lavina's letter home, dated August 29, 1975, tells how the church was developing in Teppi and about her personal ministry with the women:

*"Eveything here is okay and we just rejoice in what God is doing in the hearts of the people. On Sunday morning at our worship service, a man from the Shako tribe stood up and asked the evangelist to come and remove the three bracelets he had on his arms. They were put there by the witchdoctor to please the spirits. But now that he was a Christian, he no longer needed them and he wanted to trust in Jesus only. It is encouraging to see the response of the people. ...*

*Last Sunday they elected elders in the church and we are hoping that they will choose a man to be recognized as their pastor soon. The little mud house we rent for a church is getting too small, so they are wanting to build a church near our home. .*

*I have a sewing class for the women on Friday after noons. There are 14 women and more are wanting to come. Fourteen women is about all I can handle at one time. We are making patch-work quilts and I don't have enough of the squares of material for more people.*

Lavina and her sewing class in Teppi.

*On Friday afternoon we have a women's Bible study. One of the Amhara speaking girls leads the meeting and does real well. It is a joy to see the girls taking a share in the worship services. I go out visiting the women in their homes, trying to make one or two calls a day. I take one of the school girls with me to translate as I don't know Amharic well enough to do it on my own. The women love to have me come and they are very hospitable, always serving tea, strong sweet black coffee, hot sweet milk, bread and honey or the national food of injira-ba-wat. It's great to have this contact with the women. ..."*

In another letter, dated September 21, 1975, Lavina shares her joy in seeing what God is doing in Teppi.

*"It is a joy to see God so mightily at work in the hearts of the people in this area. There is a significant response to the Gospel among the Shako people.*

*Yesterday was a busy day. We had a very good service, some 150 people in the little house we use for the church and about 40 or so on the outside. Our services are about two hours long and it gets hard on my back to sit that long on the benches without a backrest, but the people don't seem to mind that much. They just love to sing and really have a great time. ..*

*After lunch we were invited to a Shako family's home. The couple are new Christians so a group of us went to their home and had a little Bible study, prayer and song service. The tiny hut was simple and crude with a huge fire burning in the middle of the floor where the wife was preparing coffee. It was a joy to see how radiant they were and the love and presence of Jesus was in our midst.*

*She served us coffee, thick and black, with a pinch of salt and red pepper in it along with roasted ears of corn. When the chickens began coming in to roost on a board above our heads, we knew it was time to go home. As we walked through the forest in the semi-darkness and drizzling rain, our hearts were full of joy, overflowing for this family and their new life with Jesus."*

# CHAPTER TWENTY-SIX
# BACK WITH THE MAJANG

It was time for us to take a vacation. We'd come to Addis to pick up our car from Jim's house and head north toward Gondar and Axum, site of the ancient rock churches of the Orthodox church.

Paul was a boarding student at the Good Shepherd School for missionary children located in Addis Ababa. Our son, Jim, and his wife Betty and little girl, Andrea, were at Good Shepherd, where Jim taught and was in charge of their physical education program. Down the road leading from the school to the city, another son, Denny, and his wife, Carol, and three boys lived. Dave was married and living in Holland, Michigan. Carol Joy had graduated from Hope and was about to be married. Mark was pushing ahead with his aeronautical training in California.

## THE REVOLUTION BEGINS

After enjoying a few days with our children and grand-children in Addis, Lavina and I headed on the road going north. Revolution was in the air. Rumors of an impending coup were rife. At that moment, however, things appeared to be calm enough for us to take that long anticipated holiday.

The first night out we were alarmed to hear the news on our trusty, little, portable radio which went with us wherever we went. The government in Addis Ababa was under siege, parliament had been disbanded and His Majesty's palace was surrounded by rebel soldiers loyal to Mengistu. They told of roadblocks being erected, making travel hazardous and uncertain.

407

Instead of vacationing, the very next morning Lavina and I headed back toward Addis Ababa. We made it through just in time as roadblocks were being put in position to prevent any movement in or out of the city. These were ominous days. Ethiopia would never be the same.

While still in Addis, we had a small taste of what lay ahead. Here is part of a letter to my folks, March 5, 1974:

*"We are all well and safe! These have been days of uncertainty, but better than we had feared. Lavina and I were very nearly mobbed one day in the car. We were shaking like leaves. ...The teachers and students are all on strike. ... Good Shepherd School may have to close too.*

*There have been some who were killed and shots have been heard at night. Most say it is not yet settled. Last week our Embassy had us all pack emergency bags with water, a blanket, food and passports. But for now all is relatively calm except for rumors and more rumors."*

During those early days of the revolution there was a great release of energy and enthusiasm among the people, especially among the students. Many thought that democracy had come at last. During those first few weeks the newspaper was exciting to read. News never printed before was circulating freely. The radio and television seemed to have no restraints on what they showed or said.

But, alas the freedom was short lived. Very soon censorship returned and freedoms were restricted. Eventually, the same students that had marched leading others to bring down the government, were again demonstrating against the abuses and lack of freedom under the new government. On the streets of Addis Ababa scores of people, even hundreds were eventually mowed down and killed. We were told that bodies lay in piles on the streets with permission refused to identify them and remove them being denied for many hours. We were told of one mother who lost six sons during a massacre on the streets of Addis.

## THE KEBELE

The university had long since closed and the students

were being dispersed throughout Ethiopia to educate the masses and help organize local communities to have their own political action groups, police and administrative structures. Every city, town and rural area had these students among them promoting and giving direction to the revolution. Chairman Mao's "little red book" was as common in the hands of these students as is the Bible in the hands of believers on their way to a Bible believing church. In every community Kabeles, local people's organizations, were formed where the people were reeducated and organized to act together. Students were sent out in groups of various sizes to provide communist leadership within these Kabeles throughout Ethiopia.. Regular weekly meetings were held where attendance by the local people was mandatory. Ominously, the Sunday meetings were scheduled for the same hour as Sunday morning worship. Where the church was strong, people continued to worship as before and showed up late for the Kabele meeting. Where Christians were weak, attendance at worship services suffered. Later, when Ethiopians had learned to suffer under communism, Christians refused to compromise and endured the consequences with joy for the sake of Christ.

In the Kabele meetings people were encouraged to express their likes and dislikes. Everything now belonged to them and they had power to make decisions. Enemies of the revolution were to be identified and dealt with. People who possessed too much were despised and abused. Some paid dearly, even with their lives.

In our area, these kinds of meetings stopped after a few months. Like in other areas, the dissidents had by this time been identified, as people expressed themselves in their new, democratic meetings. These "enemies of the revolution" were dealt with appropriately and it was not uncommon throughout the country for such to be imprisoned for varying periods of time, and some were killed.

In Teppi, as in other places, the traditional functions of government manned by a local administration and police continued. Along side, almost like a parallel government, the local Kabele organized and controlled the people. They built crude jails of sticks and poles to imprison those who broke their rules. Before they had guns with bullets, we would see them practicing with hand carved, wooden replicas of the real thing. Local people were required to be at their appointed places of work in the fields or on the coffee plantations. No one was permitted to leave the area controlled by a local Kabele without permission. Anyone entering the area of another Kabele had to check in, report his reason for being there and confirm that he had permission to be away from his own Kabele.. Eyes and ears within a Kabele reported any suspicious movements or activities. All the roads had countless check points where all vehicles were stopped and searched and people were questioned. The control over the people was unrelenting. Some, even in Teppi, were killed for perceived non-conformity and disobedience. Fear and suspicion tainted relationships and produced intolerable tensions.

## NATIONALIZATION PRODUCES SHORTAGES

Property was seized and redistributed by the new people with power. Regulations and more regulations restricted what people could say or do. People suffered much and many were disillusioned. Shops and stores began to run out of staple products because trading licenses were refused and the new cooperatives intended to replace them were not yet functioning. In Teppi even soap, salt, sugar and cooking oil were in short supply.

Food also became expensive and often there was little to buy in the local markets. Why should this be so? What happened in Dembidollo shows how this came about. Prior to the revolution this area was prosperous and thriving. Perhaps the mission's educational program taking students all the way through secondary school contributed to this relative prosperity in that area.

When the revolution began, there were some thirty one tractors with an assortment of needed implements to go with them in that area. The local Kabele leaders required the farmers to turn these tractors and their implements into a designated place with the promise of compensation. One year later, Bill Deeters, a Presbyterian missionary builder based in Dembidollo, reported that only two or three of those tractors was still operable. Tires on some were ruined when assigned drivers refused to change flats and instead drove them without inflation back to the center where the tire man could deal with it. Bill reported seeing open crankcases being rained on. The inevitable result was that food became expensive and scarce in the local market at Dembidollo. An area in Ethiopia which was once supplying surplus grain to other parts of the country, was now hardly able to feed its own people. These kinds of policies contributed to the national disaster when rains failed, causing widespread starvation in other parts of the country.

The revolution was undoubtedly provoked by obvious injustices of too few having too much property, prestige and power. Tragically, in the attempt to rectify long standing grievances, this same revolution unleashed horrendous displays of jealousy, envy and revenge. Thousands of innocent people were vilified, harassed and hounded. Countless thousand were falsely accused and imprisoned or killed. Ethiopia was far from being happy. Before it was finished, the country was destroyed and the revolution failed.

## REVOLUTION FELT IN TEPPI

It wasn't long before we began to experience the effects of the revolution in Teppi. The Kabele meeting of local people was held at least once a week under the shade of a big tree on the corner just outside our compound beyond the fence. Often their meetings were characterized by anger and shouting. Sometimes Lavina and I would look at each other as we were eating about that time and wonder if they began shooting how much protection the thin asbestos siding on our house would offer.

We had planted several hundred Eucalyptus trees along the front of our property outside the enclosure. By this time they had grown to about three inches in diameter and some of them were thirty feet tall. One Sunday morning when we returned from church, we were astounded to find that every tree had been chopped down. The local Kabele had done this while we were gone without asking permission or offering a word of explanation. Later they told us that everything now belonged to everybody, including our small grove of several hundred trees. This was communism playing itself out!

One Sunday afternoon our Christian young people were putting on a special Easter program. Extra chairs and benches had been arranged on the lawn in front of the office where the group would be performing on the cement platform there.

CHAPTER TWENTY-SIX

Many guests as well as our own church people were present. During the service, I noticed that several young men sitting near the front were turning around frequently and communicating with other young men nearer the back. At one stage, about ten or twelve of these young men, mostly out of town university students politicizing the Kabele, on signal, jumped to their feet and demanded that the service stop. They began wildly turning over chairs as people jumped to their feet in shock and dismay.

Our Christian young people tried to calm the situation. I saw that one of them was motioning to me not to say anything and leave it in their hands. The situation was chaotic and fraught with danger. I had determined to remain silent, when those causing the trouble demanded that I answer their questions.

I found myself standing on one of the benches near the front. Chairs were strewn about in disarray and these young men were dispersed among them. One of them in a very loud, threatening voice demanded to know what we were doing in Ethiopia. He ridiculed our ministry saying that we were spoiling the people and doing nothing for the country. I chose my words with great care, but reason was thrown to the wind. I explained how the village people were now receiving medical assistance through our itineration airstrip ministry. I spoke of our language learning programs on cassettes helping people understand the national language. It was apparent that they didn't want rational explanations. They simply wanted to show their power and intimidate the Christians and us. I was shocked by the way they unashamedly, blatantly blasphemed the name of Jesus.

Just as abruptly as it began, so it ended. One of them said, "That's enough for this time. Let's get out of here." They kicked over a few more chairs and left through the open gate. As they began crossing the airstrip, we saw them attack some of our people who were carrying their hymn-books and Bibles. They began ripping pages out of them and scattering them in the air. (once we were told that this same crowd had put a Bible in an outside privy in town to be used as toilet paper)

After they had all gone, an amazing thing happened. Instead of our group being angry over the abuse they had suffered, they knelt down among the scattered chairs and praised God and prayed for the salvation of those who had just treated them so shabbily.

We gave thanks that God had protected us in a situation that might well have gotten out of hand with serious consequences.

That evening, there was a knock on our door. Kani Naro had come from his village, Bible in hand. He had come to comfort us and to pray with us. It was such a beautiful experience to have this young man show his concern for us and to hold us up before the Lord. It had been a rather terrifying experience. Kani's coming was a token of God's goodness as He ministered to our need that night before we tried to sleep.

## ASSIGNED BACK TO GODARE

During this same period, Harry and Pat Miersma left the Godare and returned to America. Harry and Pat felt called to a different kind of ministry and having received the required additional education and training, they began their long-term missionary career with Wycliffe Bible translators. We thanked God for the good years they had given to Ethiopia, for the way they had helped us in Teppi and especially for their years among the Majang people in the rain forest at Godare. The big question now was, what do we do about the Godare?

The mission felt that Harvey and Lavina should return to the Godare. John and Gwen Haspels and their children, new missionaries ready to be assigned, would soon be available. The mission said that we should remain in Teppi long enough to orient the Haspels to the ministry in Teppi. In their opinion, we were needed at the Godare more than in Teppi.

During those deliberations, our hearts were sometimes heavy. We loved the Majang people and the years we had spent at Godare. But, we also loved the ministry in and from Teppi. God had led us into a fruitful, challenging ministry with a strong itineration outreach from seven new airstrips. We were happy and fulfilled. The mission was urging us to be open to the change and to seek God's leading with them. In the end, they came forward with an argument that was beyond dispute. "Look," they said, "you are the only missionaries in the entire world who speak the Majang language. You have the gifts, experience and language ability needed there now."

It was, indeed, a powerfully, persuasive argument. In the end, the Lord convinced us that we had to surrender the work at Teppi to another, and return to the rain forest, Godare, and the Majang people.

While we were wrestling with our decision, I took my Suzuki 185 hsp. trail bike past Metti in the direction of Godare and turned south on the trail toward Korme. I had gone about fifteen miles, when I was abruptly halted by a log across the path that I couldn't get over or go around. This was the end of my journey for that day.

Leaving the bike there, I walked some distance ahead until I ran across two young lads whom I had known at Godare. Almost immediately, they shared with me that one of their friends was very ill with a fever and they would like me to go with them so that I could see what was wrong. They assured me that the village to which they wanted me to go was near. As I had so often experienced in Africa, the word "near" has a very wide area of meaning. It was a long hike. But, eventually, we were in a very dark hut and I discovered a terribly sick young man burning with fever.

I began reminding the young men whom I had known at the Godare of how we had taught them to pray and to believe that Jesus has power to heal. I asked them if they still remembered and believed that. Assuring me that they did, I asked them if they would pray with me and they said they would. These two young men and I laid our hands on this body burning with fever and we prayed. The young lads and I were all praying at the same time, just talking to Jesus and asking Him to please make this young man well again. Before leaving, we arranged for someone to give him some hot tea and to be sure that he drank plenty of water.

I arrived in Teppi well after dark and shared my experience with Lavina. About a week later, one of those two fellows was clapping outside our gate. He brought the good news that the lad we had prayed for was well. Less than two weeks later that very sick young man, now well, was clapping at the gate. He was praising God with us for his recovery.

## IN NAIROBI

While we were living in Teppi, I took three weeks out to attend the Fifth Assembly of the World Council of Churches. I went as a reporter for the "Church Growth Bulletin" of the

School of World Missions, Fuller Theological Seminary in Pasadena, California. During our previous furlough I had begun a doctoral study program there relating to the World Council of Churches. Attending the WCC Assembly in Nairobi was part of my research activity. The magazine I represented entitled me to that coveted badge, indicating I was an accredited member of the press corps registered to cover the meeting. My press corps identification badge entitled me to go anywhere the representative from Time magazine or any of the larger publications went. It was a marvelous way to cover the meeting.

It was a great experience to sit beside Dr. John Stapert, editor of the Church Herald, every day for three weeks sharing reactions, observations and our evaluation as to what was happening. My account of those events is covered in my dissertation which was published by Tyndale Press, 1979 under the title, **The World Council of Churches and the Demise of Evangelism,** My book was well received by both the evangelical community and the ecumenical community. It received favorable reviews and was commended for fairness and good documentation. My only regret is the title itself. Had I been in America when the publishers chose the title, I would have insisted on a positive title like "The World Council of Churches and Its 'New Mission'."

## AN INVITATION FROM WEST AFRICA

While in Nairobi, God used a very small hinge that would have profound effects on our future ministry. We'd already stopped off in Accra, Ghana on our return from the states to Ethiopia. We had done that to test the waters to see if there was a need for and possibility of our extending our cassette ministry to other parts of Africa. In our minds, we were beginning to dream of the possibility of using Ethiopia as a base to reach out to other African countries during extended working vacations.

In that context, I found myself riding with another African church leader on a small commuter bus on the last day of the WCC meeting in Nairobi. He introduced himself to me as moderator of the Presbyterian Church in the English speaking province of the Cameroon in West Africa. As I shared with him briefly about our ministry using cassettes in various languages

415

as an evangelistic tool, he said, "You must come to West Africa. In my province there are 105 languages spoken. We preach in two or three of the major languages and the rest we do in pidgin. With your kind of ministry, we could preach the Gospel using cassettes in all these languages. You must come to the Cameroon." The next time we met was in his church in Buea, the Cameroon. God sometimes swings His door on small hinges, indeed!

## FINAL MONTHS AT GODARE

In the summer of 1976, Lavina and I returned to the Godare and the Haspels took over the work in Teppi. Al and Sue Schreuder had come out as part of Al's internship program from Western Theological Seminary in Holland, Michigan. When the Haspels went for furlough, Al and Sue were there alone, standing in the gap!

We had six wonderful months among the Majang. They are among our happiest times in Ethiopia. It was marvelous meeting old friends like Ocoor, Elong and Argeem.

I hadn't seen Elong for two and one half years. When he one day appeared on the compound, I learned how, on his own, he had been using cassettes all those months. He said he had moved across the river and was living way out there beyond the highest mountain peak on a ridge sloping down toward Gambela and the Barro River. He told how he had gathered a small group around him whom he had taught and who worshipped regularly. He would buy new batteries in Gambela and had kept his player functioning that entire period. Elong was with us only a couple of days, picked up new and additional cassettes in the Majang language, and then disappeared in the forest heading down toward the river and in the direction of Gambela. I never saw him again.

Only Eternity will reveal what people like Elong and others are doing to share the Gospel among their people. But, this I do know, it was the cassette that enabled them to get started and to learn the essential truths about Jesus Christ. I suspect that most of those machines have long since fallen silent. But the foundation has been laid and with their phenomenal memories, they are still drawing on that foundation of information and instruction from God's word, first made plain to them in their own language from cassettes. To God be the praise, honor and glory!

## A LETTER HOME CONFIRMS OUR HIGH HOPES

It was Elong who had gone across the Bako river and witnessed among the Daniir people. His grass string with 105 knots on it was his record of what had happened. One hundred and five people had said to him, "Elong, take some grass and make a string. Tie a knot on your string for me. I want to become a person of your Jesus."

Some period of time after Elong had been in that area, several people came in from that general direction way out beyond the Bako river. They had come to bring in a sick person, found the help they needed and also confirmed their commitment to Jesus Christ.

At that time, I was hesitant to do so, but felt this family should be baptized on the basis of their faith before they went back to their distant village beyond the Bako river.

Our letter home written three years later, dated April 1, 1976, seems to confirm that we'd made the right decision and our hearts were greatly encouraged:

*"Do you remember about 3 years ago when I wrote about this father and his three sons from the Daniir tribe that came and wanted medicine, but who believed while here and were baptized in my office before they left. They also took a cassette player back with them with two cassettes. Well, this week Ojatiin, the first person among the Majang to believe and be baptized, told me of a Majang friend of his who has visited them from time to time. They are three or four days across the Bako River from here. Ojatiin said their faith has been firm and that there are about 20 believers in this family's village now. We were thrilled and encouraged by this."*

The first seed had been sown with the help of a cassette player by a middle aged, illiterate, barefoot Majang named Elong.

## BALTI DIES AND IS BURIED

Chief Balti had become an old man since we had last seen him. He had moved closer to the mission and had a little shack just off the airstrip near where that huge tree had once stood. I visited him frequently, but he was already too ill to really comprehend clearly. It was heart breaking to see him slipping away without ever having committed his life to Jesus. During our years at Godare he would sometimes attend our worship services. He was often in the clinic. There were times when he would come into our house. We would sit together on the veranda. When he was alone, I could share with him about Jesus and he would respond with understanding and appreciation. If others were with him, however, he never entered into a serious discussion with me. He would always respond with some joking comment that didn't always make sense.

In many respects, Balti was a very weird person. Other members of his family were all a bit peculiar too. It's strange, but I had noticed already in the Sudan that frequently persons who were odd or who had had a traumatic experience like having been knocked unconscious or who had fainted and revived again, were the ones who frequently had become witch-

Balti, the most powerful Majang chief.

doctors. There was something weird about many of them and most of them I met were extremely clever and captivating. Some of them were well off, judging by the standards of their own people.

Balti, also, could be extremely cruel and unforgiving. He once shot his twenty year old son in cold blood. Shot him right in front of the young man's mother when the son and he argued. He was under the influence at the time. When Balti was under the influence of that fermented honey water, he was cantankerous and unpredictable. I had been afraid of him more than once.

He died while we were there during these last few

months. I was there beside him. He lay in his hut unaware of those around him. His breathing had become heavy as his chest heaved up and down. The Majang knew that the end was near. Earlier in the day they had come to borrow shovels and pick-axe with which they were preparing his grave. When they had it prepared, it was typical -- a circular hole about three to four feet in diameter going down less than five feet. Half way down along one side was a ledge of soil they'd left on which to base the bark strips they'd lean over him to shield the body from the dirt when they filled in the grave.

Even before he'd breathed his last, a woman was busy stripping layers of thin bark off a foot pole from a tree that was used for that purpose. She was rapidly accumulating many thin strips about a half inch in width. A very few people were sitting there with us waiting for Balti to take his last breath. When he did, Alemayu and another man went inside to remove all the bracelets and charms from his body. There were many of them. While they were doing this they asked if I could send home and ask Lavina for a white sheet in which they might wrap the body.

Once the body had been stripped of everything, they tied him tightly with these strips of green bark, tying him in a fetal position. When finished, he was a ball shaped figure less than two feet in diameter. Around these tied remains, they wrapped our white sheet and again tied it with the bark strips.

Men had come with a crude, homemade stretcher of poles between which there was a square platform of poles tightly laced together. The platform was about three feet square. Before Balti's tightly wrapped, ball shaped body was carried out and placed on this platform, someone blew long blasts on a bugle Balti had owned. It was blown only on very special occasions and this was one of them. Several people with guns also fired shots into the air. Balti's body was placed on this simple stretcher and four men carried him slowly down the hill along the edge of the airstrip to the waiting grave. At the grave site the same clearing described in an earlier chapter was being done. Women were soon throwing themselves on the ground. One woman was singing a lengthy and mournful funeral dirge. At one stage, a young woman went completely berserk, threw all caution to the wind and ran in among the stumps and vines and threw herself on the ground repeatedly. People ran out to catch her lest she injure herself on one of the sharp, protruding small stumps hidden everywhere among the vines and brush. Many shots were fired during this whole procedure.

After the burial, the people who had prepared the grave and carried the body took water and washed themselves carefully some distance from the onlookers. Again, the hopelessness of the whole situation with its pagan practices was overwhelming and depressing.

The next morning when I returned to visit the village in which the grave was located, I found several men sitting on a small log. They had been cutting their heads to show their grief. In front of one was a small hole in the ground. In it I saw at least a cup or more of fresh blood.

## CHOPPING DOWN BALTI'S BEEHIVE TREES

Once during the weeks immediately following Balti's death, I was working in the outside office just in front of the clinic. It was nearly noon and time to go home for lunch when all of a sudden we heard a nearby tree come crashing down. A few minutes later two men were walking down the mission road in the direction of the airstrip each carrying a small Majang ax over his shoulder.

When I went for lunch I noticed one of our trees on the compound just behind where the saw mill was located was missing. It had been chopped down. When I inquired who might have done such a thing without permission, I was told that when a chief like Balti dies, his people go throughout the forest and cut down any tree in which he may have once placed beehives. After fifteen years, I was still learning things about the Majang that I had never known before. I would probably have been much more perturbed had it been the stately shade tree overshadowing our house!

## WITHOUT MAF

During our last weeks at the Godare, MAF was grounded. Revolutionary forces had forbidden them to fly into several areas, including ours. Our radios were still functioning but we couldn't fly anymore. The Haspels had been assigned to live at the Godare during our upcoming furlough. Because they would be delayed, we had been asked to stay over an extra month so that we could overlap with their coming and turn the work over to them responsibly. We were quite happy to do that, the only problem being that we wouldn't have sufficient food for that additional month. With MAF grounded, we had a first class problem. Even if we somehow managed the food problem, we still wondered how we would all get out of the Godare to catch a flight from Teppi to Addis and then on to America. We decided we should take one step at a time. It was essential that we bring in additional food supplies as there was nothing we could find in Metti or Teppi to tide us over.

## USING THE TRAIL BIKE TO FETCH FOOD

Paul, who was fifteen then, and I decided we should go out with the trail bike as far as Teppi. I would fly on to Addis, have discussions with the mission about possibilities after furlough, and bring back sufficient groceries to supply our need until the Haspels arrived. Majangs encouraged us saying that the trail between Godare and Metti had been cleared and we should make it easily on the bike.

On that Sunday afternoon, Paul and I made an exploratory trip in the direction of Teppi. We went several miles and found the trail was indeed cut. We encountered a problem with logs lying across the trail which we would have to cross over. We solved this problem by cutting two boards measuring about two and a half feet in length and six inches in width. We drilled two holes in one end of each through which we put a rope that would be draped over the log and could be lengthened and shorted to accommodate whatever size log we encountered. This actually worked very well except on the three or four foot diameter logs we sometimes encountered.

On Monday morning, Paul and I started for Teppi with a small bag of sandwiches and a couple of chunks of cheese. Lavina told Sue Schreuder in Teppi by radio that we hoped to be there by late afternoon. We had just over fifty miles to go and with the path cleared like the Majangs had said, it should be a lark! It turned out to be anything but!

About two hours out, we came to a river over which they had failed to put a little bridge. The water was about chest deep. Paul and I were there alone. Should we turn back or wait for things to develop. We decided to wait. In about an hour, at least a half dozen Majang men and a couple of boys had reached our point and were sitting around with us. We solved the problem by cutting two poles, lacing the handlebars and the seat to them and getting the bike across with the help of strong, willing Majang men who were sure footed even on the slippery stones in the water. They literally hoisted the bike above their shoulders so that only the tires were wet.

Once across the river, we discovered that the trail ahead was uncut. The path was slippery, overgrown and wet. We literally had to pull bike up these steep hills with a rope and restrain it similarly when going down. Two boys about fourteen or fifteen years of age stuck with us the remainder of the day. Finally, it was totally dark and about eight o'clock at night the chain of the bike came off and we gave up. The Majang boys said they could lead us to a place where we could sleep. We walked over an hour to a tiny Majang village. In the open-sided shack, were several men and boys with their sleeping mats, a narrow bed made with sticks laced together with vines. A bright fire was burning in the center of this hut. That would be our hotel for the night.

The people were extremely hospitable. They said Paul could sleep on the stick mat and they would let me have the bed. We had no padding to lay over the sticks on which we later tried to sleep. Our clothes were wet up to our hips from the wet vines and undergrowth. We found places in the roof over the fire to dry our tennis shoes and socks. We tried drying our trousers, but I'm not sure how successful we were. About one in the morning, Paul came around the fire over to where I was lying and said softly, "Dad, I haven't slept yet."

I said, "Paul, why don't you take my bed for awhile and I'll see if I can get our clothes dry."

Paul tried my bed but soon decided it was too hard and rough. He discovered a filthy bark cloth somewhere, rolled himself up in it and fell asleep under my bed beside the fire. Later when I lay down, I could feel it whenever he turned over and gave the bed a bump.

When morning came, the Majang shared a gourd of black coffee into which they always put hot peppers. Quite some brew! I have always said that it takes only a little to remove one's hair. I'm living proof for the truth of that statement! We had only one small piece of cheese left about the size of my thumb. I offered to share it with Paul but he refused. Years later he told me, "You know, dad, the reason I didn't take that cheese is that I thought you needed it for strength." Bless his young, caring heart!

Majangs accompanied us back to the bike and when the mud and brush that had caused the chain to come off the previous evening had been remedied, we resumed out journey. Majang men helped greatly by cutting bad spots. Our pace was very slow. During the day we found roasting ears and survived on that until we reached Metti around five that afternoon. We were warmly welcomed and they fed us tasty *injira* and *wat*, the normal Ethiopian highland food. We still had ten miles to cover between Metti and Teppi. It was nearly nine o'clock when we showed up on the compound and were welcomed by Sue Schreuder. She said Al was out for a few days north of Teppi on trek.

Lavina was greatly relieved in the morning to learn we had arrived safely It's an experience Paul and I will never forget and one we would prefer not to repeat!

## PAUL RETURNS TO GODARE ON FOOT

I took Paul the ten miles back down to Metti in the morning on the bike. There we arranged for companions to accompany Paul on his trek back to the Godare. Forty miles from Metti! Quite a hike for a young missionary kid, all alone in the forest except for his Majang companions. On the way he survived on roasted, shelled corn and sweet honey water. Paul said that home looked awfully good to him. It took him several days to recover from the rigors of the journey with inadequate food, no place to sleep properly and that long way to walk.

I returned that morning with the Suzuki to Teppi, caught the plane in the afternoon and flew to Addis Ababa. Before leaving I asked Sue if she could buy a horse for me in the market on Saturday. I had no intention of trying to ride that bike home and knew a horse would be much easier. I already had a saddle in Teppi so when I returned from Addis, the horse was waiting and my transportation was assured.

## RETURNING TO GODARE ON HORSEBACK

I engaged three men to accompany me and carry the cartons of groceries. That night, I slept in a Majang village, using a new Majang beehive for my bed. This was a village where they were making these hives. They would cut ten to twelve inch logs four and a half to five feet in length. These logs were split in half and hollowed out. When they put them up in the trees they would band the two halves together again to constitute a whole log. In it were small openings for the bees to enter. The ends were stuffed with grass and brush. When they collected the honey, they would go up into the tree, carrying a smoking torch to the hive to drive out the bees and give a little protection.

That night in the village, I took two halves and laid them side by side. The reins and bridle along with some extra grass and leaves filled the empty depression. I had a sleeping back with me on this return trip. Using the saddle for my pillow, I had quite a good night. The major problem, as usual, was those village dogs that kept barking non-stop all through the night. I was home by two o'clock the next afternoon. This distance as registered on the trail bike was 52 miles from Godare to Teppi. The original trek we made going into Godare nearly fifteen years earlier before the trail was straightened was an estimated seventy miles. What took us ten days then, I now did in a long day and a half, riding comfortably on my new horse. The only problem with that horse was that he stumbled much too often. I had wondered why it might be that Sue was able to buy this horse, that is, why they were willing to sell him. It was only a few miles down the trail when I thought I had the answer. I nicknamed him, "Stumbler!" Stumble or not, it was a vast improvement over the bike trip in. Sue Schreuder had done the right thing in that market when she clinched the deal! I have long since forgotten how much she paid!

Within a few days, our hearts were gladdened when MAF came on the radio and reported that the government ban had been lifted and that they would be able to fly us out whenever we had to leave. We had been trying to figure out how we were going to make it out with just one horse. Some of us were likely to have a long hike. But, with MAF again operating, we flew out in one plane, first class. How can we ever be grateful enough for MAF's marvelous ministry.

## OUR LAST DAY AT GODARE

On that final day when MAF came in to fetch us for the last time, perhaps as many as eighty or a hundred Majangs had gathered to bid us goodbye. The afternoon before, women would come into the house, sit quietly on the floor where they felt most comfortable, and talk softly together. There was real sadness among them as they realized we were going away for a very long time. They seemed to sense that we wouldn't soon return. In the morning, the women were again at the door. They began gathering early in the morning, sitting around until the plane would come. Some of them shared memories of things we had done together and some spoke of when they had first become believers. Lavina prepared many pots of tea, while serving ripe bananas and peanuts as she finished off last minute packing.

It was Max Gove who flew in, arriving just after the noon hour. Majangs helped carry our luggage down the mission road, past the clinic and school buildings, depositing them under those two gigantic trees that formed a gateway between the airstrip itself and the compound. They were incredibly large, stately and tall, measuring between five and six feet in diameter.

It was under these towering trees that the crowd had gathered. But, now it was time to get into the plane. Max had finished loading our luggage in the pod located under the fuselage and said it was time to leave. Roket, the man whom we had ordained, whose finger I had sewn back on when he was a boy, led us in prayer. In the middle of his prayer he broke down and began to cry. Unable to continue he said, "Muse (Moses), you pray."

Moses finished the prayer. When we opened our eyes we saw that a number of them, along with ourselves, were crying. Even Bakle, chief Balti's son, who had at one time made life difficult for us, was wiping back tears. He had become a brother in Christ and a personal friend, but I never expected to see him cry.

Argeem, who had brought in those first knotted strings, had slipped away behind the big tree to weep there by herself.

We were now in the plane with our safety belts fastened. In a moment the door would shut. People would be warned to move back and the engine would start and be revved up for a final check of the instruments. We would be on our way for the last time

## THE LAST WORDS FROM THE RAIN FOREST AT GODARE

But, before the door of the aircraft closed, Argeem came quickly from behind the tree, thrust her head in through the plane's still open door and, speaking in English, the language she had first learned from our daughter, Carol, and the Zudweg girls when they played together as children, said to Lavina, "Nyijobi, (Lavina's African name) you come back. Okay? You come back." Before Lavina could answer, she continued, "If you don't come back, I'll see you one day in Jesus' house."

These were the last words we heard at Godare! The pilot pulled the door shut and fastened it. Soon we were in the air heading for Jimma and Addis. Argeem's words were God's gift for us to treasure in our hearts forever!

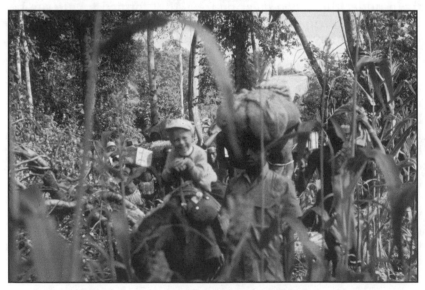

Paul was a tiny boy when we first made our way through the rain forest. So much had happened since first trekking into the rain forest. God was faithful!

426

# CHAPTER TWENTY-SEVEN

# THE NEXT DOZEN YEARS

Our original vision had been to extend our cassette ministry to other African countries from our base in Ethiopia. We intended to continue our work in Ethiopia but we would also spend several months elsewhere in Africa promoting and establishing cassette ministries. We had already begun this. During our last two years in Ethiopia we had gone twice to West Africa for three-month periods. We had recorded our 12-minute, oral, tract-like messages in some 37 languages in the Cameroons, where we were welcomed by the Presbyterian Church. We had also worked with one of their pastors to record the entire New Testament in Pidgin English. These new possibilities were exciting.

However, when Colonel Mengistu clamped down on Ethiopia with his repressive, terrorist, communist regime, our lives and future ministry would change dramatically. Instead of basing in Ethiopia, we would base in the USA. And instead of extending the use of the cassette in Africa only, we would be led of God to venture into India, Bangladesh, Singapore, Indonesia, and South East Asia as well as expanding the fledgling work we had started in Africa beyond Ethiopia.

We left Ethiopia in December of 1976 and returned to live temporarily in Pasadena, California. Here I worked on finishing my doctoral program at Fuller Seminary's School of World Missions. While doing this, a representative from Portable Recording Ministries in Holland, Michigan came out and said they would like us to consider basing on the West Coast. You may recall that the Reformed Church in America had loaned us to PRM so that we could develop overseas cassette ministries under their auspices. It was a good arrangement.

We moved from Pasadena to Rancho Bernardo where we opened a small office. Our ministry would be known as PRM's World Cassette Outreach. It was to be funded by designated funds which I was responsible to raise. The Lord wonderfully prospered the ministry with adequate funding for continued growth.

During my first extended overseas exploratory trip, I traveled with Dr. Ron Beery, President of PRM. We visited East and West Africa, India, Bangladesh, and Hong Kong. Since I had already been in Korea, Ron did the Korean part of the trip on his own. We next met with PRM's Board of Directors; they were excited to accept the new challenge. I was thrilled with their encouragement and the freedom they gave me to follow the Lord's leading. I thank God for this happy relationship, a relationship which continued until I founded Audio Scriptures International.

In serving as director of PRM's World Cassette Outreach, my primary objective was to establish cassette ministry centers in strategic locations overseas. I worked closely with the national Bible Societies in several countries. During those early years not many Bible Societies were interested in Scriptures in audio. Only a limited few within the Bible Society ranks showed any desire to commit funds or people to record and make the Scriptures available in different languages. I sometimes felt that I was a voice crying in the wilderness. Praise be to God, however, this would all change over the next dozen years. Many of the national Bible Societies began to fund and implement programs which provided the people with the Bible in audio format. They had come to recognize that a printed Bible is of little use to a person who cannot read. They came to see that by making their printed Bibles available in audio, non-readers would have the precious opportunity to learn God's Word by listening.

But, I'm ahead of myself. My own understanding as to what God wanted us to do with cassettes changed rather radically. I was excited about the potential of the cassette as a tool for evangelism and as a medium for teaching new believers how to live. Our experience in Ethiopia had confirmed how effective the cassette was. Someone carrying a simple cassette player with a cassette in a local language could introduce people to Christ who would otherwise never be reached for Him. The cassette became the essential difference between

428

being saved and being lost. In one hearing, the listener was introduced to the central truths about Jesus Christ in messages which were carefully crafted and contextualized. Through the power of the Holy Spirit, many of them came to saving faith in Jesus Christ. I was excited to do all I could to start cassette ministries where this would happen.

While I was personally excited about the potential of the cassette from the very beginning, our friends at Gospel Recordings were still wed to the disk recordings that they were using so successfully. I felt, therefore, that if the cassette was to realize its full potential, I was the one God was calling to make it happen. It is amazing how the Lord uses us with our limitations to accomplish His purposes!

Later, when it became apparent to me that Gospel Recordings had caught the vision and was now putting an increasing emphasis on the use of cassettes, I sensed that God was calling us at World Cassette Outreach to focus on putting many more translated Scriptures into audio format. My own experience of spending more than twelve years translating the New Testament into the Anuak language was undoubtedly used of the Holy Spirit to redirect my commitment.

I was so grateful for the new Bible translations which were being completed every year, but I was also very burdened that millions of non-readers, many of them new believers, could not read a single word of these translations. I was convinced, therefore, that we had to do whatever was required to provide these non-readers with Scriptures in a form from which they, too, could benefit. When I thought of the tremendous effort and cost involved in translating a New Testament, I said, "The relatively small amount of effort and cost involved in making these translations available to non-readers makes it unthinkable that we would not do so." My heart was burning with a fire that could not be extinguished.

We therefore immediately began the process of recording the Scriptures in several new languages. In Africa our first recording was done in Kenya in the Maasai language. In India our first recording was done in Tamil. The ministry in Africa had the full support and encouragement of the Bible Society in Kenya. In fact, the Bible Society there loaned us buildings on their campus to house our ministry. Our first recording studio in Africa was located in one of those buildings. Tesfahun Agidew, the first director of the work, was recommended to us by the director of the Bible Society. The recording of new language translations in Africa had begun!

## WORLD CASSETTE OUTREACH OF INDIA

While I was completing my graduate work at Fuller Seminary in Pasadena, my chief mentor was Dr. Donald McGavran. Dr. McGavran had grown up in India, had a great love for India and was recognized as the world's foremost expert on the development of the Christian movement in India. As we worked together, I would sometimes share from our experiences in Ethiopia. I told him how ordinary, uneducated Majang still wearing their leaves and grass became powerful witnesses for Christ using the recorded, tract-like messages on the cassette. I told him how Majang would return from visiting distant village with grass strings having knots tied on them. Each knot represented someone who had said, "Tie a knot on your string for me. I want to become a person of your Jesus."

When Dr. McGavran heard how God had blessed the use of the cassette in our ministry in Ethiopia, he would say, "Mr. Hoekstra, you must take this ministry to India. This is what India needs!" He would go on to talk about the 1600 plus languages spoken in India. He would tell of those vast areas in India where there were then almost no Christians. We prayed over it and in the end this great man of God put me in contact with those leaders in India that I would one day meet in person. McGavran laid the groundwork and God used him to enlarge my vision.

Eventually, in the late seventies, Lavina and I arrived in India. We had developed a pattern of spending from five to seven months overseas and then returning to California. Here we would recover our strength and try to raise additional funds for our next trip and the growing overseas ministries.

On our first trip to India, I met with leaders there whom Dr. McGavran had suggested. I spoke both with individuals and in larger gatherings. The response was always the same: "Yes, this is what India needs, but we have no cassette players in India."

Eventually, we were able to get the needed players by importing cassette player components from Gospel Recordings in Australia. Gospel Recordings sold us 333 cartons of these components weighing approximately five tons and costing $60,000. These components were assembled by the Katpadi Industrial Institute in India with the help of people from the Reformed Church in South India. All of them worked under the technical direction of Tom Van Wynen who, with his wife Sue, had been sent out to India by PRM. Churches in America provided the extra funding needed to purchase the components and pay the excessive import customs demanded by the Indian government. Truly, it was the Lord who made the entire operation possible!

## CHOOSING A DIRECTOR

Now we had a new challenge. Who would be the Director of this promising new ministry? Once again, we found that the Lord Himself had gone before us and had everything in place. Here's the story.

Three years earlier, when Lavina and I first set foot on Indian soil, two young Indians had met us at the airport in southern India. One was Pastor Ezra, a graduate from Fuller Seminary. His companion, Sundara Rajan, was a young evangelist associated with him in the Lord's work. They immediately took us to our moderately priced hotel room in the city where Sundara Rajan recorded our very first cassette for India. Later, we went out into the corridors of the hotel, rounded up a few employees and played it. Our hearts were glad. The ministry in India had begun!

I later learned that, long before we met, Sundara Rajan had a vision for using cassettes in his ministry in India. He once showed me a copy of a letter he had written to Dr. Vigo Sogaard who was then with the Voice of Peace Studio in Chiang Mai in Thailand. Unknown to me at the time, Dr. Sogaard had a vision similar to ours concerning the potential of the cassette. Sundara Rajan also showed me a copy of the Christianity Today magazine in which he had read about the ministry of Portable Recording Ministries. We knew in our hearts that God had brought us together.

The following year Sundara Rajan and I were together in the same room in a little hotel in Madras. That night we took sheets of paper and made a covenant together before the Lord. We made promises to each other if the Lord would lead and bless our ministries. I made a commitment to do all I could to help this young man use the cassette in his ministry. To get him started, I gave him a cassette recorder, 100 blank cassettes and a small high-speed duplicator. We prayed together that night and I turned in to sleep. It had been a busy day. In the middle of the night, I awakened and discovered this man on his knees in prayer at the foot of his bed. He never knew that I would see him. I knew then that God had led me to work together with a young man in India who had a pure heart and who loved the Lord Jesus.

Eighteen months later, when the cassette players were being assembled at Katpadi, in India, we had to consider what kind of organization we should form and who would head it up. You probably won't be surprised to learn that the first director of the newly formed World Cassette Outreach Ministry in Bangalore, India was Sundara Rajan. This young man and his lovely wife, Priya Raani, would develop that ministry to bless all of India. Theo Williams served as the first chairman of the Board. Our hearts were glad.

## THOSE EARLY DAYS IN INDIA

During the first few years, World Cassette Outreach of India was located in rented quarters. A garage was converted into WCOI's first recording studio, and the cassette library with the new recordings of Scripture and other teaching cassettes was in a building five minutes walk up the street. The ministry was growing and God was blessing. The first New Testament recorded was in the Tamil language, which Sundara Rajan himself read. Telugu, Kannada, Hindi and scores of other languages followed, as readers came in from different parts of India. One-day seminars were held to teach people how to use the cassette players effectively.

Lavina and I made annual visits to India to encourage and to teach. The work soon grew to the point where we were unable to fit in our trips to India while continuing to supervise the work in Africa. So I asked PRM to be relieved of the Africa work and they assumed responsibility for it. I was now free to focus my energies on India, Bangladesh, Singapore, Indonesia and SE Asia in general.

As we returned from these overseas trips, we shared

our experiences with God's people in our churches. Sometimes people would suggest that we videotape what was going on in India. We agreed with the idea, but we weren't sure how we should go about it.

## FRANKLIN KIEFT VIDEO TAPES
## THE MINISTRY

God had an answer to the video challenge that we could never have anticipated. Our dear friend, Franklin Kieft, was visiting us in Pasadena for just a few days. One evening, just in passing, I mentioned to him that folks were saying we should videotape the way our cassettes were being used overseas. As the evening went on, we also shared many other things together. Frank had been a wonderful donor partner for many years. He had come out to Ethiopia years earlier and did Herculean work to help us open that station in the rain forest. He had given generous financial support whenever there was a special need that he could help meet. But even in my wildest dream, I would never have thought of Frank operating a video camera. He was a skilled, retired engineer who had built his own Screw Machine Specialties factory. He was obviously very intelligent, but he had only a 6th grade education. As a result, he would often murder the King's English. But, he loved the Lord and his daily, life-long commitment was that he be available to the Lord for whatever God had for him to do.

That night, after we enjoyed a wonderful evening together, we bade each other goodnight. Another day had come to a close. Little did I know what the next day would bring. In the morning, when Mr. Kieft came out of his room, he wanted to talk. He said he couldn't sleep that night, and that he kept turning from one side to the other. The words kept ringing in his mind, "Harvey wants somebody to video tape the cassette ministry." He said, "I'd turn the other way and I'd hear, 'Harvey wants somebody to video tape the cassette ministry.'" He shared with me that he finally got out of bed, got on his knees and told the Lord that if He wanted him to do that job, he was willing.

Frank continued, saying, "Harvey, if an old man like me would put some money into buying one of those cameras, do you think I could learn how to run it and do that job for you?"

I was appalled. It never occurred to me that Frank could do that. I couldn't picture his huge hands operating a small video camera. But I didn't want to disappoint him. So I said, "Frank, if you could learn to operate a ten spindle, semi-automatic machine in your shop, you ought to be able to learn how to operate one of these little cameras." I definitely believe that it was God who put those words in my mouth!

Frank returned to Florida and purchased a video camera. One month later we met him in India as he stepped off the plane with that video paraphernalia in hand. He learned to run it well and took thousands of feet of beautiful video telling the story of how the Lord was using cassettes to His glory in India and other Asian countries.

## LOOKING FOR PROPERTY IN INDIA

While in India, Frank saw how the ministry of WCOI was handicapped by having to conduct its activities in two different locations. With his encouragement we began looking around for a larger, single facility. After pursuing various possibilities, we were told of an elderly Indian couple who had been praying to sell their home to some Christian ministry. After a period of negotiation and discussion, WCOI was able to purchase this home for the ministry.

Adjacent to the home was a small piece of land which we knew would make an ideal site for the WCOI administrative offices and all the activities of the ministry. The house itself would become the home for Sundara Rajan and Priya with their two sons, John Paul and James. The only problem was that the lady who owned that little piece of land lived in New Zealand and no one knew how to reach her. Years earlier she and her husband had been in India working with the Shell Oil Company. When her husband died, she had returned to New Zealand, but all we had was her name and the city in which she was thought to live.

When I got back to the U.S., I began telephoning New Zealand trying to locate her. Imagine my joy when I finally found where she was living. She was working on the night shift as a nurse in one of the local hospitals. Eventually, all the legal hurdles were overcome and Mr. Kieft wrote her a check for $8,000. The property was ours! We now had a house and a piece of land, but we had no money to put up a building. Mr. Kieft headed for the States and his home in Florida.

Some weeks later Lavina and I returned home from a trip overseas when our phone rang. It was Frank. He said, "Do you still want to put up that building in India?" One of his stocks had doubled in value and there were other funds that had become available to him. He wanted to see that building erected on the new property—if we still wanted it! My response to him was strong and clear: "Of course we want it, Frank!"

Within a year, WCOI was able to dedicate a beautiful two-story building. On the lower floor were the administrative offices, an area for duplicating and storing cassettes, and a room for technical services. The second floor housed a professional-quality recording studio, an editing room, the cassette listening library, and a small apartment for Lavina and me. Instead of living in cheap hotels and temporary improvised quarters, we would now have a clean, comfortable place to live during our stay in India. Later, our son Paul would enjoy these same accommodations on many occasions. How can we ever be grateful enough for God's provision through this humble servant, our dear friend, Mr. Franklin Kieft! The cassette ministry in India continued to grow and God continued to bless it. New Testaments were being recorded all the time in different languages from different parts of India. Cassette players with these Scriptures in audio were going out to individuals, to churches and to various village ministries. In some places the Scripture cassettes were even being played over loud- speaking systems in the towns and villages.

We personally participated in the dedication of a new congregation of believers who had come to faith largely through listening to God's word on cassettes recorded and duplicated at World Cassette Outreach of India in those beautiful new facilities. Our hearts were full of praise and thanks to God.

## BEGINNING IN SINGAPORE

In the early 1980s we had made a short exploratory trip to Singapore to see whether there was a need for audio Scriptures in that modern city. We decided to begin a limited cassette ministry there, renting two rooms in the building of the

435

Bible Society of Singapore. Though our beginning was very small, we were confident that the Lord would lead us into something much larger and more challenging in time—if He wanted us to be there. We soon learned that He had some wonderful surprises in store for us.

The evening before we were scheduled to leave California for Singapore, we received a phone call from Oklahoma State University. The caller was Tom Stewart. Tom had never called before and we had never met. Somehow or other, however, he had learned about our ministry in Singapore, and he was calling to give me a couple of names to look up when I got there if I had opportunity. One of the names was of a student whom he had met through his ministry with international students. The young man was from Malaysia, and he was Chinese speaking.

The next day Lavina and I flew to Singapore. Soon after arriving, I called one of the telephone numbers Tom had given me and reached one of Tom's former students. Within minutes of completing our call, he called back and mentioned that he and other students who had been in Oklahoma were getting together that night for a social gathering. He warmly invited us to join them. Without hesitation we went.

At the gathering we met a young man from Malaysia who was visiting Singapore in search of employment. Since he spoke Chinese and I had editing to do on a recording we had done in the Chinese language, I asked if he would be interested in proof listening to it and helping with the editing. He agreed. The next day he came to our apartment and began working. Lavina and I both liked him. We liked his attitude and he handled the work well.

About three nights after he began, Lavina and I were already in bed and were talking about this young man when suddenly I said, "You know what? I wonder if, by any chance, this could be the same young man that Tom Stewart had told me about on the phone?" I put on the light, reviewed my notes and sure enough, it was Joseph Chua, the very same young man from Malaysia of whom Tom had spoken. Did this just happen by chance--or was this the work of God? You know the answer! There is only one explanation. God had put it together. Later we invited Joseph to join the ministry of World Cassette Outreach of Singapore. Joseph accepted our invitation and we soon traveled together to Indonesia. There, using the professional studio of the Mission in Batu Malan, I trained Joseph in the techniques used by a recordist. Together we recorded our first New Testament in Indonesia.

After going back to Singapore again, Lavina and I returned to the USA and Joseph went out to record the entire New Testament in Malaysia in eight different languages. Before the work was completed, our son Paul took over the work of supervising the recordings. Paul would spend more than ten years in SE Asia directing and expanding the ministry that Lavina and I had begun. He eventually became the director over all the fields that we had started during those dozen years while on loan to PRM serving as director of their World Cassette Outreach program.

Before Paul took over my responsibilities in Southeast Asia, he had been appointed as a missionary by the Reformed Church in America and loaned to PRM. During his early years with PRM, Paul studied in London, recorded his first New Testaments in Africa in the Maasai language of Kenya and the Bambara language in West Africa. He also graduated from the Full Sail Recording Institute in Florida. He was well trained and well qualified for a very special task the Lord was entrusting to him.

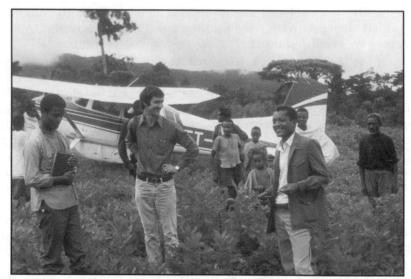

The MAF plane was essential for our living and our ministry both in the Sudan and in Ethiopia. The pilot is Max Gove from England with medical person and evangelist.

Our first recordist trained in Bangladesh.

# CHAPTER TWENTY-EIGHT

# AUDIO SCRIPTURES INTERNATIONAL

Lavina and I served with PRM from 1977 to 1989. Before retiring as a Reformed Church in America missionary, we had been loaned to PRM. The RCA provided our salary, housing and health insurance. As director of PRM's World Cassette Outreach program, we raised donor support to fund the ministry and the travel involved. As the WCO ministry grew, it was included in the PRM budget with gifts designated for WCO now being included in the total support for PRM's larger ministry. It was a good arrangement and we were happy with it– grateful to God and to all the faithful partners who were praying for the ministry and supporting it with their gifts.

After we retired as RCA missionaries, PRM provided our housing, medical insurance, a modest stipend and funds for the WCO ministry. Again, we praised God and knew that we were favored and blessed. We thrilled at what God was doing through the World Cassette Outreach program. The work had grown to where we had national centers in Bangalore, India, Singapore and Indonesia. All were staffed by nationals we had trained and equipped for fruitful cassette ministries. In each location the primary focus was on recording translated Scriptures and making them available to individuals, churches, and other ministries. The number of New Testament recordings continued to grow.

## "SHANTIR BANI" IN BANGLADESH

In India the New Testament was being recorded in some fifty different languages while in Bangladesh, Albert and Mindy Hamstra were heading up a new cassette ministry. Here the program was called the "Shantir Bani" audio ministry, the "Voice of Peace." Al trained national leaders how to record the Bible in their own languages while working closely with the Bangladesh Bible Society. He worked diligently to lay a solid foundation for work that would continue long after he and Mindy moved on to larger responsibilities with their sending agency, The Christian Reformed Church.

The Lord was truly blessing the work in Bangladesh. I personally once met with a pastor who had come in from a remote area to share with us how God was leading him and his people in their outreach ministry. He reported that they were using 15 cassette players and that well over a hundred people had already come to Christ and been baptized. He was full of the joy of the Lord and wanted to say, "Thank you for what you are helping us do because of the cassette players and recordings you have given to us." As I listened to his testimony, I wished that each of our donor partners could have been there. They, too, would have been praising the Lord. It was our donors who had made it all possible, and we thanked God for them as well as for His wonderful grace that made the harvest a reality.

## THE MINISTRY IN AND FROM
## SINGAPORE

The World Cassette Outreach program in Singapore was also flourishing. A small, local board of directors was supervising the ministry and a national was being trained to head up the work. When my son Paul took up residence in Singapore, he put in a professional-quality recording studio, loaded his own cassettes into the recorders, and helped to expand the space available for the ministry. He was also able to put in a new recording studio in Bangladesh with the result that the quality of the recordings was vastly improved.

A number of important Chinese language recordings were made in the new Singapore studio, including recordings in Mandarin, Foochow, Hokkien, Hakka and others. Dorothy Chen recorded the entire Bible in Mandarin. Many congregations in Singapore were blessed by hearing this beautiful recording through daily Bible-listening programs. Today, multitudes of people in China are hearing this recording over the radio through a ministry operating out of Beijing. And most recently, ASI has made the recording available to multitudes of people via the Internet where they can download it at their leisure and without charge.

Paul traveled extensively from Singapore to various other locations to supervise field recordings and the distribution of cassettes. He visited East Malaysia to assist and en courage Joseph Chua, the young man about whom I wrote earlier. Malaysia was the country with those famous long-houses where several closely related families lived together under one extended roof. Lavina and I had once gone there ourselves and were enthralled. We found that these long-houses are wonderful places to reach extended families with Bible listening programs.

Joseph was able to record New Testaments in eight different languages during his two years in East Malaysia. The final editing and initial duplicating of cassettes in those languages was done at the WCO office in Singapore.

Earlier Lavina and I had initiated a program in Indonesia where we had trained Joseph in the art of making good recordings of the Scriptures in new languages. Since there were already some existing recording studios there, we were able to rent these rather than build new studios ourselves. When we were ready to record a new language, we would engage a national speaker to read the entire New Testament while we carefully and patiently did the recording. Together we were able to record the entire New Testament in the Javanese language as well as in a number of other languages, such as Bahasa Indonesian, Bali, Toraja and others.

Lavina and I personally delivered the first albums of the Toraja New Testament to people on the island of Sulawesi. I shall never forget the time we stepped out of the taxi and onto the street where many people were passing by and started playing one of these Toraja language cassettes. We couldn't understand it ourselves, but they could! With great excitement, they began to exclaim with joy and surprise, "That's my language! That's my language! That's Toraja!" Their joy increased our own as we realized that many people there would soon be listening to the Word of God in their own language—most of them for the very first time.

We had seen this kind of response to the cassette many times before, but it never ceased to make us want to give thanks and praise to God for letting us help make it happen.

## AN EXPERIENCE FROM WEST AFRICA

Once, in West Africa, Lavina and I had been staying in a youth hostel where we regularly ate with the young people. After several days of eating fish and boiled vegetables twice a day, we said, "Let's see if we can find a place where we can get a cup of coffee or tea and a piece of bread." After walking about a third of a mile, we came to a coffee shop. The place was empty--and Spartan. The wooden floors were adorned with nothing more than some simple wooden tables with straight-back, locally-made chairs. From somewhere in the back of the shop a young man came to take our order. As he made his way to our table, we took out our cassette player and began to play one of the messages we had recorded just the day before. I wish you could have been there. This young fellow stood ram-rod straight and exclaimed in Pidgin English, "That's my language! That's my language!" For the next 12 minutes—the entire length of the tape—he just stood there and listened before asking for our order. We were thrilled to wait!

Over and over again we found that the lowly cassette is a wonderful and powerful medium to tell the good news about Jesus Christ in any language. I have seen it too frequently not to be totally convinced.

## WONDERFUL YEARS FOR LAVINA AND ME

Those years of recording the Scriptures in new languages were wonderful years for Lavina and me. Each year we went out to some distant mission field for a period of three to seven months. Once, we extended our tour to more than a year. We concluded, however, that this was much too long to be living out of a suitcase. Three to five months was just about right.

The work we had been doing was richly blessed by the

Lord. Responsible national organizations had been founded to carry out cassette ministries. National workers were being trained. Translated Scriptures were being put on cassettes in many different languages. We had developed good relationships with the various national Bible Societies. Our son Paul had joined the ministry and was more than able to succeed me as director of the World Cassette Outreach program.

## PEOPLE LEAVING THEIR HOMELANDS

While all of this was taking shape, Lavina and I began asking important questions. Each time we returned from overseas to our home in California, we could see the tremendous changes taking place in our own country. We began to ask ourselves, "Where are all these new people coming from?" We soon observed that many of them were speaking the same languages in which we had been recording the Scriptures overseas. The Lord began speaking to us. We saw how important it was that churches and individuals reach out with the love of Christ to these new neighbors--"the stranger within our midst", and we wanted to do something about it.

We began by doing some research. We found that more than 80 different languages were being spoken in the city of Bakersfield. In the Los Angeles School District children were coming from homes representing more than 200 different languages! In one large city after another the picture was the same. But it wasn't just a California phenomenon. Similar reports were available from Texas, Florida, New York, Michigan and also from Canada.

Our hearts were burdened. We wanted to find a way to make our overseas Scripture recordings readily available for outreach and teaching ministries in the new mission field taking shape in our own country. I began to share my vision and burden with the people at PRM since I was still working under their auspices. I wanted them to take up the challenge of being a resource center to provide Scriptures in audio for people in the U.S. as well as for people in other countries. Recordings which were made overseas could be brought over to the U.S. for use by local ministries, churches and individuals. This would enable our new neighbors to hear God's Word in their mother tongues. This kind of ministry was so very much

443

needed. And it was so very doable.

## AUDIO SCRIPTURES INTERNATIONAL IS BORN

But, to my great regret, PRM chose not to embrace my vision. They had large commitments to their work in Africa at that time, and adding another component and challenge just didn't strike fire with them. As I saw the lost multitudes of foreigners in our own backyard, I became increasingly distressed. I consulted with various friends and other Christian leaders but found no resolution to the problem. Finally, one evening, I called Les Slagh in Michigan. Les was not only a good friend of many years, but he was also the chairman of the PRM board. He explained that PRM was currently not in a position to take up the challenge I had given them. However, he encouraged me to form my own organization to become the resource center for audio Scriptures in all those languages being recorded overseas. He said, "We can still be friends and help and encourage each other." With these and other words, I was greatly encouraged and emboldened to move ahead.

Within days, the Lord's leading became very apparent. Three people confirmed my decision that the founding of Audio Scriptures International was of the Lord.

The first confirmation came just a couple days later as Lavina and I were planning to leave for our next overseas tour. I was sitting in the office when the phone rang. The person on the other end of the line was a total stranger to me. He said: "My name is Bernie Koerselman. I've been carrying a card with your name on it in my billfold for two years. Your friend, Cecil Martens, pastor of the First Reformed Church in Orange City, Iowa, gave me your name and phone number and urged me to call you. Today, I said, is as good a day as any. So here I am talking to you. Can you join me for lunch?"

I said, "I think so, but let me first call my wife. What's your number? I'll call you right back." Lavina gave me her "thumbs up" and the first thing I knew, my new friend, Bernie, and I were enjoying a leisurely two-hour conversation in a quiet restaurant booth. I discovered that Bernie was a brilliant, retired attorney who loved the Lord with all his heart. When I shared with him about the possibility of founding a new organization, he encouraged me to go ahead. He promised to help me with any questions I might have and assured me it wasn't that difficult.

The second confirmation came from an old and trusted friend who had long supported our ministry. When we left for India a couple of days after my conversation with Mr. Koerselman, Franklin Kieft was with us. In India, we spoke frequently about the possibility of forming Audio Scriptures International. Frank was strongly supportive and encouraged me to do it. One evening he said, "I'll put in $25,000 so that you can get started and not have to worry immediately about funds." Two nights later, sitting on a small outside verandah on the second floor of the little flat where we were all staying, Frank said, "I've been thinking about the new organization you'll be starting. I will extend my contribution to two years making it a total of $50.000."

The third individual who influenced my decision to found ASI was another dear friend and partner, William Ackerman, who had recently retired from his long-held position as International Director of the World Home Bible League. During his time with The Bible League, Ackerman had often greatly encouraged us. Under his leadership the Bible League had made two generous grants to help our ministry with World Cassette Outreach of India. When I called him by phone, he strongly supported the need for a resource center and urged me to move ahead with it.

The encouragement of those three men confirmed my decision to found a new organization. Audio Scriptures International in California was organized as a non-profit, 501 C3 organization in 1989. Allen Burwell became president of the Board of Directors. Bernie Koerselman and Frank Kieft both served on the Board as Directors. I was the president and Donna Sweet, who had so ably served as my part-time secretary when Lavina and I were often gone overseas, served as ASI's first secretary. Our office was located in very small rented facilities in the city of Rancho Bernardo just north of San Diego. The new work had begun!

We began with cassette masters for ten New Testament recordings from India. We soon grew out of our two-room facility and moved to a nearby but slightly more spacious office-setup with additional rooms. A small, professional-quality recording studio was built. Requests for tapes began coming i

Our hearts were full of thanks and praise to God. We had no idea at the time how large this ministry was to become.

Very soon after ASI was operational, the phone began to ring. People were wondering if we had the New Testament in Hmong. Others asked for New Testaments in Lao, Vietnamese, Khmer, Mien and other languages. Each time we said, "No, we don't have it. We'll see if anyone has recorded it; if not, we'll do what we can to see to it that it gets recorded." In each of these cases, no one had yet done it. We arranged to record these ourselves or sponsored their recording by others. With these and other recordings, the number of languages in which we had audio Scriptures began to grow. Masters of recordings done in the overseas centers kept coming to us for ASI's duplication and distribution.

We could hardly imagine how quickly we would have New Testaments in some 200 languages ready for distribution from our resource center in California. In addition, we would have available individual gospels, the Psalms and other books available in audio in another 125 languages. We praised God for His faithful provision to make the ministry possible. All was financed by donor partners – individuals, churches, Sunday schools, young people's and women's groups. Sometimes special gifts from Foundations came at just the moment of greatest need. We recognized God's faithfulness and gave Him thanks.

Very soon after ASI was formed, my son Mark and his wife Sandy and their small family moved from Michigan to California to join the ministry. Mark and Sandy both had missionary experience in Nigeria with the Christian Reformed Church. Sandy had been an assistant to the head of the CRC mission there. Mark was one of their skilled missionary pilots. Now they would serve the Lord in an entirely new venture.

Mark brought young energy and vision to the task. He was good with computers and technology of every kind and would eventually design an entirely new kind of listening device to be identified as the Talking Bible.™ After a few years, Mark would take over my responsibilities to serve as President of ASI.

## THE "PORTRAIT OF JESUS" CASSETTE

But now we must get back to the story of how the expanding ministry of ASI came about. ASI was founded to become a resource center which would have Scriptures available in audio format in as many languages as possible. Our goal was to ensure that individuals and churches and other ministries would have access to God's Word in whatever language was spoken by "the stranger within our midst."

Because the movement of peoples from their home lands to other countries was a worldwide phenomenon, requests for New Testaments on cassettes came from not only the United States but also from Europe, Australia, Canada and as far away as South Africa.

As requests for recorded Scriptures continued to increase, I came to feel that we needed some shorter Scripture recordings in addition to our recordings of the entire New Testament. Specifically, I felt that we needed an arrangement from the gospels which, in one hearing, would introduce the listener to a biblical portrait of Jesus Christ and would enable the listener to understand who Jesus was and what He had done.

My thinking was strongly influenced by our experience with cassettes during our earlier years in Ethiopia. There we had created oral, tract-like messages in several languages. Using these cassettes, the listener was introduced in one hearing to the central truths about Jesus in such a way that he could say "yes" to Him. The Majang had expressed their "yes" by tying a knot on a grass string. Over and over these knotted strings came in to us indicating those who had heard and understood the message and decided to follow Jesus. Each knot represented one more person who said from the heart, "I want to become a person of your Jesus."

How could ASI provide this kind of tract-like cassette in all these languages for which we had entire New Testaments in audio on our shelves? I thought about it and prayed over it repeatedly. Because we were a "Scriptures in Audio ministry," I didn't think it appropriate for us to write and record messages of our own. Yet, we needed something that could be used to introduce Jesus to people in a single listening session as we had done in Ethiopia. For evangelism among unreached peoples, an audio New Testament by itself was obviously very good. However, an initial shorter presentation of the person and work of Jesus in the words of Scripture might be even better. I earnestly asked the Lord for wisdom to help us meet this need.

The answer came to me with the idea that we should prepare a cassette of selected passages from the gospels which would give an accurate and compelling portrait of Jesus. This cassette would enable believers to share the essential truths about Jesus with people who needed to hear it in their own language in order to really understand and respond to the message of the Gospel.

I took my "Harmony of the Gospels" off the shelf and began to select those essential passages from the four Gospels which would connect and flow together to communicate the message most effectively. This required a great deal of time and effort as I selected and arranged and rearranged the passages until I felt we had made the best arrangement possible.

During that period of reflection and study, I made a long speaking tour on which I carried with me an album of the New Testament in English. I also had a small tape player and recorder that enabled me to put a recorded cassette on one side and a blank cassette on the opposite side. By doing this I was able to take selections from the recorded New Testament and record them on the blank tape. This arrangement was technically rather crude, but was adequate for my testing purposes. Sometimes I played for my host family those portions from the Gospels which I had selected. Each time, they encouraged me to pursue this endeavor. Several said, "When this project is completed, I want a copy for myself."

Finally, I traveled on my tour as far east as Grove City, Pennsylvania. I preached in the East Main Presbyterian Church in the morning and spoke in the Fidelis adult Sunday school class afterwards. I was totally exhausted!

After lunch Alma and Bud Wilson, the people with whom I was staying, showed me to a room upstairs where I could nap. In that room the Lord spoke to me concerning the "Portrait of Jesus" cassette. After a short nap I awakened and tingled with excitement. I sensed that the Lord was speaking to me, confirming that what I was doing was right. I went downstairs and shared with Bud and Alma what I was planning. That evening I preached again and then went to the home of Blaine and Delores Hovis for the evening. I was late for supper so Delores said, "Just make yourself at home and find what you want to eat."

Several minutes later, I was sitting alone eating at their dining room table. In the semi-darkness of that room, Blaine, whom I hardly knew at the time, came from their living room and placed a check for $1,000 on the table beside my plate. He said, "This will make it taste better." I could scarcely believe my eyes and ears. Immediately, I sensed that this was the Lord's timing. It was confirmation of what He had been showing me earlier in the afternoon in the upstairs bedroom at Bud and Alma Wilson's. After, I had finished eating, I shared all of this with Blaine. What an evening of rejoicing and thanksgiving to God. Blaine and Delores were to become our dear friends and strong partners encouraging us in ASI's ministry.

Some months later, the first Portrait of Jesus recording was done. It fit nicely unto a single cassette. We entitled it, "The Greatest Person Who Ever Lived." The first words on the cassette ask the question posed by Jesus' disciples after He had stilled the waves of the sea, "Who then is this, that even the wind and the sea obey him?"

The 'Portrait of Jesus' arrangement has proved to be very popular. Many have come to Christ through listening to it. A letter from Romania told how they had worn out their two cassettes and were now requesting two replacement tapes. They told how they had gone from house to house on the streets of their town and how many people had repented and put their trust in Christ because of what they heard. This is but one of the many testimonials from people who have used this beautiful arrangement from the gospels in their own language.

Dr. Lloyd Ogilvie was one of those who was deeply affected by the "Portrait of Jesus" recording. But his experience came from recording the tape rather than simply listening to it. After he had recorded the "Portrait" in the New King Jame

449

Version text, he shared with us the following moving testimony. "As I read this beautiful, focused, flowing narrative, I actually felt the presence of the Master right there with me. I was gripped again by the compelling account of His life and ministry, death and resurrection. And when I read His actual words, it was as if He sounded in the ears of my heart how He had actually said them. I've known Christ for 42 years. But, by the end of that recording session, I felt I knew Him better than ever before."

Giving the "Portrait of Jesus" to others is a great way to share the gospel when traveling. We encourage everyone who travels among people whose language is foreign to them to include a few "Portrait of Jesus" cassettes in their hand luggage. You can give this cassette to the taxi driver, to the person who helps with your luggage, to the waitress who serves you in the restaurant, or to people almost anywhere. The "Portrait of Jesus" cassette enables you to leave behind a lasting witness, and it can make an eternal difference in the lives of those who listen to it.

We consider it an exceptional privilege to have been used of the Lord to put together this powerful "Portrait of Jesus." May He be given all the honor, glory, and praise.

## THE TWO-POCKET ALBUM

After some time, we also felt the need for a special package that could be used effectively in international student and TESL ministries (Teaching English as a Second Language). We came up with the idea of producing a two-pocket album along with a printed booklet in English.

This album has the "Portrait of Jesus" cassette in English in one pocket and the "Portrait of Jesus" in the student's mother tongue in the other. The album also contains a printed copy in English of the message recorded on the tape. This arrangement is much appreciated by international students who are seeking to become more fluent in English. And while they use the tape to improve their English, they also have the opportunity to learn about Jesus in their own language.

The album makes an ideal gift to students when hosting them at a Sunday meal, as a graduation gift, or on some other special occasion. Giving someone one of these albums is an ideal way to share the message of Christ in a non-threatening way. In addition, when students return to their home country, the foreign language cassette can be used to teach the essential truths about Jesus to their family and friends. Because of its exceptional usefulness, we regard the Two-Pocket Album as a "tool of choice" for ministry among those who do not speak English.

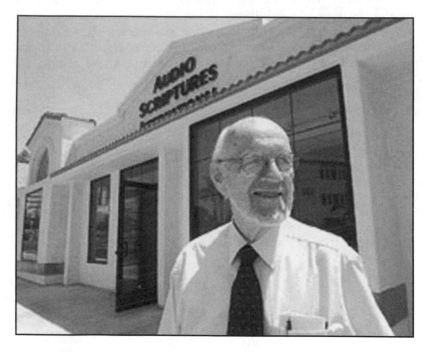

Harvey Hoekstra in front of the new home for Audio Scriptures International and the Adopt-A-Village ministries, 419 E. Grand Ave., Escondido, CA 92025. Paul Hoekstra, Executive Director of AAV supervised the extensive renovations so expertly done by Ron Lockman and his team, converting an old, burned out building into a place of exquisite beauty. The City of Escondido awarded ASI/AAV an award of $10,000 in recognition of its contribution to the beautification of the city on Grand Avenue.

*"Now to him who is able to do immeasurably more than all we ask or imagine, according to his power that is at work within us, to him be glory in the church and in Christ Jesus throughout all generations forever and ever! Amen"*

Ephesians 3:20-21

# THE MEDIA SHIFT FROM 78-RPMS TO MP3S AND MORE

During the 1950's when I was translating the New Testament into the Anuak Language in the Sudan, I could never have dreamed of the technical revolution and the media shift.. Back then all we had were those dark green, heavy-to-carry army-surplus 78-rpm record players. Gospel Recordings had come out to the Sudan and had recorded those 3 ½ minute messages in a number of languages. They then took those recordings back to Los Angeles and made the phonograph records from them. Those 78-rpm records eventually arrived in quantity back in the Sudan. We were thrilled to receive them and never dreamed there would ever be anything different.

Nyaati, a Murle speaking evangelist at Pibor, lugged this heavy record player to many distant villages. He brought back enthusiastic reports of how interested these village people were in both the message about Jesus and in this technology, which was beyond their comprehension.

During those years, we missionaries all began arriving on the field with our personal tape recorders. Don McClure, the oldest among us at our station, even had a wire recorder that appeared, and was short-lived, before tape recorders were developed. A number of those earliest tape recorders we had were as heavy and nearly as large as a suitcase. They were great, but their usefulness was tied to our running the electric generator for power. There were no small battery operated recorders during those early days when missionaries started using tape recorders.

Again, during our time at Pibor, I would sometime crank up the generator and go out to the clinic patien' were being housed and play the tape. I noted then how these listeners gave their careful attention to what the machine was saying. At that time, however, I had no idea of the revolutionary changes that were about to unfold. We never dreamed of such things as cassettes with players being powered by tiny solar panels.

By the early sixties, most missionaries in the Sudan had been expelled or denied reentry visas. We were among them. After more than a year's uncertainty and delay, we found ourselves opening the work among the Majang in the rain forest in SW Ethiopia. It was after we began work there in 1964 that we began to see dramatic changes in the way missionaries could use the new recording and duplicating possibilities. Here is an account from our experience with this shifting media.

After our furlough in 1967, we returned to Godare in the rainforest, with a totally new type of listening device. This was prior to the cassette recorder coming on the market. The device we had was designed to be a child's toy. It was a small two-track, battery-operated, cartridge-tape player that weighed less than two pounds. Our friend, Dr. Ronald Beery, who founded Portable Recording Ministries, figured out how we could record with these units. Bill Klungle, with PRM at that time, designed a machine that could duplicate three of these small cartridge tapes at the same time. Gospel Recordings people had earlier come out to do their 3-½ minute recordings from which they would make those 78-rpm records. We would wait for those records to be produced in Los Angeles and shipped to us along with those heavy army-surplus record players.

But, by the time those records and players arrived, the two-track, lightweight, battery operated cartridge players (originally intended to be marketed as children's toys) had arrived on the scene. Those heavy, army-surplus record players and those 3 ½ minute, 10 inch plastic records were never used. Instead, each of those precious GR recordings was transferred to the two-track cartridges. These new players revolutionized the way people could carry the gospel messages to others. No longer were we limited to using tape recorders on the compound where a generator would be cranked up to provide the required electrical power. And no longer did anyone have to carry those heavy army-surplus record players to take

454

the gospel to the villages.

But, this was only the beginning of change. Very soon, during this same time frame, the Phillips Corporation brought out the small, 6-volt, battery operated cassette recorder. Other models soon followed. Some of the earliest among them could be used only to play the tapes that had been recorded on that machine. This was because those units had no pinch rollers to keep the speed constant. The tape speed on those primitive units changed according to where the tape was when it went past the head. Pinch rollers soon became a standard feature on all cassette equipment and those earlier machines went to the trash bin.

The manufacture of cassettes and attendant recorders and players was a giant step forward. Cassettes could be recorded easily. High-speed duplicators enabled us to dramatically increase the number of messages we could make and duplicate. And the length of our messages could vary. We were no longer restricted to 3 ½ minutes or less that GR adhered to so that those messages would fit on the 78-RPM records.

At this same time, cassette players came on the market. We had several dozen of these at the Godare. Barefoot, illiterate Majang – men, women and children, carried them everywhere. Even before they were believers, they asked to have one to take to people in distant villages. Always they promised to return the players and, to their credit, we never lost a unit except for the one that was ruined when a man fell down in a swift stream crossing the river. All came back to be used again.

One interesting problem with that early Phillips (Norelco) recorder was that there was an electronic click that registered annoyingly on the tape each time one stopped and restarted the recording. This was later redesigned by cassette recorder manufactures, but in the beginning over a period of several years this was a real headache to us. I finally figured out a way to overcome this problem. I took a spare IBM typewriter key and pivoted it on a convenient little post on the left side of the unit's frame. Pulling this little lever-like arm, I could listen to my recording, stop it instantly at the bad place and continue the recording without that offensive electronic click. I was able to pause the tape instantly and release it permitting the tape to move to resume the recording without a click. I must have used this homemade adaptation thousands of times. It was the best pause button like arrangement one can imagine; just a small, hardened jelly-like substance, cushioned the impact on that little drive wheel controlling the movement of the tape. It was all accomplished without damage to the tape or the recorder. It was several years before the manufacturers had licked this problem in their circuitry. Meanwhile, we were able to produce excellent recordings without the slightest electronic click where we had to stop and start the recordings. This was important because most of our messages with native speakers were done sentence by sentence.

During our years in Ethiopia, we produced short 10 to 12 minute messages in a half dozen languages. Our message titles included "Who Is This Jesus?" ""The Power Of Jesus Over Evil Spirits!" "Jesus' Power Over Sickness!" "Why Jesus Died On The Cross?" "When Jesus Came Out Of The Grave." "How Jesus Went Back to Heaven." "The New Powerful Spirit Jesus Promised His Followers." "Jesus' Promised Return From Heaven."

These kinds of messages were all put on cassettes in those different languages. The voices on the cassettes were all those of native speakers. People carried these cassettes far and wide. When there were believers, they confirmed the message with their added personal testimony. The cassette multiplied the times and places where these messages were heard. The cassette became that essential difference between hearing this good news or not hearing at all. The only limiting factor was that our cassette players all required batteries to operate. When the MAF plane flew in with supplies from Jimma, they brought in batteries by the hundreds. Even so, it was one of the best uses of money ever made.

The designing of the tiny solar panel to power players directly from the sun and to recharge rechargeable batteries came soon after we had to leave Ethiopia in 1976. It was a 76-year-old man, Lloyd Swenson, in the Menlo Park Presbyterian Church who caught the vision for solar and was used of God to make it happen. Earlier, a man in Minnesota had designed a beautiful, small solar powered unit to charge a battery housed inside. He followed this up with a unit that charged batteries with a tiny 4 inch by 6 inch panel separate from the device housing the batteries being charged. We soon discovered that if we attached a shiny reflector of this same size as a wing on each side of the panel, that we could operate a cassette player using solar power without even requiring a battery for daytime listening. One had to reposition the panel frequently, but it could be done. I later discovered that if I attached these shiny metal wings to all four sides, I increased the power to around 225 milliamps – more than enough to operate players. The day I discovered that, I was ecstatic. I sent a telegram to PRM and the man in Minneapolis with this fantastic news. We now had the answer.

It was that four winged unit that caught Lloyd Swenson's attention the night I spoke in the Menlo Park Presbyterian Church. He begged me to give him one that night. He said, "Let me see what I can do. I think we have the skills in our church to make these for you. This is Silicon Valley" etc. etc. Lloyd did it. The Chargers are now history and they are still making solar panels to power cassette players. Lloyd once told me, "The night you spoke in our church, I knew why God had kept me alive." I learned that he had had a nearly fatal heart attack several years prior to that evening when God gave him a vision for the solar panel. Thanks be to God for the Chargers – volunteering their energy and skills so that others in remote areas in many different countries can say "yes" to Jesus Christ.

## DIGITAL AUDIO TAPE RECORDERS

It was a giant step forward in improving the quality of audio recordings when digital tape recording devices came on the market in the mid eighties. These wonderful digital tape recorders allowed for recordings with virtually no background hiss or noise of any kind. It was a recordist's dreams come true.

But, this dream-recording device brought with it a dangerous, unanticipated problem. Only as years moved on did we all discover that occasionally a digital tape recording goes bad. Occasionally, the recorded tape unexplainably goes completely bad. Electronic signals of strange sorts and electrical static wipe out the recording completely and it is forever lost. Unlike cassette tapes which sometimes have bleed-through, hiss and other phenomenon that make for less than perfect recordings and which involve some distortion over periods of time, the digital tape, when it goes bad, is completely gone. Lost forever!

The only thing to do then is to transfer as early as possible those wonderful digital recordings to CDs. At ASI, over a period of many months, we worked tirelessly to transfer all our digital New Testament and other recordings from DAT to CD for archiving. When doing this, we transferred from each single DAT to two CD's – one to be safely archived and the other for duplicating either as CDs or as cassettes.

## THE COMPUTER AND THE INTERNET

When Audio Scriptures International was founded in 1989, we committed ourselves to be a resource center for translated Scriptures in audio and to continue helping record the translated New Testaments into audio for non-readers.

The first facet was needed because there was and continues to be a worldwide movement of peoples from their homelands to other countries. Millions have come to America. Churches and their people need a place like ASI from which they can readily obtain Scriptures in all the different languages and in various formats. To reach our new neighbors for Christ, they need to be able to find at ASI the Scriptures in the languages spoken in their homes.

The second facet is pursued because of the unfinished task of recording Scriptures in audio for non-readers. Every translated New Testament and eventually entire Bibles, must be made available in audio for the millions of people who do not read.

While carrying out this ministry in and from ASI, we could never have anticipated these tremendous shifts taking place in the media. In the recording studio, recordings are now normally done using the computer. Sound programs facilitate editing and making whatever changes are wanted in the final product. Instead of just duplicated, recorded and edited material being available from "in house" on location, we now put it up on the Internet as well. People anywhere in the world can download an audio recording in MP3 format, listen and duplicate as many copies as desired. It can happen in China or South Africa. Words fail to convey the revolutionary implications of these shifts in the media. One knows that it all ties into God's plan that all peoples in every nation shall have their opportunity to hear the good news about Jesus Christ and be invited to say, "yes" to Him. I can see them in my mind's eye. I hear them exclaiming with joyful excitement, " We hear the scriptures in our own tongues declaring the mighty acts of God!"

Majang school-boys listening to a cassette player speaking their language.

A beautifully dressed young lady in India following along in her Bible as the cassette player narrates the same passages in her language.

459

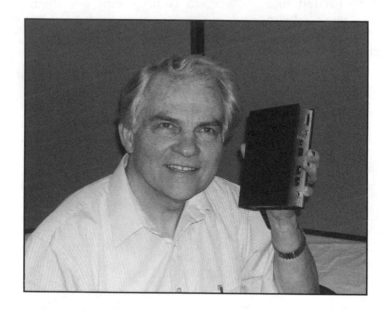

Dr. Edwin Roels checking out
this new listening device, the
Talking Bible™

*"— we hear them declaring the wonders of God
in our own tongues."*
Acts 2:11b

# CHAPTER THIRTY

# THE TALKING BIBLE™

While all of these changes were unfolding, Mark Hoekstra, ASI's President, had a deep conviction that there had to be a better way to make Scripture in audio available to non-readers. His vision took the shape of a Talking Bible™. He said we needed a simple, easy-to-operate, listening device inside which we could seal an entire New Testament in a needed language. He said it should look like a Bible and be no larger than a pew Bible in our churches.

Initially, it was his hope that this could be accomplished using the tiny digital chip. He learned, however, that current costs for such chips were still too high. Eventually, it will happen with chips, but for now, another way had to be found.

In the end, after hours and hours of experimenting and testing, Mark came up with a Talking Bible™ that uses a high quality cassette tape playing at a greatly reduced speed and using four tracks. The sound programs in the computer allow the original recordings to be manipulated and prepared for recording for use in the Talking Bible™ without degradation in sound. The final product is more than adequate for speech of good fidelity, but, which cannot accommodate music because of its playing at this slower speed.

The Talking Bible™ is a sealed device inside of which is an entire translated New Testament. It is powered by internal batteries or an external power source such as a battery, solar panel or a 6-volt wall adapter. An external speaker jack enables earphone listening or the use of an external speaker. The Talking Bible™ has a button to enable the play function, one to fast-forward and another to rewind. There is a small button enabling one to select

461

# CHAPTER THIRTY

which of the four tracks is desired and a small counter to tell where you are on the tape.. It is marvelously simple, fantastically beautiful and the answer for all who cannot read. Its primary purpose is to give non-readers the opportunity to learn God's Word by listening. It is also a tremendous blessing to the blind, those with impaired vision and those who are ill during long night hours. It is a joy and blessing to all who want to listen to the Word of God in a convenient way at any time in any place.

The Talking Bible™ is now reality. The first 10,000 units have arrived from China where they are being manufactured. In India the first 4,000 units have been manufactured and are being used in Paul's Adopt-A-Village Bible listening program there. The first units have been loaded with New Testaments in Tamil, Telugu, Hindi and Mizo. Others will follow swiftly. Hundreds of translated New Testaments will become Talking Bibles in India.

ASI's partner, World Mission, in Grand Rapids, Michigan, is distributing those that arrived from China. ASI does the recording, editing and duplicating of the New Testament tape that World Mission loads into the Talking Bibles, promotes and distributes. For promotional purposes the first five thousand units have been loaded with the KJV and NIV New Testaments and with a modern language Spanish New Testament. Other languages will follow quickly. Projects to record and make Talking Bibles are underway in Oaxaca, Mexico as I write. An urgent request for Talking Bibles in Kiswahili has just come in for a project in East Africa.

Our goal must be nothing less than seeing to it that every translated and printed New Testament be made available as a Talking Bible™. This is essential so that all who cannot read are given the opportunity to learn God's Word by listening.

When one considers the costly, disciplined, skilled and sacrificial effort of the Bible translators to complete a translation in another language, it seems unthinkable that we would not now make that translation into a Talking Bible™. The relatively small additional effort and cost to do this cries out for us to be sure it happens.

How then can it become reality? There are currently over 1000 languages in which the New Testament has been translated and put into print. More are added to this number every year. Right now there are at least 1100 translated New Testaments. Over 700 are waiting to be made available in audio. So the question is, "How can the task be completed?"

We are confident that God has led ASI to think through what is required to have every translated New Testament also made into a Talking Bible™. Consider the following important matters set forth in a document being sent to heads of mission sending agencies, Bible translators and various national Bible Societies -- matters that need to shape our thinking and commitment to this unfinished task:

### HOW TO MAKE TRANSLATED SCRIPTURES INTO TALKING BIBLES FOR NON-READERS

"Providing the translated Scriptures in audio for those who cannot read should be among our highest priorities in world mission today. It will happen when Mission and Church organizations assign personnel and funds for that purpose. The advent of the Talking Bible™ dramatically changes how this can be accomplished at much less cost and with much greater speed.

ASI presently has the ability to produce audio Scriptures in an attractive new format at a significantly reduced cost. During the past few years, ASI has developed and patented the world's first Talking Bible™ which we believe will soon become the "listening device of choice" to provide non-readers the printed, translated Scriptures in audio.

The Talking Bible™ has an entire New Testament in audio on just one tape. This tape is sealed in a tape-playing device that has the appearance of a "regular" Bible. However, instead of opening this Bible in order to READ it, the non-reader simply pushes a button in order to HEAR it. Moreover, since The Talking Bible™ is relatively light and compact, non-readers are able to carry THEIR Bible with them wherever they go—just as easily as readers do!

By putting the New Testament on just one tape, we eliminate the necessity and cost of producing the fifteen to twenty tapes usually required for each traditional audio New Testament. Moreover, the Talking Bible™ itself currently being manufactured in China and in India costs significantly less to manufacture than the tape recorders used to play other recorded Scriptures. As a result, we are able to produce audio Scriptures in a very appealing format at much less cost than those used in the past.

## TRANSLATED SCRIPTURES ALREADY IN PRINT

The New Testament is now available in print in more than one thousand of the world's 7000 languages and dialects. These numbers are increasing monthly as new translations are completed. We praise God for this truly wonderful achievement! Regrettably, however, more than half of the adults in our world are still unable to read! Consequently, multitudes of people have no direct access to the Word of God even though it has been translated into their own language.

*Therefore, a primary challenge facing the Christian movement today is to provide the printed, translated Scriptures in AUDIO form for the hundreds of millions of people who cannot read.*

## MAKING PRINTED BIBLES INTO
## TALKING BIBLES

But, how can these translated, printed Scriptures for readers become audio Scriptures for non-readers? We believe the answer lies in the advent of the Talking Bible™. Here is how it can happen.

## THE BACKPACK RECORDING STUDIO

The preferred place to record a translated New Testament is, of course, in a professional quality studio. In many situations, however, it is not feasible or cost effective to bring readers to a recording studio to narrate the text. Non-readers who have the greatest need for audio Scriptures live in places where it is difficult or even impossible to produce them because recording studios are not available in their area. We must take the recording studio to where the readers live.

ASI has designed a Backpack Recording Studio to do just that! Using the Backpack Recording Studio, Talking Bibles can be produced on site—anywhere in the world. The cost for each Backpack Recording Studio is approximately $5,000. Each recording team will require two of these Backpacks—one for the technician and the other for the proof-listener. (Just as written Scriptures require proofreaders, audio Scriptures require proof-listeners!) Trained teams are able to produce Talking Bibles on site in a language they have never studied or learned—and do so in a matter of weeks. Instead of spending thousands of dollars to bring native language speakers to where the studios are, we are now able to bring the studios to where the native speakers are! After finishing their work, the recordists bring the Backpack Studios home with them for future use.

Right now in the year AD2002, ASI is training and equipping the first teams to record and produce Talking Bibles in nearby Mexico and in distant India. ASI is also prepared to train personnel from other missions and churches who are eager to use this new technology to provide non-readers in their part of the world with God's Word in audio. What a marvelous experience this can be for anyone who is able to give up to three months to this task. By the end of three months or less, these volunteers will have actually recorded the New Testament in a new language AND will have given those people the opportunity to learn God's Word by listening just as we have who read.

### USING AUDIO SCRIPTURES EFFECTIVELY

It is not enough, however, simply to produce Talking Bibles for non-readers. Bible listening is most effective when integrated with the work of local evangelists. The Adopt-A-Village daily Bible listening program in India has demonstrated how effective this combination of structured Bible listening and the work of evangelists is when the two work together in one strategy. There are countless, thrilling testimonials from people who have come to Jesus Christ through that program. Village people listening to Scripture for thirty minutes daily tell how their lives were changed, of victory over demons, healings in answer to prayer and extraordinary experiences of God's power. People are continuing to be baptized and worship groups are taking shape. God's blessing on that strategy is evident.

There may be other models and methods. The point is that just as a printed Bible is of little value if it remains on the shelf, so the audio Bible is of little value if it is not listened to. Needed in all efforts to provide the translated Scriptures in audio, is a Bible listening plan that is integrated with the ministry of local evangelists.

## NEEDED - AN AD2000 TYPE MOBILIZATION FOR THIS TASK

We need to do far more than we are currently doing to give non-readers the opportunity to learn God's Word by listening. Something akin to the AD2000 movement is now needed to focus on providing the Scriptures in audio for all who cannot read. We need to know the size, shape and nature of this great challenge.

The advent of the Talking Bible™ makes providing the translated Scriptures in audio a doable task. The Talking Bible™ is the tool of choice for single voice narrations. Audio Scriptures International (ASI) will recruit, train and equip its own recording teams to be fully engaged in this task. For funding it is appealing to others for grants and contributions. It costs less than $10,000 to equip a team to go out with Backpack Studios to record, duplicate and provide Talking Bibles in each language. ASI's commitment is to leave behind 100 Talking Bibles with the New Testament in the language recorded in each particular project. We are beginning in Mexico and moving on to other countries

But, ASI can never do it alone. We are challenging and urging other mission and church planting organizations to assign and equip personnel with Backpack Studios to join ASI in this global effort. Unless the entire Christian community catches the vision and is persuaded that giving non-readers God's precious, saving Word in their languages is among the highest priorities in world mission today, it will never happen. If we are convinced that we now have in the Talking Bible™ a listening device that offers us a practical way -- costing less and getting the job done much more quickly -- we need to do whatever is required to be sure it happens.

The opportunity and challenge is huge. We believe this is God's calling to His people. We, urgently, invite you to partner with ASI in this great unfinished task. Our confidence is in God who provides through His people. We are appealing to you to partner with us in personnel, prayer and financial support as God enables. To Him be the honor and praise!" *

* (From the brochure, "Talking Bibles for Nonreaders" by Harvey T. Hoekstra, Chairman ASI/AAV Board, August 1, 2002)

\*\*\*\*\*

## POSTSCRIPT

World Mission and Audio Scriptures International in a strong cooperative effort believe the task is not only doable but that it can be accomplished with dispatch. If the global Christian church and its recognized world mission leaders catch the vision and provide funds and personnel, we believe every currently translated and printed New Testament could be made into a Talking Bible™ for nonreaders within the next six to eight years. World Mission and ASI are prepared to train and equip personnel that churches, missionary organizations and key lay people will help recruit and fund for this high priority unfinished task.

But, having reached that goal, we must come to grips with an additional challenge. What will we do to give Talking Bibles™ to those for whom no translation of the New Testament has been done nor is available in print? Tens of thousands of new believers need access to audio New Testaments in their own languages. World mission and church leaders need to recognize that many people are coming to faith in Christ who speak languages for which there are no translations, or at best minimal translations of Scripture in their languages.

The advent of the Talking Bible™ challenges us to take a second look at this unfinished task. We all know that it normally takes anywhere from ten to twenty years to do a translation of the New Testament. Can we afford to wait those many years before giving these new Christians the New Testament in their languages? With Talking Bibles should we not consider doing initial oral translations in needed languages. Could it be that we may no longer have to wait those ten to twenty years before we can give them entire New Testaments in audio in their languages? I say with some boldness that the answer is, a resounding, "YES!"

I am confident that under the right conditions, credible oral translations can be made of entire New Testaments in less than two years, and perhaps even sooner than that. What am I talking about? What experience is there to back up such an assertion? Let me attempt to answer and persuade you.

My comments are based on my personal experience while serving as a missionary in Ethiopia. We actually did an oral translation of several books of the New Testament and saw how God blessed those new believers who listened to his precious Word in audio in their own language. Of course, we had no Talking Bibles™ then, but we had playback cassette machines that served the same purpose, only less efficiently. I actually saw with my own eyes a group of new believers meet regularly to learn God's Word by listening to the recording of an oral translation of those New Testament books. I will never forget seeing this group of a dozen or more new Christians, led by a woman severely handicapped from polio, proceeding down the hill every Sunday morning going to their church a quarter of a mile distant. They had just come from listening to that oral translation of the New Testament and were now heading for the church to worship with other believers using the national language, Amharic. What happened there, can happen almost anywhere if the conditions are right.

So, the question is, "What are those right, essential conditions to permit a credible oral translation resulting in a Talking Bible™ in that language?

To do an oral translation it is essential that the recordist work with a speaker of the vernacular who is completely bilingual, speaking both his own language and the language of the recordist equally well. Theoretically, one would say that this informant must be a believer. However, I have personally experienced that while desirable, it is not essential.

I base my comments, in part, on my experience working with Kathy Hofmeyer, who had come out from Gospel Recordings to help us make messages in Majang in the rain forest of SW Ethiopia before there were any Christians. We used the informant's tongue like a typewriter key. And the evidence indicating that the Holy Spirit was in control was seen in the countless numbers of Majang who came to faith in Christ through listening to those messages made using the voice of a man who was not a believer.  At the end of those recording sessions, Kathy remarked, "I don't remember a time when I felt the Holy Spirit to be in more control than during these days." Let God be praised!

To do those Gospel Recording messages in Majang, there were three persons involved.   Kathy, doing the recording, and I communicated together in English. My informant and I conversed in the informant's language, Anuak, a language I knew well from my years in the Sudan translating the New Testament into that language   My informant was completely bilingual in Anuak and the Majang languages. When he understood clearly what I had spoken to him in Anuak, he would indicate he was ready to have Kathy record that sentence in Majang.  And that's the way it went, sentence by sentence.  We did a total of 11 messages in Majang before Kathy left with the recording which she had duplicated on 78 RPM records in the states to be sent out to us in Ethiopia.  It worked beautifully and it demonstrates a method that is probably being used many times by GR recordists.

Our interest here lies in seeing  this as being applicable to doing entire New Testaments as oral translations and loading these recordings into Talking Bibles. Using this method, new believers can be given Talking Bibles of New Testaments in their language without having to wait a dozen or more years before a printed, written translation is available to be recorded in audio.

My experience with the Shako language confirmed what I had observed relating to the recordings we had done in the neighboring Majang language. A good translation could be done orally and recorded in audio.  The essential ingredients were two persons,  one of whom was completely bilingual whose voice would be recorded. The other, who operated the recorder, spoke the national language only.  The conversation between recordist and informant was in Amharic, the national language. The recording was done verse by verse or with parts of a verse in the informant's language.  When properly edited, the final product communicated the text effectively and accurately. Listening, one would never have guessed that it had been done verse by verse with the recorder being paused for discussion before the next verse was recorded.   Edited to remove unwanted pauses or other sounds which inevitably creep in  during the recording process,   the end result was a hig quality recording of several books of the New Testament in the Shako language. How Shako believers were blessed by these recordings was described in the previous chapter.

Now that we have Talking Bible™ formats, we are challenged to explore and exploit this new possibility of providing Talking Bibles for oral translations. Admittedly, the finished product may not have the finesse of a printed translation. And this is not to suggest that the traditional method of translating the Scriptures resulting in a printed text should be abandoned. An oral translation should be viewed as an interim translation to meet an immediate need and to seize an immediate opportunity to give non-reading believers access to God's Word as found in the entire New Testament.

The advantages of recording an oral translation in audio rather than waiting  those dozen to twenty years for the printed version are quite compelling. And, in all honesty, we need to recognize that this sort of translation without being recorded is being done all the time when evangelists and preachers read from the printed text in another language and make an ad hoc type of translation as they stand before the people whom they want to teach. My hunch is that the carefully worked through oral translation recorded to become a Talking Bible will compare very favorably with such ad hoc translations now being done because of sheer necessity. My plea is that the need and the possibilities of doing oral translations to be made into Talking Bibles warrant our carefully exploring this possibility.

The alternative is to wait those dozen to twenty years before the contents of the entire New Testament are available to believers who will have waited all those years. And we need to recognize that many of those "once new believers" may have fallen by the way because we failed to give them the New Testament Scriptures they so urgently needed to grow in their Christian faith and walk. May God graciously lead us to think creatively and to do the right thing as this possibility is explored more carefully.

✶ ✶ ✶ ✶ ✶

# VITA

Harvey Thomas Hoekstra was born on November 20, 1920. He was the fourth of six brothers. His boyhood was spent on the farm where he grew up in the atmosphere of a Christian home. He was out of school for four and one-half years between grade school and high school. During this time he had three major operations and spent some forty-five days in the hospital. Through this experience he came to know Christ as personal Savior and was called to the ministry.

He began high school in 1938 and graduated with honor completing his work in two and a half years. He graduated Cum Laude with an A. B. degree from Hope College, and received his B. D. degree from Western Theological Seminary of the Reformed Church. He was student pastor of the Hope Reformed Church in Grand Haven, Michigan for three years while taking his theological training.

Post graduate work included the Summer Institute of Linguistic course with Wycliffe at the University of Oklahoma, a year of post graduate study at Scarrit and Peabody Colleges in Nashville, Tennessee. He also studied during two furloughs, with a term at Princeton Seminary and a semester at the Kennedy School of Missions in Hartford, Connecticut.

He received the Doctor of Missiology degree from Fuller Theological Seminary in 1978. At that time he was awarded the Donald Anderson McGavran Award in recognition of the excellence of his dissertation on the subject of the *World Council of Churches and Its 'New Mission'*. This study was published in 1979.

While in college, he was married to Lavina Irene Hoffman. With their children they have served as missionaries in the Sudan and Ethiopia for 30 years. In the Sudan he reduced the Anuak tribal language to writing, worked in the area of literacy and evangelism and translated the entire New Testament into the Anuak language which was printed by the American Bible Society. He also translated into the Murle language Mark, John, Acts and Romans which was printed by the British and Foreign Bible Society using both the Roman and Arabic script.

In Ethiopia he, with his family, pioneered work among the Majang forest people in the Southwestern part of the country. Here he developed the use of cassettes in evangelism aimed at reaching a number of previously unreached people groups with the Gospel, each in its own language. Beginning in 1977, the Hoekstras returned overseas annually serving as director of Portable Recording Ministries' (PRM) World Cassette Outreach (WCO) program.

Dr. Hoekstra founded Audio Scriptures International (ASI) in 1989 to provide Scripture on cassette in languages needed by ministries among ethnic peoples who have left their homelands and now live in other countries.

In 1979 Dr. Hoekstra was elected to serve as moderator of the General Synod of the Reformed Church in America. The Hoekstras make their home in San Diego where Harvey continues to serve with Audio Scriptures International.

In 1995 Dr. Hoekstra was awarded the "*Outstanding Alumnus Award*" by Western Theological Seminary.

Dr. Hoekstra is currently serving as Chairman of the Board of Audio Scriptures International.

The Hoekstras have six children. Three of their children are full time missionaries.

*****